The End of Sovereignty?

Author's note
Following common convention the term billion indicates one thousand million.

The End of Sovereignty?

The Politics of a Shrinking and Fragmenting World

Joseph A. Camilleri
La Trobe University
and
Jim Falk
University of Wollongong

Edward Elgar

Published by
Edward Elgar Publishing Limited
Gower House
Croft Road
Aldershot
Hants GU11 3HR
England

Edward Elgar Publishing Limited
Distributed in the United States by
Ashgate Publishing Company
Old Post Road
Brookfield
Vermont 05036
USA

A CIP catalogue record for this book is available from the British Library

Library of Congress Cataloguing-in-Publication Data

Camilleri, Joseph A., 1944–
    The end of sovereignty?: the politics of a shrinking and fragmenting
world/Joseph A. Camilleri and Jim Falk.
        p.   cm.
    1. Sovereignty.   I. Falk, Jim, 1946–   .   II. Title.
JC327.C36   1992
320.1'5–dc20   91–28764
                                                                                      CIP

ISBN 1 85278 032 0
     1 85278 699 X (paperback)

Printed and bound in Great Britain by
Billing and Sons Ltd, Worcester

Contents

Preface

We conceived the idea of this book when much of the theoretical and popular literature still focused on a world divided by the Cold War into two mutually antagonistic blocs.

It seemed to us then that this situation was potentially unstable – that the world was undergoing a process of economic, technological and political integration, but also at the same time, political fragmentation. Transnational corporations spanned the world. The number and power of new international organizations were on the rise. Evidently, the process of globalization was continuing relentlessly. But at the same time there was evidence of rising demand for regional autonomy, decay of the superpower influence, and the growth of new social movements seeking to find ways of expressing themselves politically outside the boundaries of mainstream politics. All of this raised what to us seemed an important question: to what extent does contemporary political theory or rhetoric provide an adequate basis for understanding this? For example, how realistic is it, in this emerging world, to fight for national liberation, to seek to win state power in an election, or to expect a national government to take an independent political stance?

Developing a theoretical framework for these and similar questions never appeared easy. It was nevertheless clear from the beginning that many central issues revolved around the concept of national sovereignty. The sovereign nation, the system of sovereign states, lay at the centre of a theory of sovereignty which at times explicitly, and more often surreptitiously, underlay much of contemporary political discourse. Whether in the declaratory policies of governments, or the statements of resistance by oppositional groups and movements, the concepts and often objective of sovereignty were frequently either visible, or not far from the surface. It was for this reason that we decided to focus on a single task – to examine the usefulness of the idea of sovereignty for either understanding the contemporary world or politically intervening in it.

Since we commenced this project events have certainly confirmed our earlier impressions. The two-bloc system has lost much of its meaning. The twin processes of integration and fragmentation are continuing unabated. And issues of sovereignty continue to dominate both popular and scholarly political discourse. The passage of time reinforced our initial judgement that the issues we had chosen to canvass in this study were important. Unfortunately it also demonstrated to us, in rather brutal fashion, the scale of the project upon which we had embarked.

This book makes use of our somewhat varied disciplinary backgrounds ranging over politics, political economy, social studies of science, and even the physical sciences. Although our two writing styles are compatible, they are not identical. We have not attempted to draw these artificially into a single style. We offer as a justification of this that the variation ought to lighten the density of what is inevitably a complex and layered analysis. But we leave the final judgement on this to the reader.

We have of course drawn widely on the available literature, and we have been ably assisted in this task by the research assistance of Ian Hampson, Malcolm Andrews, Mark Rix, Gail Hubble, Stewart Linden and George Myconos, whom we wish to thank for all their efforts. We also wish to acknowledge the stoic patience of our publisher, the forbearance and support of our colleagues in the Department of Science and Technology Studies at the University of Wollongong, New South Wales, and the Department of Politics, La Trobe University, Victoria, the painstaking work of the secretarial staff in the La Trobe University Politics Department, and the very generous financial assistance provided by the La Trobe University School of Social Sciences Research Committee and the University of Wollongong Board of Research and Graduate Studies. Our thanks go to Lynne Rienner publishers for permission to use some of the material from Chapter 2, 'Re-thinking Sovereignty in a Shrinking, Fragmented World', by Joseph Camilleri in *Contending Sovereignties: Redefining Political Community*, edited by R.B.J. Walker and Saul H. Mendlovitz (© 1990 by Lynne Rienner Publishers, Inc).

Finally we want to acknowledge the intellectual and emotional support of our partners Sue Rowley and Rita Camilleri, and children Anna and Michael Rowley Falk and Kristian and Emil Camilleri, who by being there have often reminded us personally that finding ways to understand the world and shape it matter.

Jim Falk and Joseph Camilleri

1. World in Transition

It is a commonplace that the times are global. Communication systems bring virtually every point of the earth's surface into close to instant contact. Few if any people are unaffected by the vagaries of the world market. Weapons systems and political alliances embrace the globe.

In many of its social and physical dimensions – politically, economically, militarily, and even ecologically – the world has shrunk and daily continues to shrink. All this is a commonplace. What is remarkable is that although all this is widely acknowledged, much of the analysis of what is happening and what should be done is predicated upon a completely different picture of the world, one whose underlying features remain steadfastly unaffected by all this change.

The world which underlies much of the political commentary and analysis, and pervades discussion of policy, is a world of sovereign nation-states. Consider, for example:

- 'Iraq' invades 'Kuwait'. Many governments deplore this violation of the country's sovereignty. 'The United States' leads an expeditionary force to the Persian Gulf with the intention of reinforcing a series of strategies intended to restore the 'legitimate' government of Kuwait to power over its 'sovereign' domain.
- The Kanaks in New Caledonia argue for a process of national liberation in which a sovereign 'Kanaky' will be created free of French colonial rule.
- Acid rain generated in one country falls in another. The government of the former refuses to be drawn into discussion about international regulation of emissions since, it claims, doing so would compromise its national sovereignty.
- A political party justifies its policies as designed to restore national economic competitiveness and national sovereignty.
- A peace organization in the Philippines deplores the presence of the huge US military bases at Clark airfield and Subic bay, arguing that they compromise the country's national sovereignty.

The list of possible examples is virtually endless. Sovereignty and the framework of ideas which surround it are a dominant feature of contemporary

1

political debate, analysis and policy. We experience what amounts to a *sovereignty discourse* – a way of describing and thinking about the world in which nation-states are the principal actors, the principal centres of power, and the principal objects of interest. Debates about national policies, national competition, national culture and national actions and objectives form part of this discourse. Measures to support the nation-state, reinforce the sense of national community and advance the national interest represent actions in which this discourse plays a key explanatory role.

This sovereignty discourse is of far more than peripheral interest. It is the way in which mainstream discussions of many of the most contentious issues in the world are advanced, arbitrated and resolved. Yet compared to the authority which the concepts exert, their basis and validity have received remarkably little attention.

True, there is (as we shall describe) a body of literature dealing with some aspects – in particular the relation between the sovereignty of nations and international law, and the relationship between sovereign states and their corresponding national communities. But overarching questions about the enduring value of the concepts as ways of explaining how power in the contemporary world is actually exercised, or how change can be achieved, remain as issues in need of urgent attention. The purpose of this book is to explore a number of these questions and begin the process of finding answers.

Put simply this book deals with the following questions: what is the theory of sovereignty, and how is it expressed in current political analysis? How accurately does it reflect the exercise of power in the world which we now experience, and the world which seems to be on the horizon? How well does it describe how the world *ought* to be? To what extent is it a guide or diversion in developing prescriptions for action to shape the future? And to the extent that the explanatory value of the ideas associated with it has been eroded by changes to the world's social, economic and technological fabric, what other ways of looking at the world are emerging which might serve us better?

In posing these questions we have laid out a framework for the issues we wish to consider. However, we should make clear that in addressing these it will also be necessary to exclude others which are canvassed elsewhere. Thus, for example, we shall not traverse in any great detail the complex skein of problems raised by the confrontation of domestic law with increasingly elaborate layers of international law. Nor do we spend much time addressing the intricate layers of international regulation which have been devised to assist economic development, nor the detail of the often subtle differences in national approach taken by different states as they seek to adjust to a wide range of different policy challenges. In place of these we examine macroscopic trends in five areas, as they bear upon our understanding of the global order: the internationalization of trade, finance and corporate organization, the globalization of the security system, the rapid transformation of technology, the accompanying spread of ecological problems, and the emergence of new social movements with both a local and transnational consciousness.

Clearly we need to begin with an examination of the nature and evolution of sovereignty, both as a conceptual framework, and as it emerges in contemporary political practice. Accordingly, in the next chapter (Chapter 2) we look at these basic issues, showing how the modern idea of sovereign nations has emerged over some four centuries as a particular way of associating the structure of political power with a corresponding structure of territorial space.

Anticipating this more detailed analysis we may note that the theory of sovereignty paints a world in which supreme power is exerted within a particular territorial boundary. Who or what exerts that power may not be straightforward, but it is usually assumed to be the national government and its agencies. Consistent with this, nation, state and national power are often considered to coincide to form the nation-state. Within national boundaries, the national state is supreme, recognizing no higher authority. Outside the national domain is the rest of the world, also partitioned into sovereign states which deal with each other, at least so far as their sovereignty is concerned, on a basis of equality.

In this picture of the world the principal actor is the nation-state. States are characterized by their particular national territories. Associated with that territory are all the people who live within it and who identify themselves, whatever their other differences, as members of that national community.

There is much more to be said. But even from this description we may perceive the outline of a theory of the world which has played an important role in human affairs for several centuries. Of course it is a theoretical construct. It is in the nature of theories that they should be violated in practice. The question is not whether this idea has changed, but whether the explanatory value of this theoretical picture of the world, which continues to underpin so much of contemporary political discourse, persists or has been eroded.

We may also anticipate an important conclusion. Not all is well with the theory of sovereignty, either as a description of how the world is, how it is evolving, or how it might be shaped. It is no coincidence that this examination of sovereignty appears at a time when human affairs are undergoing a process of relentless globalization. But not only is the world being progressively integrated but, perhaps paradoxically, it is also experiencing a process of progressive decentralization of authority and fragmentation of society.[1]

Even sophisticated models, which attempt to embroider the world of sovereign states with layers of transnational and subnational actors, may not be equal to the task of describing the diversity of contemporary politics or of explaining the origins, nature, significance or destination of that growing diversity. In this book we shall argue that much more is needed if we are to explain and successfully intervene in this complex, unified yet paradoxically fragmented world as it is now emerging.

In order to develop this analysis it is useful to situate it within the context of an intellectual moment. We live at a time when the rationalist reductionist processes of scientific and social investigation and intervention are playing an unprecedentedly powerful role in shaping our world, and the social relations which characterize it. This condition of 'modernity' has brought with it many fruits, but also acute tensions – between traditional culture and mass commodity consumerism, between North and South, between regional, national and transnational organizations, between globalization and regional fragmentation, between militarization and the desire for security, and much more.

The contemporary debate over what has been lost by adopting the intellectual approaches of modernity, and how in future we might better analyse the world both reflects and responds to the uncertainties and tensions surrounding the current moment. It is sufficiently intense for some to argue that we have entered a 'postmodern' period. In Chapter 3 we examine the relationship between sovereignty and what some call the 'postmodern condition',[2] but which alternatively can be considered as an interpretative crisis reflecting many of the same tensions, ambiguities and uncertainties that now surround the sovereignty discourse.

One central characteristic of global change which underlies many of these tensions is the extraordinary penetration of economic market relations into almost all aspects of human life. The ideology of modernity has developed around the universal goal of economic growth. It reduces all institutions – political and economic – to instruments for the achievement of that goal. Correspondingly the world political system, including the system of states, is governed by rules that embody and nurture the logic of market-oriented growth.[3] In Chapter 4 we examine the consequences of what is now the global penetration of the drive to achieve never-ending economic growth, and the institutions which articulate and facilitate it. The logic of the market both unifies and fragments. In some respects it places ever more elaborate demands on the state. At the same time in many other ways it increasingly constrains its role.

The state now finds itself confronted by ever more elaborate layers of organization which criss-cross its territorial boundaries. The role of transnational corporations in the internationalization of capital has been amply documented along with their central role in the quantitative and qualitative changes in the nature and functioning of the world economy. The growth of transnational investment, production and trade since 1945 has been accompanied by an equally spectacular expansion of international banking, with the leading American, European and Japanese banks now integrated into an international circuit of capital.

Despite considerable regional and national variation, the overall trend towards economic integration and interpenetration has become unmistakable at the global level.[4] As a result, there is a profound divergence between the territorial constraints on the state and the mobility of capital. Large corporations have become less dependent on the state for a wide range of economic functions. National governments now operate within a global environment which places significant restrictions on their powers of information, regulation and taxation.[5]

Undoubtedly one of the most remarkable, and most remarked upon features of the contemporary world is the rapid development, diffusion and application of information and communication technology. These technologies alter the effective distance between individuals, communities, branches of corporations, political groups and nations. They also assist in the contraction of time horizons, allowing information to be gathered and decisions to be made and implemented almost simultaneously, without regard to physical location.

Within these global communication webs, territorial boundaries, which once represented natural barriers to communication, now become increasingly artificial. Organization, communication, cultural and economic interchange and political strategizing extend over new communication territories which pay little or no attention to what may seem to be the increasingly ephemeral boundaries of nation and state.

The impact of the transformations in information technology is not restricted to communication. The new technologies have also contributed to the evolution of a technological and economic system which may in part be characterized as a 'regime of permanent innovation'. So rapid is this process that the characteristic way for many products to lose their value is not through their physical failure but their failure to compete with new technological innovations. Nowhere is this clearer than in the production process itself, where keeping ahead in the shifting maze of new technologies requires a flexibility of approach and investment which tests the corporate managers to their limit.

The now widely encountered choice between keeping ahead technologically, or failing, is not restricted to corporate management. Increasingly the state itself is implicated in the process, subjected as it is to a wide range of demands and pressures to maintain national competitiveness. Demands for educational and physical infrastructure, investment assistance and other forms of national, regional and local policy initiatives are some of the pressures which the state now faces on a day-to-day, and election-to-election, basis. Thus, paradoxically, we see the activity of the state expanding, but the role increasingly focused on the central objective of maintaining the environment in which locally based corporations can compete in what has become an economically cut-throat global arena.

In attempting to meet this objective, the national state is by no means the only player. International organizations such as the Organization for Economic Cooperation and Development (OECD), the international banks, UN agencies, and regional organizations such as those of the European Community, play an increasingly complex and vigorous role in cultivating and shaping corporate development in a time of intense technological and economic competition in a rapidly integrating global market.

In this environment, the discourse of sovereignty may tend to marginalize many questions which increasingly seem relevant. To what extent can we expect or rely on the nation-state to shape technological change to meet social objectives? To what extent can the state be said to be sovereign over a domain in which technological development is in part drawn and in part required from outside? To what extent can the nation-state even be said to be setting its own agenda, and indeed, to what extent can this reasonably be considered possible? Chapter 5 is devoted to examining these and similar issues in the context of an analysis of the relationship between technological change and sovereignty.

We are living in a world in rapid transition, with major implications for governments, corporations and communities. How can we best gain an intellectual purchase on a world so transformed? Should we consider the nation-state the principal actor? If not, what? The answers may not be obvious, but clearly any alternative perspective to that depicted by the discourse of sovereignty must take account of these profound economic and technological transformations. But the impact of change goes well beyond these.

Modernity has spread across the world confronting and transforming traditional structures, ideologies and values. In its wake it has brought a series of political upheavals which are still unfolding. In many parts of the Third World wars of national independence have been followed by a succession of military coups, civil wars and violent revolutions, all of which reflect in varying degrees a rising tide of collective discontent. This political turbulence is not confined to the Third World. In the First and Second Worlds, periodic convulsions have marked the Fourth and Fifth French Republics, a protracted conflict has simmered in Northern Ireland, ethnic discontent has flared in Spain, the Vietnam crisis has torn the United States, and not least, social upheaval has erupted stretching across the Soviet Union and feeding revolutionary ferment in Eastern Europe. From East to West and from North to South, rising pressures for local and regional autonomy, and the growth to prominence of a wide range of subnational and transnational institutions confront the model of a world divided into sovereign states.

If the discourse of sovereignty is to retain its explanatory power it must also attempt to accommodate the emergence of liberation movements, guerrilla organizations, terrorist groups and mercenary forces, all of which threaten what was once believed to be a defining characteristic of the national state – its monopoly on the legitimate use of violence. In addition, we now see the emergence of a far more complex and effectively global security system with which even the most powerful states now find themselves in interplay. How far can the traditi nal view of a world of sovereign states accommodate these trends? How well can it illuminate what is happening and could still happen? Are there other potentially more fruitful ways of thinking about them? We address these and similar questions raised by the shifts in the relationship between sovereignty and the global security system in Chapter 6.

The changes to the ways in which issues of security are and can be negotiated relate in no small measure to the extraordinary pace of change in military technology. Nuclear weapons may travel across the globe. Similarly, the systems which guide them and prepare for their use are formed through a network of bases, and air, land and sea-based platforms which move constantly on the globe in a dance of ceaseless vigilance. In the first phase of the development of these systems, access and ownership has been restricted to a few major nation-states. Alliance systems have been constructed around this fact, and the threat that the weapons pose to all states. Some states have co-operated with the deployment and build-up of these weapons systems, sometimes allowing them to be based on their soil, whilst others have sought to disassociate themselves from them. Recently, it has become clear that the monopoly on the weapons is dissolving. South Africa, Israel, Pakistan and India appear to have joined the nuclear 'club' whilst other countries such as Brazil, Argentina, and even Iraq, seem poised to follow suit. This proliferation of the most destructive weapons is not restricted to those powered by nuclear fission and fusion. Chemical weapons are also proliferating at a rapid pace, becoming accessible to a wide range of nation-states. So too are sophisticated delivery systems.

This proliferation of powerful weapons might be thought to strengthen the power of states, breathing new life into the explanatory model of the sovereignty discourse. Against this, these weapons also threaten the sovereign domain, rendering states more vulnerable. More generally, the technology of coercion is developing in a vast range of multifaceted applications, ranging from the subtle to the overtly destructive. Increasingly these are

available not only to states, but to other institutions as well. As the technology of coercion diffuses across a multitude of different interpenetrating
organizations, and the character of the technology transforms, central issues
are raised about the distribution of power. To what extent should we take
coercive technology as a defining feature of the most powerful actors? If we
do, does a model based on sovereign nation-states provide us with the most
useful perspective?

The emergent public understanding of the threat of greenhouse warming,
the rupturing of the ozone layer, the steadily worsening phenomenon of acid
rain, and the relentless elimination of plant and animal species, remind us
that the impact of technological development is not restricted to issues of
power and security. Over several decades the evidence has accumulated that
the single-minded application of technology, guided by the overarching goal
of economic growth, is destabilizing important characteristics of the biosphere. Temperature and radiation balance, diversity of species, purity of
life-sustaining nutrients and gases are by now all threatened.

As these problems become more significant in political life, a picture of a
world of supposedly sovereign domains seems increasingly incongruent with
the biophysical world in which we live. The issues are pressing, not least the
adequacy of existing institutions to meet the challenge of ecological disorder. The implications that environmental degradation raises for the theory of
sovereignty are subjected to closer scrutiny in Chapter 7.

The sense of ecological crisis is as much a result of growing social
awareness as a purely physical phenomenon. It is a symptom of a wider
social turbulence, indeed resistance, which has emerged in the face of the
global spread of modernity. Over the last several decades the growing complexity of political, economic and technological organization has been accompanied by the sometimes embryonic, and occasionally more mature,
development of a wide range of new social movements. Their focus varies
widely – from concern about ecological degradation to patriarchy, and from
the arms race to the denial of civil rights. Yet the domain of their activity is
often different from the social sphere delineated as the sovereign state. Some
social movements concern themselves, often intensely, with an issue which
is highly localized. Others address issues which are global in applicability,
working in a way which transcends national boundaries, sometimes forming
networks that embrace much of the world. In Chapter 8 we explore the
implications of this development for sovereignty. To what extent may these
be accommodated and explained within traditional perspectives? To what
extent do they require new explanations? And to what extent do they open
up new possibilities?

It may be clear, even from this preliminary sketch of the issues canvassed
in this book, that the theory and practice of sovereignty are facing profound

challenges from a world in a process of rapid change. The theory of sovereignty maps together particular notions of social organization and authority, with particular constructions of space and, as we shall see, time. It suggests that social and political activity does and can occur in a world compartmentalized along the boundaries and within the history and planning horizons of nation and state.

Given this, it may not seem unreasonable to expect that an alternative perspective would seek to identify not only new social formations, but social formations which effectively carve out, or have the potential to operate within, different domains of political time and space. Do such formations exist? In this book we argue that a basis for such development can be located, albeit still in embryonic form, within the contemporary political arena.

At stake is not only the size of political entities, nor even the demarcation of boundaries. It is the way in which the very nature of boundaries, actors and the political domain is defined and understood. Our analysis is neither simple nor unidirectional. But it suggests that at this moment of human history uncertainty about such issues represents more than just an accident of history. Rather it characterizes the period, suggesting that we are living at a time when the hard certainties of an older political space are giving way to new but still only partially discernible constraints and possibilities. Shifting allegiances, concepts, identities and forms of authority are characteristic of our age. The complex forms of social, economic and political organization, the multiple tiers of jurisdiction, and the uncertainties over what is to follow reinforce the conclusion that we live in a time of transition.

The times are uncertain and so is the future. Not all of the potential or predicted outcomes are attractive, and which of those outcomes will be realized remains an issue which can be settled only in the political arena. Opportunities, however, to achieve the objectives we desire (whether related to the ecology, the economy or security) will be revealed or obscured by the theories we choose to interpret the world. The analysis in this book suggests that the theory of sovereignty serves us poorly in this regard. But beyond that, it suggests that by shifting our theoretical vantage point, it is possible to begin to see, although still indistinctly, ways of grasping and fashioning new forms of less restrictive political space. It is this shift in theoretical perspective (reviewed in our concluding chapter) which opens up not only important analytical challenges, but also the tantalizing but still elusive possibility of restoring to civil society a more central and effective role in shaping our world's future.

NOTES

1. James A. Rosenau, 'Muddling, Meddling and Modelling: Alternative Approaches to the Study of World Politics in an Era of Rapid Change', *Millenium: Journal of International Studies*, **8**, (2), Autumn 1979, 130.
2. See for example, Jean-François Lyotard, *The Postmodern Condition: A Report on Knowledge*, Minneapolis: University of Minnesota Press, 1984; D. Harvey, *The Condition of Postmodernity: An Enquiry into the Origins of Cultural Change*, Oxford: Basil Blackwell, 1989.
3. See John W. Meyer, 'World Polity', in John W. Meyer and Michael T. Hannan (eds), *National Development and the World System: Educational, Economic and Political Change 1950–1970*, Chicago: University of Chicago Press, 1979.
4. See James M. Cypter, 'The Transnational Challenge to the Corporate State', *Journal of Economic Issues*, **13**, (2), June 1979, 513–42; also Richard Rosecrance, 'Interdependence, Myth or Reality?', *World Politics*, **26**, (1), October 1973, 1–27.
5. See Robin Murray, 'The Internationalisation of Capital and the Nation State?', *New Left Review*, **67**, May–June 1971, 84–109.

2.   Sovereignty in Theory and Practice

Sovereignty is a notion which, perhaps more than any other, has come to dominate our understanding of national and international life. Its history parallels the evolution of the modern state. More particularly, it reflects the evolving relationship between state and civil society, between political authority and the community. Hinsley, one of the foremost contemporary exponents of the principle of sovereignty, rightly reminds us that despite loose talk about the way it is acquired, lost or eroded, sovereignty is not a fact. Rather it is a concept or a claim about the way political power is or should be exercised.[1] Much of the confusion surrounding the concept arises from the many connotations it has acquired over the centuries, in particular from its association with notions of national interest, national independence and national security, but also with the notion of strength understood as the state's capacity to impose its will whether on its own citizens or other states.

Yet sovereignty is not just an idea. It is a way of speaking about the world, a way of acting in the world. It is central to the language of politics but also to the politics of language. It is part of the more general discourse of power whose function is not only to describe political and economic arrangements but to explain and justify them as if they belonged to the natural order of things. Sovereignty in both theory and practice is aimed at establishing order and clarity in an otherwise turbulent and incoherent world. Its historical function has been to act as 'a fundamental source of truth and meaning',[2] to distinguish between order and anarchy, security and danger, identity and difference.

Sovereignty, as both idea and institution, lies at the heart of the modern and therefore Western experience of space and time. It is integral to the structure of Western thought with its stress on 'dichotomies and polarities',[3] and to a geopolitical discourse in which territory is sharply demarcated and exclusively controlled. For all that, sovereignty may not be the last word on the subject. Given the far-reaching transformation of the social and political landscape we have witnessed this century, and especially these past several decades, there is a pressing need to rethink the concept and practice of sovereignty.

THE NEED FOR HISTORICAL PERSPECTIVE

It needs to be recognized from the outset that the theory of sovereignty is a
product of particular social and economic conditions. The quasi-universal
usage of the concept in contemporary discourse tends to obscure its relatively recent yet complex development. For most civilizations sovereignty
has not been a defining characteristic of political life. The notion would have
meant little to the tribal communities of Africa and Oceania organized
primarily around ties of lineage and kinship. The multi-state system of
ancient China with its subtle but fluid relationship between the monarchy
and feudal lords and princes could scarcely be described as a system of
sovereign states.[4] The Greek city-states, although frequently engaged in war
over territory, trade and personal rivalries, were not internally organized in
accordance with the logic of sovereignty.[5] The hegemonic principles which
underpinned the growth of the Egyptian, Persian and Roman empires bore
little resemblance to the modern notion of multiple, contending yet equal
sovereignties.[6] Similarly, the political communities constituted by the German
peoples of the Dark Ages or those reflected in the kingdoms and principalities
of medieval Europe were not sovereign states. Sovereignty, then, cannot be
understood without reference to its specificity in time and space.

To gain an insight into the concept we must turn our attention to Europe –
widely regarded as the cradle of the modern sovereign state. In the medieval
period both rulers and ruled were subject to a universal legal order which
reflected and derived its authority from the law of God. Though kings might
conclude treaties with their vassals and vassals enter into contractual arrangements with each other, it was the church which provided the feudal
order with an overarching, organizational and moral framework transcending both legal and political boundaries. As Robert Sack has aptly described
the feudal universe, 'the Christian community of the Church transcendent
was associated with the fixed and the eternal, while the earthly cities were
short-lived and changing'.[7] A maze of small kingdoms, principalities, duchies and other quasi-autonomous institutions (churches, monasteries and con-
vents enjoying special privileges and immunities, independent cities, guilds,
universities, merchants and manors) constituted a cosmopolitan patchwork
of overlapping loyalties and allegiances, geographically interwoven jurisdictions and political enclaves.[8]

In the feudal system there was no clear demarcation between the domestic
and external spheres of organization, no sharp dividing line between 'public
territories' and 'private estates'. The diverse and fragmented system of
feudal rule enjoyed a considerable level of coherence and unity by virtue of
'common legal, religious and social traditions and institutions'.[9] Benn and
Peters aptly express the legal conception of this divinely ordained hierarchy:

the law was not thought of as the creation of the political order.... Law was thought of as the external and objectively valid normative system within which all associations were contained, and from which all roles drew appropriate rights and duties.[10]

Although territorially segmented, the constituent units of the cosmopolitan order did not display the characteristics of possessiveness and exclusiveness associated with the modern concept of sovereignty. They saw themselves as the municipal embodiments of a universal community.[11]

By the end of the fifteenth century Europe comprised some 500 more or less independent political units,[12] but the old feudal order was in visible decline. Several city-states, particularly in the northern part of the Italian peninsula, became independent political entities boasting an elaborate network of banking and commercial facilities, a regular system of administration and the rudiments of a diplomatic service. With the growth of trade and the manufacturing classes, and the introduction of royal taxes, power in the rest of Western Europe became increasingly centralized in the monarchies. The strengthening of their authority, as manifested in the reigns of Henry II and Edward I in England and Philip IV in France, represented a sharp contrast with the medieval past, when the allegiance of individuals was directed primarily to their overlord, their village, their profession or their class. Monarchies developed central institutions that made and enforced the law, employed educated and competent civil servants, hired armies of mercenary troops and rationalized the collection of taxes.

By the sixteenth century several other movements were contributing to this trend. The achievements of the Renaissance in art, literature and philosophy were particularly important in the secularization of life and a corresponding decline in the spiritual and temporal authority of the church. The concentration of power in the monarchies gathered pace at the expense of the universal authorities – Pope and Emperor – and of the segmentary fiefdoms that had dominated the feudal period. The revival of Roman law corresponded to the needs of the absolutist state and the spread of capitalist relations in towns and country.[13] The strong attachment of Roman civil law to the notion of absolute private property provided the legal basis in Renaissance Europe for the growth of private commodity production and exchange in both agriculture and manufacturing. Similarly, though somewhat contradictorily, the Roman conception of absolute empirical power (enshrined in public law) became a potent weapon for the administrative centralization and territorial integration of the European monarchies.

With the Reformation and Counter-Reformation and the subsequent wars of religion, the emerging authority of the secular state appeared to be the most effective remedy for the widespread religious and political disorder that had engulfed Europe. The Reformation itself, by undermining the church's claim to universality and more particularly papal sovereignty, helped to prepare the ground for secular absolutism. Coercive authority would henceforth reside with the secular kingdom.[14] The economic practices of the merchant and the manufacturer coupled with scientific discoveries which contradicted longstanding religious doctrines contributed to the deepening schism in the church and further weakened the papacy and other religious institutions which had underpinned the ideological unity of medieval Europe.

The conclusion of the wars of religion, and especially the Treaty of Westphalia (1648) which terminated the bloody Thirty Years War, recognized the religious stalemate in Europe and resolved that henceforth religious affiliation would be determined by the secular ruler, not an external authority, be it the Holy Roman Empire or the Pope. The principle had in any case already been established through the Treaty of Augsburg (1555) which acknowledged the right of each individual German principality to decide whether its territory would be Lutheran or Catholic. The decentralized political arrangements characteristic of feudal society had thus given way to the Westphalian state system, that is a system of territorially bounded sovereign states, each equipped with its own centralized administration and possessing a virtual monopoly on the legitimate use of violence.

The consolidation of that system, which saw the development of new administrative mechanisms and forms of political control, coupled with the relocation of population and territory, facilitated the increase in trade and industrial activity during this period. At the same time the sovereign state played a vital role in redefining the concept of private property, understood as the right to exclude others from the possession of a commodity, be it land, capital or labour. Here we may note in parenthesis that the separation of the private and public spheres was paralleled and reinforced by changes in the structure of the family, the net effect of which was the consolidation of patriarchy. The enactment of laws supporting paternal authority in the household and inheritance in the male line dovetailed with the masculine conception and language of royal authority.

As Perry Anderson has pointed out, the absolutist state replaced the system of feudal domination which had relied on the institution of serfdom as a mechanism for fusing 'economic exploitation and politico-legal coercion at the molecular level of the village'. The apparatus of legal and political coercion had moved upwards 'towards a centralised, militarised summit – the absolutist state'.[15] The public authority of the state was used to enforce and legitimize a system of domestic and external – national and international – relations based on private property[16] and territorial expansion. Ownership, now understood 'as a freehold right, with no implied duties and indivisible possession',[17] had far-reaching implications for the monarchy.

Coupled with the notion of absolute sovereignty, it conferred on king or queen the right to *own* his/her domain, that is the possessions and territory over which they exercised legal jurisdiction. In this sense, the *state* became the royal *estate*. Taxation was simply a case of 'transferring his [the king's] property from one place to another'.[18] The acquisition of new territory, whether by conquest in Europe or colonization of the new world, was a means of extending the royal domain. The emergence of the sovereign state became the necessary instrument of Europe's colonial expansion.

Historians may argue over the precise date when sovereignty became a firmly established fact of political life, some focusing on the late fifteenth century, others on the Peace of Augsburg, and others still on the Treaty of Westphalia. There is also room for legitimate debate about the specific links between the legal and political framework ushered in by the absolutist state and the new economic order that replaced feudalism. These differences reflect in large part the substantial variations in the historical process as it unfolded in different parts of Europe. One thing is clear, however: sovereignty in both theory and practice was closely related to the prevailing social and economic environment of sixteenth- and seventeenth-century Europe. This is not to suggest, as is Hinsley's inclination, that sovereignty is an inevitable and virtually irreversible stage in the evolution of political institutions, or a necessary culmination of the integration of state and community.[19]

As Laski argues, the sovereign state represents not an absolute but an historical logic,[20] which is not to underestimate the power of that logic or its continued relevance to an understanding of the contemporary world. By the same token, to recognize the historical context of the concept is to highlight the close connection between political theory and political practice as well as between politics and economics. It invites us to examine whether the objective conditions which gave rise to the modern state are still largely intact, whether they have long since disappeared, or whether they are undergoing the kind of profound mutation which may in due course challenge the prevailing orthodoxy about the nature and function of state sovereignty.

THE THEORY OF SOVEREIGNTY

As we have already explained, the origin and history of the concept of sovereignty are closely related to the nature and evolution of the state, and in particular to the development of centralized authority in early-modern Europe. Most contemporary formulations of the concept are deeply indebted to the philosophical and theoretical positions advanced during that era. This is not to say that the European philosophers who developed the theory from the sixteenth to the eighteenth centuries were entirely at one in their understanding

of the concept. Many of them operated from different premises and espoused different and often contradictory views of social order. Sovereignty
could not after all be divorced from the state, itself a highly problematic
concept likely to give rise to a variety of interpretations.

Roman law, which helped to undermine the heritage of feudal ideas, was
undoubtedly one of the most important intellectual influences on the emerging theory of the state. Kenneth Dyson offers us a succinct analysis of that
influence. Whereas in medieval Europe priority was accorded to divine or
customary law, the Roman mind tended to ground law in the community or
its rulers (or some combination of the two).[21] Only the existence of a political community or state could give rise to a comprehensive legal system. The
state was understood as *summa potestas*, a Latin phrase denoting a quality of
mystique and majesty, which the sixteenth-century French philosopher, Jean
Bodin, would subsequently use interchangeably with 'sovereignty'. The intricate system of Roman law was based on the simple but fundamental
principle that a political community had the inherent power (or *imperium*) to
exact unlimited obedience from its citizens.[22]

The European revival of Roman law is clearly discernible in Machiavelli's
treatment of the state.[23] Writing in 1513–14 he offers a descriptive commentary on the Italian city-states of his own day but also a forecast of the
absolutist states that were in the making. He dispenses with medieval cos-
mology and its stress on divine authority and eternal life and gives pride of
place to the earthly political community grounded in the here and now.
Religion might still be needed, but 'a religion after the fashion of old Rome:
a religion that teaches that he who best serves his State best serves the
gods'.[24] The state, for Machiavelli, is an organization of force which ensures
security of persons and property. Its success, given the dangers posed by
internal corruption and external enemies, ultimately depends on 'a strong
hand and a clear intelligence at the helm'.[25] Only the shrewd and resourceful
'prince' can bring to fruition the aspirations of his people, and give expression to the moral and civic character of society. Machiavelli had made a
great stride towards the notion of the 'omnipotent legislator', yet fell short
of a general theory of political absolutism.[26]

It was left to subsequent theorists, notably Bodin and Hobbes, to equate
the state with the exercise of supreme authority within a given territory or
society. Institutions and individuals in charge of the state represented the
highest power in the land, acting as a court of last resort and holding an
effective monopoly on the use of force. The state was identified with the
power to make, administer and enforce laws and with the network of institutions necessary for this purpose. In time the conception of the state would be
widened to represent not just the institutions of government but the politically organized society, the body politic, the nation. According to this view,

associated primarily with traditionalists like Hooker and Burke but also with idealists such as Rousseau and Hegel, the state was a community of free people based on an implicit or explicit consensus.

In the nineteenth century the heritage of German romanticism would give rise to a further theoretical refinement with the state now conceived as 'a living, articulate force, a historic individual with a personality and will of its own, a personalised "whole" that embodied its own unique spirit'.[27] In sharp contrast to this notion was the Weberian model of the state as an autonomous, formally co-ordinated institution. Influenced by the steady expansion of bureaucratic systems of control, this model differentiated the state from other organizations by stressing its reliance on bureaucratic and legalistic methods of regulation and technical criteria of decision-making. These contrasting views of the state have deeply influenced the theory and practice of sovereignty and to a considerable extent account for the tensions that have surrounded the concept since its earliest formulation. This ambiguity, as we shall see, would become equally apparent in the external definition of the state.

The inconsistencies and ambiguities underlying the conceptualization of the state had ramifications for two closely related ideas: power and authority. If the state constituted the supremely powerful and authoritative institution of society, then the source and content of that power and authority would need to be subjected to careful scrutiny. The notion of authority has itself proved stubbornly elusive and given rise to numerous distinctions and shades of meaning. Perhaps one of the most helpful categorizations of the concept is that provided by Rees, who distinguishes moral authority (where one obeys a rule because it accords with one's conscience) from customary authority (where the rule is obeyed for fear of incurring the disapproval of another person or persons usually associated with the violation of social norms, customs or conventions), and from coercive authority (where the law is backed by force).[28] While conceptually distinct, these three forms of authority in practice often overlap, as is clearly the case with the authority of the state. It has nevertheless been argued that what distinguishes the state from other institutions is its coercive authority, or as others have labelled it, *supreme coercive power*.

According to this view, the legal sovereignty of the state, whether it is enshrined in a written or unwritten constitution, rests on the enforceability of the law, either directly by the exercise of supreme coercive power, or indirectly by the threat to exercise such power. This deceptively simple definition of sovereignty is fraught with difficulty, for what constitutes supreme coercive power is far from self-evident. Nor is it entirely clear whether such coercive power is exercised by one institution (or individual) above all others or shared by a number of institutions. If supreme coercive power is to be vested in one institution, the question arises as to whether such an institution can be readily identified. If, on the other hand, several institutions have a share in state sovereignty, in what sense can they be said to exercise supreme coercive power, especially when two or more of them are in conflict with one another? The latter problem would seem especially acute in a system based on the separation or division of powers. Here reference is often made to the United States Constitution, which enshrines a delicate system of checks and balances between President, Congress and the Supreme Court, and even limits the possibility of constitutional amendment by the provision that no state shall, without its consent, be deprived of its equal representation in the Senate.

The theory of sovereignty, then, in so far as it conceives of the state as quintessentially a structure exercising absolute power and authority in society,[29] has had to grapple with three separate but closely related questions. Are there practical or normative limits to the exercise of sovereignty? Where is sovereignty located? What is the relationship between state sovereignty and civil society? To appreciate more fully the troublesome nature of these questions, we shall briefly survey the answers offered by a representative sample of political thinkers who have most powerfully shaped the theory of sovereignty: Bodin, Hobbes, Locke, Rousseau, Kant and Austin. We shall then briefly refer to the Marxist critique before assessing the relevance of the concept for the contemporary organization of human affairs.

Bodin's *De la République* was first published in 1577 at the height of the civil war between Catholics and Huguenots. His thesis that a central authority should wield unlimited power was in part an attempt to restore order and security to the deeply divided political society that was France. His main contention was that such power had to be given legal recognition. It had to be endowed with *sovereignty*. Here he uses the words *souveraineté, majestas* and *summa potestas* more or less interchangeably. For Bodin, sovereignty was 'supreme power over citizens and subjects unrestrained by law',[30] and therefore unlimited in extension and duration. It represented absolute and perpetual legislative power, a notion no doubt influenced by Roman law and the familiar doctrines of the ruler's *imperium* and *legibus solutus*.[31] God, it is true, was above the sovereign, and the supreme power of the sovereign over all subjects was subordinate to the 'laws of God and Nature'. Bodin also referred to the constitutional or customary laws of the land, which he called *Leges Imperii* and which, he seemed to imply, even the sovereign could not change. But apart from these limitations, the practical consequence of which remained unclear, one reading of Bodin suggests that the sovereign was above the people, or, as Maritain has argued, 'separate from and transcendent over the people'.[32] On this reading, subjection to the sovereign is the defining characteristic of citizenship.

There were, nevertheless, important ambiguities in Bodin's conception of sovereignty. On the one hand, he was intent on investing the sovereign with the capacity to make and alter the law for all subjects in the realm, and with the right to do this regardless of their consent. On the other hand, he entertained a pluralist view of community life whereby the citizen acted as a member of multiple associations, including family, church, market, guild and corporation. As he himself explained: 'beside that sovereigntie of government thus by us set downe... many other things are of citizens to be had in common among themselves'.[33] If the community has a life of its own separate from that of the sovereign state, then how does one relate to the other?

Despite the lucidity of his argument, Bodin fails to grapple with this and several other questions. The sovereign is said to be subordinate to the law of God and nature, but what if the sovereign's will violates that law? Can this will still be deemed sovereign? Do the commands of the sovereign require absolute obedience? What if the sovereign contravenes the fundamental laws or *Leges Imperii* concerning the nature and form of government? To take these questions to their logical conclusion: are there any effective limitations to sovereignty and does such sovereignty ultimately rest on moral, customary or coercive authority? These unanswered questions may not have immediately affected the practical impact of Bodin's theoretical contribution, but, as we shall see, they have serious implications for the contemporary relevance of the concept.[34]

Though various writers over the following decades helped to refine the concept and vocabulary of sovereignty, the next major step did not come until *The Leviathan* in 1651. As in Bodin's case, Hobbes was writing against the background of civil war. Like Bodin and others before him, Hobbes sought to eliminate the dualism inherent in the notion of a body politic comprised of monarch and people, but unlike Bodin he swept aside all limitations on sovereignty by doing away with every right of the people. He abandoned the idea of a social contract between ruler and ruled and substituted for it a contract in which all individuals agreed to submit to the state. Hobbes describes the outcome of this universal surrender of the right to self-government as a 'Multitude united in one Person', a 'Commonwealth', a 'Leviathan'.[35] In this sense, the distinctions between society and state and between state and government are virtually abolished. Groups in the community have no independent or autonomous existence. They are merely allowed or sanctioned by the sovereign.

The omnipotent sovereign is for Hobbes the only alternative to complete anarchy. It is precisely because individuals are autonomous and equal in the 'state of nature' that they find themselves in a position of perpetual insecurity. It is only by eliminating conditions of autonomy and equality that security or 'the safety of the people' can be established. Here, Hobbes has in mind not simply physical survival, but the protection of property: 'Those that are dearest to a man are his own life, and limbs; and in the next degree (in most men) those that concern conjugal affection; and after them riches and means of living.'[36] To achieve this end, the state changes the conditions under which individuals pursue their interests. It reconstitutes society through the absolute powers of command exercised by the sovereign (legal system) and through the capacity to enforce the law (coercive power).[37] The sovereign cannot, therefore, be subjected to any criticism or limitation. No authority outside the state can sit in judgment on the state, not even religious or moral conscience, or any criterion of justice. Natural and customary law have no force of their own; it is only the sovereign's consent or command sanctioned by force which gives either reason or custom its legal status. Far from morality or convention setting a limitation on the authority of the sovereign state, it is the state which declares its own code of morals and its own religion.[38]

Not surprisingly, there soon developed a reaction to the political absolutism propounded by Hobbes on the part of those committed to constitutional theory and other more flexible forms of government. For writers such as Locke the answer did not lie in rejecting the concept of sovereignty or even Hobbes's egoistic individualism. Rather it lay in reinterpreting natural law as a claim to innate, inalienable rights inherent in each individual. For Locke, society and the state existed to preserve individual rights, including the right to property:

> men unite into societies that they may have the united strength of the whole society to secure and defend their properties, and may have standing rules to bound it by which every one may know what is his.... Hence it is a mistake to think that the supreme or legislative power of any commonwealth can do what it will, and dispose of the estates of the subject arbitrarily, or take any part of them at pleasure.[39]

The state was an instrument for protecting the 'life, liberty and estate' of its citizens. These rights were an effective limitation on the authority of the state, for the latter's legislative and executive rights were conditional on its performance, that is the preservation of the individual's rights.[40]

Locke had thus restored to natural law the importance of which Hobbes had deprived it by reaffirming the medieval tradition that moral laws are intrinsic and superior to positive law, and that governments are obliged to give effect by their laws to what is naturally and morally right. He jettisoned the Hobbesian notion of state sovereignty as supreme coercive power or at least moderated it by conceiving of government as held in trust for the people and deriving its legitimacy from their consent. Tacit though it may be, such consent could be given only in return for adequate protection of individual rights. By infringing such rights the offending government forfeited the right and authority to govern.[41] Sovereign power resided ultimately with the people. From this followed the need to divide and circumscribe state power and Locke's advocacy of majority rule and representative government.

The Lockean attempt to ground sovereignty in constitutional theory by reviving the idea of a partnership between ruler and ruled posed several problems. Not least among these was the effective division of sovereignty between ruler and ruled, thereby undermining the supremacy of power and authority which Bodin, Hobbes and others had come to regard as the essential ingredient of sovereignty.

In his *Social Contract* published in 1762, Rousseau sought to rescue the concept from the constitutionalist trap while seeking to avoid the authoritarian implications of the Hobbesian thesis. Like Hobbes, he argued that state sovereignty was unlimited and indivisible, and that the state was the result of a contract in which all individuals had agreed to submit to its will. But unlike Hobbes he equated the state with the body politic that had been formed by the social contract, 'reducing government, the rulership, to a mere commission'.[42]

For Rousseau the idea of a social contract virtually disappears, for he conceives of the community of citizens as a moral and collective personality in which each member, 'while uniting himself with all, may still obey himself alone, and remains as free as before'.[43] Having a moral identity of its own, society represented a collective good separate and distinct from the private interests of its members. It found expression in the 'general will' and endowed the body politic with absolute power over all its members. Moral authority (or popular sovereignty), at least of a kind, was reaffirmed as the basis of state sovereignty. The prerogatives of the sovereign could not 'exceed the limits of general conventions'.[44]

Rousseau's solution to the institutional dilemma posed by sovereignty was to suppress by the device of the general will the distinction between society and its political institutions, between the community and the state, between moral authority and coercive power. It was but a relatively small step to Hegel's idealization of the state as an absolute moral being, which he equated with 'the divine will, in the sense that it is mind present on earth, unfolding itself to be the actual shape and organisation of a world'.[45] Admittedly, to elevate the state to this exalted ethical plane Hegel was obliged to restore the distinction between state and civil society, but only in order to contrast the clash of individual egoistic interests that animate civil society with the *raison d'être* of the state, which is to safeguard and preserve the common good.

The dangerous implications of Rousseau's attempt to fuse the sovereignty of the people with the sovereignty of the state led Kant to reassert the principle of constitutional government. Although he accepted Rousseau's notion of popular sovereignty, he was at pains to stress the practical necessity of political organization. As Howard Williams explains, 'he sought to combine the freedom and consent of Rousseau's *Social Contract* with the domination and absolute authority of Hobbes' *Leviathan*'.[46] All members of society share in the law of the sovereign because each, as citizen, is involved in making the law – through a representative – in the legislature. But once made, the law, as administered by the executive and interpreted by the judiciary, is binding on all citizens.

This attempted reconciliation did not fully resolve the dilemma for it did not specify the necessary and sufficient conditions for the involvement of the citizenry in the making of the law. Nor did it address the complex question of whether, issues of constitutionality aside, the individual is ever entitled to disobey the law. Did the law ultimately rest on moral authority, however defined, or on the state's coercive power? It was in no small measure this unresolved question which prompted several writers to take refuge in the relative simplicity of the legal theory of sovereignty. One of its foremost exponents was the nineteenth-century English utilitarian, John Austin, whose conception of the law was limited exclusively to the category of positive law. The state, for Austin, was a legal order in which a specific authority is the ultimate source of power. This authority, which issues the commands that are habitually obeyed but which is itself immune to the commands of others, is the sovereign power in the state. Its authority is unlimited. For the purpose of this theory the moral character of the law is irrelevant. What matters is its effectiveness. The legal authority of the sovereign state derives from its supreme coercive power.

The foregoing interpretations of sovereignty, while posing more or less comparable questions and often using similar language, nevertheless indicate considerable differences of emphasis and approach. The tensions which are apparent, as much within as between the major theoretical frameworks, reflect a number of fundamental and ultimately unresolved ambiguities surrounding the concept itself. Even if we accept the meaning of sovereignty as supreme coercive power or authority, it is still not clear whether such authority is merely the attribute of an impersonal abstract state or whether it describes concrete, historically specific constitutional arrangements. Differences in conceptual or ideological disposition may help to explain why some theorists should identify the locus of sovereignty in the monarch, others in the representative assembly, others still in the people, not to speak of the more abstract formulations which proposed the Crown-in-Parliament, the constitution or simply the state as the repository of sovereignty.[47] Locating sovereignty was not merely a question of identifying this or that institution, but of determining whether sovereign authority presupposed a single or multiple locations. For many the monistic theory of sovereignty was the indispensable guarantee of the cohesiveness of state and society. For others a pluralistic interpretation was more in keeping with the requirements of a democratic polity.

Despite continual elaboration and refinements over nearly three centuries, the theory of sovereignty remained contested territory. There is nothing surprising in this given that sovereignty was generally conceived of as an attribute of the state and that the state itself was subject to numerous and sharply conflicting interpretations. By tying sovereignty so closely to the state and largely neglecting the relationship with civil society which it implied or encouraged, these theories became essentially exercises in abstraction. By divorcing themselves from the historical context, even though they themselves were often a direct response to prevailing political and socioeconomic conditions, these formulations acquired an air of unreality. They tended to accept as given assumptions about human rationality, the relevance of contractual obligations or the coincidence of state, territory and society, which only an analysis solidly grounded in history could hope to illuminate, let alone validate.

Here precisely lies the revolutionary significance of Marx's contribution. For him there is a sharp distinction to be drawn between philosophical formulation and political reality. Though the state may represent itself as sovereign and guardian of the general interest of society, this is largely an illusion. Though it may exercise power and subdue both groups and individuals to its will, the state, at least in the context of capitalist society, expresses the will of private property as the highest political and moral reality. The sovereign state is in one sense the 'official expression of civil society', yet it reflects the unhampered development of bourgeois society or the free movement of private interests.[48] It is not a 'public power' acting for the public, but a structure closely connected with particular interests and economic processes and institutions.[49] This is not to deny the relative autonomy of the state nor the fact that those who exercise state authority often think of themselves as raised above the rest of society. By the very nature of bureaucratization the state does rise above society and becomes a parasite on it.[50]

Even in the case of the Bonapartist state in France, Marx was careful to distinguish between its 'political independence' and its role as protector of the socially and economically dominant class.[51] In other words, Marx was intent on contrasting the sovereignty of the state (understood as the expression and instrument of the dominant social order) with the sovereignty of the people, for the unity and will of the nation could be realized only by the destruction of state power of which it was 'but a parasitic excrescence'.[52]

Regardless of the intricacies or validity of his class analysis, Marx's enduring insight was his appreciation of the close relationship between theory and
practice on the one hand and between politics and economics on the other.

FUNCTIONS OF THE MODERN STATE

The function of the absolutist state as conceived by Bodin and Hobbes was
to impose order in a Europe that had experienced the disintegration of the
feudal system and prolonged conflict and civil war. The more democratic
versions of state sovereignty offered by Locke, Rousseau and Kant reflected
the experience of a society increasingly conscious of its own history and the
emergence of a new economic class. The theory and practice of sovereignty
as it evolved in eighteenth-century Europe reflected, and in part anticipated,
a rapidly changing economic and political environment. To this extent at
least Hinsley is right in drawing attention to the historical origins and subsequent evolution of the theory and practice of sovereignty. He is on much
weaker ground when he tailors his argument to fit the well-known premises
of the realist paradigm, in particular when he suggests that the logic of
sovereignty is inherent in the nature of the state and that it has become and is
likely to remain the defining principle in the political organization of the
modern world. Above all Hinsley underestimates the multiple functions of
the modern state, and in particular its instrumental role in the accumulation
of capital and development of national markets.

The first and perhaps most obvious function of the sovereign state, first in
its absolutist and later in its national form, was the organization of space. By
the end of the seventeenth century most of the dynastic states of Europe had
developed centralized legal and administrative systems over clearly defined
territories. Neither outside powers (i.e. the Holy Roman Emperor and the
church) nor internal political units (e.g. duchies, cities) could challenge the
central law-making authority within its territorial jurisdiction or usurp its
exclusive right to make treaties. The sovereign state had thus asserted its
primacy in the control of geographic space, thereby reinforcing the territorial conception of community.

Social order was now more closely bound than ever before to the territorial definition of society. Within the boundaries of the state this meant a
hierarchy of jurisdictions extending from the central government at the top
to several sub-jurisdictions, which in turn might be divided into lower-order
districts.[53] The territorial fusion of society to place was an important factor
in economic organization but also in relations between states. Increasingly,
territorial defence became a primary obligation of the state, as an attack on
territory represented 'a challenge to the state's order and authority'.[54] The net

effect of sovereignty was to suggest 'permanence' in the relationship between state and space, and to emphasize patterns of continuity rather than historical transformation.[55] The demarcation and formalization of space mirrored and sustained the formalization of state authority.[56]

The territorial function of the state was inextricably linked with its economic function. It was the sovereign state which developed an intricate system of legal rights and emerging political guarantees for the maintenance of property relations – a function clearly stipulated by many of the classical political theorists. The legal framework facilitated the buying and selling of property, especially land, in ways that assisted speculative investment. Combining and recombining particular places with particular types of economic activity in profitable circumstances became an important task of government. The state also assumed responsibility for the circulation of commodities, standardization of the medium of exchange (money), and provision of the necessary material infrastructure for industrial development. As Barry Supple has observed, the state 'was a potential instrument of nationhood and of industrial power, since its sovereignty (where it could be successfully asserted) implied an ability both to transform national institutions and to dispose of economic resources by legislative and administrative means'.[57] By eradicating the power of feudal institutions, by maintaining an orderly system of law, by promoting domestic trade, and by manipulating taxes and subsidies, the state established the conditions for capitalist development.

Historically, the vigorous assertion of state authority *vis-à-vis* the market has been labelled mercantilism.[58] However, given that the term has been used loosely to describe different forms of state intervention, it may be useful to adopt the classification proposed by Miles Kahler. *Classical mercantilism*, often associated with state policies in sixteenth- to eighteenth-century Europe, perceives the international market as a relatively static zero-sum conflict and extols the virtues of a favourable balance of trade. *Developmental mercantilism*, which flourished particularly in the industrialization of the nineteenth century, uses an array of tariffs and other mechanisms to protect manufacturing industries as part of an overall policy of economic growth. *Countercyclical mercantilism* refers to the strategy pursued by most industrial countries in response to the 1930s depression, with the emphasis on trade and financial controls as a way of insulating the national economy from external sources of economic disruption.

These conceptual distinctions are important because they demonstrate the range of options open to the state and the way variations in state policy reflect different stages of capitalist development. In any case, the specific policies of the state will vary not only from period to period, but also from country to country. Moreover, mercantilist policies are likely to alternate and may even coexist with 'free-market' or *laissez-faire* policies.

In the first half of the nineteenth century the British state tended to pursue a *laissez-faire* strategy, involving a general 'dismantling of the structural, fiscal and economic barriers to the mobility of men and resources'.[59] The reduction of tariffs, the repeal of the Corn Laws (1846), the liberalization and subsequent abolition of the Navigation Laws, and the progressive deregulation of the labour and capital markets may at first sight suggest a state apparatus divorced from and unconcerned with the conduct of economic activity. This, however, is an entirely misleading impression. The state's non-interventionist stance in this period was carefully designed to enable entrepreneurs in industry, finance and commerce to take advantage of market forces. In any case, the state continued to supply the diplomatic framework and military force which would underpin the worldwide expansion of English capital.

During the same period the state played a more conspicuous role in the industrialization of continental Europe. In Prussia, in particular, the state continued its direct involvement in iron and coal production, and allocated considerable resources to the development of transport and selected manufacturing industries. Increasingly, the modern European state assumed responsibility for the control of markets and the acquisition of colonies. By the end of the nineteenth century, all capitalist states were in varying degrees involved in regulating the business cycle, overseeing industrial relations, supplying credit and subsidies to industry, funding scientific and technological research, organizing energy, transport and communication systems, and managing the external relations of the economy. The functions of the state did not derive so much from the logic of sovereignty or the will of sovereigns as from the needs of national economic expansion, the main beneficiaries of which were the emerging capitalist classes.

But the functions of the sovereign state were not purely economic.[60] It also had to resolve or at least moderate conflicts between opposing economic interests and at the same time maintain the legitimacy of the process, on which depended the stability of the prevailing order. In keeping with its legitimation function it had to offer a variety of rewards (e.g. income, education, industrial and political rights) to compensate those who would not otherwise benefit from the expansion of economic activity.[61] Further, the state became throughout the period of industrialization the principal mouthpiece for the ideology of modernization and technological mastery. The sovereignty of the state coupled with the formal enclosure of designated territories as private property provided the space, language and legitimating force for industrial innovation and the spread of modernity.[62]

Maintaining legitimacy, however, was only part of the state's stabilizing function. In a period of rapid social and economic change, it had to develop an extensive system of legal and administrative controls to ensure the efficiency of the industrial system and minimize the disruptive impact of political or electoral conflict. The power and authority of the sovereign state were thus reinforced but also significantly shaped by the very nature of the productive process and technical rationality.

There was also an important cultural dimension, not unconnected with the changing character of economic organization, namely the growth of nationalism. Some have attempted to locate the origins of the principle of nationality in the achievements of particular dynasties, whether by conquest or other means. Others have laid stress on the role of race, religion or language. Others still have interpreted nationalism as a quasi-metaphysical relationship to time and space, to the shared experience of past glories, grievances and sacrifices and of future hopes, dreams and ambitions.[63] The reality is that nationalism cannot be encapsulated by any one of these interpretations for its form and inspiration have varied considerably from country to country and period to period. As a generalization, it may nevertheless be argued that the European middle-class nationalism of the nineteenth century was much less governed by the 'personal interests, ambitions and emotions' of the ruler and more firmly planted in the 'collective interests, ambitions and emotions of the nation'.[64] The French Revolution clearly stands as a watershed in the 'democratization' of nationalism.

Nationalism, then, involves more than cultural experience. It represents a marriage of culture and politics. Its historical function has been to achieve the coincidence of state and civil society through the creation of the nation-state.[65] Yet states and nations have seldom evolved simultaneously. Whereas in some cases the nation, understood as national and cultural consciousness, preceded the state (e.g. in Germany), in others the reverse sequence applied (e.g. in France). In most parts of the non-Western world, the tendency has been for nation-building to follow political independence and the formation of sovereign statehood.[66] Regardless, however, of whether state or nation came first, the general tendency of the state has been to promote nationalist sentiment as a way of preserving its own cohesion. The attempt of the state to manipulate the symbols of ethnocentric identification and thereby reinforce its own power and authority is symptomatic of the wider bureaucratization of society and may be termed bureaucratic or state-centred nationalism.

Modern European nationalism and the various themes which gave it political potency (e.g. national self-determination, national independence, national honour) were levers which political movements and governments could use to mobilize popular energies and resources in support of their respective objectives. The end result was the creation of new national states (e.g. Germany, Italy) and the disintegration of existing multinational states (e.g. the Austro-Hungarian Empire, the Ottoman Empire). Nationalism was not, however, the mere invention of the state. It reflected a complex set of relationships and needs, of beliefs and institutions ushered in by the Renaissance and Reformation and by the subsequent scientific and industrial revolutions.

The rise of the nation was greatly facilitated by the rise of a new individualism,[67] and in particular by the emerging protestant ethic with its stress on literacy, personal achievement and rejection of a monopolistic priesthood. In the expanding world of knowledge, education became the key to identity, culture the necessary instrument and lifeblood of a shared environment. In this sense, the national principle derived much of its impetus from the combined effect of industrialization and urbanization, and especially from the uneven development to which they gave rise.[68] Although nationalism appears as a highly voluntaristic political and ideological phenomenon, it expresses the contradictions inherent in the spread of capitalism and more specifically the conjunction of economic dislocation, political fragmentation and ethnic-cultural differentiation. Nationalism, then, may be interpreted as the partly organized, partly spontaneous convergence of cultural and political experience in conditions of rapid economic change. It points to the attempted homogenization of culture within each political unit and the increasing role of the state as the main vehicle for the transmission of culture.

In this sense national sovereignty came to be seen as the defining principle of political organization, and the principal vehicle for managing, if not resolving, class, ethnic or religious conflict within and between nations.[69] It became the foundation stone of European international relations. Following the French Revolution and the subsequent downfall of Napoleon the principle was applied ever more vigorously to the external conduct of the leading European states. Increasingly the world was seen as comprising political units (states) each with a supreme authority enjoying the allegiance of its citizens and exercising an unlimited capacity to dispose of the territory and resources of that society. Outside of their boundaries, these units might act with restraint but in no circumstance would they acknowledge an external authority higher than their own.[70] In Hinsley's view, the principle was so firmly entrenched in the organization of the modern state that even when the international system broke down with the outbreak of the First World War, institutional attempts, such as the League of Nations, to suppress or limit the principle were bound to end in failure.[71] Although the status of sovereignty was at first applied exclusively to the European states system, it was eventually extended to non-Western states and inscribed in the United Nations Charter.

The state-centric view of the world or as others have subsequently labelled it the 'billiard-ball theory of international relations' or the 'international politics paradigm',[72] expressed the external dimension of sovereignty. A

system of sovereign states was one in which all states were equally independent of outside authority in the control of territory and population.[73]
Sovereignty, territorial integrity and legal equality of states were seen as the
hallmarks of international relations.[74] Several rules of international conduct
were said to derive from these three fundamental principles. First, a sovereign state could not, without its consent, allow other political entities 'to
make or apply their own rules on its territory'.[75] Secondly, and as a corollary
of the first rule, a sovereign state had the obligation 'not to intervene in the
internal affairs of other states or compromise their territorial integrity'.[76]
Thirdly, states enjoyed by virtue of their sovereignty equal rights and duties
regardless of differences in their demographic, economic or strategic circumstances.

These three basic rules, often described as the accepted norms of international conduct, rested on a distinctive though seldom clearly articulated
premiss, namely the notion of the state as person. Raymond Aron, for one,
leaves no doubt about the importance he attaches to this aspect of sovereignty. He defines the nation as a 'collective personality' which, like the
individual personality, 'is born and dies in time... asserts itself only by
consciousness, being capable of thought and action'.[77] Though the state is an
institution, its objectives may not be reduced purely to those of its members.
As collective beings states have an end in themselves. Moreover, in so far as
a state is a *national* entity, enjoying a common language, culture, history and
law, it is endowed with a unique calling or vocation.[78] Not all proponents of
the realist school of international relations theory would subscribe to this
highly voluntaristic, almost romantic personification of the state, yet most, if
not all, would in varying degrees share the conception of the modern state as
a socially and territorially cohesive entity capable of rational calculation in
pursuit of the *national interest*.

The monistic and volitional idea of the state is to a large extent a legacy
of social contract theory, which postulates the emergence of a purposeful
sovereign entity out of the structural relations of insecurity characteristic of
the state of nature. The ordered polity resulting from the Hobbesian contract
between individuals cannot, however, be replicated internationally by a similar
contract between states. The 'ahistorical moment of utilitarian calculation
informed by reason and fear'[79] that gave rise to the social contract has no
counterpart in international relations. The statist boundaries that separate
territorial spaces define and limit the scope for interaction between sovereign states as well as the freedom of action of non-sovereign entities. Domestic order is the mirror image and necessary condition of international
disorder. Anarchy thus becomes the axiomatic and unalterable principle of
global life, underpinning much theoretical discourse, not least balance of
power theory, strategic theory and game theory.

There are nevertheless variations in the way different theorists handle the anarchy problematic. For some, international relations is a crude and unrelenting struggle for power in which the supreme value is the preservation of the state. From Machiavelli's realism it was but a small step to the various doctrines of *raison d'état* that flourished in the eighteenth century and a somewhat larger step to the 'glorification of the state as force' of might as right, which reached its peak in 'the nineteenth-century German *Realpolitik* conception of *Machtstaat*'.[80] For others, international anarchy does not negate international society, that is a society of sovereign states in which the mutual recognition of sovereignty provides a basis for tolerable coexistence. Conflict and competition are tempered by a degree of co-operation reflected in the development of several institutions, notably the distinct body of rules, treaties and conventions encompassed by international law, the diplomatic system endorsed by the Congress of Vienna, and the balance of power framework proclaimed by the Treaty of Utrecht (1713) and incorporated into international jurisprudence with Vattel's *Droit des Gens* (1758).[81]

Theorists attracted to the Vattelian conception of international relations tend to argue that its emphasis on sovereignty, equality of states and voluntary adherence to commonly agreed rules of conduct makes for a more stable and predictable environment in which breaches of the rules are likely to be more difficult to justify and therefore more limited and less frequent.[82] For many writers the balance of power system captures the essence of relations between sovereign states, because it offers the most plausible account of the fragmentation of power which those relations imply. While it is possible to envisage other models of interaction (e.g. supranational integration, world government), these are deemed much less realistic precisely because they do not come to terms with the inescapable decentralization of power on a global scale.[83]

The Vattelian conception of international relations, though it allows for varying degrees of co-operation between states, nevertheless shares the fundamental premise which animates all sovereign-centred theories, namely the existence of a sharp divide between the domestic realm where order, cohesion and government are the norm and the international system whose defining characteristics are fragmentation, absence of central authority and the permanent threat of war. Maurice Keens-Soper provides us with a succinct elaboration of this premise:

> The uniqueness of the states-system as an association is that although it belongs to the gallery of human political associations, its 'constitution' is composed of institutions like diplomacy, international law and the balance of power, which are not to be found in other quarters. The political space of Europe was subject to government but to government by its independent but connected parts.[84]

International law, diplomacy and the balance of power may attenuate the frequency and intensity of conflict but they cannot obscure, much less eradicate, the distinction between intra- and inter-state order inherent in the very notion of sovereignty.[85]

OLD DEBATES, NEW QUESTIONS

Despite the entrenched position which it has come to occupy in theoretical discourse and at least declaratory policy, the idea of sovereignty has not gone unchallenged. Numerous critics have questioned the explanatory value of the concept, in particular its applicability to the twentieth century. They refer to the emergence of federal systems of government and various checks and balances, all of which are said to contribute to the internal diffusion of power and authority. Externally, they see national sovereignty as considerably limited and qualified by the growth of international law and organization. Finally, the critique of sovereignty has a normative dimension arising in part from the largely unresolved tension between democratic principles and the absolutist tendencies inherent in the concept.

Turning first to considerations of analytical validity, the key question may be phrased as follows. Does the theory of sovereignty in its various guises reflect the exercise of power in the contemporary world? Here it must be said that much of the discussion around this question has been terribly confused – partly because the implications of the relative diffusion or concentration of power are themselves ambiguous. On the one hand, it could be argued that class conflict and the fragmentation of power are antithetical to the internal meaning of sovereignty, with its emphasis on the existence of a central power in every state. On the other hand, the centralization of power and authority associated with a ruling elite or ruling class does not sit comfortably with the notion of popular sovereignty, unless we maintain the fiction that the powerful few in some mystical sense represent the will of the entire body politic. The idea of popular sovereignty, which the nation-state is meant to embody, does seem at odds with the concentration of power which typifies the modern industrial state.

In theory the *sovereignty of the people* implies that the authority of laws, leaders and the constitution itself ultimately derives from society as a whole. But this theoretical unity of the concept is contradicted by practical reality. To illustrate the argument, it can be said that in the United States the Supreme Court is the ultimate arbiter in any conflict between citizens and the courts, or between the federal government and the states that make up the federation.[86] But the size, organization and composition of the Supreme Court are determined by Congress. The Supreme Court does not exercise sovereign power in the sense in which absolute kings were said to be sovereign. It does not enjoy the executive or 'federative' power envisaged by Locke. The constitutional and practical limitations on the authority of the Supreme Court apply in different but equally effective ways to the powers and functions of both President and Congress, not to mention state governors, courts and legislatures. Clearly, in the American system, characterized as it is by the division and separation of powers, it is not possible to locate one or more clearly identifiable persons who assume ultimate responsibility for the exercise of power. Conflict is embedded at the very heart of the formal system of power.

This fragmentation of authority is also evident in unitary systems. In the British Westminster model, ultimate law-making may be said to reside in the Parliament yet, so long as it commands a cohesive majority in the House of Commons, Cabinet wields effective authority. Cabinet's hold on power may nevertheless be threatened either by internal or external crisis (i.e. within the ranks of the governing party), or by a change of fortunes at the next election. In practice, but also in theory, it is not entirely clear whether ultimate authority resides in the House of Commons, both Houses of Parliament, the Crown, public opinion or the common law. Identifying those who possess on paper the supreme law-giving or law-enforcing authority is difficult enough; establishing the unity of purpose of those who exercise such authority in practice may be virtually impossible.

Yet the pluralist attack on the legal doctrine of sovereignty is not confined to an analysis of formal institutions. Indeed, the pluralist argument revolves principally around the notion that law has its origins not in the command of a sovereign but in the multiple associations that make up the community.[87] Laski describes the dispersion of legal authority in the following terms:

> no organisation disposes in actual fact of unlimited force; and we shall fail completely to understand the character of society, unless we seek to grasp exactly how the sovereign is compelled to will things desired by bodies in the law inferior to itself.[88]

Like other pluralists, Laski calls into question the existence of an absolute authority as the source of all law and postulates instead a multiplicity of group interests, each of which possesses a degree of autonomy and contributes to the richness and complexity of social life.[89] For the pluralists, society was by definition 'multicellular and decentralised'[90] and would not therefore be represented by a single sovereign will, any more than the individual could be fully represented by a single association.[91] Divorced from social reality monistic sovereignty had little explanatory value. At best, its function would be to justify a particular form of government or the power of certain persons or institutions; at worst it could be used to obscure or conceal the reality of power by maintaining the fiction of popular sovereignty.

An added dimension of the complex environment within which modern states have to operate and which severely militates against sovereignty is said to be the expanding role of international law and international organization. Regardless of how it is that treaties and agreements arise – normally they come into being by virtue of the decisions of governments acting on behalf of sovereign states – the rapidly developing legal order both reflects the inadequacy of the state as a self-contained unit of decision-making and restricts its freedom of action. Though not legislated by a central authority, and at times lacking precision or the support of force, international law, through customs, conventions, agreements, the decisions of tribunals and the development of contemporary ethical values, has come to prescribe rules of conduct impinging on almost every facet of human organization.[92] As a consequence, international law – and the various types of international organization which accompany it – feeds on itself and becomes so closely interwoven with domestic law as to make the dividing line increasingly blurred. In these circumstances it has become progressively more difficult to demonstrate the primacy of domestic law, which is arguably one of the cardinal premisses of state sovereignty.

But there is another and more profound sense in which states are often obliged to act in ways dictated by persons and groups that do not come under their jurisdiction. The exercise of sovereignty is limited by the realities of power within and between states. To the extent that the international system normally comprises a few powerful and many weaker states, there inevitably arises a hierarchy of relations that does not easily correspond to the theoretical equality of all sovereign states. Even Austin has to concede that the predominance of powerful states (e.g. Prussia *vis-à-vis* the other members of the North German Confederation) may represent a hegemonic order inconsistent with the sovereignty of weaker states,[93] although he describes such instances as 'comparatively rare and transient'. In Oppenheim's case, power hierarchies in international relations are said to be contained by the operation of the balancing of power, which reduces the disparities between stronger and weaker states sufficiently to provide all states with the indispensable minimum of social equality.[94] But what is the meaning of such equality? Can an international system that is unable to guarantee the conditions necessary for the self-determination of most, if not all, its members be accurately described as a system of 'sovereign' states?[95]

Apart from questioning the descriptive and analytical utility of the concept, the critique of sovereignty has also contained an important normative element which stems from the tension inherent in the concept between power and autonomy and between hierarchy and democracy. Many have argued that the principle of state sovereignty, taken to its logical conclusion, undermines or at least grievously weakens the democratic ethic. Maritain, for example, focusing on Bodin's theory and in particular on his memorable phrase 'the prince is the image of God', concludes that 'the sovereign – subject to God but accountable only to him – transcends the political whole just as God transcends the cosmos'.[96] Rather than being part of and representing the body politic the 'prince' is *separate* and *transcendent*. He rules not at the peak but above the peak. The separateness and transcendence characteristic of the sovereign *vis-à-vis* the political society, and of the state *vis-à-vis* the community, are antithetical to the democratic impulse. More importantly perhaps, they reflect the legal and political separateness that divides one sovereign from another, one society from the rest of the international community. For Maritain this separateness is 'all the more questionable as the State is mistaken for the body politic itself or for the personification of the people themselves'.[97] Understood in this sense, state sovereignty becomes divorced from popular sovereignty and related notions of pluralism, autonomy, freedom and accountability.

Modern constitutional doctrines may have sought to incorporate institutional arrangements consistent with democratic aspirations. But, as Morgenthau rightly reminds us, these doctrines overlook the simple fact that 'in any [sovereign] state, democratic or otherwise, there must be a man or a group of men ultimately responsible for the exercise of political authority'.[98] In times of peace, the constitutional distribution of authority may give the impression that the supreme law-giving and law-enforcing authority is dispersed or even abolished, but this illusion is soon dispelled in times of crisis and war, when ultimate responsibility reasserts itself. For this proposition Morgenthau cites as evidence the presidencies of Lincoln, Wilson and the two Roosevelts.[99] The attempt to graft institutions on to the sovereign state rests then on a fundamental contradiction, which in practice is often resolved at the expense of the democratic principle.

A separate but related aspect of the critique – also integral to the democratic tradition – is the emphasis on the individual citizen rather than the state as the ultimate source of moral judgment. No edict, order or law, it is argued, can be absolved from the scrutiny of the citizen. No action of the state can infringe basic human rights. The real constraining force on the citizen, according to Laski, 'is not the legal obligation to obey government but the moral obligation to follow what we regard as justice'.[100] For him, the individual is the supreme arbiter of human conduct. It is the individual, not the state, that is sovereign.

Finally, it has been argued that the concept of an absolute and transcendent authority which demands an unqualified allegiance from its subjects is not compatible with the interests of humanity, by which is meant the interests of those under the state's jurisdiction as well as those beyond it. The morality of sovereign states is presumably one in which each state is a law unto itself, able to act as it pleases regardless of the consequences for others. If states are to be considered ends in themselves, morally immune to external interference, they are presumably entitled to dispose of their territories and resources without consideration for the welfare of other societies. In other words, their actions are premised on narrowly conceived self-interest much as firms and individuals are supposed to operate in the market system of nineteenth-century *laissez-faire* economics.[101] Clearly, this view has unfortunate implications for the distributive outcomes of international interaction.

In responding to these arguments advocates of the principle of sovereignty have mounted a complex and wide-ranging defence of their thesis. The more sophisticated among them concede that changes in the domestic and external environment have restricted the state's room for manoeuvre. They readily acknowledge the impact of technology in significantly reducing the capacity of states to protect their respective populations. Equally they are conscious of the implications of technological, financial and economic interdependence for the legal and moral framework of international conduct. Yet for them none of this invalidates sovereignty as the central ordering concept in political analysis. The sovereign state remains the only significant territorial actor; indeed virtually the whole world is divided among sovereign jurisdictions and virtually every person lives on territory controlled by one of these jurisdictions. The sovereign state is the political unit on which most continue to rely for their protection and security.

The constraints imposed by international law, we are told, are fully compatible with the exercise of sovereignty since the state's right to enter into international engagements is itself an attribute of sovereignty.[102] In obeying international law the state is not subjecting itself to the will of another state but to its own will. Sovereignty may be incompatible with a highly centralized system of international law, but 'is not at all inconsistent with a decentralised, and hence weak and ineffective, international legal order'.[103] Decentralization in this context means the absence of a supreme legislative power to make and revise the law, the absence of a supreme tribunal to interpret the law, and the absence of an irresistible force to impose the law. Internationally, only those rules are binding to which nations have consented, and even then the nature of that consent is likely to be so vague and qualified that the consenting nation's freedom of action will hardly have been affected. Given that the international legal order is not normally supported by physical force, there is little that can be done to violate the territorial sovereignty of the law-breaking nation.

In the case of external constraints, other than purely legal ones, the defence of sovereignty again rests largely on the legal definition of the concept, which draws the distinction between legal sovereignty and political

independence. The sovereign state, it is argued, is no less sovereign because
it does not possess unfettered freedom of action. Here a distinction is often
drawn between *de facto* and *de jure* independence,[104] or between relative and
absolute sovereignty, or again between positive and negative sovereignty.[105]
Others go so far as to suggest that sovereignty confers 'vitality' on the state
not simply by virtue of formal independence, but through co-operation with
other sovereign states.[106]

The notion of relative sovereignty (as distinct from the legal definition of
the term) has a domestic analogue. The supreme legal authority, which the
sovereign state implies, requires a supreme coercive power which ensures
enforcement of the law through the use or threat of force. But neither the
legal authority nor the coercive power, we are told, should be confused with
supreme political influence. Groups and individuals in society may share in
the exercise of supreme political influence to the extent that 'they determine
in certain intended ways the actions of the coercive and legal sovereigns'.[107]
The point of such a theoretical construction is to take account of the dispersion of power in most complex political systems. It points to the subtle
interaction of the sovereign and political society.

For Hinsley, Aron and others, the sovereign state also serves a normative
function. The coincidence of territorial state and cultural community constitutes the most appropriate and effective framework for the organization of
political, economic and technical power. The expanded functions and power
of the state parallel and reinforce the increased cohesion of the community
and facilitate the closer association between state and community evidenced
by the rise of mass politics and popular forms of government.[108] It is precisely the growing integration of the cultural and political aspects of social
life that in Hinsley's view accounts for the solidity of the modern state and
prevents the reversion to segmentary politics often associated with the decline of imperial states. Internationally, the principle of sovereignty has
played an equally important rule, justifying 'the recognition of the formal
equality of all peoples, the abrogation of unequal treaties, mandates, protectorates, in short decolonization'.[109]

The above qualifications and refinements are a useful contribution to the
contemporary restatement of the theory of sovereignty. They represent a
considered response to the criticisms that have been intermittently levelled
against the principle on both empirical and normative grounds. It is questionable, however, whether the defence can easily rest its case on these
arguments, for the structural transformation of political and economic life in
the twentieth century raises troublesome questions which require far more
careful and detailed scrutiny.

One question which the sovereignty thesis has largely neglected but which,
as we have seen, is central to any investigation of the modern world is the

nature and function of the nation-state itself. To conceive of the state as a geometric or metaphysical abstraction divorced from time and space is to conceal its historical specificity. How, then, are we to interpret the state? To describe it as a co-ordinated set of legal, administrative and coercive institutions may be accurate, but what is it that gives those institutions their content and meaning? Can we readily assume that their sole or primary function is the protection and security of citizens? Or is it analytically more fruitful to define the state as 'a mechanism for dominating, regulating and reproducing a society under given social relations'?[110] If we adopt this wider definition, then we may also need to cast the net wider to include institutions (e.g. the educational system, central banks) which perform important ideological and economic functions. This definitional approach would seem more appropriate given that a dominant characteristic of the industrial age has been the increasing integration of the productive process with the political apparatus of society.

If the state's legislative, administrative and supervisory functions enable it to enter the very fabric of the economy, it is all the more necessary to re-examine the relationship between the 'sovereign' state and civil society. Social contract theory, for example, tells us little about the relationship between the state and dominant economic interests, between bureaucratic rationality and technical specialization on the one hand and the political process on the other. This immediately raises the question as to whether the structures of the state should be abstracted and separated from those of society.

Implicit in such abstraction is the separation of the public and private spheres, with the state, understood as the political arm of society, assuming responsibility for the public interest and the private sphere consisting of the market and the relations of private groups and individuals. Whether this abstracted conception of the state, the polarities on which it rests and the ensuing autonomy (not to say sovereignty) which is ascribed to it are a reasonable approximation of social reality is, to say the least, seriously open to question.

The reification of the state as a self-contained, cohesive, purposeful agent has given rise to another dubious distinction, namely the national–international divide. This is misleading on two counts. First, it greatly underestimates the quantitative and qualitative aspects of interaction across porous state boundaries. Secondly, it greatly overstates the importance of internal social, cultural and economic conditions in the shaping of politics and the state. In a masterly review of a highly neglected tradition in the literature,[111] Gabriel Almond stresses 'the impact of international factors on internal political structure and process'.[112] He refers to Hintze's general law which holds that 'the spirit and essence of internal politics is dependent on the external conditions of the state',[113] and highlights the impact of international conflict and war on the state-building process.

Perry Anderson is no doubt right in interpreting the centralization of European monarchies in the sixteenth century and the rise of powerful armies and bureaucracies as a function of the emerging conflict between the aristocracy and a mutinous peasantry. Yet he is also attentive to the role of external pressures, particularly as they developed in the seventeenth and eighteenth centuries.[114] In Charles Tilly's analysis, external threats assume even greater significance, requiring states to extract additional resources from society in order to preserve their territorial integrity, maintain internal security and recruit and train the military and civilian personnel needed for these tasks.[115] Similarly, a number of historical studies suggest that the uneven development of the world economy was an important factor in the sharply diverging responses of European states to the process of industrialization (e.g. German protectionism in the nineteenth century compared with British liberalism). In his investigation of German, French, British, Swedish and American responses to the three world economic crises of 1873–96, 1929–39 and 1975–85, Gourevitch concludes that policy choices and outcomes in each case were greatly influenced by the structural relationship between the national and world economies.[116] Finally, mention must be made in this context of the relevance of international conflict and instability to an understanding of domestic crisis and upheaval. For Theda Skocpol international crises and war emerge as decisive influences in the French, Russian and Chinese revolutions, hastening the breakdown of the state and helping to unleash a powerful revolutionary dynamic.[117]

The point about these and other studies which stress the national–international connection is that, despite considerable differences in perspective and methodology, they all affirm the need for interactive analytical models. Two closely related forms or levels of interaction are involved: interaction between a nation-state's internal and external environment, but also between the cultural, economic, military and political dimensions in the exercise of power and authority. Such interaction is of necessity historically grounded, arising from and at the same time giving rise to periodic movements of structural transformation.

The need to rethink the notion of sovereignty is very much a function of the historical process. It reflects the widely perceived failure of the realist perspective to come to terms with the complexity of an increasingly integrated world which, paradoxically enough, coincides with the decentralization of authority and fragmentation of society.[118] Even a sophisticated model that encompasses subnational, supranational and transnational as well as national actors, while it may more accurately reflect the diversity of contemporary politics, does not necessarily explain the origins, nature or significance of that diversity. It may not correctly identify, let alone analyse, the interacting dependencies and interdependencies that cut across national boundaries.

Theorists of widely diverging ideological persuasion have recognized the declining efficacy of state action, and the emergence of issues, relationships and institutions that dissolve the national–international divide. Numerous concepts, including *aggregation, interdependence, world society, world order* and *world economy*,[119] have been advanced as a way of opening a window on the globalization of human affairs, of reassessing the meaning and function of sovereignty. To give but one example, Rosenau has sought to interpret the process of globalization by tracing a bifurcation in which the *state-centric world* coexists and interacts with a diffuse *multi-centric world* consisting of diverse, 'sovereign-free' actors largely preoccupied with issues of autonomy in contrast to the traditional security dilemma of states.[120] In the chapters that follow we shall consider this and other models of interaction. This is not to say that there is universal agreement on the scope or significance of cultural, economic or institutional interdependence. Some writers have challenged what they consider to be premature conclusions about the extent of international interdependence or of the state's declining freedom of action.[121] Certainly there is considerable evidence, especially in the light of recent trends, that international and transnational interaction is central to the organization and distribution of economic and political power. It is one more factor compounding the ambiguities which at every level now surround the principle of sovereignty.

NOTES

1. F. Hinsley, *Sovereignty*, London: C.A. Watts, 1966, p.1.
2. Richard K. Ashley, 'Untying the Sovereign State: A Double Reading of the Anarchy Problématique', *Millenium: Journal of International Studies*, (hereafter referred to as *Millenium*), **17**, (2), Summer 1988, 230.
3. For an analysis of the discourse of 'otherness' and its place in Western thought, see Simon Dalby, *Creating the Second Cold War: The Discourse of Politics*, London: Pinter, 1990, pp. 17–29.
4. See Richard L. Walker, *The Multi-State System of Ancient China*, Hamden, Conn.: Shoe String Press, 1953; Dun J. Li, *The Ageless Chinese: A History*, New York: Charles Scribner's Sons, 1965; Kenneth S. Latouretle, *The Chinese: Their History and Culture*, New York: Macmillan, 1959.
5. See T.R. Glover, *The Ancient World*, Harmondsworth, Middlesex: Penguin, 1944; Kathleen Freeman, *Greek City-States*, London: Methuen, 1948; Victor Ehrenberg, *The Greek State*, New York: Norton, 1964.
6. Adda B. Bozeman, *Politics and Culture in International History*, Princeton, NJ.: Princeton University Press, 1960; S.N. Eisenstadt, *The Political Systems of Empires*, New York: Free Press, 1963; Joel Larus (ed.), *Comparative World Politics: Readings in Western and Pre-Modern Non-Western International Relations*, Belmont, Cal.: Wadsworth, 1964.
7. Robert D. Sack, *Conceptions of Space in Social Thought: A Geographic Perspective*, London: Macmillan, 1980, p. 184.

8. See C. Tilly (ed.), *The Formation of Nation-States in Western Europe*, Princeton, NJ.: Princeton University Press, 1975, p. 15; also James Anderson and Stuart Hall 'Absolutism and Other Ancestors', in James Anderson (ed.), *The Rise of the Modern State*, Brighton: Wheatsheaf Books, 1986, p. 28.

9. See Perry Anderson, *Lineages of the Absolutist State*, London: New Left Books, 1974, pp. 37–8.

10. S.I. Benn and R.S. Peters, *Social Principles and the Democratic State*, London: Allen & Unwin, 1959, p. 256.

11. John Gerard Ruggie, 'Continuity and Transformation in the World Polity: Toward a Neo-Realist Synthesis', *World Politics*, **35**, (2), January 1983, 275.

12. Garrett Mattingly, *Renaissance Diplomacy*, London: Jonathan Cape, 1955; also R. Strayer and D.C. Munro, *The Middle Ages* (4th edn), New York: Appleton-Century-Crofts, 1959.

13. Anderson, *Lineages*, pp. 24–9.

14. See Andrew Vincent, *Theories of the State*, Oxford: Basil Blackwell, 1987, p. 48.

15. Anderson, *Lineages*, p. 19.

16. See Ruggie, 'Continuity and Transformation', pp. 275–6.

17. Vincent, *Theories of the State*, p. 62.

18. Ibid., p. 64.

19. F.H. Hinsley, *Sovereignty*, pp. 8–22.

20. Harold Laski, *A Grammar of Politics* (5th edn), London: Allen & Unwin, 1967, p. 48.

21. Kenneth Dyson, *The State Tradition in Western Europe: A Study of an Idea and an Institution*, Oxford: Martin Robertson, 1980, p. 113.

22. See Phyllis Doyle, *A History of Political Thought*, London: Jonathan Cape, 1963 (first published 1933), pp. 43–4.

23. Niccolò Machiavelli, *The Prince and The Discourses* (introduction by Max Lerner), New York: Random House, 1950; see especially *The Discourses*, 1: 2, 3, 4.

24. J.W. Allen, *A History of Political Thought in the Sixteenth Century*, London: Methuen, 1960, p. 459.

25. Ibid., p. 484.

26. George A. Sabine, *A History of Political Theory* (3rd edn), London: Harrap, 1963, p. 346.

27. Dyson, *State Tradition in Western Europe*, p. 103.

28. W.J. Rees, 'The Theory of Sovereignty Restated', *Mind*, **59**, (236), October 1950, 508–9.

29. For the standard modern definition of sovereignty as supreme law-making power see Harry Eckstein, 'On the "Science" of the State', *Daedalus*, **108**, (4), Fall 1979, 6.

30. Jean Bodin, *The Six Bookes of a Commonweale*, trans. Richard Knolles, London: Impencis G. Bishop, 1606, p. 84.

31. See Vincent, *Theories of the State*, pp. 53–4.

32. Jacques Maritain, *Man and the State*, ed. Richard O'Sullivan, London: Hollis & Carter, 1954, p.31.

33. Bodin, *The Six Bookes*, p. 11.

34. For a more detailed exposition of these questions see Sabine, *History of Political Theory*, pp.407–11.

35. Thomas Hobbes, *Leviathan*, ed. by C.B. Macpherson, Harmondsworth, Middlesex: Penguin, 1968, pp. 382–3.

36. Ibid., p. 227.

37. See David Held, 'Central Perspectives on the Modern State', in David Held et al. (eds), *States and Societies*, Oxford: Basil Blackwell, 1984, p. 8.

38. Doyle, *History of Political Thought*, p. 158.

39. John Locke, *Two Treatises of Civil Government* (introduction by W.S. Carpenter), London: J.M. Dent, 1924, pp. 186,188.

40. See J. Dunne, *The Political Thought of John Locke*, Cambridge: Cambridge University Press, 1969, part 3.

41. Locke, *Two Treatises*, pp. 219–20.

42. Hinsley, *Sovereignty*, p. 153.
43. Jean-Jacques Rousseau, *The Social Contract and Discourses*, trans. G.D.H. Cole, New York: E. Dutton, 1950, p. 14.
44. Ibid, p. 31.
45. *Hegel's Philosophy of Right*, trans. T.M. Knox, Oxford: Clarendon Press, 1952, p. 166.
46. Howard Williams, *Kant's Political Philosophy*, Oxford: Basil Blackwell, 1983, pp. 170–2.
47. Vincent, *Theories of the State*, pp. 114–15.
48. Ralph Miliband, *Class Power and State Power*, London: Verso, 1983, p. 6.
49. Held, 'Central Perspectives', p. 25.
50. John Plamenatz, *Man and Society*, Vol. 2, London: Longmans, 1965, p. 371.
51. Miliband, *Class Power*, p. 12.
52. K. Marx and F. Engels, *Selected Works*, Moscow: Progress Publishers, 1950, p. 472.
53. Sack, *Conceptions of Space*, p. 181.
54. Ibid.
55. See R.B.J. Walker, *State Sovereignty, Global Civilization and the Rearticulation of Political Space*, World Order Studies Program, Occasional Paper No. 18, Center of International Studies, Princeton University, 1988, p. 9.
56. For a more detailed examination of the spatial functions of the territorial state see R.B.J. Walker, 'The Territorial State and the Theme of Gulliver', *International Journal*, **39**, (3), Summer 1984, 534–7.
57. Barry Supple, 'The State and the Industrial Revolution 1700–1914', in Held et al., *States and Societies*, p. 171.
58. Miles Kahler, 'The Survival of the State in European International Relations', in Charles S. Maier (ed.), *Changing Boundaries of the Political*, Cambridge: Cambridge University Press, 1987, pp. 291–2.
59. Supple, 'The State and the Industrial Revolution', p. 173.
60. See R. Little and R.D. McKinlay, 'Linkage-Responsiveness and the Modern State: An Alternative View of Interdependence', *British Journal of International Studies*, **4**, October 1978, 212.
61. See Jürgen Habermas, 'What does a Crisis Mean Today? Legitimation Problems in Late Capitalism', *Social Research*, **41**, (4), Winter 1973, 656.
62. See Eckstein, 'On the "Science" of the State', p. 16.
63. Ernest Renan, *Discours et Conférences*, Paris: Calman-Lévy, 1887, p. 300.
64. E.H. Carr, *Nationalism and After*, London: Macmillan, 1945, p. 8.
65. See Hans Kohn, *Nationalism: Its Meaning and History*, Princeton, NJ: D van Nostrand, 1965; also by the same author *The Age of Nationalism: The First Era of Global History*, New York: Harper & Row, 1962; Carleton J.H. Hayes, *The Historical Evolution of Modern Nationalism*, New York: Richard R. Smith, 1931; Hugh Seton-Watson, *Nations and States*, London: Methuen, 1977.
66. See Mostafa Rejai and Cynthia H. Enloe, 'Nation-States and State-Nations', in Michael Smith et al. (eds), *Perspectives on World Politics*, London: Croom Helm, 1981, p. 38.
67. Ernest Gellner, *Nations and Nationalism*, Oxford: Basil Blackwell, 1983, p. 39.
68. Tom Nairn, 'Nationalism and the Uneven Geography of Development', in Held et al., *States and Societies*, p. 199.
69. Silviu Brucan 'The State and the World System', *International Social Science Journal*, **32**, (4), 1980, 756–60.
70. For a classic exposition of this view see Martin Wight, *Power Politics*, Harmondsworth: Penguin, 1979; also Hans Morgenthau, *Politics among Nations* (5th edn), New York: Alfred A. Knopf, 1978. For a more nuanced elaboration of the argument see Hedley Bull, *The Anarchical Society: A Study of Order in World Politics*, London: Macmillan, 1977 (especially pp. 101–26).
71. Hinsley, *Sovereignty*, pp. 210–11.
72. See J.H. Leurdjik, 'From International to Transnational Politics: A Change of Paradigm?' *International Social Science Journal*, **26**, (1), 1974, 53; also Oran Young, 'The Actors in World Politics', in J.N. Rosenau et al. (eds), *The Analysis of International Politics*, New York: Free Press, 1972, pp. 125–44.

73. Bull, *The Anarchical Society*, p. 31 .
74. Holsti, *International Politics: A Framework for Analysis*, Englewood Cliffs, NJ: Prentice-Hall, 1967, p. 83.
75. Ibid, p. 84.
76. Ibid.
77. Raymond Aron, *Peace and War: A Theory of International Relations*, trans. Richard Howard and Annette Baker Fox, Garden City, NY: Doubleday, 1966, p. 750.
78. Ibid., p. 751.
79. R.B.J. Walker, 'History and Structure in the Theory of International Studies', *Millenium*, 18, (2), Summer 1989, 174.
80. Dyson, *State Tradition in Western Europe*, pp. 102–3. For one of the most influential exponents of *Macht staat*, see Heinrich Gotthard von Treitsehke, *Politics* (introduction by Hans Kohn), New York: Harcourt, Brace & World, 1963.
81. Bull, *The Anarchical Society*, p. 37.
82. Peter F. Butler, 'Legitimacy in a States-System: Vattel's *Law of Nations*', in Michael Donelan (ed.), *The Reason of States: A Study in International Political Theory*, London: Allen & Unwin, 1978, p. 61 .
83. R.B.J. Walker illustrates this argument by reference to Inis Claude's typology of approaches to the management of power in international relations (Inis Claude, *Power and International Relations*, New York: Random House, 1962). See Walker, 'The Territorial State', pp. 540–1.
84. Maurice Keens-Soper, 'The Practice of a States-System', in Donelan, *The Reason of States*, p. 32.
85. Aron, *Peace and War*, p. 738.
86. For this purpose we rely on Raymond Aron's illustration of the problem (*Peace and War*, pp. 740–1).
87. For a detailed outline of the pluralist theory of the state, see Vincent, *Theories of the State*, pp. 181–217.
88. Harold Laski, *The Grammar of Politics*, London: Allen & Unwin, 1925, p. 51 .
89. See Harold Laski, *Authority in the Modern State*, New Haven, Conn.: Yale University Press, 1919, pp. 56–7; K.C. Hsiao, *Political Pluralism: A Study in Contemporary Political Theory*, London: Kegan Paul, 1927, p. 57; H.M. Magid, *English Political Pluralism*, New York: Columbia University Press, 1941, p. 31.
90. Vincent, *Theories of the State*, p. 201.
91. G.D.H. Cole, *Self-Government and Industry*, London: G. Bell, 1917, p. 82.
92. See Richard A. Falk and Saul H. Mendlovitz (eds), *The Strategy of World Order (Vol. II): International Law*, New York: World Law Fund, 1966 (in particular the following essays: Morton A. Kaplan and Nicholas de B. Katzenbach, 'Law in the International Community'; Roger Fisher, 'Bringing Law to Bear on Governments'). See also Quincy Wright, *Contemporary International Law: A Balance Sheet*, Garden City, NY: Doubleday, 1955; William D. Coplin, 'International Law and Assumptions about the State System', *World Politics*, 17, (4), July 1965.
93. John Austin, *The Province of Jurisprudence Determined*, New York: Humanities Press, 1965, lecture VI.
94. Cited in Georg Schwarzenberger, 'The Focus of Sovereignty', in W.J. Stankiewicz (ed.), *The Defense of Sovereignty*, New York: Oxford University Press, 1969, pp. 170–1.
95. See Mary Kaldor, 'The Global Political Economy', *Alternatives*, 11, 1986, 439.
96. Maritain, *Man and the State.*, p. 31.
97. Ibid, p. 46.
98. Hans J. Morgenthau, *Politics Among Nations: The Struggle for Power and Peace*, New York: Alfred A. Knopf, 1967, p. 315.
99. Ibid.
100. Laski, *Grammar of Politics*, p. 63.
101. See Charles R. Beitz, 'Bounded Morality: Justice and the State in World Politics', *International Organisation*, 33, (3), Summer 1979, 405–24.

102. K.W.B. Middleton, 'Sovereignty in Theory and Practice', in W.J. Stankiewicz (ed.), *The Defense of Sovereignty*, p. 153.

103. Morgenthau, *Politics Among Nations*, p. 300.

104. Middleton, 'Sovereignty in Theory and Practice', p. 157.

105. Schwarzenberger, 'The Focus of Sovereignty', p. 167.

106. J.D.B. Miller, 'Sovereignty as a Source of Vitality for the State', *Review of International studies*, **12**, (2), April 1986, 79–89.

107. Rees, 'Theory of Sovereignty Restated', p. 514.

108. Hinsley, *Sovereignty*, pp. 226–7.

109. Aron, *Peace and War*, p. 743.

110. Fred Halliday, 'State and Society in International Relations: A Second Agenda', *Millenium*, **16**, (2), Summer 1987, 218.

111. He lays particular stress on the following contributions: Otto Hintze, *The Historical Essays of Otto Hintze*, New York: Oxford University Press, 1975; John Robert Seely, *Introduction to Political Science*, London: Macmillan, 1886; Charles Tilly (ed.), *The Formation of National States in Western Europe*, Princeton, NJ: Princeton University Press, 1975; Peter Gourevitch, 'The Second Image Reversed: The International Sources of Domestic Politics', *International Organisation*, **32**, 1978, 881–912.

112. Gabriel Almond, 'Review Article: The International–National Connection', *British Journal of Political Science*, **19**, Part 2, April 1989, 238.

113. Ibid, p. 245.

114. Anderson, *Lineages*, pp. 29–42.

115. Tilly, *Formation of Nation-States*, p. 73.

116. Peter Gourevitch, *Politics in Hard Times*, Ithaca, NY: Cornell University Press, 1986, pp. 234–7.

117. Theda Skocpol, *States and Social Revolutions*, Cambridge: Cambridge University Press, 1979.

118. James N. Rosenau, 'Muddling, Meddling and Modelling: Alternative Approaches to the Study of World Politics in an Era of Rapid Change', *Millenium*, **8**, (2), Autumn, p. 130.

119. For a representative sample of these theories, see James A. Rosenau (ed.), *Linkage Politics*, New York: Free Press, 1969; Robert O'Keohane and Joseph S Nye, *Power and Interdependence: World Politics in Transition*, Boston: Little Brown, 1975; John Burton, *World Society*, Cambridge: Cambridge University Press, 1972; Richard Falk, *A Study of Future Worlds*, Amsterdam: North-Holland, 1975; Samir Amin, *Accumulation on a World Scale: A Critique of the Theory of Underdevelopment*, New York: Monthly Review Press, 1974.

120. James N. Rosenau, 'Patterned Chaos in Modern Life: Structure and Process in the Two Worlds of World Politics', *International Political Science Review*, **9**, (4), October 1988, 327–64.

121. See, in particular, Karl W. Deutsch, Lewis J. Edlinger, Roy C. Macridis and Richard L. Merritt, *France, Germany and the Western Alliance*, New York: C. Scribner's Sons, 1967; Kenneth N Watz, 'The Myth of Interdependence', in Charles P. Kindleberger (ed.), *The International Corporation*, Cambridge, Mass.: MIT Press, 1970.

3. The Interpretative Crisis

Sovereignty is in the end an idea – an invention of human beings. As the preceding chapter has shown, it has arisen at a particular moment in human history, and may be expected to serve particular needs which have arisen at that time. From this point of view it is reasonable to expect that changes in global culture and political economy may well have repercussions for the concept and practice of sovereignty. In this chapter we examine some central tensions in global culture, and their implications for the concept of sovereignty.

It is not a new insight that the worst time to assess the significance and nature of a historical period is when we are living it. The future to which it leads is unknown, and the past from which we are moving must be assessed by comparison with our present understanding. Future, past and present must all be subjected to critical inquiry. It is not altogether surprising that description of the condition of the present remains confused and contested. This is especially true at a time, such as the present, when so much is in a state of extraordinarily dynamic change.

Nevertheless, there are some highly visible characteristics of the age. There is the dominance of a complex, globalizing, economic system, motivated by a market in which various ventures compete for profit – the capitalist market. There is the central importance of technology in human affairs, and the extraordinary speed with which that technology is being reshaped. And intertwined with the processes which have created the relentless process of modernization and thus modernity as we now experience it, has been an ideology stretching back at least to the beginning of the seventeenth century. This ideology is usually referred to as *the idea of progress*.

Put most simply, the idea of progress is a belief that civilization has moved and will continue to move in a direction which is desirable and determined by natural law. As Bury puts it:

> The idea of human Progress... is a theory which involves a synthesis of the past and a prophecy of the future. It is based on an interpretation of history which regards men as slowly advancing... in a definite and desirable direction, and infers that this progress will continue. And it implies that... a condition of general happiness will ultimately be enjoyed, which will justify the whole process of civilisation.[1]

This idea is so deeply embedded in contemporary Western culture that it seems scarcely plausible that people could imagine the world differently. Nations, political ideologies and cultures are all commonly ranked according to their level of progress along an imagined evolutionary path of human attainment, and 'progress' itself is often treated as an unqualified term of praise.[2]

The idea of progress, however, is relatively recent and primarily a Western phenomenon. As has been described at some length elsewhere,[3] the rise of the idea of progress occurred in parallel with the replacement of the feudal order by mercantilism and capitalism. Amongst its most powerful early proponents was Francis Bacon, who published his *Novum Organum* in 1620. In it he made clear that whilst the 'Ancients' had provided the youthful beginning to the world, the present enjoyed the accumulated wisdom of all the ages. Bacon discounted miracles and accidents as the base of history, looking instead to natural laws and causes. The rising capitalist class found the idea to resonate with their own desire to destroy and replace the old feudal order with new relations of power based on their ownership of new means of production.

Modernity

If the idea of progress is an important ingredient of recent history, it is only that. We still require some way of describing and understanding the present moment. Here we are faced with several dilemmas, not least being the inadequacy of any given term to perform such an ambitious, inevitably distorting, and in many circumstances damagingly simplifying act of representation. One such term, which may help, despite its own complex and evolving connotations, is that of 'modernity'.

Arising at the end of the Christian Middle Ages 'modernity' designated a world which no longer seemed trapped by the past and overshadowed by the extraordinary achievements of classical antiquity. Instead, there emerged an awareness that new wonders could be built upon those of the past. Modernity connoted a sense of unrepeatable time. And human history began to be seen as having progressed from the brightness of classical antiquity, through the darkness of the Middle Ages, into modernity and a 'renascence' towards 'a luminous future'.[4]

The concept of 'modernity' is problematic, not least because it is continually being transformed into the past. By its nature modernity is subject to a continuous and relentless process of modernization transforming that which was modern into the past, only to reveal the latest emerging moment of modernity. 'Modernity' may be considered as a condition – physical, economic, cultural, psychological – which people now experience at this 'modern' moment. What constitutes 'modernity' can be understood only as relative to our place in the evolution of time. In this sense, reference to modernity without qualification, really means 'our modernity'.

Central to this experience are the tensions and exhilaration produced by a world seen to be grinding forward through a relentless process of destruction and creation. Walter Benjamin captures these tensions in his haunting image of the 'Angel of History':

> His face is turned towards the past. Where we perceive a chain of events, he sees one single catastrophe which keeps piling wreckage and hurls it in front of his feet. The angel would like to stay, awaken the dead, and make whole what has been smashed. But a storm is blowing from Paradise; it has got caught in his wings with such violence that the angel can no longer close them. This storm irresistibly propels him towards the future to which his back is turned, while the pile of debris before him grows skyward. This storm is what we call progress.[5]

It is these tensions in 'progress' which Marshall Berman takes as the universal characteristic of modernity:

> To be modern is to find ourselves in an environment that promises adventure, power, joy, growth, transformation of ourselves and the world – and, at the same time, that threatens to destroy everything we have, everything we know, everything we are. ... modernity can be said to unite all mankind. But it is a paradoxical unity, a unity of disunity... to be part of a universe in which, as Marx said, 'all that is solid melts into air.'[6]

It is hardly surprising that the interpretation of experiences of modernity, even when they may appear from outside as caused by the same environment, should differ considerably. From the first half of the nineteenth century two sharply conflicting images of modernity arose – the first, seen positively as a stage in Western civilization reaping the results of scientific and technological progress, industrialization, and the development of capitalism; and the second, developed particularly in art and literature, displaying an attitude of radical optimism about the future, but dismayed by modernist values and profoundly rejecting the world of 'bourgeois modernity'.[7]

These two concepts of modernity do nevertheless have one thing in common. The world is perceived (whether heroically or disastrously) as bent upon a process of rapid destruction of all that is old, and the construction of ever more transitory and ephemeral replacements giving rise to a 'distinctive experience of time, space and causality as transitory, fleeting, and fortuitous and arbitrary'.[8]

It is not necessary to understand this condition of modernity as the result of some historical process of unmotivated autonomous development. It can be understood, at least in part, as the result of a recognizable project of intervention, intertwined with the development of capitalism itself, mounted from the Enlightenment and coming into clear view in the eighteenth century. This is what Habermas calls the *project of modernity* – a concerted effort by Enlightenment thinkers 'to develop objective science, universal morality and law, and autonomous art according to their inner logic'.[9]

Modernism

If the concept and interpretation of our modernity is so contested and ambiguous, so too is the intertwined and partly interpenetrating concept of 'modernism'. Calinescu[10] profitably devotes some 90 pages to these two concepts and we should be warned that anything much less is an oversimplification. But we do need some idea of the significance of each. In short we can say that modernism arose in the mid-nineteenth century as the collective intellectual and aesthetic response to modernity and the relentless processes of modernization:

> These world-historical processes have nourished an amazing variety of visions and ideas that aim to make men and women the subjects as well as the objects of modernization, to give them the power to change the world that is changing them, to make their way through the maelstrom and make it their own. Over the past century, these visions and values have come to be loosely grouped together under the name of 'modernism'.[11]

But once again this response is by no means uniform. On the one hand, modernism's vision of the world may be seen as rationalistic and instrumental:

> Generally perceived as positivistic, technocentric, and rationalistic, universal modernism has been identified with the belief in linear progress, absolute truths, the rational planning of ideal social orders, and the standardization of knowledge and production.[12]

On the other hand, modernism contains much that is critical, perturbed, or even sickened by the enticing yet chaotic and treadmill experience of modernity.

Crises within modernity

The drive towards modernization which has led to our modernity has never been more intense, more promising, or more threatening. We need only review a few aspects of our modernity to recognize the extraordinary way in which the process of modernization has constructed a world built, ever more precariously, upon profoundly opposed opposites.

Central to this perspective of modernity we note the desire to control – whether it be control of humankind, or the processes of the biosphere. The desire to control combines with and is reinforced by the incremental accumulation and use of knowledge of the world, which produces at times extraordinarily powerful results, the dynamic incentive to utilize these provided by the market, and organizational structures to implement them provided through the vast transnational systems of corporate and state power.

The result is the complex set of modern contradictions which beset humanity. Social division and tension is in part controlled through the extraordinary panoply of military hardware (including nuclear weapons) which threaten to destroy much of humanity in a single convulsion. The physical impact of the process of relentless modernization so profoundly remoulds the world that it creates new dimensions of ecological crisis and insecurity. The modernization of the world economy simultaneously integrates the world and creates local regionalism and fragmentation. Citizens begin to be identified as part of one global family, but at the same time they experience the alienation and anomie that arise from the uniformity and reduced emphasis on spiritual and ethical values which appears to be characteristic of modern mass consumerist society. Economic transformations release the riches of the earth on an unprecedented scale, but also give rise to a profound division between North and South, as a result of which the vast bulk of the earth's inhabitants find themselves in a state of increasingly abject poverty.

Postmodernism and interpretative crisis

It is within the context of these critical problems that the phenomenon of postmodern interpretation and culture arises. There is much debate about precisely what the various terms – postmodernism, postmodern interpretation, or indeed postmodernity – are to be taken to denote and connote, and about the validity of the connotations which are invoked. Clearly these gain their meaning by their claim to a disjunction from, if not opposition to, the ideas, conceptions and representations of modernism and modernity. Given the multiple ambiguities in these latter terms, it should be no surprise that the new alternatives also refract into many possible interpretations. Here we will simply sketch enough of the relevant terrain to explore its implications for sovereignty.

A simple but quite possibly highly misleading approach to the issue is to *define* this moment of late capitalism as 'postmodernity', and the response to it as 'postmodern'. That leaves unexamined all the interesting questions about what we are to understand by this, and whether the moment (or interpretation of it) is indeed better understood as a continuation of the past, or a disjunction from it.

The claim to disjunction is reinforced by what Jameson calls 'an inverted millenarism' – a wide range of strident claims that we are coming to 'the end' – of ideology, class, Marxism, industrial society, mass manufacturing, high-modern art and architecture, and much else.[13] These resonate with the reaction in art and architecture to an aesthetic modernism now seen to have lost its radical edge, and to have accommodated to mainstream modernity. There can be no doubt that the reaction in art and architecture is there, seen in the images and structures drawing, often playfully, on images not of the future but the past. Similarly, one need not look far to encounter the inverted millenial claims to the end of many of the underlying themes and practices of modernity. However, whether all this represents yet a further twist of style and fashion in what is essentially still the project of modernity and the response to it, or is something more is open to debate.

Harvey, for example, argues that there is far more continuity between modernism and 'postmodernist' thought than rupture. Even Lyotard, an influential theorist, concedes that postmodernism is 'not modernism at its end but in the nascent state'.[14] In any case, the outpouring of literature in the area makes it quite clear that there is at minimum a self-styled 'postmodern' intellectual movement. It also seems clear that it raises such a vast range of critical issues that if it is a continuation of modernism it is a continuation in which the tensions within that set of interpretations has reached crisis point.

The body of 'postmodern' literature falls primarily into two areas. First there is an account of major changes to global technological, political and economic arrangements, which argues that these are so profound as to represent a shift from modernity to postmodernity. (The central elements of these changes are described elsewhere in this book.) Secondly, there is the cultural and intellectual response to these changes. These constitute 'postmodernism'.

To specify some of the essential characteristics of what is often considered to be the postmodern perspective, it is useful to explore the contrasts between particular examples of modernist and postmodernist interpretation. Inevitably the use of such examples will leave much untouched. But the problem of describing the differences between modern and postmodern styles of thought is a symptom of the difficulty of reflecting upon and untangling changes in interpretation at the time that they are happening.

Central to postmodern sensibilities is a deep suspicion of the use of metanarratives – broad interpretative schemas (such as those of Marx, Freud, or indeed Einstein) which purport to provide 'the truth' about how vast ranges of things are connected. Rather, theorists such as Foucault enjoin us to study the many tiny mechanisms, each with its own history, dynamics and significance, which make up the whole. Thus for Foucault power is better understood by studying the detail of its operation in a hospital, gaol or asylum than by attempting to deal with power as a function of the global political economy.

Both modernist and postmodernist interpretation are confronted by and recognize the fragmentation and discontinuity which characterize modernity, but whilst modernist theorists seek to develop metanarratives to unify and transcend this fragmented reality, postmodernism 'swims, even wallows, in the fragmentary and the chaotic currents of change as if that is all there is'.[15]

One such metanarrative whose legitimacy is thus undermined is the idea of progress (together with much of the accompanying intellectual baggage of the project of modernity). The belief in the emancipation of humanity through the application of science, technology and abstract reason is now replaced by a 'growing sense that we are not bound to complete the project of modernity...and still do not necessarily have to lapse into irrationality or into apocalyptic frenzy'.[16]

For the physical sciences the neat metanarratives of scientific method have been broken apart under the critical examination of sociologists, historians and philosophers of science.[17] The history of science dissolves from a tale of discovery of the new, and proof of the discovery or falsification of the old, into a world of simultaneously competing claims of truth and falsity which can (usually partially and temporarily) be resolved through a process of social negotiation.

In the physical sciences there is also an increasing interest in the regimes of in principle unpredictable motion (chaos), which turn out unexpectedly to be experienced by very simple systems,[18] the imprecision in many common quantities that were previously considered to be precise (such as 'the length' of a coastline) and the very considerable errors of judgement which may be engendered by the reductionist approach (which underlies so much of scientific analysis) of seeking to understand complex systems by simplifying them to the point where they can be viewed as a set of individual components of known behaviour.[19] Compatible with this latter conception, the environmental critique, at least in essence, can be interpreted as a postmodernist view in which the traditional approaches of science in particular, and more generally the project of modernity, are reaching their limits.

Here we have a sharp example of the claim, perhaps overstated, that we are confronted with sharp disjunction in the most holy preserves of modernity (science itself). Lyotard is not alone in perceiving the possibility and early development of a new 'postmodern science'. For example, biologist Charles Birch argues for a 'postmodern worldview' in which nature is treated as organic and ecological, the emphasis on reductionism is reduced, monism replaces dualism, biocentric as opposed to anthropocentric perspectives are emphasized and the boundaries between disciplines are surmounted.[20] Never timid about putting his case strongly, Lyotard goes even further.

Postmodern science – by concerning itself with such things as undecidables, the limits of precise control, conflicts characterized by incomplete information, 'fracta', catastrophes and pragmatic paradoxes – is theorizing its own evolution as discontinuous, catastrophic, nonrectifiable, and paradoxical. It is changing the meaning of the word knowledge, while expressing how such a change can take place. It is producing not the known, but the unknown.[21]

Lyotard is obviously arguing for a postmodern science which rejects the desire to describe the world in a single, unified, centralized narrative.

Whether or not we agree with Lyotard's verdict on the implications and extent of the tensions he detects within science, tensions do exist. A similar critical tension stretches across many (if not all) fields of modern intellectual practice. In literature there is a shift from the examination of one reality to the examination of a world in which different realities coexist and interpenetrate.[22] In linguistics and the social sciences, the approach of structuralism, which seeks to understand phenomena in terms of the system of structures and interactions which underlie them, is now challenged by poststructuralism, in which all structural divisions are viewed as simply contingent socially produced artefacts, always open to challenge, and artificially dividing the whole. Here, rather than seek to construct 'improved' totalizing accounts of social action, history, political economy, literature, or art, there is an emphasis on 'deconstruction', in part by examining those features, issues or even people which are marginalized or rendered invisible by the accounts and language which have traditionally dominated interpretation.

One important strand of this critique is the deconstruction of personal identity itself (the 'decentring of the subject'). Much of social science, and indeed art and literature, has been constructed around the idea of individual actors. They are conscious. They make decisions. And the totality of culture, political economy and much else is constructed from their collective actions and interactions. This is to draw a boundary around the individual, and whether in literature (the 'subject') or in social theory, this privileging of individual identity is open to challenge. After all, a person's self-concept (conscious and subconscious) does not spring from a vacuum, but is constructed out of the interactions, interpretations, stories, explanations which a person experiences during life. In literature this is twice reinforced since the subject ('I') which appears in a text is not the person, but the person's presentation of the person's perception of 'who they are'. These considerations lead to a project which, rather than privileging subjectivity as a given, examines how the construction of particular subjectivities marginalizes, shapes or represses other possible subjective experiences and perceptions.

In short, amongst a significant cross-section of writers there is a growing tendency to seek out the virtues of past achievements which have been trampled under the rush to modernize, and to challenge boundaries, deconstruct categories (including individual identity), dispense with totalizing narratives (including those which have centrally supported modernity), and accept, even celebrate, the simultaneous validity of multiple coexisting, conflicting, often interpenetrating realities.

All this still merely sketches a picture which may be filled in and greatly elaborated. The rejection of the modernist narrative of progress, and the desire to embrace many simultaneously different and even contradictory accounts of reality, and to deconstruct and challenge all boundaries and unifying metanarratives tends towards a sort of intellectual geography which replaces depth with an expansive breadth composed of a fragmented collage, whose overall shape must remain forever hidden.

Further, several pitfalls are hidden in this landscape, not least being that the metanarratives, which are to have been obliterated, may in fact merely be submerged where they still play a powerful but covert role. For example, as Jameson points out, the claim to be 'post' (that is that we are experiencing a sharp disjunction with modernity) is consistent with an ideological mission of demonstrating that the global system no longer obeys the central dynamics of capitalism. In this sense there is a partly submerged implication that existing critiques of capitalism have lost their value. This appears somewhat more explicitly in the writing from the neo-conservative wing of postmodern theorists. Thus, despite the desire to abandon metanarrative, each statement about postmodern culture also implicitly represents a political stance on the nature and implications of the global economic system.[23]

Harvey summarizes the danger in blindly allowing our postmodern guides to lead us into and lose us in this postmodern intellectual landscape:

> its penchant for deconstruction bordering on nihilism, its preference for aesthetics over ethics, takes matters too far. It takes them beyond the point where any coherent politics are left, while that wing of it that seeks shameless accommodation with the market puts it firmly in the tracks of an entrepreneurial culture that is the hallmark of reactionary neoconservatism. Postmodern philosophers tell us not only to accept but even to revel in the fragmentations and the cacophony of voices through which the dilemmas of the modern world are understood. Obsessed with deconstructing and delegitimating every form of argument they encounter, they can end only in condemning their own validity claims to the point where nothing remains of any basis for reasoned action.[24]

There are indeed serious pitfalls.

If, as a result of entering on to the postmodern landscape, we find ourselves wallowing in a relativist morass, searching for suppressed meanings, but having abandoned all metanarratives by which we may envisage the shape of the landscape as a whole and thereby develop a sense of direction, then we may indeed find ourselves distracted from determining political strategies to deal with a vast range of critical problems – from the threat of greenhouse warming to the increasing economic gap between North and South. But whilst this danger is real, it is only likely to be realized if we are determined to *confine* ourselves totally to this landscape. Here we should stress that the term 'postmodern' in fact relates to a wide range of voices which by no means constitute a single entity. At best, as a global label, it represents a general trend or tendency in thinking.

One political strength of this postmodern trend is to place value on the voices which are normally marginalized, and to explore how this process of marginalization occurs. In this way it seeks to render 'the invisible' visible. Clearly this is of particular relevance to marginalized, disempowered groups which seek to reverse their situation, and those from 'outside' who wish to help. Examples of the use of postmodern tools to this end range across a broad spectrum – from the writings of feminists to those of activists in 'the Third World'. Gayatri Spivak, who can be said to come from both locations simultaneously, is a case in point. She criticizes 'post-Marxists' for rejecting or trivializing the notion of class because it is a universalist concept. Instead, she argues, the contemporary virtues of the concept can be developed by exploring its multiple possible roles and connotations – by 'complicating and expanding it'.[25]

It is possible to find political insight within postmodern thinking, yet it is also true that there is a tendency within it to be distracted from action to contemplation. However, it is not necessary either to understand or accommodate to the postmodern as the sole means of representing or comprehending the world. Instead we may recognize virtue in the postmodern correctives to the dogmatic polarized utilitarian-centred thinking to which they react, whilst still refusing to accept them as all there is. In short, we may, in exemplarily postmodern fashion, refuse to accept the postmodern as a 'totalizing discourse'.

It is important to recognize that the 'postmodern' emphasis we currently find abounding in a wide body of literature does not arise in isolation. It reflects tensions in thinking as people strive to interpret life and society at a moment when capitalist society is undergoing vast areas of reorganization. The economic system is emerging as a force which is now unmistakably global. Financial flows circle the globe in a matter of seconds, along invisible networks of communication. People, goods, information, entertainment, 'news' and rhetoric flow across national boundaries as never before. Transactions are sealed by transnational entities invisibly in multiple regions of the globe simultaneously. Labour and production materials are moved between regions, to the rhythm of the global market, with increasing velocity. And the divisions of the time scale in which the market operates are continually contracted towards each other.[26]

It is within this globalizing, accelerating and highly mobile world that the tensions, of which postmodernist thought are a symptom, arise and must be faced. Many of those tensions evoke the problem of coming to terms with the current and future role of national states – a role which is increasingly under challenge by the very nature of these developments. It is from this perspective that we propose to examine some of the interpretative approaches which have arisen, at least partly in response to these developments, and their implications for the notion and practice of sovereignty.

SOVEREIGNTY AND (POST?) MODERNITY

The Narrative of Nation

Our examination of sovereignty occurs at a time when the underlying tenets of centred action and the metanarratives of political economy and control by the state are, from a postmodern perspective, very much in crisis. This crisis, in turn, has very considerable implications for the theory and practice of sovereignty.

The concept of a sovereign nation begins with the idea of a nation. As we have already indicated in our discussion of the emergence of nation-states, these are relatively new phenomena. Postmodern approaches remind us that these concepts are social constructions. They are concepts which have arisen at a particular point in time and serve particular functions at a particular moment of history. In this sense they are inventions. Similarly, the ideas of nation and sovereign nation are inventions. That is they are part of a metanarrative – a story through which vast numbers of people construct a picture of the world and organize both their understanding and their action.

As Benedict Anderson points out, nation is a concept which draws upon the image of a large imagined *community*. This in itself is a remarkable invention. It suggests to this group of people that, despite all the inequalities of power and wealth which may otherwise divide them, there is something which also unites them characterized by 'a deep, horizontal comradeship'.[27] What is invented here is a national political community which is imagined 'as both inherently limited and sovereign'.[28]

Once invented, this concept has proved to have exercised considerable power. Although it may be an overstatement, Anderson may be not too far from the truth when he claims that 'nation-ness is the most universally legitimate value in the political life of our time'.[29] But to the extent that this may be true, it is very much a product of the circumstances in which it has arisen. As Anderson notes, the eighteenth century in Western Europe marks not only the dawning of nationalism, but also the waning of religious modes of thought. It is the time of modernity – the replacement of secular fatality by rationalist, secularist modernization and progress. And argues Anderson, 'few things were (are) better suited to this end, than the idea of nation'.[30]

Central to the idea of the national community is the idea of vast numbers of people envisaged in some sort of connection at the same time, and developing together. The idea of national community, then, evokes an idea of a horizontal vision of the whole society at once. Both these ideas, notes Anderson, are characteristics of a society which can construct them, at least in imagination.[31] The particular developments which aided these constructions were the interchange of messages through commerce, the development of print capitalism which enabled people to think and relate in these profoundly new terms, and the development of standardized popularly accessible time, again a development which became deeply embedded in the rise of industrial production.

The above developments, greatly facilitated by the bureaucratic apparatus of the modern state, led, amongst other things, to the development of monoglot mass reading publics. The vast diversity of dialects and languages was reduced, simplified and homogenized through the creation, sale and acceptance of a far smaller number of more widely spread print languages. Further, the sale and consumption of these particular languages, and the increasingly 'national' messages inscribed in them conformed to particular territorial boundaries, further reinforcing and communicating the idea of the national community. According to Anderson, 'The convergence of capitalism and print technology on the fatal diversity of human language created the possibility of a new form of imagined community, which in its basic morphology set the stage for the modern nation.'[32] It is as if the print media have aligned particular languages to particular territorial units.

However, the sense of horizontal community is only one of two central features of the imagined national community. The other is a sense of national history (a vertical vision of the community through time). The concept of a nation which is in some sense eternal seems deeply rooted in the rhetoric of nationalism, even though nation-states are comparatively recent formations. The late Indonesian President Sukarno could speak of hundreds of years of colonialism endured by Indonesia, even though the concept of Indonesia was only invented in the twentieth century.[33] The community not only exists but its existence is naturalized through the apparent historical inevitability of its emergence and future. Those who comprise it may identify common roots and work for a common future. Central to the idea of the national community is the idea of community defined by both a history and a concept of its future. For Anderson the idea of a social organism moving calendrically and inexorably through time 'is a precise analogue of the idea of the nation, which also is conceived as a solid community moving steadily down (or up) history'.[34]

In the above two senses, the culture of modernity has over the last two centuries provided fertile ground for the emergence of imagined national

communities, complementing the growing structural importance of national
state formations in the development of industrialized societies (both East
and West). The idea of progress and the intertwined celebration of modernization have reinforced the idea of a national community with a common and
determined history and future. At the same time the scale of organization of
the communication systems, the process of commerce, the legal and other
official interactions have extended across the national territory, and can be
pictured as predominantly confined to it. We have now reached a point
where that picture is increasingly challenged by other ideas and images
(including those 'postmodern' perspectives which we have discussed). As
the tensions within modernity sharpen this may well have significant implications for the narrative of the imagined national community and its usefulness in making sense of the world in which people live.

Three Structural Considerations

It is useful to begin our discussion by considering several features of the
contemporary world which appear to be playing central roles in shaping the
context within which the debate about 'postmodernity' and the challenge to
the concept of national sovereignty simultaneously arise. We shall deal with
these only briefly here, since they are considered in much greater detail in
later chapters.

First, we have the rapid structural change occurring in the technology of
communication. Recent developments in communication technology clearly
play an important role in the development of the tensions around the concept
of nation. The impact of these technologies are not unambiguous, since the
national information technology systems, from radio to television to the
telephone, have not only helped forge a concept of an accessible national
community but also allowed the national government and its agencies to
communicate nationalist rhetoric to the entire citizenry.

Nevertheless, in terms of the history of these developments the national
reach of government was accomplished several decades ago, whilst the
international flow of messages, images and money through the increasingly
integrated global communication systems is still growing at an extraordinarily rapid rate. Further, these systems are by no means solely dominated by
national entities. More and more transnational corporations utilize them for
advertising, sponsorship and similar purposes. Images of international consumption permeate all borders; the message and the medium increasingly
form part of the culture, goals and accomplishments of the global market as
much as of the nation-state.

This is true not only in the advanced industrialized countries but also in
the Third World. Gamani Corea, who chairs the UN General Assembly

Committee on an International Development Strategy for the fourth UN Development Decade, warns that under the pressures of global capitalism

> Third World countries are one by one becoming 'ungovernable'. No matter what the complexion of the governments – right wing, left wing, military, or democratic – they are all in situations of not being able to respond adequately to the expectations of their people: expectations aroused by the media, by communications, by education. ... it is my feeling that turmoil and tension in the Third World will eventually spill over national boundaries and threaten and endanger the very fabric of global peace and stability. ... Such disturbances, if widespread, could interfere with the workings of the entire global economy.[35]

Significantly, Corea goes on to argue that the nation-state cannot rescue itself from this predicament. A new form of international regulation is needed (including a form of international social security which would allow redistribution of funds from North to South where necessary) coupled with a corresponding change in the lifestyles in the North.

Secondly, as we have already hinted and shall more fully examine in the next chapter, major structural changes in the global market pose another powerful challenge to the concept of the national community. As the market globalizes, the truism that commerce knows no boundaries becomes ever more starkly evident. One way in which this is revealed is the extent to which production is 'dispersed and deterritorialized'.[36] Similarly it is reflected in the considerable ideological pressure for free trade and dismantling of national protective barriers, the growing presence in national economies of transnational economic entities, the increasing interdependence of most economies, the increasing vulnerability of national financial markets to international fluctuations, the concomitant decline in the ability of national states to regulate their own economies, and the increasing influence and importance of international or regional regulatory bodies such as the German Bundesbank for the European Community, or the World Bank and International Monetary Fund for many other nations.

The calls for greater rather than less international regulation, whether to guard against market excesses or to regulate market fluctuations, are likely to grow with the internationalization of economic activity. For example, Jan Pronk argues:

> We need a global mixed economy including a strong and clear international framework of powerful public institutions, a kind of global public sector, enhancing the wealth and welfare-creating capacities of the global private sector. We need an internationalisation of the concept of the welfare state with international transfers to correct gross inequalities. We need an international pluralistic democracy within which Third World countries can participate effectively in international decision-making.[37]

These calls may or may not be appropriate or efficacious. They may or may not attract official support. Yet they are suggestive of a new and increasingly influential voice.

Thirdly, the economic impact on the environment leads in some respects to the strengthening of state power, hence of the image of national community. Local pollution of rivers, soil erosion, regulation of radiation hazards and the like are often appropriately controlled by national governments, and to the extent that the national state accepts the responsibility it gains in legitimacy. But recently the increasing technological sophistication, intensity and scale of production and consumption have also led to the development of transnational environmental effects (including, for example, the global deterioration of the atmosphere and oceans). As these develop, they provide a sharp demonstration of the limits to the state's ability to regulate crucial aspects of the environment. As a result, these problems, which are now emerging with alarming speed, undermine the supposed virtues of the national community. Instead they suggest an image of global civil society artificially partitioned into national communities which are thereby insulated from the global co-operation needed to prevent the rapid deterioration of their global environment.

Poststructuralism, Postmodernism and the Sovereign Nation

Each of the above aspects of modernity poses a direct challenge to the concept of the sovereign national community. But they also interrelate with the growth of the broader intellectual and interpretative tensions expressed through the new 'postmodern' perspectives which we have already described. The result is a combined shift in both analytic perspectives and their physical, economic and technological context, which together have significant implications for the enduring legitimacy of national community and therefore the sovereign nation-state.

Let us begin with the consciousness of environmental disturbance. If we accept Lyotard's view that recent work in the physical sciences, which focuses on the limited extent of our knowledge of the world, may be considered part of the postmodern, then several observations seem appropriate. First is the new insight that, contrary to earlier expectations, various forms of human intervention, far from disturbing the environment in small ways with the effects naturally dying out over time, may produce disturbances which grow exponentially and eventually lead to an alteration to a system's behaviour. This is the so-called 'butterfly effect' – the suggestion that the beating of a single butterfly's wing one day may significantly alter global weather patterns weeks later. In short, recent developments in mathematical modelling suggest that small random perturbations to the global ecosystem may cause significant alterations to its future behaviour. As a result the future of such systems is in principle, perhaps within certain limits, unpredictable.

Secondly, it is a truism, but at the popular level only a relatively recent one, that in the environment 'everything is connected to everything else', and as a consequence 'there is no such thing as a free lunch'. This is a reflection of a general critique of reductionist approaches to the environment. This critique stresses that the process of reducing the environment to a conceptual model based on some set of known interactions between a set of indentified simplified components is likely to obscure from our attention many critical phenomena based upon synergistic interactions between those components which we have identified, and those we have misrepresented or overlooked because of our inevitably partial understanding of the system. An example is the way in which the 'nuclear winter' effect of nuclear war was completely overlooked for decades. A similar example is the surprise with which the ozone hole was only recently greeted by physical scientists.[38]

This last observation meshes with a more general postmodern critique of determinist models of the world. The tendency to view the physical environment as ultimately controllable is being challenged by the less confident relativist postmodern analyses which concentrate not so much on what is controlled, as on what is not. This emphasis on the truths that are marginalized by the application of the metanarratives of the physical sciences constitutes a loss of confidence in the project of modernity, and the state's ability to guide the national community in relation to it.

Decentring and the will of the state

So far we have dealt with ways in which the power of the nation-state to act autonomously are limited, or the conception of the national community is undermined. However, postmodern analysis draws our attention to a more fundamental limitation on the sovereignty of the nation-state, relating not so much to its *power* as to its *will* to act.

The critique begins with the state itself. The concept of the nation-state is, as we have already remarked, an invention. The national community is itself a construction held in imagination, and potent only to the extent that it is shared by those who are imagined as comprising that community. But the concept goes beyond the *existence* of the community. The nation is viewed not just as an entity which *exists*, but as an entity which *acts*. More generally, the nation-state is traditionally envisaged as a single, conscious agent, capable of conscious sovereign desire, judgement and action.

The model of nation as a single agent is of course not the only model. Indeed, contemporary critical theory of the state goes to some lengths to undermine it, unpacking the various agencies of the state and examining the interplay between them, other institutions, and the community in general. Nevertheless, the single agent image is still prevalent. It can be found widely used in international relations (the billiard-ball model), in strategic theory and in newspaper reports of daily international events. The 'US' is said to have condemned 'Iraq's' invasion of 'Kuwait'. The 'USSR' is said to be joining the 'US' in economic co-operation. Similarly, it is this single national actor which is invoked when we speak of the sovereign nation. We can put it this way. The discourse of national sovereignty privileges a view of the nation as a single, autonomous, conscious agent. It is here that contemporary postmodern perspectives have much to say that is relevant to the problems of a discursive emphasis which invokes autonomous subjects.

As we have noted, even for human beings the construction of the subject in texts is highly problematic. This is because what is conceived by an individual human as a conscious, autonomous decision is conditioned by a self-consciousness which, far from being autonomous, is constructed out of the interactions, interpretations, stories and explanations that a person experiences during life. If this is true of a person, it is certainly true of the complex of institutions, interpretations and interactions which constitute the imagined national actor.

In short, from a poststructuralist treatment of decentring, the constraints on the state's power to act may be far less important than the constraints on the state's will to act. Indeed, as Foucault stresses, the distinction between power and will is itself an artificial dichotomy. He stresses that power operates not simply 'on' us (from outside) but in us. This representation of power has radical implications, since it emphasizes the extent to which power is not only pervasive and dispersed but also reciprocal.[39] The act of having to construct power within also constrains the actions of those seeking to achieve this. In this sense the servant exerts power over the master in many sophisticated ways which in more traditional perspectives might well remain invisible.[40]

Similarly, we may seek to investigate the ways in which power operates not merely on but in the nation. The nature of the imagined 'sovereign' will of the nation-state, or even the government, will depend upon a vast range of factors including the dominant orthodoxy about what is possible and what is not, what is realistic, what is rational, what is profitable, and what is desirable. These judgements do not arise in a vacuum but are conditioned by a vast range of factors including the arguments and inducements offered to those making them, and the cultural norms and shaping of ideas provided through the dominant discourses of the time.

Here we reach the bottom line of this argument, since the above factors are in a process of rapid change. A global shift in culture, of which the postmodern tensions are an indicator, is accompanying the global reshaping of production, consumption and the market. Part of that shift is a belief that certain actions are no longer rational or legitimate. In particular, the dominance of orthodox economic considerations over many others is by now a feature of national official discourse both East and West. Other components include the marginalization of socialist concepts, the growing emphasis on the importance of certain processes which are said to constitute 'democracy', and the broad dominance of consumerist values and desires. All these condition what the nation (whether state or community) will conceive as being within its legitimate desire or reach. In this way the power of global culture, global communication, the global market and related factors, including that which has been called postmodern, penetrate through the imagined boundaries of nation and national state, conditioning and shaping the national will and constructing the perspective of the possible and the desirable from which its relative 'power' to exert sovereignty will be exercised.

Some postmodern distractions

The above are useful insights which both follow from and are emphasized by contemporary postmodern approaches. Further, as these perspectives, with their potential to undermine the notion of nation itself, develop further and gain wider adherence, they have the potential to challenge and undermine the associated theory of sovereignty. However, as a feature of contemporary culture, the social implications of postmodern perspectives extend well beyond this.

The emphasis on the decentred subject has had a corrosive influence not only on the imagined sovereign will of the nation but also on the perception by individuals of their own autonomy and ability freely to exercise judgement. The stress on the relativity of all values, judgements and data, and the continual reminder of the extent to which any perspective of reality marginalizes other perspectives of reality, which if enunciated might well be accepted as more persuasive, tends to be politically disempowering. The pluralist acceptance of the validity of multiple, contradictory and interpenetrating accounts both reflects and reinforces a disempowering feeling of malaise in relation to, and detachment from, the development of events in the physical, social, economic and political environment.

There is, then, a tendency to see disorder and fragmentation everywhere and to eschew grand global pictures. For example Lash and Urry, in their valuable book *Disorganised Capitalism*, make much of the disordering forces currently at work within the global market.[41] However, as Harvey points out, this is to stamp a very peculiar perspective on events – one that systematically marginalizes the very considerable areas of coherence which exist at the global level.[42] Further, there is a tendency to avoid discussion of systematic change in the global system as a whole. The stress on 'disorganization' ignores the possibility, emphasized by Swyngedouw,[43] that the apparent disorder we observe at this moment is simply a by-product of a global system undergoing transition from one highly ordered regime of accumulation to another.

In short, there is a contemporary tendency to construct a discourse in which overtly enunciated metanarratives, whether liberal, psychological, cultural or from political economics, are viewed with the deepest suspicion. As a result the study of the global market, the global shaping of technology, the global contours of culture and political geography and much else is marginalized in the discourse, undermining explicit analytic approaches to issues which may well have much to do with current perceptions of the world, including the sovereignty of nations. Further, by marginalizing these insights the debilitating implications of the remaining perspectives are left uncontested, diluting the challenge experienced by dominant institutions, including governments, as they participate in the reshaping of contemporary society and its power relations and practices.

Deconstruction and Reconstruction

One thing does seem to stand out. We live in times when, as Karl Marx predicted, much of what was thought to be solid has indeed lost its firmness. The project of modernity has produced extraordinary tensions not only between the physical and the social, but in understanding itself. The crises which surround the relentless process of modernization have compounded an increasing distrust in modernist perspectives. But contemporary 'postmodern' analysis which has arisen in response has features which tend to reinforce an unsettling and disorienting sense of uncertainty and disempowerment. Taken together these suggest that we are currently at a moment of interpretative crisis. As with all crises, this raises both dangers and opportunities – both intellectually and in action.

One central opportunity afforded by the erosion of the image of the sovereign nation and the effectiveness of the national state is that it creates a clearer need to deconstruct, rethink and reconstruct political agendas. With the ability of the nation-state to deal effectively with a bewildering array of vital issues in serious doubt, old recipes for change, including most obviously the idea of 'gaining power' by capturing control of legislatures or the armed forces, becomes increasingly problematic.

In principle, poststructuralist perspectives invite a radical deconstruction of the process by which state power is constructed and legitimized. An understanding of the way in which 'nation-ness' is constructed as a narrative, and the way in which this narrative may be deconstructed, has the potential to undermine the parochial nationalism of community and state, to allow global problems to be tackled in a more flexible and innovative context. Whether that potential will be lost in a generalized project of deconstruction, with the way all narratives of power are constructed and stabilized becoming the central focus of attention, is a political (and intellectual) question which remains to be resolved.

At the same time the postmodern analysis of 'individual' identity promises to provide a powerful counter to the legitimizing power of so-called 'democracy'. It is by no means a new insight that the process of 'democracy' practised in advanced Western societies has more to do with a common acceptance of a particular form of process (rooted in the British Westminster system) than with a reality in which a politically conscious community, with access to necessary information and a full understanding of the spectrum of available options, determines the issues that affect them. Enough has been said about the dominance of central communication systems, the pervasive role of dominant discourses and the social construction of the subject to make it clear that there is a great gap to be explored between the form of 'democratic' decision-making as it actually is and the ideal which it purports to serve.

It is the constructed association of the form of decision-making with the democratic ideal which imparts so much legitimacy to the operation of national states in 'democratic' countries. It is clear that the tools of deconstruction can play an important part in opening up this issue, and that they will become increasingly important as political institutions are stressed and rendered problematic by the shifting patterns of modernization, which are themselves closely tied to a globalizing market.

Both the danger and the promise of contemporary postmodern approaches is that they render more complicated the present and future of the aesthetic, social and technical order in which the nation is constructed. The danger is that the complication may act as a bewildering maze. The promise is that it may free us from the image of inexorable single-minded progress (irrespective of destructive 'by-products') which has been so deeply embedded in the project of modernity.

In particular, the postmodern movement promises to re-present the future, not as something which is fixed, but as a tangle of many constructions, and to render many of these disrupted possibilities visible. As Ross comments:

> The question common to postmodernism and technology is of the presence of the future. ... The future is at once the presence and disruption of rules. ... Just as practice must find its form, and will do so under criticism from within and without, technology will both define the shape of the future and disrupt it, under criticism from within and without. In this sense, modern and postmodern criticisms of modern technology that sound simplistic frequently have a profound purpose: to find the alternative forms within it that can bring the future under practical control.[44]

Unfortunately it is difficult, once again, to see how we can make such an examination without at least provisionally accepting some of the instrumental metanarratives of science and technology. So it may well be that the emphasis of the postmodern may in the end represent not the end of the project of modernity but, more realistically, the tensions within that project which may, with the development of appropriate political action, allow the continuing but ambivalent project of modernization to be reshaped, and to select the better rather than worse possibilities from the available concepts of the future.

What then can we say about the politics of reconstruction in a world in which the boundaries of nation and the construction of sovereignty have been penetrated, constrained and deconstructed through the intellectual and political changes associated with the current reorganization of society and economy? Following Jameson, we should note that the 'postmodern' culture accompanying these changes is characterized by the qualities of flatness and expansive breadth. Many of the solid signposts upon which individuals and communities have depended to navigate their actions have become less distinct, or have disappeared: the linear narrative of unfolding determined progress melts away; the inherent benevolence of scientific and technological intervention erodes; time horizons within which to initiate and react to technical and social change compress; the solidity of the rightness of our interpretation of the world against that of 'the other' dissolves; the confidence in mechanical historical mechanisms softens; the security of national community and the legitimacy of 'our' government's 'sovereign decisions' begin to evaporate; and even the confidence in our own placing as autonomous individuals is clouded in worrying complication.

But if such flatness is indeed increasingly characteristic of this moment of human culture, it is from this terrain that human beings, both individually and collectively, must forge their future. And if this is true, it is equally true that the politics of the reconstruction of the future must provide an alternative to the past grids of community and nation, in which individual people can locate themselves in a world which is now increasingly global, develop credible images of useful action, and seek to construct them in practice.

The challenge here is considerable. But, as we shall explain in more detail later, there are a number of fruitful possibilities which individuals, groups and communities are exploring. Let us consider just three of them here.

First, at the level of individual consciousness, there is the development and strengthening of the 'politics of identity'. It is already well understood, from the experience of the feminist movement amongst others, that it is necessary to extend the conception of what is political to the construction of individual consciousnesses and action. 'The personal is political' has an enduring theoretical as well as practical importance in a world in which the tidy external categories by which we might otherwise have defined our political character are melting. Postmodern literature provides a discovery, and in some cases rediscovery, of many of the significant components through which individual subjectivity is constructed, and so in principle we may work upon ourselves in a process of self-reconstruction to reconcile our values, aspirations, subjective understanding and action.[45]

Secondly, the deconstruction and reconstruction of subjectivity is a political project which extends beyond each person. There is a growing sense that new collective social anchor-points are needed in a world in which national community is losing its solidity and strength. Here we are already beginning to see not only the value but also the potential strength of local or regional communities, where common work, leisure, consumption and production build a mutually reinforcing basis of aspirations and action for change. Hierarchical political parties, and other bureaucratic and commercial organizations, in this sense may have diminishing appeal whilst local organization, built not so much around the politics of production as increasingly around the politics of consumption, is already acquiring renewed vitality.

Finally, we can even now discern a worldwide consciousness which understands that to locate the individual politically in a world that is increasingly globalized means developing structures and systems which allow him or her to map his or her actions and understanding within a perspective of the world as a whole. Here we see multiple efforts and initiatives consolidating new forms of global consultation, education and international action through which individuals, and local, national and regional organizations for change can position both themselves and those who comprise them.

There is reason to think that despite the ambiguities associated with them the new communication systems may be playing a positive role. Whilst the initial market imperatives for much of the development of these systems derive from the needs of transnational corporations and associated regulatory agencies, the logic of the market – and the associated technological change – is such that, almost as a by-product, significant access to these systems is coming within the reach of a wide range of smaller groups, and indeed significant sections of whole communities. It has been observed in recent literature that a central dynamic of capitalism is to act, as it were, to compress global space. Clearly, given the initial cost of the technology, this compression has been selective. The first to see dramatic reduction in global space were the large corporations and government agencies. In a sense, however, there is a diminishing economy of scale. The first gains are the largest, and it may well be true that the major agencies of the market are already 'global'. As the price of access to these systems drops, the possibility of transcending the gap between regional and global for a vast range of other, less orthodox organizations rises rapidly. The potential for this is already seen in the growth of international environmental networks such as 'Greennet' which provide international interconnection and news for a wide range of environmental and other citizen action groups in regions spanning the entire world.

The communication systems are of course only a technology – one piece of hardware which can at best (certainly not always) assist in the social project of constructing a grid against which a new politics may be constructed. Coupled with this but perhaps more important, is the emerging possibility of deconstructing 'democratic' institutions, and of reconstructing a much more radical vision of global participatory democracy. This is a project mobilizing the energies and resources of individuals and movements drawn from diverse cultural and political streams, spanning all continents and bridging the North–South and East–West divides. In later chapters we shall review the intellectual and institutional obstacles that stand in the way of a plausible and compelling image of the global community. But it would be wrong to overlook the very potent though not always predictable impulses that are encouraging its emergence.

Thus, one conclusion we may draw from the present tension in interpretation and representation is that the search for an effective politics of the future is already giving rise to new frameworks, which not only replace those which are eroding but are sufficiently robust to allow people, whether individually, regionally or globally, to have the confidence to take part in its construction. As Harvey also observes,[46] one of the implications arising not only from postmodern analysis but from the contemporary state of human affairs of which it is a symptom is that the 'local' and the 'global' are rapidly assuming something of the political priority once exclusively reserved for the national arena. The decentring of power is no longer just a useful avenue for intellectual inquiry but a revealing signpost for political action.

NOTES

1. J. Bury, *The Idea of Progress*, New York: Dover, 1960, p. 5.
2. S. Pollard, *The Idea of Progress*, London: C. A. Watts, 1968, p. v.
3. See ibid., and Bury, *The Idea of Progress*.
4. Matei Calinescu, *Five Faces of Modernity*, Durham, NC: Duke University Press, 1987, p. 20.
5. Walter Benjamin, *Illuminations*, London: Fontana, 1973, p. 259.
6. Marshall Berman, *All that is Solid Melts into Air: The Experience of Modernity*, New York: Verso, 1982, p. 15
7. Calinescu, *Five Faces of Modernity*, p. 42.
8. D. Frisby, *Fragments of Modernity: Theories of Modernity in the Work of Simmel, Kratauer and Benjamin*, Cambridge: Polity Press, in association with Oxford: Basil Blackwell, 1985.

9.   J. Habermas, 'Modernity: An Incomplete Project', in H. Foster (ed.), *Recodings: Art, Spectacle, Cultural Politics*, Port Townsend, Washington: 1985, 1983, p. 9.
10. Calinescu, *Five Faces of Modernity*.
11. Berman, *All that is Solid Melts into Air*, p. 16.
12. Vergani, Shinoda and Kesler, 'The Culture of Fragments – Notes on the Question of Order in a Pluralistic World: Towards a Structure of Difference', *PRECIS*, **6**, 1987, 7.
13. Frederic Jameson (1984), 'Postmodernism, or The Cultural Logic of Late Capitalism', *New Left Review*, **146**, 53.
14. Quoted in Steven David Ross, 'Power, Discourse, and Technology: The Presence of the Future', in Garry Shapiro (ed.), *After the Future: Postmodern Times and Places*, New York: State University of New York Press, 1990, p. 265.
15. David Harvey, *The Condition of Postmodernity: An Enquiry into the Origins of Cultural Change*, Oxford: Basil Blackwell, 1989, p. 44.
16. Andreas Huyssen, *After the Great Divide: Modernism, Mass Culture, Postmodernism*, Bloomington: Indiana University Press, 1986, p. 217.
17. See for example, J. Schuster and R. Yeo (eds), *The Politics and Rhetoric of Scientific Method: Historical Studies*, Dordrecht: Reidel, 1986.
18. See James Gleik, *Chaos: Making a New Science*, London: Cardinal, 1987, and references contained therein.
19. See for example Jean-François Lyotard, *The Postmodern Condition: A Report on Knowledge*, Minneapolis: University of Minnesota Press, 1984, p. 55.
20. See for example Charles Birch, 'Eight Fallacies of the Modern World and Five Axioms for a Postmodern Worldview', *Perspectives in Biology and Medicine*, **32**, (1), Autumn 1988, 12–30.
21. Lyotard, *Postmodern Condition*, p. 60.
22. B. McHale, *Postmodernist Fiction*, New York: Methuen, 1987.
23. Jameson, 'Postmodernism'.
24. Harvey, *Condition of Postmodernity*, p. 116.
25. Gayatri Chakravorty Spivak, 'Political Commitment and the Postmodern Critic', in Aram H. Veeser (ed.), *The New Historicism*, New York: Routledge, 1989, p. 284.
26. Harvey, *Condition of Postmodernity*.
27. Benedict Anderson, *Imagined Communities: Reflections on the Origin and Spread of Nationalism*, London: Verso, 1983, p. 16.
28. Ibid., p. 13.
29. Ibid.
30. Ibid, p. 19.
31. Ibid., pp. 40–1.
32. Ibid., pp. 46, 49.
33. Ibid., p. 19.
34. Ibid., p. 31.
35. Gamani Corea, 'Global Stakes Require a New Consensus', *ifda dossier*, **78**, July/September 1990, 77.
36. Stanley Aronowitz, 'Postmodernism and Politics', *Social Text*, **18**, Winter 1987–8, 99.
37. Jan Pronk, 'We Need a Global Mixed Economy and a Global Public Sector', *ifda dossier*, **78**, July/September 1990, 44.
38. See Jim Falk and Andrew Brownlow, *The Greenhouse Challenge: What's To Be Done?*, Melbourne: Penguin, 1989.
39. Michel Foucault, *The History of Sexuality Vol. I, An Introduction*, trans. Robert Hurley, New York: Pantheon Books, 1978 and related comment in Steven David Ross, 'Power, Discourse, and Technology: The Presence of the Future', in Garry Shapiro, *After the Future*, p. 264.
40. Although this point may seem obvious it is omitted from many contemporary analyses. See, for example, Held's account in Stuart Hall and Martin Jacques (eds), *New Times: The Changing Face of Politics in the 1990s*, London: Lawrence & Wishart in association with *Marxism Today*, 1989, p. 191.
41. Scott Lash and John Urry, *The End of Organised Capitalism*, Cambridge: Polity Press, 1987.

42.   Harvey, *Condition of Postmodernity*.
43.   E. Swyndgedouw, 'The Socio-Spatial Implications of Innovations in Industrial Organi-
      zation', Working Paper, No. 20, Johns Hopkins European Center for Regional Planning
      and Research, Lille, 1986, cited in Harvey, *Condition of Postmodernity*, pp. 173–6.
44.   Ross, 'Power, Discourse, and Technology', p. 270.
45.   Hall and Jacques, *New Times*, p. 150.
46.   Harvey, *Condition of Postmodernity*, p. 305.

4. World Economy

It has taken the stock market crash of October 1987 to bring home to many the multifaceted character of economic globalization: the rapid flow of information made possible by new electronic information systems; the availability of large funds which can be moved from one corner of the globe to another at a moment's notice; and the integration of national economies into 'one increasingly seamless global market'.[1] Technological change, particularly in the field of computers and electronics, has vastly reduced the physical and financial obstacles to global transactions and stimulated the creation of a bewildering array of financial instruments which enable investors and borrowers worldwide to trade around the clock and react almost instantaneously to each other's moves. The sharp rise in the velocity of money, the vast capital flows across national boundaries and the complex linkages of the world's leading financial centres are but the most evident symptoms of the rapidly changing economic landscape.

These symptoms are especially noticeable in periods of economic downturn or financial crisis, when markets tend to be doubly volatile and panic and over-reaction are transmitted swiftly and widely across the globe. Yet they are part of a long-term trend which has been with us for some time, and which points unmistakably to the internationalization of economic activity. The question arises: how does this trend affect the political organization of the world, and in particular the division of political space into discrete, state-centred, sovereign jurisdictions? Before answering this, it is first necessary to examine the nature, scope and pace of economic internationalization, for this process mirrors and closely interacts with the evolving structure of power and authority within and between nations.

ECONOMIC INTERNATIONALIZATION

In the new economic order created after 1945 under the aegis of Pax Americana, trade, investment and technical advances soon outstripped their pre-war equivalents. National economies became ever more sensitive to international pressure, particularly as domestic electorates came to believe that national prosperity was dependent on growth in the world economy.[2] The integration and interpenetration of national economies would in due course have the most far-reaching consequences not only for 'national' economic policy but for the political process as a whole, both domestically and internationally.

Transnationalization of Trade

Expanding trade was perhaps the first clear indicator of the process of global integration. A particularly striking example was provided by the United States, whose exports and imports as a proportion of gross national product (GNP) both rose from about 4 per cent in the early 1930s to 10 and 12 per cent respectively in 1984. But this was no isolated example. Between 1948 and 1971 world trade had increased by 7.3 per cent per annum. It was not simply that worldwide trade increased dramatically during this period, but that it played a key role in promoting growth and cementing the bonds of interdependence between the leading Western economies.

A key agent in the growth and changing character of international trade has been the transnational corporation (TNC). Using their global organizational networks often involving a long chain of affiliates and subsidiaries, the core corporations became dominant actors in the international division of labour. They accounted for a large and growing proportion of the total system of production and exchange, a trend increasingly evident in the manufacturing sector.[3]

In 1960 the top 200 global industrial corporations accounted for some 17.7 per cent of GNP in the non-planned economies. By 1980 their share had increased to 28.6 per cent.[4] Transnational firms based in the United States accounted for 80 per cent of its exports and for over one half of its imports.[5] A significant fraction of world trade – in excess of 30 per cent – is now represented by the movement of goods and services from one productive unit to another within the same enterprise. Intrafirm transfers are estimated to account for as much as half of some countries' total imports. A variety of TNC strategies encouraged the internationalization of markets.[6] According to one assessment, the transnational corporation is transforming international trade into 'internal movements in which products replace goods to the extent that certain types of subsidiaries may be regarded simply as workshops'.[7]

We shall return to the TNC in chapter 5 for a more detailed analysis of its relationship with the state on the one hand and technological change on the other. For the moment suffice it to say that the reproduction of capital now occurs primarily through global rather than purely local or national strategies. There exists a world market for goods, capital and labour, but this market no longer corresponds with the traditional notion of international trade as the exchange of national products. The world market connects countries, regions and cities and is reflected as much in the transnationalization of production as in the transnationalization of trade. Labour, materials and credit are transferred from one location to another in line with global corporate strategies aimed at minimizing the costs of production and maximizing productive capacity. Although capital accumulation is still equated with the performance of national economies and measured largely by rational accounting systems, in practice the influences which govern capital accumulation cannot be understood simply within the decision-making framework of national sovereign states.

Transnationalization of Production

The growth of foreign investment since the late 1940s has been amply documented. By 1967 the book value of all foreign investment was estimated to be nearly $110 billion. By 1971 it had jumped to $165 billion. In 1975 the inflow of foreign investment to all countries was estimated at $21.5 billion. By 1980 the annual inflow had reached $52.2 billion.[8] The expansion of transnational corporations continued unabated in the 1980s, although the growth rate of foreign direct investment eased considerably. There has also been a significant shift in the pattern of foreign investment among the capitalist economies. Whereas during the 1950s and 1960s American capital accounted tor the bulk of foreign investment, the export of European and Japanese capital gathered considerable steam during the 1970s and 1980s.[9]

Side by side with the transfer of capital has come transfer of labour. Although migrations of workers, both forced and voluntary, have a long history, three recent developments in the global reorganization of labour are playing a key part in the changing structure of the world economy. First, rural to urban migration has facilitated industrialization in several Third World countries by providing a cheap and compliant (largely female) workforce. Secondly, millions of migrant workers in OPEC countries, (e.g. from India, Pakistan, Sri Lanka, the Philippines) have contributed directly and indirectly to the recycling of petrodollars. Thirdly, the employment of migrant workers in low-paid, labour-intensive industrial and service jobs has significantly augmented and helped to discipline the workforce of advanced capitalist countries.[10] In time the world market for capital has combined with the 'world market for labour-power' to produce a 'world market for production sites'.[11] This is not to suggest that the process of internationalization is equally apparent in all sectors of the world economy, or that all social, cultural or political roadblocks restricting the free flow of labour, materials and credit across national boundaries have been eliminated. A clear trend

has nevertheless emerged making internationalization the defining characteristic of the contemporary world economy.

A particularly revealing aspect of the worldwide reorganization of capitalist production has been the shift of manufacturing capacity from the
established industrial countries to the newly industrializing countries (NICs).[12]
During the 1970s these countries, notably Hong Kong, Singapore, Taiwan,
South Korea, Brazil, Mexico and Argentina, sharply increased their exports
of manufactured goods. For the first four of these, exports of manufactured
commodities rose from 35 to 59 per cent over the period 1963–76.[13] During
1963–81 the export of manufactured commodities from the Third World
rose by an average of 46.87 per cent per annum compared to 27.18 per cent
for the world as a whole.[14] Several preconditions contributed to this trend.
The availability of a cheap, virtually inexhaustible and compliant labour
force in the Third World was an important factor,[15] as was the deskilling of
production tasks made possible by new technology. In addition, technical
advances in transportation and communication (e.g. freighters, containeriza-
tion, air cargo) have meant that the technical, organizational and cost factors
previously impeding the relocation of industry could be largely discounted.
Finally, the international concentration and centralization of capital, coupled
with the growth of an elaborate international infrastructure which included
the International Monetary Fund (IMF), the World Bank and the Organisation for European Economic Co-operation and Development (OECD), provided the necessary support for the financing of foreign investment almost
anywhere in the world.

The new international division of labour does not, however, treat the
Third World as a homogeneous entity. We need to distinguish the East
Asian NICs (recipients of export-oriented foreign investment) from the Latin
American NICs (where foreign investment is directed largely to the home
market), the oil-exporting countries, and the bulk of the less developed
countries.[16] Even within these categories there are likely to be significant
variations at the national and even local or regional levels. As we shall see in
the next chapter, the processes of integration are far from uniform, yet this
uneven development is itself an integral part of the dynamic of global
competition and therefore a factor in the internationalization of economic
activity. In any case, rapid technological change, in particular the application of microelectronics, has breathed new life to manufacturing industries
in the core capitalist countries, suggesting a more fluid international division
of labour than seemed likely even a decade ago.

The severe recession experienced by most Western economies in the
early 1970s provided a powerful stimulus for the restructuring of the world
economy. There was more to this, however, than the relocation of industry.
The reorganization of capital accumulation was 'a complex process involv-

ing the disappearance and creation of firms through mergers, takeovers, purchase of shares, bankruptcies and the formation of new companies'.[17] The process occurred in a trans-sectoral direction (by merging different sectors of the economy) but also transnationally (by merging enterprises in different economies). Between 1973 and 1978 European firms were involved in 4,612 mergers, and in the same period 623 US firms were taken over by Canadian, European and Japanese firms. In 1979 alone and again in 1980, more than 600 US firms were taken over by foreign transnationals.[18]

Economic internationalization has been reinforced by the accelerated fusion of industrial and financial capital. Transnational corporations have accumulated large portfolios of stocks in banks, insurance and investment companies. For their part, banks control an increasing proportion of the world's largest corporations (26 per cent in 1978 up from 13 per cent in 1965). For example, a leading American bank, Morgan Guarantee Trust, is reported to have accumulated controlling shares in 12 TNCs and to have a significant ownership or controlling interest in 60 other large companies.[19] The large banks now play a key part in co-ordinating capital investment programmes, maintaining credit lines and extending preferential loans to large firms. They are directly involved in the complex web of transactions that result in reorganizations, mergers and acquisitions.

Transnationalization of corporate activity is not, however, purely a function of size. In recent years the most rapid growth has occurred among small and medium-sized firms, which have sought to exploit their specific advantages in a transnational setting. Very often this means operating in only one or at best a few host countries. Moreover, as already indicated, strategic alliances are emerging between American, European and Japanese firms with a view to pooling specialized services, sharing the high costs of research and development and spreading investment risks associated with fierce competition and uncertain market prospects. These alliances, once concentrated in the primary and manufacturing sectors,[20] have now spread to the services area, notably to financial and trade-related services. They constitute an increasingly important mechanism in the continuing integration of the world market.

Transnationalization of Finance

Needless to say the new technology, notably in the area of telecommunications and data processing, has been a decisive factor in almost every aspect of global economic restructuring. Nowhere has this been more apparent than in the globalization of financial markets and the rapid expansion of international banking and foreign exchange trading. At the same time the development of new technologies has come to depend on the availability of vast financial resources.[21] The net effect of these two mutually reinforcing trends has been the expanded capacity of financial institutions to link diverse and distant markets, thereby reinforcing the internationalization of trade and production.

The development of a global money market gained considerable impetus during the 1960s, with the leading US banks seeking to establish themselves in the main commercial and financial centres of Europe and East Asia, while consolidating their foothold in Latin America. The same trend soon emerged in European banking, giving rise to an unprecedented growth of credit business. In 1982 total international bank lending amounted to $2,387 billion.[22] International banking activity, expressed as a proportion of world trade, had risen from a little over 10 per cent in 1964 to 45 per cent in 1972 and reached nearly 120 per cent in 1985.[23]

An important vehicle for the internationalization of commercial banking has been the spectacular growth of the Eurocurrency market.[24] Under this system banks of many nationalities, holding currencies (e.g. US dollars, German marks, Swiss francs) outside of their countries of origin, issue debt instruments on the basis of these deposits, thereby creating both long- and short-term capital and money markets. In 1973 total Eurocurrencies were already larger than total government international reserve assets.[25] Measured in US dollars at current prices the net size of the Eurodollar market had risen from $9 billion in 1964 to $132 billion in 1973, reaching approximately $1,200 billion in 1980.[26] Financial transactions within this market have tended to operate in ways that erode the capacity of national governments or international governmental agencies to regulate the flow of money and capital.[27]

The creation of a vast transnational credit system is a complex phenomenon whose origins are likely to be the subject of continuing controversy. The chronic US balance of payments deficit and the associated breakdown of the Bretton Woods system were no doubt important contributing factors. It is, however, with the consequences rather than the origins of this phenomenon that we are primarily concerned here. International liquidity is estimated to have trebled between 1969 and 1975 and again between 1976 and 1983. The volume of money as measured by the IMF expanded at an average annual rate of 7.5 per cent in the 1960s. The corresponding rate for the 1980s was at least 14.3 per cent. Large and rapid money flows ultimately produced a circular but frenetic paper chase fuelled by interest rate differentials and exchange rate fluctuations. The net effect was to circumscribe the range of policy instruments in the management of national economies and greatly increase the role of private banks in meeting the foreign exchange requirements of national governments.

A critical element in the new equation of international finance was the debt structure of several national economies, especially the less-developed oil-importing countries,[28] but also those that had embarked on ambitious programmes of export-oriented industrialization. Third World debt rose from under $100 billion in 1972 to over $500 billion in 1981, exceeding $1,000 billion in 1985. It had reached $1,300 billion by the end of 1989. By 1986 the debt service ratio had risen to 50 per cent for Latin American countries and 35 per cent for African countries.[29] Although much smaller in absolute terms, the debt incurred by the poorest countries (e.g. Bangladesh, Guinea, Madagascar, Somalia, Tanzania) had an even more debilitating impact given the size and underdeveloped character of their economies.[30] Several factors, beyond the control of Third World governments, had compounded the problem: the steep and unexpected rise in interest rates, the high value of the dollar resulting in a hefty increase in dollar-denominated debts, and the slump in export revenue reflecting in part the continuing recession in key Western economies. The combined impact of these exogenous influences highlighted the declining capacity of boundary-maintaining systems (i.e. sovereign states) to predict, let alone control, an increasingly complex environment and therefore to formulate, let alone implement, autonomously determined priorities and objectives.

Viewed from the vantage point of state sovereignty, the debt crisis is particularly instructive in its consequences for the core as much as for the periphery. A significant proportion of the debt, it should be remembered, was the direct result of the lending practices of a handful of private banks. By June 1984 America's 209 largest banking organizations had $132.6 billion outstanding in loans to the Third World. But 24 banks accounted for 84 per cent and only 9 banks for just under two-thirds of this debt. The fortunes of these banking giants were now inextricably tied to the responses of the major debtor countries. Were the latter to default on a significant scale, individual banks could be severely affected as could the entire financial sector given their size, strategic role within the American banking system and the close connections with their European counterparts.

The response of the leading banks was to embark on a damage limitation strategy with the support of their respective governments and especially the IMF. Most newly industrializing and less developed countries had little option but to comply with IMF conditions, which included devaluation of the currency, reduced consumer demand (through cutbacks on social programmes and wider application of the user pay principle), privatization of government enterprises, higher taxes and interest rates, and reallocation of resources to the export sector.[31] Failure to comply offered the prospect of accumulating arrears, a drastic fall in their credit rating and the drying up of new loans from both bilateral and multilateral, private and official sources.

The impact of IMF intervention and more generally global financial integration was as much political as economic. Debtor countries were more often than not driven towards authoritarian responses, as they sought to quell the dissent provoked by economic hardship and social dislocation. The trend was particularly conspicuous in parts of the Third World but not altogether absent from the First or Second Worlds. More and more the function of the state apparatus was to neutralize opposition to global integration and manage as best it could its negative consequences. To this extent the international mobility of money capital represented a significant new stage in the evolution of the system of sovereign states, for it not only challenged the notion of state authority as the repository of the popular will but called into question the force of national boundaries, or to put it differently, the analytical as well as practical relevance of the dividing line between national and international society, widely regarded as pivotal to the theory and practice of sovereignty.

Third World debt was the most striking symptom of a rapidly unfolding trend, namely the increasing role of private markets in international financial relations. The same trend was apparent in the decline of the Bretton Woods system, which had provided for a degree of national regulation over international capital movements.

The shift to flexible exchange rates encouraged the rapid movement in and out of currencies and set the stage for 'casino capitalism', a term used by Susan Strange to describe a game where unpredictability itself became the great attraction, drawing to it more and more players and vastly accelerating the speed of each move and countermove.[32] A closely related characteristic of this game was its international dimension. Despite the long distances often separating them, the leading players (i.e. financial managers of the large corporations) were able to respond to each other's moves almost instantaneously. They were, moreover, geographically diversifying their assets and liabilities as a way of hedging against unfavourable changes in exchange rates, thereby giving added impetus to the already explosive growth of the international financial market. Estimates put the daily turnover of the New York foreign exchange market in 1977 at some \$10–12 billion, a figure that was to double within three years. The turnover in the London exchange market was even greater, reaching the staggering figure of \$45 billion in 1985. According to one estimate, 'an average of \$420 billion crossed the world's foreign exchanges each day in 1987', of which more than 90 per cent represented financial transactions unrelated to trade or investment.[33]

The international integration of trade and finance, most strikingly reflected in the shift to flexible exchange rates, has dramatized the nation-state's diminishing capacity for economic regulation. To put it differently, it has severely constrained the effective range of strategic options and policy instruments available to governments. Even those with considerable financial muscle have not been immune to the trend. For example, the decision of successive US administrations to maintain high interest rates was in part a response to America's chronic balance of payments deficit, which in turn reflected the changing structure of the world economy. The vicissitudes of US monetary policy are a striking demonstration of the powerful constraints which international capital markets now impose on all governments, irrespective of the strength or size of national economies.

What is at issue is not just the capacity of governments to regulate their respective financial systems. Over the last fifteen years there has been, it is true, a marked decline in government controls over financial transactions. Countries with a long-standing bias towards 'liberal' policies (e.g. the United States, West Germany, Netherlands) have almost completely eliminated controls on foreign borrowing and lending. But even countries with a long history of government intervention (e.g. France, the United Kingdom) have drastically eased restrictions on the flow of foreign capital.[34] It is nevertheless conceivable that in years to come the trend may be at least partly reversed. The more significant conclusion is that the ebb and flow of national financial regulation is itself governed by external factors, in particular the pressure generated by an increasingly integrated, geographically unrestricted system of transnational trade, production and finance. In this emerging global system, characterized simultaneously by centralization and fragmentation, the key influences, decisions and outcomes do not correspond with the choices of sovereign wills and are not contained by the boundaries within which they operate.

THE WORLD SYSTEM

From the foregoing survey the following picture emerges. National economies have become increasingly interdependent and the closely related processes of production, exchange and circulation have assumed a global character. Much labour-intensive manufacturing industry has been relocated to regions with relatively low labour cost structures, although new technologies are putting increasing emphasis on the availability of a highly skilled workforce, hence the recent development of new manufacturing capacity in the advanced industrial countries. Contributing to the restructuring of economic activity have been the twin factors of rapid technological change and increasing integration of international finance. The ensuing international division of labour is able to utilize regional variations in technical infrastructure, market conditions, industrial relations and political climate to achieve globally integrated production and marketing strategies. The transnational corporation is the most conspicuous but not the only significant agent in the process. As Immanuel Wallerstein and others have observed, what we are witnessing is another stage in the development of a 'world system',[35] whose defining characteristic is the transnational scope of capital.

Making sense of the large and elusive puzzle that is globalization is central to our reassessment of the meaning and relevance of sovereignty. In order to clarify a number of the more intriguing aspects we propose to turn to world system theory, and in particular to Wallerstein's contribution.[36] The main drift of his thesis is that the 'world-economy' has been in the making for some considerable time. Though the date of origin cannot be specified with complete precision, the process has roughly paralleled the growth of capitalism and the formation of the modern state.[37] But whereas in the early stages of capitalist development national economies and nation-states were decisive in the internationalization of economic activity, in the contemporary period systemic interaction on a global scale appears to have acquired a dynamic of its own.

For Wallerstein the 'world-economy' is now universal, in the sense that all national states and national economies are in varying degrees integrated into its central structure. Though socialist systems in the post-1945 period accounted for a significant fraction of the world's population and territory and one at least could boast awesome military power, he nevertheless argues that their role in the world system is ultimately governed by the world market, which is itself the expression of global capitalism. Communist states, however different their internal economic and political institutions, or antagonistic their foreign policies, have had to operate within a larger diplomatic, strategic and economic framework whose *modus operandi* derives from the logic of the world market. To this extent a single division of labour may be said to cut across both national and ideological boundaries.

A distinguishing characteristic of Wallerstein's unified system is a pattern of global stratification which divides the world economy into core areas (the beneficiaries of capital accumulation) and peripheral areas (which are consistently disadvantaged by a process of unequal exchange). The system of states, which institutionalizes and legitimizes the core–periphery division, also concretizes, through an intricate web of legal, diplomatic and military relations, the distribution of power within the core. Wallerstein has further refined his explanatory model by postulating the existence of a semi-periphery which acts as an intermediate link in 'the surplus extraction chain'[38] and enhances the adaptability of the international division of labour by providing for mobility along the vertical organization of economic roles.

Here we are not concerned with the detail of Wallerstein's conceptualization. Nor indeed do we wish to offer a case for accepting or rejecting all the assumptions, methodologies and conclusions that are part of his theoretical project. Our purpose is simply to identify those aspects of the theory which can help to make sense of the process of transnationalization, as well as the problems it poses for an adequate reinterpretation of the nature and function of the modern state.

The first important point to note about world system theory, as developed by Wallerstein and his associates, is that it ascribes a major role to the system of states. It is that system which enforces the relationship between capital and labour and permits the extraction of surplus from the periphery to the core. States are the political instrument used by dominant classes to maintain their share of the world surplus product.[39] The use of political power for this purpose combines with efficient production for a competitive world market to produce a delicately balanced system in which the hegemonic centre will sooner or later lose its relatively dominant position to more efficient producers.[40] Corporate and financial interests mobilize the resources of the nation-state to enhance their position *vis-à-vis* their competitors. The state provides the political framework within which is conducted the competition between capitalist classes.

The second valuable feature of Wallerstein's approach is his historical perspective, with its emphasis on the evolving character of the capitalist world-economy. He postulates a series of stages: the emergence of the European world-economy, that is the transition from feudalism to capitalism (1450–1640); the establishment of British hegemony; the shift from agricultural to industrial capitalism; and more recently the consolidation of industrial capitalism under American hegemony.[41] Wallerstein is at pains to characterize the state system as integral to the world system at every stage of its development. Though one may wish to dispute the particulars of his periodization, what clearly emerges in this historical account is the functional role of the state – a theme to which a number of other writers have since returned.[42] In each case the aim is to trace the evolution of the global political economy by connecting the processes of capital accumulation on a global scale with the geopolitical rivalries associated with the state system.

The third and closely related dimension of Wallerstein's analysis, which we wish to highlight, is precisely its systemic quality. National states are still important actors, but their function is no longer interpreted simply in terms of their relationship to national society, to the national economy, or to each other. They have acquired global functions and are integrally related to global structures of production and exchange. The world system is not merely the summation of its parts. By virtue of its universality and the regularity of its mode of operation, it exercises a constraining influence on all its subsystems, including nation-states. To use Brucan's expression, 'the systemic acquires a drive of its own'.[43] Though functioning across a multiplicity of states, the world system is characterized by a single division of labour.

Rich in historical detail and bold in conceptual architecture, the Wallersteinian model is nevertheless prone to overstatement and oversimplification. To begin with, its notion of the international division of labour is too rigid and monolithic. Like much of dependency theory,[44] Wallerstein's 'worldwide division of labour and productive specialisation' no longer identifies the proletariat as those who sell their labour within a given national economy. Rather it is seen as comprising nations or groups of nations which have become victims of exploitation on a global scale, hence the pattern of global stratification that pits the 'world bourgeoisie' against the 'world proletariat'. One form of crude analysis, it seems, has been substituted for another. The notion of a series of closely interwoven 'centre–periphery relations', forming a subtle but unbroken chain of economic, political and cultural domination, does not easily square with existing reality.[45] As several studies have shown, the economic dynamism of the metropolitan centre (and the export of capital to the periphery) may well result in reduced profit rates in the 'centre' relative to the 'periphery' and the relocation of industry from the centre to the periphery. The diffusion of growth in the newly industrializing countries is partial evidence of this process.

Wallerstein's notion of the semi-periphery[46] represents an attempt to modulate the dualistic image of unequal exchange by postulating the existence of semi-peripheral nations and markets which act as 'intermediate elements in the surplus-extraction chain'. Although this threefold division may more accurately describe the pattern of global stratification and the increasing integration of newly industrializing countries and oil-exporting countries with the advanced capitalist economies, it still does not fully reflect the complexity of the world system. It does not characterize, let alone explain, the rapidly evolving relationship between core states, nor does it adequately conceptualize the nexus between production, distribution and political organization.

The strength of world system theory, it seems, is also its weakness. Frankel is right in suggesting that once history is presented 'as a succession of hegemonic states from the "core" which preside over unfolding stages within the world-system',[47] we are left with a 'homogenizing' theory which equates interdependence with full integration. There is a tendency in such theorizing to assume that the relationship between the world economy and the state system is entirely or overwhelmingly functional.[48] The historical evidence suggests a much more contradictory process. The state may not be sovereign, but this does not necessarily mean that the system of states performs a purely instrumental role. The functions states perform cannot be understood purely in terms of the requirements of global economic integration. Individual states and the state system as a whole retain a degree of autonomy, even though that autonomy may fall far short of the attributes of sovereign statehood.

As several writers have pointed out, there are two competitive mechanisms at work: the market and the state system.[49] Private firms compete by seeking low-cost production operations and/or markets that promise high rates of return. States seek power, influence and prestige and to this end form alliances and acquire military power. But what concerns us here is neither of the two mechanisms taken in isolation but their interaction, for it is this interaction which holds the key to the structure of power and authority, both nationally and internationally, and therefore to the meaning and efficacy of state sovereignty.

Chase-Dunn and Rubinson have attempted to establish a connection between market competition and state rivalry by postulating the notion of 'power-block formation'. Here they have in mind a process by which 'the interests of a political-economic coalition are institutionalised within the state apparatus'.[50] Once certain economic interests, as reflected in production and trade, become dominant the tendency will be for their economic ascendancy to acquire a political dimension. Similarly, once political ascendancy has been achieved in a core area it is likely to be duplicated in the periphery. As a consequence a power block emerges based on an economic and political alliance not only within the core but also between elites in the core and the periphery. Initially, the alliance may entail a strict division of labour between industrial production in the core and agricultural and mineral production in the periphery. Over time the alliance may encourage the development of export-oriented industrialization in certain parts of the periphery. To this extent, the territorial structure of the state system provides both a framework and a stimulus for economic competition.

Suggestive though it is about the nature and function of international alliances and the dependencies and interdependencies which they institutionalize, the notion of power-block formations leaves several questions unanswered. It does not explain the combination of factors which gives rise to power blocks, how authority is exercised within them, how they relate to one another, or what function is performed by the discourse of state sovereignty. Power blocks are certainly important players in the internationalization of economic activity. On the other hand, such internationalization has a profound impact on the distribution of power within and between power blocks. Economic internationalization also carries with it far-reaching repercussions for national societies, provoking a variety of sectional responses which may considerably limit or qualify the state's integration within either the power block or the world system at large. Even where an alliance is buttressed by a strong integrationist ideology, the state may be inclined, in the interests of its own legitimacy and survival, to adopt a mercantilist strategy as a way of reconciling or at least appeasing a number of competing interests. In other words, the individual state is not reducible to a mere superstructure entirely subordinate to the requirements of the international accumulation of capital. Its actions cannot be interpreted as the expression of the general capitalist will. The state retains a degree of political autonomy even though the manner and context in which it is exercised will vary greatly from state to state, issue to issue, and one period to the next.

Conceptually at least, the critical question is not just the relationship between the individual state and a particular sectional interest (e.g. a transnational corporation) or set of interests (e.g. manufacturing capital), but also the relationship between one state and the power block of which it is a part and, perhaps most importantly, between the state system as a whole and the world market. How does the state relate to the global totality that is the productive process? Posing the question in this form may help to explain why several critics of world system theory have rightly taken issue with its overemphasis on trade and unequal exchange as the key to the reproduction of the core–periphery division of labour. Instead, it is argued, the world economy should be reconceptualized as a 'world mode of production' in which the world rather than the nation is the unit of analysis and where 'world class relations', not just 'world exchange relations' are subjected to probing scrutiny.[51]

While analytically useful, the notion of a world class must be treated with considerable care and subjected to several qualifications. To begin with we are not dealing with a homogeneous class operating within a clearly defined national society but with what is at best a heterogeneous coalition of interests that operates across national boundaries. The direct and almost exclusive relationship that may once have tied a national class to its national state clearly does not apply. If the concept of class is to be usefully extended to an analysis of global politics, then this cannot be done by positing a new pattern of class relations that pits the core against the periphery and groups together nations according to their function in the global division of labour. A more promising avenue would be to view capital accumulation as a national and international process which involves relations of production but also a 'complicated field of power relations' and social and ideological conflict.

World system theory has yet to develop this wider theoretical agenda. On the other hand, it has added weight to the proposition that the periodic reorganization of society is dictated by the requirements of capital accumulation and anchored in the relations of global production. This helps to explain why national economic policy can no longer be interpreted as reflecting a sovereign national will. More specifically it helps to explain why the substitution of monetarism for Keynesian demand management came to dominate the policy process not just of one or a few but of virtually all OECD countries through the 1970s and early 1980s. Old Keynesian solutions were no longer adequate in conditions of stagflation. For capital accumulation to resume its upward curve it was necessary to place a higher priority on combating inflation, curbing wages and reducing public spending. Equally important in the drive to cut production costs and restore profit margins were the introduction of new technology and relocation of industry from metropolitan to peripheral regions. The leading role played by many social democratic parties since the early 1970s in managing this process is indicative of the powerful integrative pressures bearing on the contemporary capitalist state.[52] National states remain dominant political and economic institutions, but their function can no longer be understood simply in terms of their relationship to national society or the national economy.[53] They have acquired global functions and are integrally related to the transnationalization of production and finance. The actions of nation-states are not reducible to the interests and priorities of a coherent, self-contained, sovereign national will. The limited autonomy characteristic of the modern state should not be equated or confused with the traditional concept of sovereignty understood as supreme coercive power and authority.

THE STATE AND THE PROCESS OF INTERNATIONALIZATION

We have previously referred to the state and the market as the two pre-eminent institutions of the contemporary world system. We have also seen how the state performs both political and economic functions, and operates both nationally and internationally. What is in question is not the importance of the state but its sovereignty. The modern industrial state has played a leading role in protecting and expanding the international capitalist relations of production. It has provided the structural underpinning for each stage of the international division of labour: the internationalization of nineteenth-century trade in the so-called competitive phase of capitalist expansion; the internationalization of money capital in the late nineteenth and early twentieth centuries; and the internationalization of production which has become the dominant feature of the contemporary world economy.[54]

Equally important has been the function of the Third World state which, in the post-independence period has provided the labour force, administrative and political structure and military power needed to integrate peripheral economies with the world market. Strange as it may seem, the socialist state has also contributed to the process. Its central role in the development and co-ordination of the productive apparatus of these societies made it an attractive partner for transnational corporations and the necessary link between centrally planned economies and the world market.[55] In all three cases the state has in varying degrees and in different ways offered an effective mechanism for regulating and diversifying economic activity within and across national boundaries. States have largely been instrumental in securing for their economic producers access to overseas resources and markets, and have provided the diplomatic and legal framework necessary for the rapid expansion of international transactions.

But there is a deeper sense in which the state has assisted the internationalization of capital. It is the competitive state system, that is the differential in profit-making opportunities between national economies, which acts as a stimulus for the mobility of capital. Prices, industrial relations, financial conditions and exchange rates are obviously important factors governing investment decisions. The fluctuation between import liberalization and protectionism is another critical consideration. These policy variables represent incentives and penalties that influence resource allocation and corporate perceptions of comparative advantage. It does not follow, however, that state policies are the prime movers in the decision to invest. These policies are themselves strongly influenced by the relations of production which, as we have seen, increasingly operate in an international setting. State intervention in the economy and various forms of mercantilism need not therefore be interpreted as expressions of national sovereignty. They are just as likely to reflect the dynamic of the world market and the interests and priorities of transnational organizations.

Two other state functions are worth highlighting: military protection and legitimation. The first relates to the role of armed forces and military alliances in underpinning the existing relations of power and production – a theme to which we shall return in the next chapter. The second relates to the role of modern systems of education in promoting and justifying economic growth. It is not simply that educational expansion has provided the necessary skills and expertise to operate the rapid growth of the productive apparatus but that educational curricula have become a powerful tool for the 'homogeneous modernization of domestic social structures'.[56] They have helped to inculcate in otherwise diverse societies the modernizing ethic that has become the ideological hallmark of economic growth. Through the intermediary of educational institutions, which it largely funds and administers, the state provides the intellectual basis on which rests the global technological edifice. In a wider sense it can be argued that, notwithstanding periodic fluctuations between *laissez-faire* and interventionist policies, the state embodies the institutional authority which stabilizes and rationalizes the operation of the market.

The numerous functions performed by the modern state and the elaborate administrative, legal and military, not to mention ideological, apparatus it has established in the performance of these functions are often cited as evidence of the 'strength' of the state. Here the precise meaning of strength is a matter of legitimate debate. It should not, however, be assumed that state strength is synonymous with state sovereignty. The two concepts are related but not identical. The distinction between strength and capability on the one hand and between sovereignty and autonomy on the other is central to our thesis, and must therefore be subjected to careful analysis.

In Wallerstein's model we are offered five 'independent' measures of political strength: the capacity to assist owner-producers to compete in the world market; military power; the ability to perform these tasks without endangering the profits of the dominant class; efficient and effective administration; and a mode of action which maintains a balance between competing interests within the dominant class or 'hegemonic' bloc.[57] Core states are strong because they are able to tax more plentiful surpluses and offer the dominant class military protection and the infrastructure needed to gain control of international markets. By contrast peripheral states are weak because they have much less access to world trade and because their dominant classes are more likely to depend for their survival on the strength of core states. Although military power is one of the indicators of state strength, for Wallerstein the decisive factor is 'productive capacity for success in the world market'.[58]

For others the key to state strength lies in the centralization of its administrative apparatus. In 'neo-Weberian' circles there is a tendency to distinguish between strong and weak states in terms of the degree of administrative control or bureaucratic centralization they have developed.[59] The assumption is that such strength is indicative of the state's capacity to impose its will. Organizational structure is thereby seen as a key variable governing the ability of the state apparatus to pursue autonomous goals and priorities.

Centralization and strength, however, may not be as closely connected as the above argument would suggest. In the case of peripheral states the centralization of authority, as evidenced in one-party systems and military rule, is a sign of weakness rather than strength, for the function of dominant elites is to preserve the conditions that underpin the dependent status of their society. On the other hand, in the semi-periphery, where the emerging owning-producing class may need the support of direct state involvement for the extraction of economic surplus, a centralized institutional structure may assist competitiveness in world markets and may therefore provide a measure of state strength. Similarly, in the core, where the function of state intervention is in part to mediate between the conflicting interests of civil society, centralized decision-making and administration may be taken as an indicator of strength.

It still does not follow that strength and centralization are synonymous, or that either is a necessary and sufficient condition of sovereignty. Though Wallerstein concedes that the mediating function gives the state a degree of autonomy, he is at pains to show that state conduct remains closely tied to the interests of the dominant class. In this he is clearly at odds with Krasner's conceptualization of state autonomy, according to which state aims are not reducible to the immediate or long-term interests of the capitalist class, or even to the long-term survival of capitalist society. In Krasner's view, states pursue the 'national interest' to the extent that their objectives 'reflect general societal goals, persist over time, and have a consistent ranking of importance'.[60] 'Strong' states are better able to pursue the national interest in that a centralized form of government can more effectively articulate the general interest of society, whereas 'weak' states, characterized by fragmented public institutions, are more likely to be vulnerable to pressure groups seeking to achieve particular ends.

The direct linkage between strength and centralization is also asserted by Katzenstein, although in more sophisticated fashion. Taking France and America as a point of comparison, he offers the following contrasting assessment of their domestic structures:

> In France the state is centralized and strong because a feudal society had to be modernised. In America the state is decentralised and weak because society was already modern. The French state is united and controls an atomistic society. The American state is divided and is controlled by a pluralist society.[61]

This analysis is perhaps helpful in contrasting the American and French political systems so far as the nexus between private and public power is concerned. But it does not necessarily tell us a great deal about the nature of state strength or the relationship between strength and centralization.

That the French state has traditionally played a more interventionist role than the American state in the regulation of domestic economic activity is plain enough. It does not follow, however, that the French state is stronger than the American state. In several respects it is much weaker: it commands fewer economic and military resources and is much less able to influence international outcomes.

One thing is clear: the yardstick of state strength cannot be confined to purely domestic relationships. Centralization of power and authority may demonstrate or even enhance state strength. By the same token it may obscure and even accentuate state weakness. Centralization simply describes the structural forms developed by the state in the performance of its functions, whereas strength denotes the success with which these functions are performed. The two concepts are closely related but neither is synonymous with sovereignty, for theoretically at least all states, regardless of their strength or degree of centralization, are equally sovereign. If by sovereignty is meant the supreme authority that gives expression to the unity and will of the nation (i.e. civil society), then strength may be said to serve a purely instrumental function. The sovereign state may need to be strong if it is to overcome the domestic or external forces seeking to obstruct its will. Strength, then, may be a necessary condition of sovereignty but not necessarily within the reach of every state. In any case, it is not a sufficient condition.

Nor can sovereignty be equated with centralization and bureaucratization. Even if sovereignty is divorced from any notion of general interest and more narrowly defined to mean supreme coercive power and authority, strength and centralization are likely to remain largely instrumental in character. They may influence the way sovereignty (i.e. supreme coercive power and authority) is exercised, but they are unlikely to give it its meaning and content. The state may be strong and centralized, but it may not be sovereign. As we shall argue in more detail in the next chapter, the state, despite the resources at its command, may not have the freedom to assert its will independently of outside forces or domestic private interests. Sovereignty implies a particular relationship between the public and private spheres and a particular concept of territoriality which defines the boundaries between the internal (national) and external (international) environments. However, as we have already observed, these distinctions have been substantially eroded by rapidly evolving forms of economic and social organization. Paradoxically, the increasing strength of the state may result in its declining sovereignty.

The paradox is most strikingly evident in the area of economic policy. We have already seen how large-scale movements of capital across national boundaries have greatly circumscribed the scope for macroeconomic regulation available to either home or host states. It is not so much that transnational capital accounts for an increasing slice of the national economic cake, but that it is closely intertwined with the operations of local firms which often act as the customers and suppliers of transnational firms. The complex web of contracting and subcontracting 'has qualitatively weakened the links between nation-states and transnational capital'[62] and greatly exacerbated the difficulties of national economic management. National governments have come to operate within a global environment which they do not control but which substantially shapes the strategic options as well as policy instruments at their disposal.[63] Much the same trend is suggested by the transnationalization of financial institutions and the growing pressure exerted by transnational banks for the deregulation of domestic banking and finance.[64] By the late 1980s the deregulatory ethic which had already engulfed Western Europe, North America and Australasia was making serious inroads in Japan and beginning to create large cracks in the Soviet bloc economies.

But it would be a mistake to think that the internationalization of finance and the state's declining capacity to regulate financial transactions within its boundaries are an entirely new phenomenon. The trend has been steadily gathering momentum for several decades, despite recent signs pointing in the opposite direction. In a fascinating account of key decisions, 'which have altered the course of world economic history in recent times',[65] Susan Strange has highlighted the progressive abdication of state surveillance and control, particularly in relation to the world's monetary and financial system.

Over a period of little more than two decades a significant shift has occurred in the balance between private and public power, and between national regulation and economic internationalization. A situation has arisen where the operation of private banks and other leading financial institutions is shaping the framework and agenda of national policy. Some have argued that in a context of mounting trade rivalries the trend may be reversed, and that 'embedded liberalism' may soon give way to moves for 'greater autonomy and the delinking of national economies'.[66] There is little evidence, however, to support this scenario of an international regime in which nationally defined priorities triumph over transnational pressures and connections. There may well be a revival of trade protectionism but more as temporary leverage in an intensified competitive struggle which, in any case, cuts across national boundaries and is more likely than not to hasten the internationalization of economic activity.

Increasing protection of domestic markets cannot of itself restore national control over the instruments of economic policy, much less over economic outcomes. The decline of state autonomy (and therefore effective sovereignty) is a long-term and universal trend arising from both endogenous and exogenous influences. Governments formally retain the power to impose tariffs, regulate the flow of capital and levy exchange controls. But whether, how and to what extent that power is exercised depends very much on the prevailing ideological and institutional climate. While the extraction of concessions from governments and the imposition of bank-defined fiscal discipline have been most evident in the case of Third World countries experiencing crippling foreign debts, the trend may be said to have reached global proportions. The financial power of private institutions has assumed a decisive role in shaping the structure and processes of the public sphere not only in advanced capitalist economies but increasingly in the Chinese, Soviet and East European economies.[67] The changing relationship between the public and private spheres and the virtual collapse of the dividing line separating the domestic from the external environment suggests a fluid but closely integrated global system substantially at odds with the notion of a fragmented system of nationally delineated sovereign states.

CHANGING NATURE OF HEGEMONY

Our discussion of the state must now be taken a step further. We need to turn our attention from the state in general to the role of dominant states, and the implications of such dominance for the theory and practice of sovereignty. For in contradistinction to the assumed legal (i.e. authoritative) equality of sovereign states stands the disproportionate concentration of power in a few states, hence the long-standing distinction between great and small powers. Some writers go further and suggest that the international order prevailing at any one time, and by implication the management of an otherwise anarchic system, depends largely on the institutional and ideological primacy of an imperial power or, as others have described it, a 'hegemonic core power'. The concept of hegemony is directly relevant to our study since by definition the existence of a hegemonic system contradicts the notion of a fragmented system comprised of sovereign states each exercising supreme coercive power within the territory it controls and unrestrained by external authority or force.

According to hegemonic stability theories international relations since the sixteenth century have been dominated sequentially by one of these states: Portugal, the Netherlands, Britain and the United States.[68] For some theorists this imperial or hegemonic position derives principally from military power and the manipulation of alliances. For others – among them Wallerstein – hegemony involves 'a situation wherein the products of a given state are produced so efficiently that they are by and large competitive even in other core states, and therefore the given core state will be the primary beneficiary of a maximally free world market'.[69] Hegemony is thus equated with productive, commercial and financial dominance, although political and military power is seen as a necessary instrument in establishing and maintaining the domestic and external conditions conducive to such dominance.[70]

Wallerstein's notion of hegemony represents a significant advance in our understanding of the world system, rightly stressing the role of productive capacity, the close connection between the economic, political and military dimensions of power, and the way these combine in the conduct of the hegemonic state. Yet, as Robert W. Cox points out, there is still more to hegemony. Drawing on the Gramscian interpretation of the concept as 'a unity between objective material forces and ethico-political ideas', he conceives of international hegemony as state power based on economic dominance but stabilized and justified by 'an ideology incorporating compromise or consensus between dominant and subordinate groups'.[71] A hegemonic order is precisely one in which one state has been able to establish the legitimacy of its dominance.[72] Hegemonic leadership is exercised when a state is able to institutionalize its economic and military dominance through a complex web of relationships and control mechanisms that elites in secondary states find beneficial and are willing to administer. Though the international order will generally work to its advantage, the hegemonic power may have to make periodic sacrifices in order to consolidate its prestige and the legitimacy of its leadership.

Expressed in general terms, the overriding function of hegemonic power is to ensure stability for the world system, particularly in a period of rapid economic change. For Kindleberger, the hegemon performs three specific functions in a liberal economic order: it offers an outlet for surplus production; acts as a lender of last resort, thereby maintaining monetary stability; and generates the outflow of capital and credit needed to maintain capital accumulation on a global scale. All three functions are critically important given that certain tendencies inherent in the market system may, if unchecked, result in bursts of sustained recession and even depression. Britain, it is argued, successfully performed this role in the three or four decades prior to the First World War and the United States in the two decades after the Second World War.[73] The failure of both powers to play a stabilizing role in the inter-war years is seen as the catalyst for the severe economic depression that was to afflict most capitalist economies. This interpretation is largely consistent with Gilpin's explanation of the rise and fall of 'liberal economic orders', although in his case the hegemonic power's capacity 'to manage and stabilise the system' is said to diminish as profit rates in the 'core' fall relative to those in the 'periphery' and the export of capital by the core state weakens its political and economic power.[74]

Within hegemonic stability theory there are considerable differences regarding the structural forms that hegemony can take, and regarding the relative weight to be assigned to the economic, military and ideological components of hegemony. For all these variations, one thing is clear: hegemony is inconsistent with sovereignty for any state other than the hegemonic state. The dominance exercised by one state by definition encroaches on the effective sovereignty of all other states. A hegemonic system is precisely one in which one state enjoys privileges, responsibilities and functions not shared by other states, in which one state's authority effectively prevails beyond its own sovereign jurisdiction, thereby qualifying if not undercutting the jurisdiction of other states.

Needless to say the leadership exercised by any hegemonic centre will not be permanent. Sooner or later that leadership will be challenged by other centres intent on retrieving their autonomy or aspiring to establish their own hegemony. The question is whether the decline of hegemony can give rise to a new and fragmented system of competing states, more conducive to the principle of sovereignty. To examine this possibility we shall turn our attention to the changing fortunes of American hegemony.

Indicators of America's diminishing influence usually include the loss of nuclear monopoly, the fall in America's GNP as a proportion of world GNP, the even more dramatic reduction in the US share of global manufacturing capacity and the corresponding decline in America's share of world trade.[75] As Gill and Law have argued, the Reagan presidency may be interpreted as an attempted 'remobilisation' of the dominant elements of American political culture, or 'internal reconstruction of American hegemony in a Gramscian sense'.[76] The revival of Cold War rhetoric, the greatly expanded defence budget, the reaffirmation of American authority within the Western alliance system, and the more assertive stance against Marxist or revolutionary forces in the Third World were perhaps the external (and more overtly ideological) façade in a wide-ranging campaign to revitalize American hegemony.

The attempt, however, to recreate the social, psychological and political conditions conducive to American dominance could not obscure changing economic realities. The privileged position of the US dollar could no longer be used as effectively to support prolonged foreign military expeditions, buy foreign assets, and at the same time maintain the productivity of the domestic economy. By the end of 1988 the United States, which as recently as 1983 was still the world's largest creditor nation, was now saddled with a foreign debt burden of $532.5 billion. In short, the military resources and residual economic leverage at the disposal of the American state, though formidable, were no longer sufficient to sustain the hegemonic order established by Pax Americana at the conclusion of the Second World War.

In the wake of the relative decline of American power there has been a tendency for regional economic blocs and alliances to form as core states and sectional economic interests seek to advance their position at the expense of others. The question arises: do these two closely related trends – economic regionalization and incipient mercantilism – point to the demise of hegemony and the reassertion of state-centric authority? Do they, in other words, express the renewed relevance of sovereignty as a central ordering concept in international political economy, particularly for those periods which represent a transition from one hegemonic system to another? Careful sifting of the evidence would suggest a rather different conclusion.

Turning first to the issues posed by the emerging mercantilism, there is no denying that the international environment has generally become more conflictual, protectionist pressures on governments have multiplied, and the discipline required by the General Agreement on Tariffs and Trade (GATT) has been eroded. By 1983 more than 40 per cent of Japanese exports to Western Europe were restricted by measures that violated the letter or the spirit of GATT rules.[77] As a consequence of European barriers Japan and the newly industrializing countries have sought to sustain their export performance by targeting the American market, thereby provoking a fierce protectionist backlash in the United States. Since the early 1980s the Japanese–American trading relationship has become increasingly acrimonious as has the relationship between the United States and the European community, particularly in the agricultural sector where each side has sought to gain an advantage through a policy of subsidy and counter-subsidy. The West Europeans, for their part, have been reluctant to expose their economies to greater international competition fearing the likely repercussions for the fragile social and political compromise, if not consensus, so painstakingly established since the war. As for the Americans, they have steadfastly retreated from their free trade commitments, imposing import quotas on textiles, cars and goods in a range of other industrial sectors where American interests have been severely hurt by European and Japanese competition. The pressure of high interest rates and the over-valued dollar have greatly accentuated the protectionist tendencies of American agriculture, but also contributed both directly and indirectly to 'the de-industrialisation of significant sectors of the American economy'.[78]

At face value the 'newest mercantilism'[79] points to the diminishing political impact of interdependence. Yet the verdict of a definitive shift from 'openness' to 'closure' in the global political economy is seriously misleading. The rising tide of protectionist sentiment is itself largely a response to the interpenetration of national economies, to the transnationalization of production and finance, and not least to the volatility of flexible exchange rates and structural and geographical changes in the pattern of investment. There is little indication that these trends will be reversed as a result of increasing demands for protection. To begin with, transnationalization has created in its wake powerful interests, in business but also in organized labour, within the centralized bureaucracies and the consuming public at large, which have a stake in economic liberalization.[80] Indeed, the growth of trade barriers coincides with, and is in part neutralized by, unprecedented levels of financial deregulation and increasing international economic integration. Indeed, rising trade barriers merely accentuate the incentive to penetrate closed markets through such mechanisms as equity investment, mergers and takeovers, joint ventures and cross-licensing of technologies and products.

What, then, of the emergence of regional blocs? It is now commonplace to describe the world economy as coalescing around three axes: the European Economic Community, centred on the economic weight of a reunified Germany, a North American bloc in which the Canadian and Mexican economies are increasingly tied to the United States, and a Pacific Basin region centred primarily on Japan and its East Asian and Pacific trading partners.[81] It is difficult, however, to envisage any of these three alliances developing the required self-sufficiency in resources, markets, access to capital or technical infrastructure to consider relinquishing the opportunities offered by an integrated world market. The establishment of relatively self-contained, unrelentingly antagonistic regional economic alliances (i.e. undiluted imperial rivalry) is belied by the growing evidence of transnational corporate alliances and instruments of financial integration. Such regional trading blocs as may be formed are likely to be characterized by undefined or overlapping membership, porous boundaries, and an intricate pattern of transnational and transregional trading, commercial and financial relationships.

The decline of American hegemony may accentuate the competitiveness evident in the world market and inter-state relations, but this tendency is likely to be offset by the integration arising from the transnationalization of capital and the interpenetration of national economies and regional trading blocs. As we have already observed, this second tendency is itself antithetical to the principle of sovereignty. Over time the transnationalization of trade, production and finance is giving rise to interests, perceptions and organizational forms which cannot be equated with those of any one state.

To speak of an emerging global class is to oversimplify. By the same token, there have emerged networks, contacts and ideological affinities which overlap with, yet cut across nationally defined social classes. Key participants in this process include the managerial elites associated with transnational corporations and financial institutions, but also a sizeable fraction of the bureaucratic elites which administer national states and international governmental organizations. The interests of this loose international coalition are far from uniform, and are probably best served by a collectivist or *ultra-imperialist* strategy which strives for a degree of co-operation between metropolitan centres cemented by a web of regional and international institutions designed to preserve the stability of the system.

Despite continuing tensions and instability, the international 'liberal' or capitalist order has survived the demise of American hegemonic leadership. Several factors account for the persistence of this global order which Keohane and others equate with continuities in the international trading and monetary regimes.[82] First, the decline of American economic power has been gradual and partly offset by the network of military alliances which tie European and Japanese security to the American nuclear deterrent. Secondly, other powerful state structures have emerged in which capitalist ideology is also firmly embedded, making possible, in the Gramscian sense, a normative consensus within the core which minimizes the prospects of significant deviation in economic or foreign policy by any one state. Thirdly, as we shall see, international institutions have assumed many functions previously performed by the American state. In the process they have developed a co-ordinating role which is no longer a mere reflection of US interests and priorities. These institutions, of varying size, status and function, may not be able to formulate, let alone enforce, strict rules of international conduct, but they do provide an avenue for multilateral macro-economic surveillance and co-ordination. They also constitute a channel for building and publicizing support for values, ideas and interests which contribute to a dominant discourse about political and economic action. The decline of US hegemony has thus given rise to a more subtle, less statist, centralized or predictable form of hegemony. The ensuing system of co-ordination, though in part still dependent on the state's administrative apparatus, is in no way constrained by the boundaries of the state. Nor does it in any meaningful sense respond to the state's 'sovereign' will or to its supreme coercive power and authority.

ROLE OF INTERNATIONAL ORGANIZATION

The diminishing capacity of the state to regulate national economic activity in a period of mounting conflict in the international market-place has strengthened the integrative function of international institutions. The severe economic recession of the 1970s, the decline of American hegemony and the consequent restructuring of the world economy have greatly enhanced the role of international organizations in promoting and regulating the transnationalization of economic activity. This is not to say that all forms of international regulation have found equal favour. For example, the numerous conferences and institutional initiatives (e.g. UNCTAD programme) that brought together representatives of the advanced capitalist countries, the less developed countries and the oil-exporting countries in the early to mid-1970s proved largely abortive. The attempt to resolve problems of energy supply, raw materials, economic development and international finance in the context of a New International Economic Order were clearly not palatable to those interests spearheading the push for global integration. On the other hand, the World Bank and the IMF, GATT, the Food and Agricultural Organization (FAO), the International Labor Organization (ILO) and other United Nations agencies have become important elements of an emerging global superstructure which facilitates multilateral monetary and trade transactions, greater compatibility of training and educational systems, the flow of technical and managerial expertise, taxation agreements and treaties for investment protection.[83]

The functional importance of international organization is not, in any case, a recent phenomenon. Quite apart from its security role, the United Nations system has since its inception had as one of its main functions the more effective reproduction and accumulation of capital. The IMF and the World Bank in particular were entrusted with the task of promoting the consolidation and expansion of the capitalist world economy. To this end they are endowed, by virtue of their statutes, with a dual capacity for global intervention. At one level they are able to use the substantial resources placed at their disposal by member countries to promote a particular pattern of international trade and investment, and set rules or guidelines on the form of the trade and payments regime. But at another level they are in a position to make the provision of economic assistance to member countries conditional on the latter's acceptance and implementation of their policy prescriptions.[84] The power to withhold economic and financial assistance or cut off sources of international loans has enabled the World Bank and the IMF to exercise substantial and continuous leverage on a great many national economies. The key to their power lies not only in the financial resources at their disposal but in their capacity to influence the aid programmes of major governments and the lending policies of banks and other key financial institutions. Though less dramatic, the role of other UN agencies and assorted regional and international governmental organizations has also been influential in shaping the structure of the rapidly evolving world economy.

These institutions have, if anything, acquired increased significance. The debt crisis, probably more than any other factor, has propelled the IMF to the forefront of international decision-making. Both Third World and Eastern European countries with sizeable debt problems have almost without exception had to rely on the IMF for emergency relief. However, to gain such relief and have their creditworthiness restored, they have had to accept the IMF's harsh fiscal discipline. The structural fragility of many dependent economies has also ensured a central role for the World Bank. The aid offered to the very poor countries is in a sense an attempt to offset the disintegrative tendencies of the world system, that is, to prevent the sharpening domestic and international inequalities of income and wealth from endangering the stability and legitimacy of existing power relationships. The reverse side of the coin is the financing of infrastructure projects needed for the development of manufacturing industry, agribusiness and international trade. Nowhere has this function been more apparent than in the export-oriented strategies of the newly industrializing countries.

Although the World Bank accounts for only a small fraction of the total loans disbursed to the periphery and semi-periphery by the core sectors of the world economy, its role is more important than the raw figures would suggest. Operating in concert with the IMF, it helps to shape the credit rating of recipient countries and evaluates the performance of their development programmes. By virtue of their global reach, organizational strength, professional expertise, and close connections with core governments and private banks and corporations, these international institutions have acquired an authoritative status within the world economy comparable in some respects to that enjoyed by the state *vis-à-vis* the national economy.[85] To this extent, the leading international organizations, of which the World Bank and the IMF are the most conspicuous, may be said to play an increasingly important initiating, monitoring and regulatory role in the reorganization of economic activity on a global scale.

The Western economic summits since 1975 represent a less structured, at times less tangible, but nonetheless significant form of international coordination.[86] On the one hand, it could be argued that the impact of the decisions they have taken over a decade and a half is relatively meagre. The tendency has been not so much to innovate as to support existing policies, to legitimize the prevailing neo-classical philosophy with its emphasis on checking inflation, cutting public spending and reducing budget deficits. A key theme has been cutting taxes, encouraging international competition and reducing government intervention. On the other hand, summit exhortations, while not always fully or consistently implemented, have helped to create a political climate more conducive to their realization. The summits may be interpreted as a symbolic instrument of collective management in the era of declining US hegemony. Underpinning this exercise in economic summitry have been the financial bureaucracies of the biggest capitalist powers (that is, the Group of Five; later Seven) which, together with the managing director of the IMF, were responsible for 'multilateral surveillance' of economic policy and, especially since 1985, for the development of new procedures for policy co-ordination. The Louvre and Plaza accords of September 1985 and February 1987 respectively represented tentative but significant steps towards the pluralist adjustment of foreign exchange rates.

It should not, however, be inferred from this brief survey that the functionality of international organization is either comprehensive or unproblematic. In the area of banking, where the need for international supervision and regulation has become most acute, the major Western governments responded to the banking crisis of 1974 by setting up the Committee on Banking Regulations and Supervisory Practices. But the efficacy of the rules devised by that Committee, the so-called Basel Concordat, was at best limited, depending as it did on the co-operation of home and host governments in the sharing of information and the establishment of adequate inspection procedures. In December 1987 these governments went a step further by committing themselves to creating by 1992 a uniform international definition of bank capital and common higher standards for evaluating risk and defining capital adequacy for banks in these countries.[87] However, the success of such multilateral co-ordination was conditional on more rigorous financial regulation within each state and greater uniformity in financial policy and administration between states.

The discrepancy between national regulatory environments has in large measure contributed to the qualitative and geographical expansion of financial innovations, the combined effect of which has been to accentuate the problems of international regulation and weaken further the willingness of national governments to apply stringent controls on financial markets. Ironically, the competitiveness of the international system has acted as a disincentive for domestic regulation even though the latter remains the *sine qua non* of international regulation. Core corporations have consistently argued that in a highly competitive world environment greater regulation threatens higher productivity and business confidence. As a consequence, national policymakers, fearful of politicizing their financial and economic decisions, have refrained from extending the scope and efficacy of state intervention, thereby limiting, albeit indirectly, the reach and effectiveness of international organization.

Notwithstanding these impediments, international organization, of both the formal and informal variety, has acquired an important co-ordinating role in the transnationalization of economic activity. Such co-ordination complements but is not subsumed by the many administrative functions still performed by the state. International bureaucratization is itself evidence of the diminishing capacity of national bureaucracies to provide an adequate institutional framework for the complex task of economic regulation. Paradoxically, the growth of international organization accentuates the constraints of national regulation, and highlights the widening discrepancy between the institutional requirements of an integrated world economy and the institutional capabilities of a fragmented system of 'sovereign' states.

DIFFUSION OF POWER AND AUTHORITY

The foregoing analysis points to a rapidly evolving world system whose distinguishing characteristic in the current stage of evolution is the progressive integration of economic activity on a global scale. The fragmentation of the state system and the economic rivalries and military conflicts that it expresses both hinder and facilitate the transnationalization of capital. At one level it seems as if the horizontal organization of the world economy is at odds with the vertical organization of the international political order. But this tension, real though it is, does not fully describe the complexity of the situation for it suggests that these two institutions (or sets of relationships) are theoretically and practically distinct. A careful reading of the historical process suggests otherwise.

The progressive integration of the world market is reflected in the transnationalization of trade, production and finance, which in turn dictates the periodic reorganization of industrial activity across national boundaries. The ensuing interpenetration of national economies coexists with the continuing fragmentation of the system of sovereign states. The interaction of these two mutually reinforcing trends accounts for the self-sustaining dynamic of uneven development which characterizes nations, regions and the world as a whole. The fundamental contradiction, then, is not between the objectives of the national state and the strategies of transnational capital. Rather the contradiction is internalized within each state or national society, although the international division of labour greatly influences how that contradiction manifests itself at any given time or place. The effect of this contradictory dynamic is to blur the neat dividing line between national and world markets as much as between domestic and foreign policy. It is as if global processes and institutions are invading the nation-state and as a consequence dismantling the conceptual and territorial boundaries that have traditionally sustained the theory and practice of state sovereignty.

All of this is not to argue that the vast legal, administrative, military and ideological apparatus of the state is no longer powerful or functional. Our analysis suggests instead that the sovereign state, though it remains a key instrument for the co-ordination and expansion of the productive process on a global scale, can no longer perform this function single-handedly. More importantly, the very performance of this function requires the state to act in ways that weaken its claim to sovereignty. The laws and regulations that the state promulgates and enforces under the rubric 'economic management' correspond less and less to the priorities of a cohesive, easily identifiable (let alone popular) sovereign will. The transnational integration of capitalist production, precisely because it creates and feeds upon differential rates of productivity, technical innovation and economic growth within and between national societies, tends to sharpen the conflict of economic interests and weaken the integrity of national economies, thereby placing added pressure on social and political cohesion. To make matters worse, the periodic reorganization of the productive process, and even of the labour force, accentuates the need for state intervention at the very time that external forces are greatly increasing the pressure for industrial and financial deregulation.

Faced with these conflicting demands and the prospect of virtual paralysis, the state may adopt one of two strategies: delegation or reassertion of authority. The first strategy, which we have already explored, involves the formal or implicit transfer of authority through various forms of institutional innovation. This delegation of powers usually occurs in the context of specific functions and is reflected in the establishment of ad hoc or long-term mechanisms of consultation, co-operation and co-ordination. These may be supranational or transnational in character; they may operate regionally or internationally. Though it remains subject to legal and practical constraints, the growth of international organization has gained considerable impetus in recent decades and is now a significant influence in the processes of systemic and subsystemic regulation. Even where the trappings of legal sovereignty remain intact, the net effect is to reconstitute the practical meaning of sovereignty with the consequent dispersal of power and authority to diverse institutions and locations.

The state may choose the second option (i.e. reassertion of its own authority) by resorting to force (the tendency is especially striking in the Third World but by no means confined to it) or by reactivating primordial ethnic-cultural-religious ties. Though either mechanism may provide it with breathing space, neither is likely to resolve the fundamental contradiction that reflects the inner logic of a still unfolding historical process. Political repression, even where it demonstrates the coercive power of the state, is likely to weaken its legitimacy and with it the validity of the claim to sovereignty. The use of coercive power may not in any case produce the desired outcome. As for the partly engineered, partly spontaneous appeal to nationalism, the strategy, as we shall see in a later chapter, is at best a double-edged sword likely to be as much a source of political division as of social solidarity. The changing face of economic organization is calling into question Weber's notion of the state as a territorial entity exercising a monopoly on the legitimate use of violence. It is not that the Weberian interpretation has been proven false, but that it has lost much of its explanatory power precisely because it fails to take sufficient account of the intimate connection between economics and politics, between national and international phenomena, in short the simultaneous internationalization and denationalization of economic organization. In the second half of the twentieth century we are witnessing the emergence of a complex yet relatively integrated world system which encompasses, and in part operates through the state system, but whose logic and *modus operandi* are no longer subordinate to the will or organizational priorities of sovereign jurisdictions.

NOTES

1. Joan E. Spero, 'Guiding Global Finance', *Foreign Policy*, **73**, Winter 1988–9, 114.
2. R. Rosencrance et al., 'Whither Independence?', *International Organisation*, Summer 1977, 437.
3. P. Dicken, *Global Shift, Industrial Change in a Turbulent World*, London: Harper & Row, 1986, p. 60.
4. Frederick F. Clairmonte and John H. Cavanagh, *Transnational Corporations and Global Markets: Changing Power Relations*, Washington, DC: Institute for Policy Studies, 1982.
5. See United Nations Centre on Transnational Corporations, *Transnational Corporations in World Development: Trends and Prospects*, New York: United Nations, 1988, figure VI.I, p. 90.

6. Ibid., pp. 16–17.
7. Bernadette Madeuf and Charles-Albert Michalet, 'A New Approach to International Economics', *International Social Science Journal*, **30**, (2), 1978, 256.
8. United Nations Centre on Transnational Corporations, *Transnational Corporations in World Development*, p. 507.
9. Ibid., pp. 75–80.
10. See Saskia Sassen-Koob, 'Issues of Core and Periphery: Labour Migration and Global Restructuring', in Jeffrey Henderson and Manuel Castells (eds), *Global Restructuring and Territorial Development*, London: Sage, 1987, pp. 60–87.
11. Folker Fröbel, 'The Current Development of the World Economy: Reproduction of Labor and Accumulation of Capital on a World Scale', *Review*, **5**, (4), Spring 1982, 539–40.
12. See Folker Fröbel, Jürgen Heinrichs, Otto Kreye and Oswaldo Sunkel, 'The Internationalisation of Capital and Labour', *African Review*, **4**, (3),1974, 328–9.
13. Ibid., p. 40, table 2.14.
14. Dicken, *Global Shift*, p. 38, table 2.11 .
15. For a more detailed characterization of the production process and of the way it has been structured to take advantage of the emerging international industrial reserve army, see Folker Fröbel, Jürgen Heinrichs and Otto Kreye, *The New International Division of Labour*, Cambridge: Cambridge University Press, 1980, pp. 34–7.
16. See David Gordon, 'The Global Economy: New Edifice or Crumbling Foundations', *New Left Review*, March–April 1988, 54.
17. Vladimir Andreff, 'The International Centralisation of Capital and the Re-ordering of World Capitalism', *Capital and Class*, Spring 1984, 59.
18. The evidence is cited in Andreff, 'International Centralisation of Capital', p. 60.
19. Stanislav Menskikov, 'Transnational Monopoly and Contemporary Capitalism', *Political Affairs*, June 1986, 32.
20. For a discussion of strategic alliances between American and Japanese firms as a response to economic crisis in the semi-conductor industry, see Dieter Ernst, 'US–Japanese Competition and the Worldwide Restructuring of the Electronics Industry: A European View', in Henderson and Castells *Global Restructuring*, pp. 38–59.
21. See Stephen Gill and David Law, *The Global Political Economy: Perspectives, Problems and Policies*, Hemel Hempstead: Harvester-Wheatsheaf, 1988, p. 202.
22. Cited in Jerry Coakley, 'The Internationalisation of Bank Capital', *Capital and Class*, Summer 1984, 114.
23. Ralph C. Bryant, *International Financial Intermediation*, Washington, DC: Brookings Institution, 1987, p. 22.
24. For a useful historical survey of the factors contributing to the birth of the Eurocurrency market, see Eugene Versluysen, *The Political Economy of International Finance*, New York: St Martin's Press, 1981, pp. 21–7.
25. *Business Week*, 21 August 1978, p. 76.
26. See Gill and Law, *Global Political Economy*, p. 151.
27. Jim Hawley, 'The Internationalisation of Capital: Banks, Eurocurrency and the Stability of the World Monetary System', *The Review of Radical Political Economics*, **11**, (4), Winter 1979, 79.
28. Michael Moffitt, *The World's Money: International Banking from Bretton Woods to the Brink of Insolvency*, London: Michael Joseph, 1984, pp. 99–101.
29. *IMF Annual Report* of the Executive Board for financial year ended 30 April 1987, Washington DC, p. 30; Alain Lipietz, 'How Monetarism has Choked Third World Industrialisation', *New Left Review*, **145**, May/June 1984, p. 78, table 1.
30. Robert E. Wood and Max Mmuya, 'The Debt Crisis in the Fourth World: Implications for North–South Relations', *Alternatives*, **11**, (1), January 1986, 107–31.
31. See Susan George, *A Fate Worse than Debt*, Harmondsworth, Middlesex: Penguin, 1989, p. 52; also Manuel Guitain, *Fund Conditionality*, IMF Pamphlet Series No. 38, Washington, DC, 1981.
32. Susan Strange, *Casino Capitalism*, Oxford: Basil Blackwell, 1986, pp. 9–11; see also

Frank E. Morris, 'The Changing World of Central Banking', *New England Economic Review*, March–April 1986, pp. 3–4.

33. *Forbes*, 22 August 1988.

34. Gunter Dufey, 'International Capital Markets: Structure and Response in an Era of Instability', *Sloan Management Review*, Spring 1981, pp. 40–2.

35. See Immanuel Wallerstein, *The Modern World System*, New York: Academic Press, 1974; Barbara Hockey Kaplan (ed.), *Social Change in the Capitalist World Economy*, Beverley Hills, CA.: Sage, 1978; Immanuel Wallerstein, *The Capitalist World Economy*, Cambridge: Cambridge University Press, 1979; Albert Bergesen (ed.), *Studies of the Modern World-System*, New York: Academic Press, 1980; W. Ladd Hollist and James N. Rosenau (eds), *World Systems Debates*, special issue of *International Studies Quarterly*, **25**, March 1981.

36. See Wallerstein, *Capitalist World Economy*, pp. 152–64.

37. Immanuel Wallerstein divides the process into four major epochs, starting with the fifteenth century when the world system emerged in what was then its predominantly European form (Wallerstein, *Modern World System*, pp. 25–32).

38. Immanuel Wallerstein, 'Semi-Peripheral Countries and the Contemporary World Crisis', *Theory and Society*, **3**, (4), Winter 1976, 461–84.

39. See Christopher Chase-Dunn, 'Interstate System and Capitalist World Economy: One Logic or Two?', *International Studies Quarterly*, **25**, (1), March 1981, 19–42.

40. Ibid., p. 29.

41. Wallerstein, *Capitalist World Economy*, pp. 26–33.

42. See, for example, Attila Agh, 'The Dual Definition of Capitalism and the Contemporary World System', *Development & Peace*, **4**, (1), Spring 1983, 193–204; Mary Kaldor, 'The Global Political Economy', *Alternatives*, **11**, 1986, 457.

43. Silviu Brucan, 'The State and the World System', *International Social Science Journal*, **32**, (4), p. 761.

44. Among dependency theorists possibly the most influential has been André Gunder Frank, author of *Latin America: Underdevelopment or Revolution* and *Capitalism and Underdevelopment in Latin America*, New York: Monthly Review Press, 1969. Much of his work reflects the influence of Paul Baran, who may be considered the pioneer of this approach and possibly the most important contemporary innovator in the Marxist theory of imperialism. In addition to *The Political Economy of Growth* (New York: Monthly Review Press, 1957) see Paul Baran and P. Sweezy, *Monopoly Capital*, (Harmondsworth: Penguin, 1963) and P. Baran, *The Longer View* (New York: Monthly Review Press, 1969). Other significant contributions to the 'dependency' model include: S. Amin, *Accumulation on a World Scale*, 2 vols, New York: Monthly Review Press, 1974; S. Bodenheimer, 'Dependency and Imperialism: the Roots of Latin American Underdevelopment', *Politics and Society*, **1**, (3), May 1971, 327–58; Fernando Henrique Cardoso, 'Dependency and Development in Latin America', *New Left Review*, **74**, July–August 1972, 83–95; Johan Galtung, 'A Structural Theory of Imperialism', *Journal of Peace Research*, **8**, (2),1971, 81–117; P. Jalee, *The Third World in World Economy*, New York: Monthly Review Press, 1969; Theotonio dos Santos, 'The Structure of Dependence', *American Economic Review*, **60**, May, 1970, 231–6.

45. Many of these qualifications are examined in J. Camilleri, 'Dependence and the Politics of Disorder', *Arena*, **44/45**, 1976, 34–59.

46. Wallerstein, 'Semi-Peripheral Countries', p. 464.

47. Boris Frankel, *Beyond the State? Dominant Theories and Socialist Strategies*, London, Macmillan: 1983, p. 178.

48. For a wide-ranging critique of the world system approach see Theda Skocpol, 'Wallerstein's World Capitalist System: A Theoretical and Historical Critique', *American Journal of Sociology*, **82**, (5), March 1977, 1075–90; Theda Skocpol, 'The Origins of Capitalist Development: A Critique of Neo-Smithian Marxism', *New Left Review*, **104**, July–August 1987, 25–92; Peter Worsley, 'One World or Three? A Critique of the World System Theory of Immanuel Wallerstein', in R. Milliband and John Saville (eds), *Socialist Register 1980*, London: Merlin Press, 1980; Vincente Navarro, 'The Limits of

the World Systems Theory in Defining Capitalist and Socialist Formations', *Science and Society*, **46**, (1), Spring 1982, 76–90.

49. Terence K. Hopkins, 'The Study of the Capitalist World-Economy: Some Introductory Considerations', in Terence K. Hopkins, Immanuel Wallerstein et al., *World-Systems Analysis: Theory and Methodology*, London and Beverley Hills: Sage, 1982, p. 13.

50. Christopher Chase-Dunn and Richard Rubinson, 'Toward a Structural Perspective on the World-System', *Politics and Society*, **7**, (4), 1977, 467.

51. Albert Bergesen, 'From Utilitarianism to Globology: The Shift from the Individual to the World as a Whole as the Primordial Unit of Analysis', in Bergesen, *Studies of the Modern World System*, p. 10.

52. This trend is examined in some detail in J.A. Camilleri, 'After Social Democracy', *Arena*, **77**, 1986, 48–73.

53. Bruce Andrews is right to insist on the role of the productive process but seems insufficiently conscious of its international dimensions. See Bruce Andrews, 'The Political Economy of World Capitalism: Theory and Practice', *International Organisation*, **36**, (1), Winter 1982, 135–63.

54. This argument is largely derived from Palloix's historical conceptualization of the state. See Christian Palloix, 'The Self-Expansion of Capital on a World Scale', from *L'Internationalisation du capital* (Paris, 1975), *The Review of Radical Political Economics*, **9**, (2), Summer 1977, 11–12.

55. Fröbel et al., 'Internationalisation of Capital and Labour', p. 331.

56. Andrews, 'Political Economy of World Capitalism', p. 142.

57. Christopher Chase-Dunn and Joan Sokolovsky, 'Interstate Systems, World-Empires and the Capitalist World-Economy: A Response to Thompson', *International Studies Quarterly*, **27**, (3), September 1983, 357–67; at p. 360.

58. Immanuel Wallerstein, *The Modern World System II: Mercantilism and the Consolidation of the European World Economy 1600–1750*, New York; Academic Press, 1980, p. 113.

59. Peter B. Evans, Dietrich Rueschmeyer and Theda Skocpol, 'On the Road toward a More Adequate Understanding of the State', in Peter B. Evans, D. Rueschmeyer and Theda Skocpol, *Bringing the State Back In*, Cambridge: Cambridge University Press, 1985, pp. 350–1.

60. Steven Krasner, *Defending the National Interest: Raw Materials Investments and U.S. Foreign Policy*, Princeton, NJ: Princeton University Press, 1978, p. 13.

61. Peter Katzenstein, 'International Relations and Domestic Structures: Foreign Economic Policies of Advanced Industrial States', *International Organisation*, **30**, Winter 1976, 17.

62. Hawley, 'Internationalisation of Capital', p. 79.

63. This conclusion clearly emerges in Harold Van B. Cleveland and Ramachandra Bhagavatula, 'The Continuing World Economic Crisis', *Foreign Affairs*, **59**, Spring 1981, 600.

64. See John G. Ruggie, 'The Politics of Money', *Foreign Policy*, **43**, Summer 1981, 151–2.

65. Strange, *Casino Capitalism*, p. 25.

66. Robert Gilpin, *The Political Economy of International Relations*, Princeton, NJ: Princeton University Press, 1987, pp. 389, 407.

67. See Beth Minz and Michael Schwartz, 'Capital Flows and the Process of Financial Hegemony', *Theory and Society*, **15**, 1986, 77–106.

68. See G. Modelski, 'The Long Cycle of Global Politics and the Nation-State', *Comparative Studies in Society and History*, **20**, April 1978, 214–35; W.R. Thompson, 'Uneven Growth, Systemic Challenges and Global Wars', *International Studies Quarterly*, **27**, (3), September 1983, 341–55.

69. Wallerstein, *Modern World-System II*, p. 38.

70. For a succinct exposition of these contrasting views, on which this analysis draws heavily, see Chase-Dunn and Sokolovsky, 'Interstate Systems'.

71. Robert W. Cox, 'Labor and Hegemony', *International Organisation*, **31**, (3), Summer 1977, 387.

72. Robert W. Cox, 'Social Forces, States and World Orders: Beyond International Relations Theory', *Journal of International Studies: Millenium*, **10**, (2), Summer 1981, 153.
73. Charles Kindleberger, *The World in Depression, 1929–1939*, Berkeley: University of California Press, 1973; see also his 'Dominance and Leadership in the International Economy', *International Studies Quarterly*, **25**, (3) June 1981, 242–54.
74. See Robert Gilpin, *War and Change in World Politics*, Cambridge: Cambridge University Press, 1981, p. 156.
75 See Gill and Law, *Global Political Economy*, p. 340; also David Calleo, *Beyond American Hegemony: The Future of the Western Alliance*, New York: Basic Books, 1987; Paul Kennedy, *The Rise and Fall of the Great Powers*, New York: Random House, 1987.
76. Gill and Law, *Global Political Economy*, p. 349.
77. *Economist*, 26 November 1983, p. 52.
78. Gilpin, *Political Economy of International Relations*, pp. 370–4.
79. See David Sylvan, 'The Newest Mercantilism', *International Organisation*, **35**, 1981, 375 9.
80. Gill and Law, *Global Political Economy*, pp. 244–5.
81. See Gilpin, *Political Economy of International Relations*, pp. 397–9.
82. See Robert O. Keohane, *After Hegemony: Cooperation and Discord in the World Political Economy*, Princeton, NJ: Princeton University Press, 198, pp. 182–216; also John Gerard Ruggie, 'International Regimes, Transactions and Change: Embedded Liberalism in the Post-War Economic Order', in Stephen D. Krasner (ed.), *International Régimes*, Ithaca, NY: Cornell University Press, 1983.
83. Fröbel et al., *New International Division of Labour*, p. 37.
84. Daniel A. Holly, 'L'O.N.U., le système économique international et la politique internationale', *International Organisation*, **29**, (2), Spring 1975, 478–9.
85. Volker Bornschier, 'The World Economy in the World System: Structure, Dependence and Change', *International Social Science Journal*, **34**, (1), 1982, 50–1.
86. See Robert D. Putnam and Nicholas Bayne, *Hanging Together: Co-operation and Conflict in the Seven-Power Summits*, London: Sage, 1987, pp. 229, 233, 234.
87. Spero, 'Guiding Global Finance', pp. 123–4.

5. Technological Change

For the industrialized world, the period since the Second World War has been one of intense technological change. Waves of technological innovation and restructuring have rolled across the globe. With them has come the retooling and reorganization of production, a broad-scale reshaping of transport, profound changes to rural and urban life, and the institution of potent new forms of mass communication, leading to a much more integrated global system of social and economic interaction. This raises the following question: to what extent is technological change affecting the ability of national communities and national states to assert their sovereignty in the international arena and over their national destiny?

We may address this question by placing the changing characteristics of some key elements of technological change in their political and economic context. As a preliminary it is useful to elaborate some aspects of the idea of sovereignty itself. We have already alluded to the fact that in most societies the monarch has to all intents and purposes been displaced by the modern state. This leaves open the question of where sovereignty is to be vested. Is it to be popular sovereignty (where the people are sovereign), or state sovereignty (with the state exercising sovereignty on behalf of the people)? It is often unclear in contemporary discussions which of these alternatives is intended. Frequently they are linked, so that even where popular sovereignty is invoked, the state is taken to express the popular will because of some democratic process or consensual contract. Indeed, if sovereignty is not articulated by some institutional actor or process it is difficult to see what practical meaning sovereignty can have.

If the state is taken to be the sovereign actor, then it is useful to distinguish between two aspects: internal and external sovereignty. Internal sovereignty refers to the relationship of the state to events inside the sovereign domain, whilst external sovereignty refers to those outside the domain's boundaries. As mentioned earlier, externally the sovereign state is assumed to enter the international arena on the basis of legal equality with other states. Internally, the sovereign state exerts supreme authority, uncompromised in this authority either from without or within.

These are of course gross abstractions. In actual practice, externally the nation-state faces a range of constraints as it manoeuvres within a complex system of alliances, security arrangements and economic and political institutions. Internally the state also faces several potential constraints. This becomes clear once we step beyond the gross simplification in which the state is conceived of as a single unified entity. We may do this by taking into account the interaction of the various organs of the state with a great many other informal regional and national institutions within society. The resultant picture is one of a more pluralist system in which the ability of the state to exercise internal sovereignty may be severely qualified.

It follows that more than one type of capability is required for a state to exercise sovereignty. As discussed in the previous chapter, the state must have the capacity to act effectively in relation to the goals it has set itself within its own domain. Wallerstein analyses the 'strength' of the state in relation to various economic and military capabilities. But for the state to be sovereign, it is not enough for it to be strong. It must also be sufficiently autonomous to be able to conceive of a diverse range of possible goals which it desires to implement. We therefore need some analytic devices to distinguish the various components which go to make up not only the strength but the sovereignty of the state.

It may be useful to break down the state's capability to act into a number of different components. First it is useful to distinguish between internal and external sovereignty. Secondly, it is important to distinguish between the state's capacity to act, and the extent to which it is able to conceive autonomously of its objectives.

In short, when considering the extent to which a state may be considered sovereign, it is useful to refer to several aspects of the state's capabilities: its 'capacity', 'internal autonomy', 'external autonomy' and 'subjective autonomy'. 'Capacity' refers to the level of resources which the state has available to it to implement its objectives. (This has a more limited meaning than the 'strength' of the state as considered in the last chapter, since it is clearly distinguished from the autonomy of the state to use those resources.) 'Internal autonomy' refers to the extent to which the state may act independently of other actors within its domain. 'External autonomy' is the corresponding freedom which the state has to act independently of other states or external institutions. 'Subjective autonomy' (or the state's 'will') refers to the extent to which the state finds itself able to formulate and seek to implement a wide range of possible objectives.

The relationship between these variables and sovereignty is relatively simple. A sovereign state will have high levels of capacity, and external, internal and subjective autonomy. To the extent that a state is restricted in any of these areas, its sovereignty is correspondingly compromised. The positioning of a state in relation to these variables is not necessarily static. In particular, the capacity of the state to act, whether internally or externally, will be affected by changes to the political, economic or other structures within which it must operate. Not least, changes to technology, often cutting across state boundaries and playing a central role in transforming the state's environment, are likely to exert a powerful influence, as much on the state's capacity as on its internal, external and subjective autonomy. One key question, therefore, is: how are changes to technology actually affecting the position of the state in relation to the principle of sovereignty?

COERCIVE TECHNOLOGY AND THE POWER OF THE STATE

One central if not defining characteristic of the state is often said to be its virtual monopoly over the use of armed force. The power of the state to act in the international arena is often directly associated with its capacity to wield military force. Similarly, the power of the state to determine events within its domain is often considered to depend critically on its capacity to exert coercive force within that domain.

We have already remarked that the concept of a system of sovereign states assumes also a set of sovereign domains. At least in theory, the boundaries of these domains are fixed for ever since the violation of one state's territorial integrity by another, particularly through military action, constitutes an infringement of the sovereignty of the former by the latter.

This ideal is clearly not met in practice. States frequently intrude upon one another's space for a variety of reasons – including the desire to assure long-term security, or to expand the national domain. Nevertheless, this way of infringing sovereignty is not infrequently considered a serious international incident. A case in point is the international response to Iraq's invasion of Kuwait.

Over the last couple of decades the spectrum of techniques available to the state for applying force has considerably widened due to the development of a broad array of coercive technologies. Force may now be applied with technological capabilities ranging from the massive power of the hydrogen bomb, and nerve gas bombs, fuel air explosives and napalm, to the restrained and measured coercive power of rubber bullets, irritant chemical sprays (such as mace and tear gas), cattle prods and rubber truncheons.[1] These may be used to apply force either inside or outside the national domain. We begin by considering their application outside the national boundaries, in the international arena.

Coercive Technology and External Sovereignty

The ability of states to defend themselves against possible attack by other states is often regarded an important symbol of their external sovereignty. To what extent does access by states to modern powerful weapons systems provide support for the theory of sovereignty?

First we should note that the development of military technology is an ongoing process, so that judgements about the balance of effectiveness should always be considered to be provisional. Nevertheless, there is good reason to go beyond what may at first sight be the appealing conclusion that the net effect of new advances in weapons technology is to reinforce the sovereignty of the state.

Whilst weapons have undergone dramatic changes, the general trend has been on the one hand to make them more precise, extend the range from which they can be delivered, and provide the greatly enhanced communication and intelligence capabilities needed for this purpose, and on the other hand to extend and fill in the level of available destructive capability. However, the increasing sophistication of the weapons does not necessarily render them effective in actual combat. As the wars in Vietnam and Afghanistan demonstrated, whilst this sophistication may produce new capabilities, it may also produce new vulnerabilities. Similarly, the advent of precision-guided munitions, which are available to most states, renders vulnerable the more expensive weapons (such as aircraft carriers). Nevertheless, as the 1991 Gulf War showed, given the right circumstances, the new weapons can be used with devastating effect. Perhaps the most accurate assessment is that weapons sophistication in itself guarantees nothing.

What of the increased destructive power of the weapons? Of all the weapons developed to date, nuclear weapons have the greatest capability for physical destruction. Granted, access to nuclear weapons remains monopolized by a handful of nations. But for those nations which do possess them, there is at least a suggestive argument that access to these most destructive of weapons systems should assist in reinforcing their sovereignty.

However, as is now widely conceded in the strategic literature, the very destructiveness of nuclear weapons constitutes a serious deficiency since it limits the ways in which they can, in practice, be used. So serious is this deficiency that nuclear weapons have not actually been used in battle since the Second World War. This limitation is compounded by the fact that, since 1945, the possession of nuclear weapons has become more widespread. This raises two fears: first, there is the problem of mutual annihilation – the use of nuclear weapons may produce a chain of events which in the end destroys the country that initiates their use. Secondly there is the problem of nuclear proliferation – once nuclear weapons are used, even in a limited engagement, this may produce a global response with the majority of states which have hitherto forsaken the acquisition of nuclear weapons deciding that they must now turn to the construction of nuclear arsenals. Despite attempts by the nuclear armed states to avoid these problems they continue to limit the utility of the nuclear armouries in times of international conflict.

Implicit in this analysis is the potential contradiction between the increasing power of weapons and their usefulness in either defence or offence. What the above illustrates is that weapons cannot be considered in isolation from the context in which they are to be used. Once constructed they become part of a system of weapons which transcends national boundaries, and which once triggered may produce detrimental consequences for many states. In this sense, whilst individual parts of the system may be 'owned' and even 'controlled' by individual states, the system as a whole is not fully under the control of any state. To the extent that this is true, the fact that individual states have an apparently powerful military arsenal is not necessarily a symptom of their enduring sovereignty so much as of their integration into (or emergence as part of) a transnational military system whose construction and operation are increasingly at odds with the theory of sovereignty.

This possibility is rendered even more plausible by one further observation. The power and range of some of the new technologies, of which nuclear weapons are the prime example, require not merely national but global deployment. As a result we now have a worldwide system of bases and intelligence systems capable of scrutinizing and targeting every corner of the globe. The five nuclear powers have spread nuclear-related activities across 65 countries and territories. The United States has deployed about 70 per cent of its tactical nuclear weapons in foreign countries or at sea. Together the five nuclear powers have deployed some 11,800 nuclear warheads outside their national territories.[2] As a result many states now house in their 'sovereign domains' components of weapons systems over which they have little or no control.

Each state manoeuvres in a system of states in which many of them have access to much of the new military technology, so that as the potency of threats has increased, so has the potency of the response. As a result, changes in military technology, although they may at times affect the balance of power between states, have generally proved an uncertain adjunct to the capacity of states to act. What is clear is that for the system as a whole the changes to coercive technology have created a much more complex system of command, control, communications, intelligence and weapons, whose transnational span and internationally interlocked character are inconsistent with the claim that contemporary developments in military technology have reinforced the capacity of states to act as sovereign entities.

Coercive Technology and Internal Sovereignty

When we consider external sovereignty, especially in the context of military power, it seems natural to focus on the state, which is the principal agent through which 'national' actions are articulated. However, when we shift our attention to internal sovereignty it is less clear whether it is the people or the state which is to be sovereign. As already noted, the apparent tension between popular and state sovereignty may be at least partially reconciled by the claim that the people are sovereign, and their will mediated by the state through some set of democratic procedures.

However, the existence of a democratic process offers no guarantee that it will express the popular will, and the link between the two is often quite indirect. The process is usually mediated by periodic elections or referenda. This requires the individual citizen to subject his or her views on a multitude of issues, which may vary from time to time, to an infrequent, discrete act of choice which is often between two not very dissimilar parties offering only partly articulated policies on what they would do if elected. Various institutions, including the state, may play an important part in presenting the information on which members of the community will base their choices. In this sense, the policies and actions of the state may be interpreted as an expression of the community's will. Alternatively, it is possible to interpret the will of the community (as expressed through the democratic process) as a manipulated response to the actions of the state but also to a range of other national or transnational institutions.

No doubt in many situations the truth lies somewhere between these two interpretations. What this tells us is that in discussions of internal sovereignty it is an excessive simplification to consider the state as the only player within the national arena. As we shall discuss later, the state operates in an arena usually penetrated by a wide range of different institutions. If it is to exercise sovereign authority over the national domain (even if notionally on behalf of the national community), it must have the capacity to prevent obstruction of its decisions and actions by sections, or even a majority, of that community. It must also have a high level of autonomy from the pressures exerted by 'private' organizations so that it can make decisions, but also conceive of them in the first place. That is, it must have a high level of subjective autonomy.

The relationship between the will of the community and the state's authority is therefore complex, with implications for internal and subjective autonomy, and hence for internal sovereignty. For example, if we are considering popular sovereignty, the state may act in ways which constrain the internal and subjective autonomy of the community. Here for popular sovereignty to be a reality, the state must serve, not dictate, the popular will.

Alternatively, if it is state sovereignty which is at issue, then the community may act as a constraint on state autonomy, reducing its hold over the national domain.

How is technological change affecting this complex relationship? Is it enhancing the authority or autonomy of the state at the expense of that of the people (consistent with the requirements of internal state sovereignty), or is it enhancing the authority and autonomy of the people at the expense of that of the state (consistent with the requirements of internal popular sovereignty), or is it moving in some other direction?

Let us first consider the impact of technological change on state sovereignty. One of the means available to the state for overcoming obstacles to its 'will' is coercive technology. During the last few decades technological change has made a wide range of impressive coercive instruments available to states. Some are now equipped with armoured 'riot control vehicles' complete with tear gas launchers, devices for expelling powerful jets of chemically treated water, electrically activated outer casing, loudspeaker systems, and ports for firing weapons. Riot police may be equipped with protective lightweight armour and weapons which hurt and maim but do not kill. Technologies for crowd control are complemented by a wide range of devices which may be applied to the coercion and control of individual citizens. These range from mind-altering drugs to new forms of torture and lie detectors.

It might seem likely that the availability of these technologies would produce a net increase in the state's capacity to control the population, thus reinforcing the state's internal capacity and autonomy. But it should not be assumed that these technologies, though sophisticated, are any more persuasive than technologies which have been available to the state for much longer. Technologies such as the hot iron, the whip, and the thumbscrew have been known for at least a millenium.

The simple fact is that in many contemporary societies there is an obstacle to the state using the more obviously brutal technology. At least in part this obstacle arises because the state's authority often relies on a discourse which legitimizes the authority of the state by reference to the ideal of popular sovereignty. Consistent with this, the dominant political discourse of most technologically advanced nations tends to place a greater emphasis on individual rights than on those of the state, a doctrine which does not favour state actions in relation to civil society that are perceived to be arbitrary, unjust or brutal.

Coercive technology may be effectively employed by the state only if two criteria are fulfilled. First the threat posed by the technology must be sufficient to induce the desired change in the behaviour of those against whom it is directed. (This threat may well be reduced by the deployment of the new technologies.) Secondly, the threat must be credible in the circumstances – that is, it must be feasible for the state to use the technology. If the state's legitimacy to act is in doubt, and if the threatened or actual use of the technology would reduce its legitimacy, then the political cost of using it may outweigh any possible gain. The failure of the Marcos regime in the Philippines to use its military forces to crush the popular uprising in 1986 graphically illustrates this limitation.

Though remarkable technical developments have occurred, it does not necessarily follow that the new coercive technologies have greatly increased the effectiveness with which the state can control either its own citizens or attain its objectives within the global system. On the contrary, for many states the development of the new technologies which coerce but do not kill, and more generally the increased subtlety of the coercive techniques, may well reflect a changing context in which the state's authority to utilize the full range of possible coercive measures against its own citizenry is increasingly constrained.

This conclusion is reinforced by a further observation: emerging with the process of technological change is a series of challenges to the state's monopoly on the use of coercive technology, which arise from the very close relationship which has emerged in many countries between military and commercial production. This has led, amongst other things, to the increasing prevalence of 'dual use' technologies which have both military and commercial applications.[3] The production of military technologies now frequently relies on the sophisticated skills gained in the production of commercial commodities. Many commercial goods are developed on the basis of experience gained in researching, developing and producing military goods.[4] Similarly, corporations are often allocated important roles in the production of coercive technologies, and these are often treated as important tradeable commodities. As a result many of the weapons designed for use by the state to assist in solving its problems may become available to other organizations for use in exerting pressure on the state. The monopoly on the legitimate use of armed force, often considered a defining characteristic of the state, is thus subtly but steadily undermined. The rise of commercial security forces, armed with a variety of coercive technologies, provides a perhaps trite example. The rise in legitimacy of the non-state actor, for example the Palestinian Liberation Organization (PLO), and its access to sophisticated armaments provides an instructive but by no means isolated instance of this phenomenon.

Overall, then, the developments in coercive technology have two important implications for state autonomy. On the one hand, the state finds itself rivalled by other non-state actors which may obtain the same sophisticated coercive technology on the world market. On the other hand, the state's ability to use coercive technology to control its own domain is challenged, to some extent, by a growing aversion to the use of more brutal methods, together with a related emphasis within much political discourse on popular sovereignty. These two constraints on internal autonomy have been discussed in the context of changes to technology which is overtly intended for coercion. But other areas of associated technological innovation are also relevant to our discussion of state capability and autonomy. Prominent amongst these are the rapid developments in the technology of surveillance based upon the extraordinary advances in communication and computing technologies.

In 1982 some 16 US government departments were estimated to possess a combined total of more than 3.5 billion files on American citizens.[5] Typically, information kept on any citizen may include data on national files associated with passport control and national security, tax, medical benefits and allied social benefits, insurance and superannuation, police criminal offence and driving licence files, and national census files. In addition, a host of other files dealing with financial transactions, credit and point-of-sale purchasing are in existence and may be accessible through agencies set up to sell credit ratings. In many countries governments are, for a variety of reasons (ranging from tax surveillance to social security considerations) moving towards requiring every citizen to possess and, in a range of transactions, use a national identity card bearing a unique identifying number.

Added to this technology, the potential for monitoring private and commercial communications by tapping telephones or receiving telecommunications from satellites (such as the US Rhyolite series satellites), the increasing sophistication of remote surveillance cameras (whether borne on moving platforms such as helicopters or built into stationary locations, for example on roads), the development of electronic devices which report their location, and the development of blood, breath and other biochemical monitoring devices, electronic fingerprint and voice recognition systems, all provide the new state with avenues for monitoring the behaviour of citizens.

Again, at first sight, the availability and widespread use of surveillance technologies may suggest a consolidation of the state's capacity and autonomy. However, this line of argument is overly simplistic. It omits any assessment of the changing context within which the state operates, and to which these technological developments are at least in part a response. Like the coercive technologies, the new technologies of surveillance are impressive in their power, as evidenced in this case by their unprecedented capacity to collect and process data. Despite this striking technological capability, it does not follow that the surveillance made possible by the new technologies renders a citizen more visible to the national administration when compared to the visibility of a citizen in a small town under the control of a local administration. The new technology is powerful, but its use is symptomatic not so much of the growing strength of governments as of the new problems posed for them by the interactions of the ever larger conglomerates of people which make up modern cities.

As with technologies of coercion, technologies of surveillance are broadly generalized across a range of national and international non-state actors. They are available not only to the state, but also to commercial enterprises and even private citizens. Mercantile credit organizations follow the movements, preferences and credit records of citizens worldwide. Banks, credit, employment and other commercial institutions purchase access to these and similar data bases. Advertising agencies, often operating in many countries simultaneously, use international data bases to target communities and mould opinion. The communication media, operated and developed for profit by large corporations, whose territory increasingly extends beyond national boundaries, are used by the state to consolidate community support for its policies, but may also be used by non-state organizations, including media corporations, to reshape or undermine the current policies and structures of the state.

The integration of global economies and communication systems thus creates a global system of interaction in which the state is but one player amongst others and state borders are becoming less and less important. As the example of South Africa suggests, increased exposure to international scrutiny may operate to limit the autonomy of the state to use traditional coercive measures, rendering what is perceived as excessive brutality or repression more vulnerable to international scrutiny and sanctions.

In short, the effect of the changes in either the technologies of coercion or those technologies which may legitimize their use cannot be adequately evaluated in isolation from other changes in the technological and social environment within which the state operates. The state's environment extends beyond its borders. The market-place from which states obtain their weaponry is an international market-place from which other states can, by and large, purchase similar weaponry. The actions which states take in relation to some of their citizens is reflected back on to their own population's TV sets through international media networks. The responses of other states to these actions may become a significant factor in the internal politics of the nation, placing limits on what the government and its agencies can and cannot do in the external arena.

Increasing technological sophistication should not be mistaken for evidence that the capacity or autonomy of the state has been consolidated. The impact of technological change on the sovereignty of the state is at best ambiguous. First, the state, even if armed with the most modern coercive and surveillance technologies, faces other states many of which are similarly equipped.

Secondly, the state is faced with a more complex situation within its own domain, in which far larger populations must be regulated in the process of more complex and wide-reaching activities. Thirdly, the state's monopoly on the use of coercive technology is progressively undermined by the emergence of non-state actors who have access to the same technology. Fourthly, other forms of coercion have emerged such as the technology of surveillance, which, when coupled with a more complex economic system, create powerful levers of social coercion which are available to organizations other than the state. In sum, whilst it might be supposed that developments in coercive technology represent a reinforcement of the idea of sovereignty, in practice they frequently reflect and provoke an overall diminution in the power of the state to shape the course of events within its national domain.

One final point should be made. Whilst changes to the technology of coercion seem to produce a picture increasingly *inconsistent* with the idea of *state* sovereignty, they do not necessarily produce a picture which is correspondingly *consistent* with the idea of *popular* sovereignty. For example, access to new technologies of coercion may assist the emergence of powerful new non-state actors. Yet this trend does not necessarily represent any increase in the autonomy of the citizen. Indeed, there is reason to expect that non-state actors may well be less accountable to the popular will than the state. The new communication technologies make available to the citizen a torrent of information. But so far they have not led to the development of mechanisms favourable to the assertion of the popular will, other than those already available through traditional democratic processes which relate citizen to national state.

Whatever the quality of the information that citizens receive, they are likely to continue to conceive of their choices as those which relate to the future actions of the state. As a result the range of choices which the citizen imagines as possible is unlikely to be any wider than the range of choices which seem to be available to the government and its agents. In short, the subjective autonomy of the 'people' is no greater than the subjective autonomy of the state. And, as we shall see, there is good reason to conclude that the range of possible choices for both state and citizen is increasingly constrained, as the state finds itself operating as just one actor in an increasingly elaborate and integrated global technological, political and economic system.

A GLOBAL ARCHITECTURE OF POWER

As the above discussion emphasizes, technological development is just part of a more general reshaping of the political, economic and social terrain, and the effect of such development is to reshape a global system of power in which the actions of states and the influences bearing upon them are only one component. This suggests a view of the world very much at odds with the traditional 'billiard-ball' model of international relations with its emphasis on the primary role of national actors. A new metaphor is needed to encapsulate more aptly an increasingly fluid and complex environment.

We find it useful to consider political actors as now interacting within a global *architecture of power*.[6] As with the architecture of a city, the ability to exercise power is shaped by an integrated technical, physical and social environment. Also, as in a city, the exercise of power occurs in a recognizable if complex pattern. In this sense, as with the architecture of most cities, the architecture of power has a design although no single designer. In invoking this description we are seeking to avoid the trap of privileging one particular mechanism or structure of power (the nation-state, military force, the market, ideology, technology) before we begin our analysis. Rather, we are approaching the exercise of power, constraint and control as a systemic phenomenon. From this perspective we may inquire into the current and developing form of the architecture of power and its effects on individuals, institutions (whether corporations, states, or elements of states, markets, ideology), and much more. Each of these both shapes and is shaped by the architecture of power.

In the globally integrated social world of the 1990s, although the actions of corporations and local, national, regional and international government agencies influence, and are in turn influenced by, the development of worldwide systems of technology, the resulting architecture of power has a form which is not simply determined or planned by any individual or single institution. Its form develops dynamically, according to the results of struggles and alliances between the various social and physical components which make up that architecture. At any given time it allows some actors to be more powerful than others, but the power configuration is neither fixed nor immutable, since the shape of the architecture is itself undergoing change. It is within this more complex and integrated architecture of power that states must now act, and it is in relation to its dynamically developing form that the validity of the picture of a world of sovereign states and communities must now be assessed.

The shape of the architecture of power is by no means uniform. For example, elites in many Third World countries are considerably more compact than in First World countries, and in the Soviet Union ownership patterns are very different from those in the United States. There are differences yet there are also many commonalities – in the way workers are controlled, in the technology of production and the direction of its development, in the technology of coercion, in the desire to trade, in the increasingly important intrusion of transnational corporations of various complexions and in the potent dynamics of the global market. Further, as we noted earlier, there is an evident process of convergence. As trade, finance and production are increasingly transnationalized, the commonalities multiply and spread across the world. Nowhere is this clearer than in Eastern Europe and the Soviet Union, where extraordinarily rapid changes are now occurring with the explicit aim of restructuring these economies upon market principles, revamping their industrial infrastructure with infusions of Western capital and technology, and fully integrating them into the global market.

From the above vantage point, sovereignty appears not merely as a single idea, constructed out of a series of historically established ideas and past political formations, but as part of a living discourse which is itself the subject of an ongoing contest over how the future is to be shaped. 'Sovereignty' may be invoked as a principle in order to support the continuing importance or expansion of the state, the programme of particular political parties, various ideological or policy positions, and a range of different commercial initiatives. 'Cultural sovereignty', 'economic sovereignty', 'technological sovereignty' and 'national sovereignty' have become widely used terms, appealing in part to the traditional authority and respect vested in the concept, yet modifying and stretching the term to try and paper over the contradictions which now confront its original meaning.

From this perspective, the 'sovereignty' of states cannot be adequately examined unless it is placed in the context of the other principal features of the emerging global architecture of power. As a step in this direction, we now briefly review the extent to which the impact of technological changes on some of the key components of that architecture – in particular, trade, communication, production, and corporate organization – impinges upon the idea, practice and discourse of sovereignty. We begin with a discussion of the architecture of corporate organization.

THE ARCHITECTURE OF CORPORATE ORGANIZATION

In Scammell's view, the Second World War constitutes 'a great dividing line.... For the first and last time in modern economic history there was to be a fresh start.'[7] As we outlined in Chapter 4, this fresh start, utilizing the technological developments from the war, and the growing consumer demand within the rebuilding economies, produced spectacular growth in manufacturing, production and trade.[8] It also presaged the parallel era of corporate expansion and integration.

It is by now well understood that the phenomenal growth and expansion of corporations carries enormous significance for global politics. As one writer enthused over twenty years ago:

The international corporation is acting and planning in terms that are far in advance of the political concept of the nation-state. As the Renaissance of the fifteenth century brought an end to feudalism, aristocracy and the dominant role of the Church, the twentieth-century Renaissance is bringing an end to middle class society and the dominance of the nation-state. The heart of the new power structure is the international organization and the technocrats who guide it. Power is shifting away from the nation-state to international institutions, public and private. Within a generation about 400 to 500 international corporations will own about two-thirds of the fixed assets of the world.[9]

This may be a crude analysis of what is actually taking place, since these corporations, whether national or transnational, continue to rely upon the functioning of states to facilitate and define their operations.[10] Nevertheless, the growth in the scale of the corporations is uncontested.

Since the late 1940s the scale of corporate activity has grown rapidly, as corporations have undergone a series of mergers. In the first stage they sought to integrate their operations horizontally (absorbing other corporations involved in similar activities). This was followed by a phase of vertical integration (in which corporations sought to gain ownership and control of the entire chain of production from raw material inputs to retail distribution).[11] Later corporations engaged in conglomerate mergers in which they absorbed companies of entirely different types – oil corporations first became energy corporations, and then developed interests in everything from satellites to banks. In the most recent phase, corporations have turned their attention outside the boundaries of what they once saw as their home country and reorganized their production and sales on a truly global basis. It is this last phase of activity which has given rise to the phenomenon we now label the transnational corporation (TNC).

According to one contemporary study, 'of the 100 largest economic units in the world today, half are nation-states and the other half TNCs'.[12] Nevertheless, the impression created by some studies in the 1960s, largely focusing on the experience of American TNCs, that most if not all TNCs are extremely large, is erroneous. Despite the impressive scale of some of these global entities, the tendency to go international has infected much smaller entities as well. Most TNCs are much smaller, and many TNCs (45 per cent of the 9500 surveyed in one study) have operations in no more than one foreign country.[13]

Over the last two decades the tendency to organize at an international level has spread, with TNCs originating from many countries. Some TNCs have developed in the Third World (in particular, in Asia – Hong Kong, South Korea, Taiwan, Singapore, Malaysia and India; and in Latin America – Brazil, Argentina and Mexico). In absolute terms these TNCs still represent a relatively small component of overall global investment. According to one study, in 1980 the total stock of foreign direct investment by such TNCs was no more than $10 billion.[14]

However, whilst the rise of Third World TNCs may not represent a major proportion of global investment, their actual significance is much greater when compared to the scale of the economy of the host Third World country. TNCs in Third World countries may be very big business indeed. They may carry far-reaching implications for the way in which the governments of these countries view their objectives and policies. Third World elites have traditionally been both smaller and wealthier, in relation to the size, assets and income of the population at large, than their counterparts in First and Second World countries.[15] As more of this small elite is shifted across into corporations operating transnationally, strategies designed to promote the interests of the nation may become decoupled from those pursued by corporations. 'In other words, a significant part of the national bourgeoisie is being transformed into a private transnational technocracy, losing legitimacy as part of a national ruling class.'[16]

In summary, the transnationalization of business, at least for the capitalist world, is a global phenomenon cutting across the divide between the First and Third Worlds. The way in which corporations go transnational is far from uniform. Some are huge global organizations comparable in economic scale to nation-states, whereas most are much smaller with more restricted international operations. Nevertheless two simple conclusions can be drawn:

- Every year more and more companies go transnational, their operations cutting across the borders of the domain supposedly under the control of the sovereign state; and
- Within the global architecture of power the wealth and activity of more and more of those in positions of influence depend upon corporations with increasing levels of transnational activity.

The expansion in the size of state agencies reflects, to a considerable extent, an increasingly symbiotic relationship between state and corporations. It has been argued that the expansion of the agencies and activities of the state is a symptom of the reassertion of the state's sovereignty in the economic and political realms.[17] But this pays too little attention to the changing relationship of the state to its rapidly evolving domestic and external environment. Whilst the state has grown, its role has been steadily transformed (and constrained) by the very process of economic internationalization. The state operates in a world in which it must interact with other institutions of equivalent economic scale, in a system of economic organization which conforms less and less to state boundaries, and is increasingly divorced from control by any particular state.

Reference to 'TNCs' is of course a simplification. TNCs as well as national corporations differ considerably in their strategies and forms of organization.[18] For example, within the organization of a single firm it is not uncommon for one level of management to pursue a global strategy, and for others to pursue national or regional strategies.[19] Similarly, there is considerable variation in TNCs' relationships with host governments, the extent to which they regard themselves as based in a particular nation, and the degree with which they equate the likely success of their own strategies with that of their 'home base'.[20]

But despite these variations, it is possible to generalize to this extent. First, the globalization of corporate operations is subjecting the state to powerful and conflicting demands. On one side are the demands emanating from the national community pointing to particular policies and priorities (for example, in Australia, the preservation of wilderness). On the other are the pressures exerted by transnational corporations for policies and initiatives which are widely perceived to be in conflict with community goals (for example, guarantees to logging companies that they will have continued rights to harvest natural forest). More and more, however, community priorities are required to bend before what is regarded as the greater national need to maintain economic compatibility with corporate objectives.

Secondly, in many countries the state is aggressively seeking to develop its 'national competitive advantage'. One approach to this is to foster conditions in which the number and value-added productivity of leading corporations are maximized. Here the nation-state has an important role to play, but one which is increasingly constrained as it struggles to maintain and develop the competitiveness of locally based national and transnational corporate activity in an ever more demanding global market. Moreover, as we saw in the previous chapter, the limitations on the options available to the state are compounded by the policies and actions of international organizations (e.g. the World Bank, OECD).

Of course, states experience a range of competing pressures. Historically, when external pressure was exerted on states to deregulate their economies and allow the entry of new foreign competitors, those corporations with an existing base in the national market which benefited from protection, tended to argue for the retention of trade barriers. As a result, especially in the more powerful countries, the state's response often lacked consistency. For example the United States, which after 1945 acted as the leading advocate of free trade, has more recently been described as moving 'simultaneously toward free trade and protectionism'.[21] Nevertheless many states have considerably lowered trade barriers over the last two decades. To the extent that they bowed to pressure to liberalize trade and dismantle fiscal controls, they have had their ability to regulate investment and industrial development within their domain correspondingly reduced.

However, the major constraint on states is not so much the removal of trade or other restrictions (which can in principle be restored) but the increasingly powerful pressure to achieve and retain national competitiveness and so, it is sometimes suggested, retain the ability to exercise at least residual national sovereignty. Political parties now find that they 'may oppose prevailing policies but not the state functions themselves, or the underlying discourse of economic growth that propels them'.[22] This perception is not restricted to political parties, but has come to be widely shared in the community at large. One may reasonably conclude that, at least so far as subjective autonomy of either state or community is concerned, much of the latitude traditionally attributed to the state in the setting of policy directions has been sharply reduced. To this extent at least, the underlying claim of the sovereignty discourse, that either state or community exercises supreme authority within the national domain, is increasingly open to challenge.

THE ARCHITECTURE OF COMMUNICATION

The changes to corporate organization have been greatly facilitated by dramatic increases in the power of computers and communication. But, as we have already suggested in relation to the technology of surveillance, these also have implications for state sovereignty.

Through the advent first of the telephone, telex, radio and television, and then the integration of computer technology and information transmission through the facsimile machine, modem, optical character recognition scanner and digitized telephone systems, information has been reduced to electronic form and then transmitted over electronic networks worldwide. Side by side with these developments information has come to be understood as a commodity itself. The electrical signals which stream down the optical cables and through the satellite channels may represent computer software packages, media reports, corporate intelligence, or instructions to transfer huge sums of money.

We have already noted that the new information technologies have provided the state with the ability to collect, analyse and utilize unprecedented quantities of data associated with the running of both the state apparatus itself and civil society. So sophisticated and comprehensive is the potential for this data gathering and processing, that some analysts have referred to the 'self-reporting state'. But, as we have already discussed, this is at least in part a symptom of the increasingly complex requirements of modern industrial society. There is little convincing evidence that these data flows are significantly enhancing the internal autonomy of the state, which is a necessary condition for sovereignty.

While the new information technology provides the state with increased volumes of information it gives community and commercial organizations similarly increased access to information. Though it is often suggested that the information society is likely to open up a new era of popular control, this is by no means assured. Indeed, other trends may be identified which are restricting this potential. For example, the pressure to privatize public resources is extending into the sphere of state information gathering. As a consequence, much information is progressively transferred from the public sphere where it was previously available to all free of charge, to the private sphere where it is available only for what is often a very substantial fee.[23] As a result, though the technology has the potential to place information at the disposal of civil society, opening up new possibilities for the formulation and expression of informed choice, in practice much of this potential appears to be circumscribed.

The major conduit for the newly enhanced information flows is the telecommunication network of undersea cables and satellite relays which transmits not only business information, but newspaper, radio and television images worldwide. The US-managed INTELSAT network, for example, links over 100 countries. Taken as a whole the system is dominated by a few large companies, including the US giants AT&T, ITT and RCA, as well as several Western European and Japanese corporations.[24] In many respects the system may be regarded as a new 'vertical dimension' of global territory, constructed by the telecommunication companies (often in collaboration with state agencies), which extract a toll for its use. The territory is not naturally bounded by national borders, but offers a potentially global market to those who can exploit it.

Within this territory, different developments in communication technology are tending to reduce all transmitted information, whether pictures, speech, software or text, to a common digital form. This convergence in the form of transmitted information has limited the technical capacity of the state to regulate flows of information across national boundaries reducing, as they do, the traffic across the state's boundaries to a featureless stream of binary bits. The trend presents a difficult challenge to the sovereignty of the state, reducing its capacity to control what is an increasingly valuable and voluminous flow of electronic commodities. As a result, the licensing of information use, and the policing of trans-border data flows, have become major issues for public and private sector alike.

To illustrate the difficulties of policing the new forms of information flow we need only consider the emergence of the global network of computers, informally interconnected through the existing telecommunication networks, which now provides a form of global electronic mail service. As one writer puts it:

> Over the past decade and a half there has been established an effective global
> electronic mail system – without carrier or government sanction, without planning,
> and without even a fully agreed upon data transfer protocol.... It generally works
> well though it has no directory, no map can be drawn of it, [and] it collects no
> direct revenue.... Though its services are illegal in some jurisdictions and ignored
> in others, its official non-existence makes it impossible to monitor.[25]

This new form of international electronic mail service, which, in contrast to
the official mail service, has grown with little help from the state, is much
more efficient than the state-operated service, allows the duplication and
transmission of documents at high speed and at little cost (thereby undermining such things as copyright legislation), pays no respect to state
boundaries, and to the extent to which it could (in principle) be policed,
would require the most severe intrusions into the privacy of its users. As
such it illustrates how older sectors of state responsibility are being undermined, how the state's ability to regulate the flow of information is declining
at the very time that information flow is assuming greater importance, and
how artificial and irrelevant state boundaries appear within the electronic
territory of the new world of information flows.

In addition, though the state now has greater access to information, much
of the relevant information is generated outside its geographical domain.
This information tends to become the province of supranational or international organizations (e.g. EEC, OECD) or comes under the control of a
transnationally organized private sector, for which information is a steadily
more valued commodity. At the very time that the state gains access to
highly sophisticated information technology, it also becomes more dependent on information over which it has little or no control.

Finally, the way citizens perceive themselves is now mediated by information services (for example those available in newspapers and on television)
which not only escape the control of the state, but are derived from private
firms situated outside the state's boundaries. As a result, the 'imagined community' which underpins the ideology of nationalism[26] is now vulnerable to
influences and processes which are themselves outside the state's control.

Amongst those corporations which have been quick to make use of this
new channel are the large US corporations which sell news and entertainment worldwide (or from another point of view, manufacture and sell the
viewing audience to their advertising customers).[27] Considerable concern has
since arisen about both the culturally homogenizing impact of the images
they transmit, and the economic impact of their domination of the market.
The state has, as a result, come under pressure to take measures to reinforce
national 'cultural sovereignty'.[28]

This immediately raises the question: what does the expressed demand
for cultural sovereignty represent? Is it a demand for sovereignty in the strict

sense of the word? Examination of the issue would suggest otherwise. First, the question of controlling information channels does not pivot simply around national boundaries. Inside the national domain the production and transmission of much print and electronic information is often monopolized in a few powerful hands. In this sense, the debate is about exchanging one level of manipulation for another.[29] Secondly, the idea of national culture is itself a particular construction, often doing violence to many regional and other cultural variations. Thirdly, as Robin Mansell notes in his study of the US–Canadian relationship, when policies for cultural sovereignty are implemented, they often amount to little more than ensuring a role for the state in developing the communication infrastructure and export outlets for indigenous cultural products. This policy model, notes Mansell, 'creates incentives for the homogenization of communication/information products even though it is designed ostensibly in support of Canadian sovereign control over its communication/information sector'.[30]

In short, national culture is itself a notion whose value is called into question by the same changes which are challenging the authority of the state from within and without. In particular national culture is becoming a commodity subject to the same external influences as other commodities mediated by the global market. In the case of national cultures that process is facilitated by the rapidly expanding communication networks. These provide the state with greatly extended techniques for mustering and controlling information. But they also play a role in mediating the state's aims and actions in relation to that information. The result is that the function of the state is steadily emerging as a component of a global communication system, rather than as that of a sovereign autonomous actor. What is true of the state in relation to the production and transmission of information is equally true in relation to the parallel production and transmission of physical commodities.

THE ARCHITECTURE OF PRODUCTION

As with the modernization of the technology of communication, the associated modernization of the technology of production is a focus of intense debate. It is widely understood that the relentless and often dramatic changes to this technology have profound relevance to the fate of communities, nations and regions. What then are its implications for the theory and practice of sovereignty?

As with communication technology, the most widely visible impact of technological change on manufacturing is that made possible by the introduction of information technology. In particular, the introduction of computer-programmable robotic tools, combined with computer-aided design, has opened the doors to a much more flexible form of manufacturing, in which a wide range of different components can in principle be produced on demand from the same programmable tools. In a highly influential book, Piore and Sable[31] have claimed that the advent of new flexible manufacturing technology and techniques challenges the trend towards mass production (sometimes referred to as 'Fordist' methods of production), opening up the possibility of new political and technological arrangements.

Piore and Sable claim that the flexible specialization approach provides a way forward for many corporations which are currently organized around mass production principles but face a deepening crisis as their markets saturate with the goods which they have supplied. But, they argue, if flexible specialization is to be taken up broadly amongst manufacturers, this will require not only technical change but profound social reorganization. In particular, they point to the possible development of regional communities formed around particular flexible but specialist enterprises (such as already exist in northern and central Italy), federations of economically and socially interlocked but not hierarchically ordered firms (exemplified by the Japanese corporate federations), or 'solar systems' of central firms surrounded by associated constellations of collaborating workshop factories and suppliers. The picture they draw is one in which localism is greatly strengthened and the advantages of centralism greatly weakened. They suggest that this type of social organization could produce a kind of 'yeoman democracy' constructed from a democratic association of regional free producers.[32]

Piore and Sable do not argue that these changes are inevitable, but that we stand at a 'second industrial divide' where they are at least possible. Their argument has proved both controversial and influential. They have been criticized, for example, for not providing the criteria which would enable their claims about the relative dominance of the two forms of manufacturing to be empirically measured, for an excessive and misleading simplification of the present and historical process of production, and for a failure to examine the relative economics of the choices they consider.[33] As Mahon points out, changes towards flexible manufacturing are only occurring in one segment of the manufacturing industry. It may never be economically attractive to introduce them in other segments.[34]

Others offer at least partial responses to these counter-arguments.[35] But for the purpose of this chapter we need go no further. The 'second industrial divide' is important to this analysis because it represents one of the more interesting attempts to canvas the sorts of future currently foreseeable changes in technology, combined with appropriate political change, might produce. The future envisaged is one in which both capitalist and socialist planning are replaced by a system of production fine-tuned to respond sensitively to the market. As Gough observes, the flexible specialization strategy is one in which 'the specificity of capitalist planning and the capitalist state disappear'.[36]

It is of course quite possible that none of these analyses will in the end prove accurate indicators of future possibilities. But within the perspectives offered, and the controversy that surrounds them, one thing stands out. Whichever of the proposed futures we examine – the transnational arrangements which would support multinational Keynesianism based on extended mass manufacturing, the market-driven localism of the pure flexible specialization world, some combination of these two, or the continuation of the unfettered growth of transnational production as we currently know it – the sovereign state seems increasingly squeezed from the picture. Moreover, no other mechanism emerges through which the national community may express its control over the national domain.

Placed in this context, the only hope for salvaging the system of sovereign states as a useful explanatory model of the functioning and shaping of the world is if some decisive role could be found, beyond these accounts, for the sovereign state in designing the architecture (including the technological architecture) of the national domain. One piece of evidence which is sometimes offered in support of this contention is the state's role in the contemporary rise of the newly industrializing countries.

LESSONS FROM THE NICS?

For some two centuries, the unequal terms of trade, in which raw materials flow from the 'developing' countries on 'the periphery' to the 'core' industrialized nations and smaller flows of processed goods flow in the reverse direction, have underpinned the base of the dramatic gaps in affluence between the bulk of people in the First and Third Worlds.[37] This pattern of uneven development between core and periphery which was made possible by the innovations in transport, and more generally communication, has more recently come under challenge by new directions in the development and deployment of technology and by the tendency of TNCs to make their plans on a global chessboard in which national boundaries are often increasingly irrelevant.

As indicated in Chapter 4, transnational corporations, by taking advantage of the new communication technologies, have been able to utilize the availability of particular sets of resources, and particular economic, social and cultural circumstances in different regions, so as to minimize the costs of production. Transnational firms are by definition those capable of conducting an integrated global strategy. For example, in the case of steel commodity manufacture, steel smelting can be sited next to coal and iron ore, whilst the labour-intensive parts of the process are sited in quite different regions of the world where labour protection laws are weak, and labour is cheap. Similarly, the more polluting processes may be sited in places with weak pollution controls, whilst the processes of design may remain in places where the necessary skills of a highly educated workforce are readily available.

The result, as we know, has been the partial relocation of manufacturing industry from the advanced industrial nations to the newly industrializing countries. The point here is not that the Third World has overtaken the advanced industrialized countries. The latter still account for the bulk of trade in manufactured goods. On the other hand, far-reaching social and political changes have occurred in those Third World countries experiencing rapid growth in manufacturing capacity.

This trend is of particular significance to our inquiry because it sheds additional light on the complex relationship between technology and sovereignty. Further, the conclusions it illustrates are by no means limited to the NICs. They apply with even greater force to other Third World states, and have considerable relevance even for advanced capitalist countries.

The process of industrialization in the NICs is often presented as evidence of the 'strong state' at work, and as a practical demonstration of the viability of sovereign decision-making. However, in the case of most of the newly industrializing countries a considerable proportion of manufacturing investment has come from transnational corporations, often as part of transnationally organized chains of development, production and marketing. In this sense, though industrial development has taken place, and though it may generate both direct and indirect employment in the host country, the plans, allegiances and ultimate uses made of the profits may not be significantly influenced by the host government or by any discernible strategy pursued in the name of the 'national interest'.

The above characterization applies most clearly to the weakest NICs, and beyond them to the rest of the Third World. It would seem to apply much less to the leading NICs, of which Korea provides the most striking example.[38] Korea, it is true, has relied heavily first upon American aid and then upon outside borrowings to finance the extraordinary development of textile, transport equipment and microelectronics industries which constitute the leading edge of its increased economic productivity. But this growth has been so rapid that by the late 1980s it seemed likely that Korea would over the next decade become a net creditor nation. What, then, follows from this experience?

In Korea the state has played an interventionist role, providing education, infrastructure, export incentives and financial assistance, thereby establishing the necessary conditions for the encouragement of investment in new industry, whilst at the same time intervening to hold back wages and wage-related costs. However, even here, the effectiveness of government intervention in targeting individual industries to shape an effective economy is generally recognized to have had mixed results.[39]

For example, attempts to hold back wages are now provoking considerable worker unrest.[40] As Porter points out, whilst the role of the government in targeting and encouraging technological development was effective in the 1960s and 1970s, the choices it made were often counterproductive.[41] As the economy reaches greater maturity, and as local competition gives way to international competition as the guiding principle of industrial strategy, the state steadily phases out its direct intervention. Protection is declining and the government is playing a different and diminished role. In this sense, the function of the state becomes more problematic as the logic of the external market penetrates more pervasively into the Korean economy.

More generally, the NICs face the same dilemma as other states. As they become more integrated into the global economy and progressively succumb to pressures to abandon controls over the movement of trade and money across their boundaries, they find themselves increasingly vulnerable to the goodwill of international and transnational organizations. Local stock market or currency crashes may be triggered internationally and unseat governments. Attempts by countries such as the United States or Japan to resolve imbalances in their economies may precipitate rapid global recession or inflation. In addition, US credit agencies are now responsible for the credit ratings of governments as well as corporations. As a result, government actions can prompt external agencies to lower a country's credit rating, with serious domestic political and economic consequences.

Taken together these features of industrialization in the NICs amount to a particular form of economic growth which, even where it has occurred with the direct encouragement of the agencies of the state, is increasingly subject to a number of forces which lie outside the control of that state. It is true that rapid industrialization has included the development of large indigenous corporations. But even here the state is forced to adjust to the prospect that if these are to endure they must plan to compete in a global market.[42] Especially within the relatively authoritarian systems of the NICs, this may also mean subordinating the interests of the national community (for example in relation to environmental or labour protection) to the priorities of corporations intent on maintaining profitability and increasing productivity. In this sense, even with the significant development of indigenous corporations, the latitude available to the state in asserting sovereign national policy goals is increasingly constrained by the needs of corporations which have to engage in fierce transnational competition in the context of an international institutional structure, and an unmistakably international market.

The conflict between industrial development and the sovereignty of the state is not restricted to NICs, or even to the Third World as a whole. Any government attempting to set the agenda for internal industrial development cannot but be influenced by the interests and priorities of TNCs operating within its jurisdiction. The actual or implied threat by a strategically placed firm that it may be forced to relocate its plant to another country is bound to carry considerable force. States, operating in the competitive environment of the global market, often feel obliged to lure foreign companies to their shores and retain them in order to maintain the necessary access to capital, markets or technology. A situation may thus obtain in which decision-making by governments, far from determining the direction of development in their domain, has precisely the reverse effect.

However, as we have observed in other contexts, the key conclusion to emerge from this does not concern the specific relationship between a national government and a single corporation (whether indigenous or foreign). A great deal has been written about the particular advantages the TNC enjoys with respect to its host (or even home) state by virtue of its privileged access to technology (through a variety of patenting arrangements), its superior access to financial resources, and its capacity to evade taxation and other regulations (through transfer pricing and a range of other technical and legal instruments). The very considerable leverage the TNC can extract from these advantages cannot be overlooked.[43] But the challenge to sovereignty is both more subtle and more profound.

First it should be stressed that the national state does not relate simply to one or even several TNCs. Rather it has to function within the more pervasive constraints imposed by an increasingly integrated global system of production and finance, of which TNCs are both agents and beneficiaries. Secondly, the penetration of national economies by firms is neither comprehensive nor uniform. The highly profitable corporate sector with its bias towards high technology, relatively high wages and capital-intensive methods of production stands in sharp contrast to the more labour-intensive sector of the economy geared to small-scale production, less advanced technology, low productivity and low wages. Uneven development is thus reproduced within the society,[44] compounding the process of fragmentation and calling into question the notion of a cohesive, let alone popular, sovereign will.

Thirdly, and perhaps most tellingly, the transnational corporation, which may be aptly described as the vanguard of modernity, represents a model of development which often stands in sharp contradiction to the values, lifestyles and institutions of the host country, especially in a Third World setting. The more domestic elites interact with foreign interests and international agencies, the more receptive they become to their demands. As a consequence, national structures and policies are progressively shaped to suit the specifications of transnational strategies and programmes. Schiller has described this loss of control as a 'fundamental change in the country's cultural ecology ... that fit[s] nicely with the requirements of the multinational goods producers that are financing the new system'.[45] The subjective autonomy of the state is thus undermined from within and with it the exercise of sovereign authority over the national domain.

THE STATE AND TECHNOLOGY POLICY

It is against the background described above that we now consider more generally the implications of technology policy. If the NICs are not an example of the enduring reality of sovereignty, can we find such an example, perhaps less dramatically but more widely dispersed, in the actions of the state in the more mature industrialized countries? In the 1980s a wide range of different technology policies were introduced across many countries. Not infrequently their justification was couched in terms of the need to develop policy which would ensure the long-term preservation of national sovereignty.

In considering the implications of such technology policy we may usefully distinguish between internal policy, which represents the set of official statements about how the state intends to direct the course of developments within the national domain, and external policy, which outlines how the state intends to relate to other states and institutions outside its boundaries. In practice these two areas of policy are increasingly linked as the boundary between 'inside' and 'outside' is steadily eroded.

Consistent with this, we may distinguish between internal technology policy which deals with the development of technology and supporting infrastructure within the national domain, and external technology policy which deals with exports, imports and transnational joint ventures which in one way or another cross the domain boundary. These two interlinked areas of policy provide both a resource that potentially adds to the capacity of the state and a body of strategic and organizational considerations relating to a range of state objectives, including those bearing on the long-term maintenance or erosion of the state's capacity as well as internal and external autonomy.

What, then, in contemporary political discourse, constitutes a 'successful' technology policy? How does it relate to the state's capacity to act? How in practice do policies which are judged to be successful relate to the state's autonomy, and therefore to its sovereignty? Determining the success or failure of technology or, more broadly, industry policy is made difficult because these terms have become catch-phrases covering a multitude of government actions that may directly or indirectly affect the structure of production in the economy.[46] Nevertheless, it is reasonable to suggest that the main publicly stated aim of much industry policy has been to achieve industrial vigour and avoid industrial stagnation.

Initially this objective was approached through a strategy of 'targeting' leading industries for assistance. Against this, exponents of the free market have tended to argue that government intervention is inappropriate and that there is no reason to assume that a group of government planners 'targeting' and stimulating the growth of a range of industries are any more likely to pick the likely successes than their private industry counterparts. Indeed, one could argue that since the incentives for success and penalties for failure in the private sphere are greater than in the public sphere, the former is more likely to encourage success than is the latter. One analyst has put it this way: 'The idea of picking winners is the pot of gold at the end of the rainbow that keeps the hopeful trudging in the same direction as those with clearer ideas.'[47]

More recently the discussion has shifted from 'targeting' leading edge industries for assistance to a more sophisticated strategy of developing national systems of innovation. Here an effort is made at the national level to develop combined systems of infrastructure and companion industries which will enable continued development of at least some vigorously innovative and highly productive industry.[48]

Whether the selected strategy is 'targeting', or something more sophisticated, it is clear that, whilst the world is increasingly internationalized, national governments still have a range of policy tools with which they can attempt to influence the comparative advantage of micro-regions, and the skills and industries located within their national boundaries. As Dicken puts it:

> even in the market economies the importance of political involvement in the economy should not be underestimated. All governments intervene to varying degrees in the operation of the market. Hence political factors may create, alter or destroy the bases of comparative advantage.[49]

The tools available include the application of tariffs, import quotas and other trade policies, subsidies through the tax system, direct subsidies and grants to particular industries, special aid through targeted government procurement policies, and a host of 'offset' and other arrangements which governments can require of foreign investors. If these tools are to be used solely in the pursuit of selecting the likely winners and helping them along – that is in seeking to enhance the competitiveness of individual firms or industries operating in the national domain – then the anti-intervention exponents of the free market may have a point.

There are, however, much wider considerations which may motivate industry policy. One of these, which is relevant to our analysis, is the aim of maintaining and maximizing so-called national 'technology sovereignty'. One author defines technological sovereignty as:

> the capability and the freedom to select, to generate or acquire and to apply, build upon and exploit commercially technology needed for industrial innovation. It is present to the degree that there is the technological capability to undertake such tasks: it is absent to the degree that others are able to restrict or prevent subsequent development or exploitation of that technology.[50]

The aim here is to decrease a nation's technological dependence. Traditionally many communities have relied on a range of naturally endowed resources as a way of maintaining their competitive advantage. Possession of the resources relevant to the needs of the expanding manufacturing industries obviously makes a region more attractive to some of the more profitable enterprises. But resources are often finite. Minerals once dug from the ground are then lost to the region which once possessed them. Resources which are useful one year may be displaced by others a year later as new technology is introduced. The alternative to relying on natural resources is to create intellectual resources. Accordingly, access to technological skills and know-how, especially in those industries which are destined to grow, is now often considered a crucial element in any strategy for enduring economic success.

Communities now participate in an international competition in which the only option is to match the lowest-cost producers or lose economic ground. As transnational corporations gain greater global reach, their freedom to choose between different regions on the basis of preferred characteristics increases. This enables them to play off regions to extract the lowest possible cost for resources. But at the same time, developments in telematics and the globalization of the TNC organization enables a 'branch plant' strategy to be deployed where technological know-how is, even if developed abroad, effectively sealed within the organization and returned to headquarters in a form of 'reverse technology transfer'.[51] Partly as a result of the internationalization of production many communities face the danger of gradually losing the vital base of knowledge and skills which they need to compete effectively in the future. Technological strategies aimed at enhancing technology sovereignty seek in one way or another to counter this trend and gain stable access to an enduring base of vital technological know-how. How effective then, are these strategies? Do they suggest a viable strategy for reasserting sovereignty?

An affirmative answer to this question is suggested by the frequently cited examples of countries which have instigated ambitious industry policies overseen by powerful state agencies, and experienced high rates of economic growth. Apart from the NICs to which we have already referred, Japan provides perhaps the most striking example of a country where the public sector has exercised considerable direct and indirect influence on the performance of the private sector. Despite limitations on the government's statutory authority to control business, there has developed an extraordinarily close, symbiotic relationship between the state and private capital. Lockwood puts it this way:

> The Industrial Bureaux of MITI [Ministry of International Trade and Industry] proliferate sectional targets and plans; they confer, they tinker, they extort. This is 'economics by admonition' to an extent inconceivable in Washington or London. Business makes few major decisions without consulting the appropriate governmental authority; the same is true in reverse.[52]

Japan's case is striking. Here decisive state intervention and strong economic growth have occurred side by side. Does this signify a higher level of internal or external autonomy for the state than our analysis has so far suggested?

A necessary but not sufficient condition for autonomy is that policies must be effective, which in turn raises the central question: would Japan have enjoyed comparable or even greater economic growth in the absence of these policies? Unfortunately, this is not easy to determine. As one well-regarded analyst of Japan's interventionist strategy concludes: 'The favourable and unfavourable possibilities arising from ministerial guidance are strong enough to leave the net evaluation in doubt.'[53] Some analysts also suggest that there is a danger in assuming that Japan is an example of unusually extensive state intervention, since its policies replace other forms of collaboration that exist in other countries, in particular military research orchestrated by government, and state-funded research in universities.[54] So even for this 'clear' success story there is considerable ambiguity about the reasons for its success. The common strategy of trying to draw conclusions from single case studies may thus be flawed. But this does not mean that no conclusions can be reached. Indeed, a broader survey of a range of countries suggests that it is in fact possible to draw a number of general conclusions about the institutional and policy characteristics which have contributed to a resilient base for successful economic competition.[55] The necessary characteristics include a well-developed system of technical and scientific education, a wide base of existing industries, and a comparably wide spectrum of supporting economic institutional structures. Whether these historical observations can be confidently used to derive a set of criteria for future successful national policy is more debatable.

For our purposes it is not necessary to pursue this debate. It is sufficient to note that success in economic development should not automatically be equated with sovereignty. Certainly technological and scientific capability appear to contribute to a state's economic performance, and perhaps more generally to its capacity to act. So far as Japan is concerned, even though it may be uncertain whether its economic success has vitally depended on any especially effective targeting, there can be little doubt that it has successfully built a base of technological know-how in the post-1945 period. There is also some evidence that the special collaboration between Japanese indigenous corporations and the state played an important and purposeful role in achieving this.[56] One example which is often cited is Japan's deliberate decision to build up its microelectronics industry, allowing fierce competition to take place between its indigenous companies operating in its own large domestic market, but shielded from foreign competition behind a protective tariff wall.[57] In this sense it can be argued that Japan's strategies have helped reinforce its technological sovereignty. However, even if this is true, the question remains: what is the relationship, if any, between 'technological sovereignty' and the concept of sovereignty in its wider sense?

The definition we have applied does not restrict technological sovereignty to any particular domain. Yet it is quite common to speak of the technological sovereignty of a single firm.[58] From this point of view it is possible to refer to the technological sovereignty of transnational corporations in the same breath as local firms, regions or nation-states. Clearly this is a different concept from national sovereignty. Thus we may ask: does increasing one or other of these forms of technological sovereignty shed much light on the practice of state sovereignty? The answer must lie in the relation between the institutions which are supposed to enjoy a modicum of technological sovereignty and the institutions which are supposed to exercise sovereignty in the national domain – whether on behalf of the national community or, more commonly, the national state. If greater technological sovereignty is to mean anything for national sovereignty it must at least enhance the ability of the national community, or the state acting on its behalf, to select, generate, apply, build upon and exploit technology needed for industrial innovation within its domain.

But the concept of technological sovereignty used in these discussions relates almost entirely to the sovereignty of either individual firms, industry sectors, or industry as a whole. The impact may well be positive in the places where those firms operate. If as a class they span the national domain, it may be argued that this form of technological sovereignty provides enduring economic health, and therefore jobs, additional cash flow and more consumer goods and services to be enjoyed by the community at large. This outcome need not be specific to the nation but may also apply to micro-regions within the national domain as well as to macro-regions of which the national domain is a part. The state, true enough, may be able to tax these enterprises and so derive additional revenues which can be used to further its objectives. But, as we have already pointed out, whilst this may increase the state's capacity, it will not necessarily render it sovereign.

Greater economic flows mean more access to new military technology and greater prominence in the planning of supranational organizations. But, more subtly, access to military technology (as discussed earlier) does not necessarily mean greater power or freedom of action on the international stage. Moreover, participation in the production of commodities, though it may lead to higher living standards for some, if not the majority of the population, need not lead to any greater space for autonomous decision-making by the state. Regardless of the economic fortunes of the population, the space for autonomous decision-making is increasingly filled by the busy presence of international organizations and corporations, and shaped by the demands of a global market and a transnational corporate culture and ideology.

In the case of technological sovereignty, as we have used it in this section, technological dependence in key industrial sectors weakens the capacity of the state to act. Although it seems clear that for many states the attempt to reduce existing levels of technological dependence may be a long and uphill battle, the degree of success in achieving this goal is not central to our analysis. What must be stressed is that even if the state succeeds in this enterprise its claim to national sovereignty is not automatically reinforced. There is no guarantee that such success will improve the state's competitive position in relation to other institutions within its domain, or alleviate the constraints within which the state has to manoeuvre. Indeed, the net effect may be to consolidate the constraints upon the state's subjective autonomy.

In principle, the search for technological sovereignty can be centred around many goals – the desire to implement a more ecologically sustainable technology, the desire to distribute more equitably the spoils of industrialization, the desire to provide greater work satisfaction, the desire to produce more healthy cities, and much else. However, it need not be, and is usually not, expressed or conceived in these terms. The dominant motivation described in almost all of the technology policy literature appears to revolve around the desire to keep ahead in an unending race for technological, hence economic, survival and, if possible, 'strength'.

The tenor of the debate reflects what is perceived to be the political reality in which the state has to operate. It mirrors the state's instrumental role in economic organization, to which we have referred more than once in this and previous chapters. The very fact that the question of the technological options open to corporations is now blended into the discourse of sovereignty under the label 'technological sovereignty' is evidence of the extent to which the roles of state and corporation are increasingly blurred in both theory and practice. Nor is this trend restricted to 'indigenous' corporations, which are in any case progressively extending their operations outside the national domain. It also applies to transnational corporations which operate from outside extending into the national domain. As Susan Strange puts it:

'there is a symbiosis between state and transnational corporation from which both benefit ... they are allies as well as competitors or opponents'.[59]

In short, some governments have instituted imposing programmes of national planning for technological development. Judgements about the relative success of these are usually based upon how much international investment will be attracted, how much industry will be constructed, and how successfully indigenous industry can compete in a now globalized market. But it should not be assumed that industrial reorganization, which may entail the dismantling of old industries and the establishment of new ones, with all the social and economic tensions that such a process inevitably unleashes, derives from the state's or the nation's autonomously determined preferences and priorities. The policies of the 'smart state',[60] striving to secure the benefits of economic competition and offset its more undesirable consequences, may be doing no more than adjusting the national economy to the ceaseless shifts in international comparative advantage, over which it may have at best marginal influence.

It should by now be clear that success of this kind, even when loosely couched in terms of reinforcing sovereignty, does not necessarily constitute success in the light of this broader objective. Technology policy may make new technological resources available to the state, in this way strengthening its technical and economic capacity to act in the future. But these resources are made available in the context of a seemingly endless race in which all other states are seeking and to some extent also gaining access to the very same resources. Internally and externally the autonomy of the state is challenged by the multiplicity of actors, each of which influences in complex ways the development of new technologies. National technology policy is integrated into chains of production, organization and finance, into market forces, and into patterns of demand which link across the world with little regard for national frontiers. The national arena is increasingly crowded by a wide range of non-state actors, often transnational in character, which add to the pressures responsible for the final shape of the processes of production and consumption in the national domain.

Whether we consider the technologies of coercion, surveillance, transport, communication, data storage, or the emerging patterns of corporate organization, production or technological innovation, the same general conclusion obtains. Whilst each of these may in some way increase the capacity (or strength) of the state (as revealed, for example, by its size, activity, or the sophistication of the resources at its disposal), its internal and external autonomy to exercise this capacity is simultaneously constrained. This is mediated by the intractable problems with which the state must now deal, the activities of a greatly elaborated structure of organizations which cuts across the boundaries of the national domain, and the emergence of new global communication territories (bearing little relation to national boundaries), which have been opened up by the relentless march of technological change.

None of this is to say that no role remains for the state. In one sense its role is expanding. The agencies of the state, and its policy-making and administrative functions, are increasingly called upon to facilitate the extension and development of the international system, to support the activities of a wide range of local, national and transnational economic actors, and by these means to establish the conditions for economic growth within the national domain. Yet as the objectives and discourse of state policy increasingly focus on this narrowly instrumental role, the last remaining area of autonomy, the subjective autonomy of the state, is severely circumscribed.

There is by now an evident tendency for the state's sovereign will to contract, marginalizing many of the normative concerns of civil society, in order to focus on what is perceived to be the paramount objective of economic growth. To the extent that this occurs, the state becomes less and less able to consider, let alone resolve normative questions. To the extent that civil society continues to be preoccupied by such questions, it must look elsewhere for their resolution. This itself has implications for the theory of sovereignty, as we shall see in Chapter 7 when we examine the tension between the current emphasis on economic growth, the environment and national sovereignty, and in Chapter 8 when we deal with the rising phenomenon of the new social movements.

But we may already conclude from our discussion in this chapter that an examination of the effects of technological change on the state, civil society and global organization does little to support the claims of state sovereignty. In practice, whilst the dynamic interplay of technological, social and economic development may tend to increase the sophistication of the coercive and manipulative resources available to the state, it simultaneously engenders a process which reduces its overall autonomy in the use of those resources, a situation which both in theory and in practice seems increasingly at odds with the notion of a territorially bound sovereign authority autonomously guiding affairs within the national domain.

NOTES

1. Carol Ackroyd, Karen Margolis, Jonathan Rosenhead and Tim Shallice, *The Technology of Political Control* (2nd edn), London: Pluto Press, 1980.
2. William M. Arkin, and Richard W. Fieldhouse, *Nuclear Battlefields: Global Links in the Arms Race*, Cambridge: Ballinger, 1985, p. 4.
3. See for example, F. Karl Willenbrock, 'Technology Transfer and National Security', *IEEE Technology and Society Magazine*, September 1985, 13–15.

4. For a historical overview see David F. Noble, *Forces of Production*, New York: Alfred A. Knopf, 1984.
5. 'Who Is Watching You?', US News and World Report, p. 32, cited in Jerry L. Salvaggio, 'Is Privacy Possible in an Information Society?', in Jerry L. Salvaggio (ed.), *The Information Society*, New Jersey: Lawrence Erlbaum, 1989, p. 117.
6. This concept has been used, albeit somewhat differently, in Stephen Hill, *The Tragedy of Technology: Human Liberation versus Domination in the Late Twentieth Century*, London: Pluto Press, 1989.
7. W.L. Scammell, *The International Economy Since 1945*, London: Macmillan, 1980, p. 2.
8. W.W. Rostow, *The World Economy: History and Prospect*, London: Macmillan, 1978.
9 R. Barber, 'Emerging New Power: The World Corporation', *War/Peace Report*, October 1968, 7.
10. See James F. Petras and Morris H. Morley, 'The U.S. Imperial State', in James Petras, *Class, State, and Power in the Third World: with Case Studies on Class Conflict in Latin America*, London: ZED Press, 1981, pp. 1–35.
11. Richard J. Barnet and Ronald E. Muller, *Global Reach: The Power of the Multinational Corporations*, New York: Simon & Schuster, 1974.
12. I. Benson and J. Lloyd, *New Technology and Industrial Change*, London: Kogan Page, 1983, p.77.
13. P. Dicken, *Global Shift: Industrial Change in a Turbulent World*, London: Harper & Row, 1986, p. 55.
14. Cited ibid., p. 82.
15. See for example, Ankie M. Hoogvelt, *The Third World in Global Development*, London: Macmillan, 1982.
16. Osvaldo Sunkel, 'Big Business and "Dependencia"', in George Modelski (ed.), *Transnational Corporations and World Order: Readings in International Political Economy*, San Francisco: W. H. Freeman, 1979, p. 222.
17. See for example, Robert Gilpin, 'The Politics of Transnational Economic Relations', in Modelski, *Transnational Corporations*, pp. 66–83.
18. See for example, Michael E. Porter, *The Competitive Advantage of Nations*, New York: Free Press, 1990.
19. James Leontiades, 'Going Global – Global Strategies vs National Strategies', *Long Range Planning*, **19**, (6), 1986, 96–104.
20. Ibid.
21. John Zysman, *Governments, Markets and Growth: Financial Systems and the Politics of Industrial Change*, Ithaca and London: Cornell University Press, 1983, p. 277.
22. Stanley Aronowitz, 'Postmodernism and Politics', *Social Text*, **18**, Winter 1987–8, 101.
23. See Herbert I. Schiller, *Who Knows: Information in the Age of the Fortune 500*, Norwood, NJ: Ablex, 1981, pp. 47–78; and Herbert I. Schiller, 'Privatising the Public Sector: The Information Connection', in B. D. Ruben (ed.), *Information and Behaviour*, Vol. 1, New Brunswick: Transaction, 1985.
24. Vincent Mosco and Andrew Herman, 'Communication, Domination and Resistance', *Media, Culture and Society*, **2**, 1980, 351–65.
25. Richard Jay Solomon, 'Vanishing Intellectual Boundaries: Virtual Networking and the Loss of Sovereignty and Control', *ANNALS, American Academy of Political and Social Sciences*, **495**, 1988, 40–8.
26. See Chapter 3 of this book.
27. D. Smythe, 'Communications: Blindspot of Western Marxism', *Canadian Journal of Political and Social Theory*, 1, Fall 1977, 1–27.
28. See for example, Raquel Salinas and Leena Palda'n, 'Culture in the Process of Dependent Development: Theoretical Perspectives', in Kaarle Nordenstreng and Herbert I. Schiller (eds), *National Sovereignty and International Communication*, Norwood, NJ: Ablex, 1979, p. 95.
29. Nordenstreng and Schiller, *National Sovereignty*, pp. xi–xii.
30. Robert E. Mansell, 'Contradictions in National Communication/Information Policies: The Canadian Experience', *Media, Culture and Society*, **7**, 1985, 337.

31.   M. Piore and C. Sabel, *The Second Industrial Divide*, New York: Basic Books, 1984.
32.   Ibid., p. 303.
33.   K. T. Cutler, J. Williams and C. Haslam Williams, 'The End of Mass Production?', *Economy and Society*, **3**, 1987, 405–39.
34.   R. Mahon, 'From Fordism to New Technology, Labour Markets and Unions', *Economic and Industrial Democracy*, **8**, 1987, 5–60.
35.   Richard Badham and John Mathews, 'The New Production Systems Debate', *Labour and Industry*, **2**, (2), 1989, pp. 194–246.
36.   J. Gough, 'Industrial Policy and Socialist Strategy: Restructuring and the Unity of the Working Class', *Capitalism and Class*, **29**, 1986, 70.
37.   Pierre Jalée, *The Third World in World Economy*, New York: Monthly Review Press, 1969.
38.   See in particular Porter, *Competitive Advantage of Nations*, pp. 455–79.
39.   See Kimmo Kiljunen, 'Transnational Corporations and Third World Industrialisation', *Corporation and Conflict*, **19**, (1), March 1984, 39–57; also Luc Soete, 'International Diffusion of Technology, Industrial Development and Technological Leapfrogging', *World Development*, **13**, (3), 1985, 409–22.
40.   Porter, *Competitive Advantage of Nations*, p. 686.
41.   Ibid., p. 475
42.   Peter O'Brien, 'The New Multinationals: Developing-Country Firms in International Markets', *Futures*, August 1980, 303–16.
43.   See Franklin B. Weinstein, 'Multinational Corporations and the Third World: The Case of Japan and Southeast Asia', *International Organisation*, **30**, (3), 1976, 387–404.
44.   See J.A. Camilleri, *Civilization in Crisis*, New York: Cambridge University Press, 1976, pp. 107–10.
45.   H. F. Schiller, 'Madison Avenue Imperialism', *Trans-Action*, March–April 1973, 53.
46.   B. Hindley, 'Empty Economics in the Case for Industrial Policy', *World Economy*, **7**, 1984, 277.
47.   See for example ibid., pp. 277–94.
48.   See Henry Ergas 'Does Technology Policy Matter?', in Bruce R. Guile and Harvey Brooks (eds), *Technology and Global Industry: Companies and Nations in the World Economy*, National Academy of Engineering Series on Technology and Social Priorities, Washington, DC: National Academy Press, 1987, pp. 191–245; Christopher Freeman and Bengt-Ake Lundvall (eds), *Small Countries Facing the Technological Revolution*, London: Pinter, 1988; and Porter, *Competitive Advantage of Nations*.
49.   Dicken, *Global Shift*, p 136.
50.   P. Grant, 'Technological Sovereignty: Forgotten Factor in the High-Tech Razzamatazz', *Prometheus*, **1**, (2), 1983, 240.
51.   Ibid., p. 248; Rahat Nabi Khan, 'Multinational Companies and the World Economy: Economic and Technological Impact', *Impact of Science on Society*, **36**, (141), 1986, 15–25.
52.   W.W. Lockwood, *The State and Economic Enterprise in Japan*, Princeton, NJ: Princeton University Press, 1965, p. 503.
53.   Richard E. Caves and Masu Uekusa, *Industrial Organization in Japan*, Washington: Brookings Institution, 1976, p. 152.
54.   G. Saxonhouse, 'What is All This About Industrial Targeting In Japan?', *World Economy*, **6**, 1983, 271.
55.   Richard R. Nelson, *High-Technology Policies: A Five-Nation Comparison*, Washington: American Enterprise Institute for Public Policy Research, 1984, pp. 78-87.
56.   Grant, 'Technological Sovereignty', pp. 252–4.
57.   Nelson, *High-Technology Policies*, pp. 68–71.
58.   Grant, 'Technological Sovereignty', pp. 241–9.
59.   Susan Strange, 'Subnationals and the State', in John Hall (ed.), *States in History*, Oxford: Basil Blackwell, 1986, p. 301.
60.   Miles Kahler, 'The Survival of the State in European International Relations', in Charles S. Maier (ed.), *Changing Boundaries of the Political*, Cambridge: Cambridge University Press, 1987, p. 307.

6. The Security Dilemma

Though sovereignty is a multifaceted legal and political concept, it is probably the external meaning of the concept which has captured the public imagination and dominated recent academic discourse.[1] Internal sovereignty connotes, as we have seen, the exercise of supreme authority within the state's boundaries, whereas external sovereignty connotes the legal equality of states, with no state subjecting itself to a higher external authority. Supremacy within and equality of status without are considered complementary and mutually reinforcing manifestations of sovereign statehood. Arising from this central premiss, several closely interrelated principles have come to govern the conceptualization of sovereignty: that internal and external sovereignty are analytically if not practically distinct; that political authority resides exclusively in the institutions of states; that states are the discrete entities which make up international society; that there is a substantial correlation between the formal rights implied by state sovereignty and the actual capacity of states to exercise these rights.

These principles suggest in different ways and to varying degrees that political authority rests with states understood as relatively distinct, self-contained institutions separated by clearly demarcated boundaries. The purpose of this chapter is to examine whether, and to what extent, these principles accurately reflect the political realities of the modern world. We have already seen in Chapter 4 how in the era of economic transnationalization states are severely restricted in their capacity to manage their domestic economies by the actions of other states, more importantly by the behaviour of non-state actors, perhaps most importantly by the rapidly evolving structure of the world economy. In this chapter we shall argue that similar trends, albeit in more subtle form, are at work in the security field[2] where the state had traditionally prided itself on being the architect of policy and on exercising a monopoly on the use of force.

Central to our thesis is the argument that the external or international function of the state is inseparable from the internal or societal one. To put it differently, the state operates in a complex environment in which policy decisions, processes and outcomes cut across state boundaries and in which the pattern of authority corresponds less and less to that implied by a system of sovereign states. According to Nettl, 'the state acts for the society interna-

tionally, and internal matters relating to foreign affairs are a state preroga-
tive... . In short, the state is the gatekeeper between intra-societal and extra-
societal flows of action.'[3] This is a sophisticated restatement of the familiar
argument that the state, regardless of its power or size, has a relatively free
hand in formulating foreign policy, and that whatever may be its status or
efficacy in the domestic context, its external sovereignty or autonomy is not
under serious challenge. The difficulty with this characterization is that it
assumes that the state represents a recognizable collective will or interest
which it effectively represents in its dealings with other states, even though
such a collective will or interest may be less easily discernible in its internal
policies. There is, however, little evidence to support this line of reasoning.

If interaction between the state and other associations or collectivities
within society points to a pluralism that constitutes a limitation on the
sovereignty of the state, there is no reason to think that such interaction,
when placed in an international setting, is any less limiting of state sovereignty. If domestically, the state performs an instrumental role on behalf of
sectional interests or if the actions and decisions of the institutions that make
up the state are inseparable from the preferences and influence of private
interests, then there must be a presumption that similar factors are at work in
the state's external conduct. As we pointed out in Chapter 2, several recent
studies have drawn attention to the close connection between the state's
external environment and its domestic policies.[4]

The aim of this chapter is to explore the political, strategic and cultural
ambiguities that cut across the sharply demarcated boundaries implied by
the notion of external sovereignty. Attention will focus on the way these
ambiguities, themselves the expression of a still unfolding process, are alter-
ing the significance of territorial boundaries, hence of the theoretical division between the domestic (intra-state) and international (inter-state) environment. In this context we shall see that power and authority are dispersed
across a far more diverse and complex set of interactions and institutions
than is postulated by the system of sovereign states. This is not to suggest
that state sovereignty does not still constitute, at least formally, the dominant
vehicle through which authority is exercised but rather to highlight the
widening gap between form and substance.

The use of force and nationalism are no doubt still potent factors in world
politics, but neither of them, either alone or in combination, may be regarded
as synonymous with external sovereignty. The nature of national identity
and military power and their function in the international system are themselves subject to profound change, thereby contributing to a much more
heterogeneous and even contradictory pattern of relationships than is implied by the concept of sovereign statehood. Nowhere are these tensions and
ambiguities more strikingly reflected than in the rapidly evolving East–West

relationship which has dominated international politics for more than four decades. A re-examination of the Cold war–*détente* phenomenon in the latter part of this chapter will be used as a case study to clarify our understanding of the larger trends that are visibly reshaping the meaning and practice of sovereignty.

BOUNDARIES

Since the Treaty of Westphalia (1648) the division of the world into clearly delineated jurisdictions has been widely regarded as the organizing principle of politics. Yet the boundaries that are an integral part of the notion of territorial sovereignty are much more fluid than is often assumed.

Unquestionably, the twin principles of sovereignty and legitimacy have been closely associated with territory, that is with the demarcation of boundaries and the violent conflicts that often surround such demarcation.[5] Over the last 200 years a succession of local, regional and global conflicts – many of them waged in the name of existing or aspiring state sovereignty – have helped to establish the territorial boundaries within which sovereign authority could be exercised. Writing in 1939 E.H. Carr concluded: 'In no previous period of modern history have frontiers been so rigidly demarcated, or their character as barriers so ruthlessly enforced, as to-day.'[6] The role of such international organizations as the League of Nations and the United Nations, but also of numerous regional collective security arrangements, may be seen as having consolidated this process by affirming the inviolability of boundaries and at least on occasions acting to defend boundaries when they were violated or under threat.

Yet several trends, many of which are at an embryonic stage, indicate a progressive erosion of the exclusivity associated with notions of territorial sovereignty. There is no suggestion here that territory has ceased to perform a central function in social organization or that territorial behaviour is the invention of the modern nation-state. All political communities regardless of their stage of development – from the nomadic tribe to the Greek city-state, the imperial state, the feudal state, the dynastic state, and most recently the nation-state – express and nurture a certain attachment to territory. In this sense, the distinction between nomadic tribes and sedentary communities is itself a fine one, for nomads depend for their survival on familiarity with the territory in which they roam.[7] Territoriality is not an all-or-nothing proposition. It can vary significantly in intensity and form depending on prevailing cultural, economic and technological conditions. This qualification is especially pertinent to the contemporary period despite the pervasive influence of territory and frontiers on both domestic and international politics.

The European balance of power system, as it evolved in the eighteenth and nineteenth centuries, became synonymous with the idea of exclusive sovereignty, which 'made defence and internal administration the primary and increasingly exclusive task of the central authorities'.[8] Here Kratochwil contrasts the rigidly delineated boundaries separating modern European states with the much more loosely defined frontiers separating earlier empires. He cites the case of the Roman Empire where the public domain (*ager publicus*) had no legal boundaries. The outer edge of the empire constituted not so much a boundary as 'a floating zone within which tributary tribes as well as Roman legions with local barbarian recruits were used to keep the peace'.[9] But is the contrast with the contemporary system of sovereign states as complete and definitive as this initial assessment would suggest? After all, an integral part of the European balance of power was the succession of territorial adjustments which the major European powers devised at the edges of their colonial empires. Buffers, protectorates, trusteeships, spheres of influence, suzerainties, and neutral or demilitarized zones were a few of the mechanisms used for the purpose. All of these served to blur the dividing line between competing jurisdictions.

Elements of the same strategy were also used within Europe itself as a way of containing potential conflicts and injecting a degree of flexibility into an otherwise dangerously rigid system. In this context Kratochwil himself cites the nineteenth-century example of the Balkans, which he describes as a 'frontier zone in which Austrian, Russian and British influence met, and which could not be effectively dealt with by the nominal power, the Ottoman Empire'.[10] At first sight it may appear as if the twentieth century has seen the geographical extension and political consolidation of territorial sovereignty in its most rigid form. The relative stability of European boundaries, particularly after 1945, the establishment of sovereign states throughout the greater part of the Third World in the aftermath of decolonization, and the moral and institutional weight accorded by the UN Charter to the principle of national sovereignty, all testify to the normative importance that fixed and universally recognized boundaries have achieved in international relations.

Yet closer inspection suggests that a great many bilateral and multilateral arrangements – some formal, others informal – have considerably diluted the logic and political force of territorial demarcation. A striking instance of this trend is the increasing salience of the principle of collective security in the twentieth century, particularly in the aftermath of the Second World War. The considerable degree of political and military integration, necessitated by the formation of these security systems, was most vividly exemplified by the functioning of the Eastern and Western blocs at the height of the Cold War. Each bloc consisted of a complex network of bilateral and multilateral agreements governing the establishment and operation of military bases, the stationing of troops, combined military exercises, weapons procurement and the adoption of joint conventional and nuclear strategies. These agreements, concluded between seemingly sovereign entities, in effect constituted the legal instrument used by the dominant powers to intrude inside the boundaries of their allies. Despite differences in policy profile separating one ally from another, it seemed, at least for a time, as if the political map of the world revolved around the boundaries of the bloc rather than the boundaries of the state.[11]

In time the sharply drawn boundaries between the two opposing blocs (i.e. the 'Iron Curtain') would succumb to many of the pressures that had previously moderated the territorial demarcation of national sovereignties. Kratochwil's description of the three devices – spheres of responsibility, spheres of abstention and functional regimes – which have been used as instruments of conflict management within the international system[12] is particularly relevant to the analysis of Cold War politics. A complex web of arrangements, ranging from formal treaties to unspoken rules,[13] has given rise to an elaborate set of expectations, rights and obligations which have greatly modified the fragmented system of sovereign states. In the post-1945 period the United States and the Soviet Union saw themselves, and were seen by others, as playing a leading role in the maintenance of world order. The diplomatic, military and economic ramifications of this extended far beyond the outer edge of the two alliance systems.

INTERNATIONAL ORGANIZATION

Though the two adversaries did not reach a formal agreement on the scope or limits of their respective spheres of responsibility, and though their interventionist and policing actions did as much to provoke as to contain conflict, they gradually developed a *modus vivendi*. This understanding was seldom formalized and often gave rise to dissatisfaction because of perceived asymmetric outcomes, yet it provided the breathing space needed by both sides to retreat from the consequences of nuclear brinkmanship. Complementing these unspoken or unwritten agreements were a number of formal arrangements – designated by Kratochwil and others as 'functional regimes' – which eroded the importance of national boundaries by establishing a framework for transnational co-operation. The Partial Test Ban Treaty, the Nuclear Non-Proliferation Treaty, the Law of the Sea, the Universal Declaration of Human Rights, the Antarctic Treaty, are just a few of the elements of a rapidly expanding body of international law which reflects the reality of power relationships yet at the same time constrains the behaviour of states, including the two superstates.

The concept of functional regimes, and the intricate web of laws, rules and regulations on which they rest, also helps to focus our attention on the role of international organizations which are both a product and a primary source of international law in the contemporary world.[14] Apart from the League of Nations and the United Nations, which represent the most comprehensive attempts at international co-operation in modern times (in both inclusiveness of membership and breadth of objectives and activities), the twentieth century has witnessed an explosive growth in the number and variety of international governmental organizations (IGOs), some concentrating on particular regions (e.g. the Organization of African Unity), others confining themselves to one area of policy or facet of international interaction (e.g. UNESCO). Notwithstanding the considerable differences in membership, geographical spread, function, administrative infrastructure and access to resources, IGOs have become central to the functioning of the international system. Though their efficacy may sometimes be limited, particularly where security conflicts are involved, they have created a psychological and institutional framework which constrains or at least qualifies state actions and perceptions.[15] Through the collection and dissemination of data, the preparation of policy options, and the exchange of views and personnel these organizations provide a forum for discussion and contribute to a more flexible problem-solving environment. While they owe their existence to the decisions of states and are dependent on states for their continued survival, IGOs help to set timetables and agendas and facilitate decision-making processes which acquire a life of their own and are distinct from the preferences or priorities of any one of their member states.

Over the last thirty years a vast literature has emerged describing, analysing, predicting and prescribing the behaviour of non-state actors.[16] Here we are not referring simply to IGOs but to a wide range of other politically significant groupings, whether subnational, transnational or supranational in character, whose actions are not under the direct control of any one state or group of states, yet contribute directly to the complex interdependencies that comprise the world system. The significance of these organizations is not merely that they encourage collective rather than unilateral responses to problems, but that they reinterpret the nature of a given problem by evading, overcoming or at least diluting the territorial prism through which states normally perceive political reality. The World Council of Churches, the International Olympic Committee, Amnesty International, Friends of the Earth and Greenpeace are examples of transnational organizations which multiply available channels of international communication and create new avenues for common socialization. All of this is not to suggest that such organizations, whether they be transnational corporations, churches, trade unions, liberation movements or development agencies perform comparable functions or that their actions and policies necessarily reflect the same values. On the other hand, they all undermine in varying degrees political and even physical restraints imposed by the territorially bound state. In short, they redefine the political terrain by occupying political space and areas of decision-making which contrast sharply with the territorial delineation of sovereign jurisdictions. In the process they establish a framework of interaction which diminishes the importance of physical and legal boundaries.

As one would expect, the qualitative and quantitative growth of international institutionalization has wide-ranging ramifications for the security dilemma and even for the strategies and techniques devised by states to resolve it. We have already referred to the integrative features of military alliances and to the asymmetric interdependencies they have created, particularly since 1945. But quite apart from collective security institutions, national liberation, separatist and other revolutionary movements have also influenced popular and official perceptions of security. Such movements often threaten to dismember existing sovereign entities; at the very least they complicate the security dilemma confronting sovereign authorities, in part by accentuating the already considerable interconnection of internal and external threats.

The role of institutions is more extensive still. Even organizations that have no immediate or apparent stake in security issues are bound to influence the way these issues are interpreted and managed by the state. Particularly instructive in this respect is the recent experience of European integration. The functionalist argument that the process of economic unification would progressively undermine the independence of national institutions and eventually spill over to other areas of political and military co-operation can now be seen to have been simplistic and premature. The policies of de Gaulle's France and Thatcher's Britain have effectively shattered any illusion about the rapid transfer of national power and authority to supranational institutions.

Yet the not infrequent reaction of many political commentators, who saw in the slow and painful progress of European integration evidence of the centrality of the state-centric paradigm, was also a case of misinterpretation. The European Economic Community, established by the Treaty of Rome in 1957, has been described as 'a strange hybrid, its decision making intergovernmental, its normative law supranational within its own areas of competence'.[17] Yet, for all its ups and downs European unification has made steady advances, particularly since the 1985 decision of the European Council to complete a single market by 1992. By confirming the principle of weighted majority voting, the Council took a significant step towards the 'pooling of sovereignty'. The drive to establish a single market, in the context of mounting trade rivalries and a rapidly changing Atlantic relationship, has given added impetus to proposals for monetary union as well as closer political and military collaboration.

It may be argued that the initiative for a European Community represents no more than a potential union of states, which, if successful, would in due course replace a number of states with one new superstate. The point, however, is that such a process is not irreversible and does not occur overnight. What we may be witnessing, well before the new supranational entity has emerged, is a prolonged form of 'incremental federation',[18] which itself implies a substantial dilution of sovereign power and authority, and calls for a re-examination of the thesis that the territorial coincidence of state and nation as traditionally understood remains the governing principle of contemporary political life. If this is an accurate characterization of the trend, then those member states (e.g. Britain under Thatcher) which present sovereignty as an all-or-nothing proposition may be underestimating the degree to which the rapid and continuing changes in technological, industrial and financial integration have already blurred the dividing line between states and the capacity of national governments to act unilaterally within them.[19]

INTERCONNECTEDNESS OF THE INTERNATIONAL SYSTEM

A voluminous literature now exists describing and interpreting the complex interdependence that characterizes present-day international reality.[20] While much of this writing is simplistic in its treatment of power relations and insufficiently attentive to the ways in which interdependence may coexist with and even reinforce deeply embedded forms of technological, economic and military dependence, the concept nevertheless represents an accurate observation in so far as it refers to the numerous and inextricably interwoven threads that link almost every corner of the globe. Interdependence theories have rightly emphasized the numerous linkages associated with modern methods of production, communication and transportation, but have largely neglected the interconnectedness which is no less apparent in the field of security relations. It is not simply that the war system, understood as the actual or potential confrontation of armed forces, is now a global phenomenon as both world wars, the Cold War, the Vietnam War and the Gulf War clearly indicate, but that the conflicts and contradictions that underlie the preparation for war are themselves global in character.

Internationalization of Conflict

The rival nationalisms that collided in the First World War and again two decades later were themselves the product of a multifaceted competition for markets, resources and power that had long since overspilled the boundaries of the nation-state. Many of the protagonists were successful or aspiring imperial powers entangled in a competition for spheres of influence that encompassed every continent. There was, moreover, a close if not always transparent connection between the decisions of states and the evolving structure of national economies increasingly propelled by the engine of international trade and the export of capital. The contest between competing ideologies in the Second World War and the even starker confrontation between communism and capitalism in the aftermath of that war point to the importance of ideology as an instrument of legitimation and a vehicle for the internationalization of conflict.

One of the most striking manifestations of the internationalization of conflict was the deepening interconnection of different regions on the one hand and between those regions and the global strategic system on the other. Set in the context of nuclear stalemate, American and Soviet capacity to project military power abroad, even though US capabilities were more extensive and sophisticated than those available to the Soviet Union, provided a powerful impetus for military interaction, which in turn contributed to the polarization of regional conflict. Even where such intervention did not dramatically change the global or regional balance of power, both superpowers normally felt obliged to respond to each other's moves for fear of appearing to abandon their respective clients or allies. Where it was deemed imprudent to commit substantial military power in a given theatre, perhaps because the adversary enjoyed an overwhelming military or diplomatic advantage (e.g. the United States in Latin America), the inclination was to maintain a low-key presence, waiting in the wings to seize any opportunities that might emerge.

A second option, not necessarily incompatible with the first, was to seek, as part of the global contest for spheres of influence, a more secure foothold in another region where the adversary's position was perhaps less impregnable. To this extent at least, regional conflict and instability became inseparable from the global axis of geopolitical and strategic rivalry. With the superpowers reluctant to engage in direct confrontation because of the nuclear stalemate, domestic and regional rivalries and disorders situated far from the centres of Soviet and American power (in Korea, Vietnam, Cuba, Angola, Mozambique, Afghanistan, Nicaragua) became, in Bloomfield's phrase, 'surrogates for systemic war'.[21] By internalizing the logic of international bipolarity, regional conflicts tended in turn to rebound on each other even where the connections between issues and leading protagonists seemed remote or at best indirect. In each case, the East–West conflict would act as a transmission belt, with the intractability of conflict in one region militating against the resolution of conflict in another. Even where separated by long distances, regional security systems had become closely interconnected by virtue of their close relationship to the central balance.

Paradoxically, the improvement in superpower relations can also serve as a stimulus for the internationalization of conflict. The international response to Iraq's invasion of Kuwait, and especially the punishing war launched by the US-led coalition against Iraq, would not have been possible without Moscow's willingness to support, or at least tolerate, American military and diplomatic objectives. In this instance the explicit or tacit understanding between the two superpowers paved the way for one of the most massive applications of military force since the Second World War. The fact that the whole operation was conducted in the name of the United Nations and to some extent legitimized by a number of UN Security Council resolutions – in practice the United Nations seemed impotent to influence the course of events – merely reinforced the process of internationalization. US military power and the prestige of the international organization combined to transform what had initially started as a regional dispute between Iraq and Kuwait into a conflict of global dimensions. The extensive transfer of sophisticated military technology to the Middle East and the far-reaching ramifications of the political economy of oil underscored the transnational as well international origins and structure of the conflict.

The Emerging Macropolitical Agenda

The interconnectedness of the international system was not, however, purely a function of geography or the omnipresence of the East–West conflict. Security, understood in its purely military sense, was increasingly linked to other facets of international life, of which the most important was economic organization and well-being. The formation of the Atlantic security community, institutionalized through NATO, complemented and reinforced the Atlantic economic community, institutionalized through the Organization for European Economic Co-operation and the Organization for Economic Co-operation and Development. In the Asia–Pacific region, the US security framework, comprised of a patchwork of bilateral and multilateral arrangements, was also connected to regional economic institutions (e.g. the Asian Development Bank) as well as to international organizations (e.g. GATT, IMF, the World Bank) that formed an integral part of global capitalism. Western security arrangements and American military power generally provided the umbrella for the successful expansion of 'free enterprise' on a global scale. Within this international order, often loosely designated as Pax Americana, states, transnational corporations and international institutions operated according to the logic of the market, with the United States as hegemonic power performing a policing and co-ordinating function, keeping open supply routes and maintaining access to markets and raw materials.

The elaborate global security framework constructed by the United States in the late 1940s and early 1950s was justified in terms of the perceived need to contain the expansion of communist power and influence. Yet the Cold War did not merely pit one system of military power against another. It also represented the collision of two economic systems, one governed by the market-based allocation of resources and private enterprise and the other by central planning and state ownership of the means of production. Placed in this context, the Council for Mutual Economic Assistance (COMECON) may be described as the economic equivalent of the Warsaw Pact, and both institutions as instruments of Soviet domination of the communist bloc. Without at this point entering into the intricacies of the East–West conflict, one conclusion seems inescapable. Inter-bloc and intra-bloc relations and the institutional forms they acquired owed their origins and rationale to a complex set of factors which could not be reduced to the interests or decisions of sovereign states. Military objectives were inextricably linked with and substantially influenced by economic and political processes which cut across national boundaries and derived from transnational interests and institutions.

In time, the North–South and East–West axes of conflict would criss-cross to produce a series of flashpoints, of which the Cuban missile crisis, the Vietnam War and the various Middle East conflicts were the most conspicuous examples. In each case, the use or threat of force, whether by superpowers, regional powers or nationalist movements, represented merely the tip of the iceberg. This most visible or external aspect of the conflict often obscured the underlying clash of economic and political interests and alliances which bore little or no relationship to the notion of competing sovereign wills.[22] Significantly, many Third World countries had sought in the early years of the postcolonial era to minimize the intrusion of strategic bipolarity and the threat it posed to their security and independence by pursuing a policy of non-alignment.[23] As time went on the focus shifted to the economic arena, with Third World governments calling for a new international economic order and redistribution of the world product. What is particularly relevant to our analysis here is not so much the relative success or failure of these two strategies as the close interaction of states and markets, and between the military-diplomatic and economic arenas of conflict which they imply.

Two types of boundaries long regarded as central to an understanding of international life, namely the theoretical and practical boundaries separating politics and economics – reflecting in part the assumed separation of states and markets – and the geographical boundaries between states were gradually dissolving under the cumulative weight of the rising curve of economic, technological and social change. National governments might from time to time reassert their independence by introducing stricter laws to regulate different sectors of the economy, and Third World states might call for a new international economic order as a way of neutralizing the loss of national control over economic policy. However, the interpenetration of national economies associated with the emerging global market and the ensuing permeability of traditional territorial divisions appeared less and less susceptible to effective counteraction by boundary-maintaining systems.

Over time the diminished salience of territorial and policy boundaries was complemented and reinforced by the slow, at times erratic, but persistent unfolding of what may loosely be described as a macropolitical agenda. Though many factors contributed to the redefinition and enlargement of the notion of security, none was more important than the growing intrusion of ecological concerns into social consciousness. We shall postpone a fuller discussion of the implications of environmental degradation for state sovereignty to the next chapter. For the moment suffice it to say that economic intervention in the natural order has unleashed a series of cumulative and interacting imbalances, some regional, others global, which threaten to disturb the delicate equilibrium established over evolutionary times between the biosphere and the world of inanimate matter. No state, however rich or powerful, could by its own unaided efforts mount an adequate response.

Numerous other problems, including international debt, trade rivalries, widespread human rights abuses – at times verging on genocide – nuclear proliferation and drug trafficking seemed to overstep the boundaries of sovereign states. It is as if the various manifestations of economic, social and political disorder had greatly exceeded the problem-solving capacity of existing institutions and rendered traditional notions of military security less central to an understanding of international order.

A macropolitical agenda may be said to have gradually emerged as a consequence of three related factors.[24] First, the contemporary human predicament has assumed global proportions in that it threatens the existence of a large fraction of humanity. Secondly, and perhaps more importantly for our analysis, the various threads of global disorder are closely interconnected, cutting across policy and institutional boundaries. Thirdly, the radical acceleration of change, coupled with almost instantaneous methods of communication, has heightened awareness of the challenge to human adaptation, and the institutional limitations of the state as it struggles to elaborate appropriate responses. Over time these have combined to shape a macropolitical agenda which calls into question the analytical and practical utility of the principle of sovereignty and the absolute priority it ascribes to territorial demarcations between sovereign jurisdictions.

Global Military Order

The above conclusion may at first sight appear to contradict the observable emphasis which governments continue to place on formal boundaries and the sovereign authority they exercise on behalf of the state or body politic. However, the outward trappings of sovereignty, firmly grounded though they may be in constitutional theory and diplomatic practice, may obscure more than clarify the reality of economic and political power. Two arguments are often advanced in support of the claim that no formal alternative to the system of sovereign states 'has been effectively articulated and legitimated'.[25] One relates to the use of force and the other to nationalism. Both arguments seek to demonstrate that the formal mode of political organization continues to enjoy legitimacy, and holds the key to the decision-making process. As such both arguments deserve careful scrutiny, particularly as they impinge on the notion of national security.

A fundamental attribute of sovereignty is said to be the monopoly the state exercises on the legitimate use of force. It is this attribute which enables the state to maintain internal order and sustains its claim to external recognition. According to Richard Haass, 'the inability to marshall sufficient force against an adversary will result in a diminution of influence, territory or sovereignty'.[26] As states ceaselessly struggle to maintain their privileged access to force, the ensuing, often violent, conflict between competing states is a living testimony to the primacy of state sovereignty. Underlying this whole argument is the premiss that the management of force and the exercise of sovereignty are, if not synonymous, at least complementary and even mutually reinforcing.

The assumed relationship between force and sovereignty is open to the criticism, as Haass himself recognizes, that 'force has become less important relative to other forms of influence in which the nation-state does not possess a monopolistic or even dominant position'.[27] Rosenau reaches much the same conclusion, when he observes that conventional war has become 'increasingly less viable and credible as a policy option'. As a consequence, states are deprived 'of that which Waltz argues gives them the advantage when the "crunch" comes, the ultimate sanction inherent in the call to do battle, to legitimately impose their will by coercive means'.[28] Any argument about the declining use or utility of force must, however, take account of the widespread incidence of violence in the twentieth century. Quite apart from wars of national independence and interventionist wars by the great powers, the post-1945 period has witnessed a seemingly endless succession of wars, for example between the United States and North Korea, China and India, India and Pakistan, the United States and Vietnam, China and Vietnam, Vietnam and Cambodia, Israel and its Arab neighbours, Iran and Iraq, Iraq and Kuwait, Algeria and Morocco, Morocco and Mauritania, Libya and Chad, and Ethiopia and Somalia.[29]

That the destructive power available to the modern state is immeasurably greater than in any previous epoch is obvious enough. That states have been prepared to accumulate, threaten and on occasions use that power is also clear enough. There are nevertheless, as the previous chapter has shown, several limiting factors in the use of armed force, of which the most important is perhaps the advent of weapons of mass destruction. Able to travel long distances at unprecedented speeds and inflict indiscriminate violence on civilian populations, these weapons tend to undermine conventional notions of territorial defence. It is precisely this limitation which initially prompted John Herz to stress the negative impact of nuclear weapons on territorial defence.[30] The destructiveness of the new weapons is an important factor in the reluctance of those who possess them to risk a major confrontation. Whereas the list of wars since 1945 is depressingly long, none has so far entailed a head-on collision between nuclear powers. So technological innovation may limit the strategic options available to modern statecraft.

The precise impact of technology on the territorial state no doubt remains problematic and will vary with changing circumstances.[31] One thing is nevertheless clear: the capacity of the state to defend territorial boundaries against armed attack has been in steady decline throughout this century. The ability of one state to use lethal force and penetrate the boundaries of another state of necessity implies the vulnerability of that other state to such force. Vulnerability is crucial because it affects not only military personnel and installations but above all civilian populations, which the use of armed force is intended to protect in the first place.

The widespread incidence and rising intensity of armed conflict do not therefore offer conclusive evidence either of the existence of sovereign authority or of the close relationship between the state's sovereignty and its security function. Neither of these conclusions is sustainable so long as several closely related questions cannot be answered in the affirmative. Is the use or threat of force primarily the outcome of decisions made by sovereign states? Can military power be used in ways consistent with the principle of state sovereignty? Does the sovereign state determine the character and function of military technology? Does armed conflict strengthen state sovereignty?

These are troublesome questions, to which there are no simple answers. Even a cursory examination is sufficient to cast serious doubt on the assumed connection between sovereignty and military power. To begin with, one must return to the distinction between the state as *agent* and the state as *instrument*. The formal decision to use military force is, it is true, generally made by the state, or to be more precise by those institutions, be they legislatures or executives, which are vested with that supreme authority, whether by convention or written constitution. However, while appearing to uphold the principle of sovereignty, the formal exercise of authority may obscure a more complex and contradictory decision-making process. One illustration may help to clarify the argument.

Much has been written about the origins of the First World War, about the escalating pressures over which most of the protagonists had relatively little control, about the time constraints inherent in the various mobilization plans, and about the cumulative psychological stress to which national policy-makers were subjected.[32] The end result was a war that few European leaders wanted, and whose magnitude in human and financial terms they could scarcely have foreseen, much less desired. This war, like all wars, had its own peculiar characteristics and was the outcome of specific conditions prevailing at the time. Yet it may be possible to generalize to this extent: most modern wars are to a considerable degree subject to the complexities and rigidities of crisis decision-making. In conditions of prolonged stress, misperception and internal upheaval, the state may not be capable of considering the range of available options, and there may be a sharply increased probability of accidental, inadvertent or unauthorized war.[33] In other words, the conditions normally considered necessary for the exercise of sovereignty, in particular the existence of a cohesive and rational sovereign will, may be either lacking or severely qualified.

If we turn to the idea of national sovereignty as the expression of the popular will, it is possible to envisage military decisions which seriously violate accepted democratic or constitutional arrangements. A great many covert and often illegal military actions undertaken by national security organizations, of which the Iran Contragate episode is a recent example, belong to this category. Clandestine activities are significant because they tend to undo the nationalization of the state, that is the strong emotional attachment of nation to state – a potent force which the French Revolution unleashed and which subsequent wars have often reinforced.[34]

The intricate, hierarchical and secretive military apparatus, which has developed largely as a function of the new technology, tends to produce the same alienating effect. The highly specialized and esoteric language, elite professionalism and high-tech gadgetry characteristic of modern military establishments, not to speak of the destructiveness of modern warfare, have severely tarnished the image of military institutions. Their increasing reliance on covert operations, involving the establishment of secret military facilities, penetration of foreign governments and their agencies, and dissemination of propaganda at home and abroad has compounded the problem of accountability and engendered a mixture of fear, suspicion and unease within the body politic. The actions of the armed forces, in war as in peacetime, have become as much a source of political division as of social cohesion.

The adverse impact of military force on internal sovereignty is not confined to the home state. The gap between formal and effective sovereignty is exposed whenever the sovereign institutions of one state are to varying degrees underpinned, controlled or subverted by the armed forces and intelligence agencies of another state. A foreign military presence, including large troop deployments, military bases, or command, communications and control facilities of the kind associated with modern alliances, cannot but call into question the sovereignty of the junior ally. The legal claim that external force does not infringe sovereignty because it operates with the approval of the host state has limited plausibility. Even if it can be demonstrated that the invitation to the external power is consistent with the exercise of sovereign authority, it would still need to be established that such authority can effectively continue to be exercised in conditions where a substantial military force is located within its territory but not effectively subject to its jurisdiction. What is true of overt activities governed by international treaties and agreements applies with even greater force to covert operations, which may include the penetration and manipulation of the host country's intelligence services, cultivation of agents of influence, organization of insurgency, and the illicit transfer of money, drugs and arms.

Advanced military technologies militate against the exercise of effective sovereignty by virtue of their destructiveness, their capacity to penetrate national boundaries, their corrosive effect on democratic practices and institutions, but also the mounting financial burden they impose on national economies. It is partly in order to contain these costs and to cope with the new budgetary uncertainties that great and small powers alike have established complex military production and procurement policies. Even states boasting the most extensive national defence industries have found it necessary 'to share each other's markets, financial resources and technical knowledge'.[35] International collaboration can take many forms, including licensed production (e.g. the Indian production of Soviet-designed aircraft), co-production and offsets (e.g. Belgian, Dutch, Norwegian and Dutch co-production in the purchase of F-16 aircraft), joint research and development (e.g. the Milan anti-tank missile), and subcontracting from overseas (e.g. the involvement of Lucas Aerospace in the production of Swedish JAS Gripen aircraft).

These collaborative projects, however, involve much more than intergovernmental agreements. Almost invariably they depend on transnational corporations with substantial defence interests (e.g. Raytheon, Thyssen,

Hughes Aircraft, McDonnell Douglas, Ferranti International, Rockwell, Honeywell), many of which have, as a result of mergers and takeovers and varying degrees of cross-ownership, developed an elaborate and internationally based organizational infrastructure. The participation of transnational corporations holds several attractions for national governments, in particular economies of scale, ability to penetrate foreign markets and access to high technology in electronics, data processing and computing. As a result of these interlocking public–private arrangements, the development of military technology, arms transfers and even strategic doctrine are increasingly shaped by transnational industrial, financial and political pressures. Though it continues to enjoy the official sanction of the state, defence policy more and more derives its logic from the structure of the international economic and military order[36] rather than the autonomously determined objectives and priorities of the sovereign state.

Force and the Politics of Dissent

Once the assumed supremacy of sovereign authority is subjected to empirical scrutiny, it emerges that the sovereign state is not a self-contained and monolithic structure and that power and authority are substantially diffused over a political space that cuts across state boundaries. As a consequence, the rise of military capabilities and armed conflict, far from enhancing the power and authority of the sovereign state, simply points to new uncertainties and capabilities, both subnational and international, which severely weaken that power and authority. This brings us face to face with the role of nationalism and the degree to which nationalist ideology enhances the state's legitimacy and freedom of action, particularly when it comes to the use of armed force. Two trends, both of which have assumed considerable significance over the last several decades, suggest that for the state nationalism may be a strategy of diminishing returns.

To begin with, when deciding to wage war the state can no longer rely on automatic or universal compliance. In the light of recent experience, notably the barbarity of two world wars and the enormous human and financial costs associated with modern wars of intervention, the public in most Western societies has become highly sceptical of the need or appropriateness of coercive strategies. The questioning of particular policy decisions as well as of the official ideology has gone hand in hand with the demystification of the nation as an object of quasi-religious veneration. The uneven but conspicuous growth of the peace movement in many parts of the world together with the discernible rise of a more internationalist current in world public opinion[37] points to the partial delegitimation of state-centric force and a growing divide between state and society.

The erosive impact of dissent on the state's coercive power is compounded by the growth of dissident violence. Although visible in more exaggerated form in the newly emerging states, the disruptive effect of such violence is not confined to this part of the world. It has punctuated the contemporary history of several advanced industrial societies, as indicated by the periodic convulsions experienced in France under the Fourth and Fifth Republics, the protracted conflict in Northern Ireland, ethnic separatism in Spain and Canada, the linguistic polarization of Belgium, ethnic disaffection in Eastern Europe, and the increasingly powerful centrifugal forces operating in the Soviet Union. The principle that the nation should be wholly encompassed in one single state has nowhere been fully applied. Indeed, the movement for national self-determination which gave the principle of state sovereignty much of its impetus and legitimacy, particularly in late eighteenth- and nineteenth-century Europe, has in more recent times exacerbated the latent tensions between nation and state.

National or ethnic identification has become a powerful lever with which to challenge existing state boundaries. That nationalist movements themselves normally aspire to sovereign statehood (e.g. the Palestinian Liberation Organization, FRETILIN in East Timor, the nationalist movements emerging in different parts of the Soviet Union) does not alter the fact that existing sovereign states are increasingly subject to fissiparous tendencies which substantially modify the way sovereignty is interpreted and exercised. With the spread of education and mounting dissatisfaction stemming from the decisions and *modus operandi* of centralized authority, hitherto dormant minorities acquire higher levels of political self-consciousness and a greater willingness to assert their autonomy. While the technological revolution, and in particular the extremely rapid growth of transportation and communication systems, may facilitate the centralization and integration of state power, they also unleash a new social dynamic highly disruptive of the existing configuration of economic and political power. Though at first preoccupied with issues of language, education and control of media, ethnic and other minority movements soon turn their attention to more general demands which question the existing distribution of resources and constitutional arrangements.

The argument that ethnicity and nationalism are increasingly disruptive of the system of sovereign states finds indirect confirmation in Nettl's conclusion that the First World War is an important watershed in the evolution of nationalist movements. Whereas in the nineteenth century nationalism helped to shape the theory and practice of sovereign statehood, twentieth-century nationalism, both in its European setting and in the diverse forms it acquired in the colonized world, simply appropriated an existing concept and applied it to an already established cultural and political reality. The state thus became little more than a 'collective noun summarising the effective government of an independent nation and the creation of an international diplomatic persona'.[38] In many of the newly independent states of Asia and Africa the absence of anything remotely resembling the European model of the homogeneous nation merely compounded the tensions generated by modernization and bureaucratic centralization. Nationalism, religion and ethnicity, instead of legitimizing the state or endowing it with an organic structure, now became principles of rejection, promising a different model of political organization in sharp contrast to the perceived inanimateness and even depersonalization of existing state forms.

For it to survive as an institution the national or multinational state has had to pay a price: it has had to accommodate the new nationalism; and allow for a devolution of power and authority whereby submerged ethnic and other minorities could exercise a degree of autonomy. In some cases it has virtually abandoned the claim to a monopoly on the legitimate use of violence. The state, we may therefore conclude, remains a critical element in the political organization of society, but its claim to sovereignty has become politically more fluid and legally more ambiguous.

THE EAST–WEST AXIS OF CONFLICT

By virtue of its geographical, technological and ideological dimensions, the East–West confrontation which emerged after 1945 became central to the security dilemma of virtually all states. At the same time it gave rise to an intricate web of institutional and conceptual responses which considerably modified the application of the sovereignty principle. An investigation of the globalized social conflict known as the Cold War offers a uniquely valuable focus for an analysis of the practice of sovereignty as it has unfolded since 1945.

The Soviet–American adversary relationship, though it has its origins in the Russian Revolution, did not acquire its full geopolitical significance until after 1945. As a result of the drastic shift in the relation of forces, two and only two powers, the United States and the Soviet Union, could conduct a global diplomacy. Within the space of a few years a bipolar system of international politics emerged and with it two opposing spheres of influence. As one of us has argued elsewhere, the Cold War was characterized, at least initially, 'by a concerted attempt by both the United States and the Soviet Union to divide the world into two opposing camps, to impose bipolarity on a global scale'.[39] This period witnessed a tightening of political and military discipline within each camp, the establishment of integrated military alliances, in short a tendency for the locus of decision-making to shift from the nation-state to the bloc.

The Function of the Cold War

This unprecedented reorganization of the international system prompted numerous and often competing interpretations of the Cold War. For the realist school, the East–West confrontation represented first and foremost a global rivalry resting upon a bipolar conflict between the United States and the Soviet Union, the two states which, because of their economic resources, geographic position and military capabilities, had attained an unchallenged pre-eminence over all other states. A closely related but conceptually distinct explanation stressed the functionality of the Cold War, that is its instrumental role in entrenching the dominance or hegemony of the superpowers in their respective camps, a feature starkly reflected in the Brezhnev doctrine of 'limited sovereignty'. In this perspective, the primary function of the East–West conflict has been to maintain internal order or, as Halliday puts it, to provide 'a diversion, a ritual, an excuse, which masks the primacy of conflicts within the societies and between the states of both camps'.[40]

A third and perhaps more widely held view attaches a much higher priority to the ideological factor, likening the Soviet–American dispute to a great contest between two contradictory social and philosophical systems. The order-maintaining function of the Cold War is not thereby invalidated but placed in a wider socioeconomic context. Here order is equated not simply with control or power in an abstract sense but with the stability of a particular social and economic system, notably capitalism or communism. Order thus becomes inseparable from legitimacy, for the function of official ideology is usually to extol the virtues of one's own system while denigrating the aspirations and achievements of the other. Both sides portray themselves as champions of a model of development which others will want or need to emulate. Though ideological claims about workers' democracy on the one hand or political freedom on the other may entail a good deal of hypocrisy, they nevertheless reflect sharply conflicting interests and a tendency towards interventionism, both of which severely militate against state-to-state accommodation. Understood in this sense, the geopolitical, functional and ideological explanations of the Cold War are not mutually exclusive but complementary dimensions of a larger explanatory framework.[41]

While each interpretation highlights different aspects of the conflict and attaches different weights to particular factors, all three reflect to varying degrees certain common themes, namely the emphasis on the globalization of the East–West conflict, the interconnectedness of political, economic and military spheres of action, and the blurring of the dividing line between domestic and foreign policy. We are, in other words, offered a portrayal of the Cold War which, even if located within the strict confines of geopolitical analysis, takes us beyond the traditional image of a fragmented international system comprised of discrete, relatively self-contained, notionally equal sovereign states. Instead, a global security system is postulated, which rests on the twin pillars of strategic deterrence and the East–West ideological divide. Within this global architecture of power the function and importance ascribed to territorial and policy boundaries are substantially qualified.

Alliance Systems

The two opposing alliance systems established in the late 1940s and early 1950s were central to the restructuring of power.[42] Reference has been made to the integrative tendencies implicit in these collective security arrangements.[43] Not only did they accentuate military integration in time of peace but they encouraged a process of political and bureaucratic interdependence whereby the civil and military apparatus of each state became increasingly sensitive to the objectives and priorities of its counterparts in other member states, and in particular the senior ally.

A corollary of this trend was the increasing tendency for security policy in most states, especially junior allies, to be divorced from the domestic political process. Decision-making tended to evade existing mechanisms of public accountability in much of the communist world – a pattern that was generally replicated, perhaps a little less crudely or conspicuously, in many Western countries. All of this is not to suggest that alliances were entirely co-operative institutions, or that strategic planning was devoid of conflict, confusion or contradiction. Within NATO, military procurement was often the subject of fierce wrangling between governments, reflecting divergent political and economic interests and giving rise to prolonged disagreements about contract awards and operational requirements. The drive towards greater European defence co-operation, including collaborative arms procurement projects (e.g. Anglo-French Jaguar, Anglo-French helicopters, Franco-German missiles) was evidence of the European desire to limit subordination to American interests, thereby reinforcing the rivalry–cohesion dichotomy that characterized alliance relationships.

Periodic tensions within the Atlantic alliance about strategic doctrine, diplomatic conduct and apportionment of the defence burden made it clear that the United States could not exercise unlimited power and authority. The intermittent upsurge of nationalist fervour and various forms of cultural and political dissent in Eastern Europe, which often provoked the never altogether successful application of brute force, were indicative of the limits to Soviet dominance. Alliance cohesion was less than total. It did not produce either in the East or in the West a fully integrated political community with autonomous and legitimate central institutions.[44] It would be entirely mistaken, however, to conclude that sovereignty remained intact. To argue that member states were not persuaded to shift, fully or permanently, 'their loyalties or political activities toward a new center whose institutions possess or demand jurisdiction over the pre-existing national states'[45] is one thing; to suggest that the global military system was determined by the decision of sovereign states is quite another.

Even after allowing for intra-alliance tensions and rivalries, the fact remains that the strategic orientation of each bloc, especially at the height of the Cold War, was shaped primarily by superpower interests and priorities. Though the majority of Third World states formally espoused a policy of non-alignment, France withdrew from NATO's integrated military structure and China effectively ended its military alliance with the Soviet Union, even these more striking examples of oppositional behaviour did not radically alter the central strategic balance or substantially modify the domestic and external constraints within which most states – aligned or non-aligned – defined and implemented their security policies. These limitations to national freedom of action reflected in part the vast disparity in military capability between the superpower on the one hand and virtually all other states on the other. The interdependence characteristic of collective security arrangements was inherently asymmetrical. Even with the special Anglo-American relationship, it was widely recognized that 'Britain's dependence on the United States for political support in sustaining its international role, for technical assistance in nuclear matters and for military and political intelligence was markedly greater than any dependence created for the United States on Britain.'[46] In both blocs, the co-ordinating and stabilizing function was performed primarily by the superpowers.

The Function of Détente and the Decline of Bipolarity

With the rise of new centres of power and the ensuing tensions and instabilities, the United States found it increasingly difficult to maintain its hegemonic position in the world economy. Indeed, the 'second Cold War' may be interpreted in part as an attempt by the United States to reassert its hegemony over the Western alliance, particularly in the realm of defence and security, and to use its strategic pre-eminence as a lever with which to extract economic concessions from its allies. But the strategy had only limited success, as evidenced by the growing resistance of America's partners to the extension of its domestic jurisdiction in such areas as antitrust legislation, technology transfer and East–West trade. Increasingly, the United States was perceived as intervening to secure national advantage rather than the stability of the international system.

The subjective perceptions of allies combined with changes in the objective conditions of the US economy to erode the legitimacy and effectiveness of American hegemony. In the case of the Soviet Union the mechanisms at work were rather different but the end result remarkably similar. The structural weakness of the Soviet economy was an important contributing factor and its consequences were if anything more pronounced. Against a background of economic stagnation, the vastly altered strategic environment coupled with mounting domestic ferment and the profound influence exerted by Western Europe's market economies brought about an abrupt end to Soviet military and political dominance in Eastern Europe.

What, then, are the implications of these trends for sovereignty? If the establishment and maintenance of superpower hegemony during the 1950s and 1960s constituted part of a process inimical to the principle of sovereignty, could the subsequent decline of Soviet and American power and the gradual fragmentation, perhaps dissolution, of the two blocs be interpreted as paving the way for the reassertion of the principle? Though plausible, such an interpretation is seriously misleading, for the relationship between hegemony and sovereignty is both complex and variable. The rigidities injected into international relations by ideological and strategic bipolarity were obviously prejudicial to the exercise of sovereignty, but the problem did not lie merely or primarily in the large gap between first-rate and second-rate powers. Rather it stemmed from the creation of a global strategic system of which the two Cold War alliances were an integral part. The distinguishing characteristics of this strategic system were the global application of strategic doctrine, the global reach of weapons systems, and the complex interconnections of regional and global security on the one hand and of economic and military security on the other. The relative Soviet, and to a lesser extent American, decline within the global geopolitical framework and the rapidly diminishing cohesion of their respective alliances did not negate the underlying logic of that global strategic system.

To begin with, changes in the two alliance systems were not merely a function of diminishing Soviet and American influence. The movement towards *détente* which became especially conspicuous during the Gorbachev era had been part and parcel of the East–West relationship for nearly four decades. As we have already observed, oscillation between Cold War and *détente* has been a distinguishing feature of the contemporary strategic system. The Cold War served several important functions: it promoted the cohesion and integration of the two blocs, strengthened the role of ideology thereby legitimizing a complex web of social, political and economic arrangements within each bloc, and gave added impetus and justification on each side to a coalition of converging and overlapping interests, committed to high and rising levels of military expenditure.[47]

In addition the Cold War provided the superpowers with a pretext for maintaining and extending their respective spheres of influence in the Third

World. However, even when viewed from the vantage point of superpower interests, the Cold War was at best a mixed blessing. While encouraging allies to toe the line, it also heightened their fears about future security.[48] In conditions of strategic parity doubts soon emerged about the credibility or reliability of nuclear protection. The superpowers were themselves vulnerable to the risks of nuclear brinkmanship. In conditions of severe tension their military build-up might escalate to the point of unauthorized, inadvertent or accidental war. As for interventionist policies, they almost invariably entailed high diplomatic, economic or military costs. Though they might for a time contribute to this or that objective, naked Cold War politics confronted each superpower with a range of negative repercussions the cumulative weight of which could not be indefinitely ignored.

Détente was therefore an important safety valve, as useful in its own way to superpower interests as confrontation. It set limits to the nuclear arms race, particularly through the arms control mechanism, and enabled both sides to make periodic adjustments to strategic doctrine and force deployments so as to take account of the implications of technological innovation, changing domestic economic circumstances and fluctuations in the global balance of power. *Détente* also provided an opportunity for negotiation on a number of unresolved regional and other conflicts, thereby applying a brake on costly and often unsuccessful military expeditions. Equally important was the need to reassure the governments and electorates of allied countries which had become increasingly fearful of the dangers of counterforce strategies.

East–West security relations have passed through at least five phases in which co-operative arrangements were concluded or at least negotiated: towards the end of the Second World War (agreements about the future of Germany and the establishment of the United Nations); mid-1950s (Austrian peace treaty, Geneva negotiations); early 1960s (Partial Test Ban Treaty, the so-called 'Hot Line' Outer Space Treaty); early 1970s (SALT agreements, ABM Treaty, 'Basic Principles' agreement); mid-1980s (INF agreement, negotiations for strategic and conventional arms reductions).[49] Although the fruits of these co-operative phases were never fully dismantled during the subsequent downturn swing of the cycle, they did not entirely escape impairment.

Given conflicting assumptions and expectations, it is not surprising that *détente* should have proved an ambiguous and spasmodic process, often giving way to renewed bouts of ideological and strategic confrontation despite the perceived benefits of expanded trade, arms control and summit diplomacy. By the same token, the cyclical pattern of the East–West relationship cannot obscure the resilience of *détente*, which is in part explained by the confluence of powerful domestic pressures at work in allied countries as much as in the United States and the Soviet Union.

Pursued in isolation, neither Cold War nor *détente* was capable of satisfying the diverse, rapidly evolving and often contradictory interests of the Soviet and American states. The resulting pendulum swing between Cold War and *détente* represented a continuing attempt by both sides to maximize the advantages and minimize the disadvantages inherent in each strategy. What made the process both confusing and precarious was the chronological and qualitative disjunction between Soviet and American perceptions and responses.[50]

In the euphoria of the Soviet–American thaw in the late 1980s, many were ready, perhaps prematurely, to proclaim the end of the Cold War. The gradual democratization of Soviet politics, the rising revolt against political repression in Eastern Europe, the powerful domestic impetus for the reorganization of the centrally planned economies, coupled with the increasing penetration of foreign capital and growing West European sentiment in favour of denuclearization – these and related factors eventually led to the dismantling of the Berlin Wall and, more generally, the Iron Curtain. By the early 1990s several signs pointed to a new security system based on German reunification, a reduced military role for NATO, the disintegration of the Warsaw Pact and a multi-faceted European institutional framework able to fulfil important security and economic functions.

The movement towards *détente* and the related decline of bipolarity cannot, however, be interpreted as a retreat from the internationalization of the security dilemma, much less as the reassertion of state sovereignty. The international order created at the end of the Second World War rested on two pillars: an integrating world economy and a global security system. Though both pillars have been subjected to powerful and accelerating pressures, there is little to suggest that the processes of economic integration have been reversed, or that security outcomes reflect primarily the decisions of national sovereign actors. To begin with *détente* is a process which includes and to a considerable degree depends on the active participation of the two superpowers. The global strategic balance remains a dominant influence in most regional security systems, as much in Europe as in other parts of the world. Ironically, the diminishing capacity of both superpowers to impose their will on their respective blocs, and in the case of the Soviet Union, the prospect of internal disintegration coupled with the possible breakdown of centralized control over the Soviet nuclear arsenal, has provided a strong incentive for closer diplomatic collaboration and even strategic co-ordination. The East–West thaw of the 1980s was widely interpreted as paving the way for further Soviet–American arms control and disarmament agreement in the early 1990s, the containment, if not resolution, of several regional conflicts (e.g. Southern Africa, Afghanistan, Cambodia, Nicaragua), and a less paralysed UN system with an enhanced peacekeeping function.[51]

Détente and Convergence

Détente, then, may be seen as an important mechanism facilitating the integration of the world polity, world economy and global security system. These processes are, in fact, closely connected. Though the geopolitical and geostrategic equation, both regionally and internationally, remains in a state of flux, the explanation for this is to be found not so much in the sovereign will of nation-states as in the continuing impact of technological change (not least in the military sphere), the interpenetration of national economies, the mobility of transnational capital, and the growth of cross-cultural linkages and exchanges. *Détente*, Soviet–American co-operation and even Soviet decline may be interpreted as a process that has assumed a pivotal role in the globalization of human affairs, in part because it connects the internationalization of economic activity with the internationalization of security relations.

Something of the relationship between *détente* and global integration is suggested by convergence theory. *Détente*, it may be argued, mirrors and reinforces an underlying tendency towards East–West convergence, which impinges not only on superpower relations but on the network of interests tying together the two halves of Europe. The notion of convergence is, of course, neither new nor uncontested. Katchen is probably right in stating that the American conception of *détente* has been traditionally premised more on 'theories of economic, social and political interdependence and convergence' than on 'specific and limited agreements'.[52] For the Soviet Union, on the other hand, *détente*, at least until recently, has had a more pragmatic quality, focusing mainly on the need to consolidate the political and military gains made at the end of the Second World War and the desire to provide the Soviet economy with a larger injection of Western capital and technology.[53]

Notwithstanding the different versions of convergence theory that have gained currency in both political and academic circles, there is a common conceptual core which argues that industrialization and modernization will gradually bridge the gap separating divergent social political and economic systems.[54] The formulation offered in Jan Tinbergen's writings postulates a tendency for opposing systems to converge under the homogenizing influence of technical rationality as mediated by experts and machines, skilled workers and bureaucracies.[55] As evidence of this trend, reference is usually made to the gradual transformation of centrally planned economies, with the introduction of labour incentives, decentralization of economic decision-making and increased interaction with Western economies. As for the capitalist world, the post-1945 period witnessed widespread acceptance of Keynesian macroeconomic policies, which resulted in an expanded public sector and more extensive forms of state intervention. The combination of these two trends gave rise to the notion of a middle ground of which the

Western 'mixed economies' and the reforming economies of Eastern Europe were considered early manifestations. However, more recently, with the rise of the ideology of economic and financial deregulation in the West and the quickening pace of economic reorganization in the East, notions of convergence have tended to acquire a more explicitly Western bias, postulating the demise of the communist experiment and the accelerating incorporation of the Eastern bloc countries into the international market economy.

In the foreseeable future convergence is most likely to gather momentum in the European theatre. Even if NATO should retain a role, likely in any case to be more political than military,[56] the emphasis will be on pan-European structures (e.g. Conference on Security and Co-operation in Europe) and on various forms of economic integration or at least co-ordination. Though the United States will no doubt remain an interested party and an important conduit linking Europe to other theatres of conflict, the drastic reduction of the superpower nuclear and conventional presence on European soil will encourage the development of European institutions and reinforce the cultural and political message encapsulated by such slogans as 'Europe from the Atlantic to the Urals' or the 'Common European Home'.[57] In this process the role of transnational corporations, international banks, supranational institutions and the ethnic, peace, human rights and environmental movements will be no less important than that of national governments.

Convergence theory will obviously continue to be influenced by shifting ideological perceptions and sudden and often unpredictable changes in the economic and political landscape. One thing, however, seems relatively clear: convergence theory under its various guises is pointing to the increasing penetration of physical and cultural space by the global market and to the powerful integrative pressures acting on national economies and national politics. To the extent that *détente* constitutes a diplomatic or strategic manifestation of an underlying current of economic and technological convergence, it may be accurately portrayed as a mechanism of global integration. The sovereign state plays a part in shaping that mechanism, but is in turn shaped by it. What emerges from this discussion is that *détente*, like the Cold War, is part of a complex and rapidly evolving system of strategic and diplomatic interaction that is increasingly global in its scope and consequences. Though the state remains a key actor within that system, its actions and decisions do not necessarily conform to the hypothetical sovereign will or idealized national interest. Rather they are the product of a complex set of sectional interests and relationships that cut across national boundaries and weld together the economic, military and political facets of both domestic and international life.

CONCLUSION

The theory of state sovereignty is steadily losing its explanatory power because it purports to represent the world in a manner that privileges spatial and temporal uniformity. That is, the state is proposed as the irreducible unit of political analysis and sovereign statehood as the immutable principle of political organization. However, as the foregoing survey indicates, the structure of power and authority is undergoing rapid and substantial change. The outcome is a heterogeneous pattern of overlapping allegiances and jurisdictions. Even in the sphere of security relations, where the use of military force as an instrument of statecraft suggests a high degree of historical continuity, we have seen that the ways in which force is threatened or used and the institutional forms through which it is deployed and managed have undergone drastic modification. It is not merely, as Ian Clark explains, that states have changed or that their relationships have changed substantially as a consequence.[58] It is rather that the domestic and international milieu within which they operate has been so transformed as to call into question the meaning of the traditional division between 'inside' and 'outside' on which rests the conceptualization of the sovereign state as a self-contained, territorially bound decisional unit.

Though the capacities of the state have vastly expanded, partly as a function of technical innovation, it does not follow that these capacities strengthen or validate the state's claim to sovereignty. Even in the security arena where the state is supposed to enjoy a monopoly on the legitimate use of force, the proliferation of liberation struggles and separatist movements, not to mention the assortment of mercenary and other 'private' military forces supplied by an expanding black market, points to an increasing dispersion of power. There is, however, a second, more decisive limitation on the state's capacity to act. More and more, the state's military options are influenced, at times almost predetermined, by a wide array of exogenous agencies which include arms manufacturers, banks and other financial institutions, foreign governments, their armed forces and intelligence organizations, and more generally a range of institutional arrangements, including regional and international collective security agreements.

As a result of the close connection between 'domestic' and 'external' agencies, the state's boundaries, far from delineating the domain within which state sovereignty is exercised, represent instead a porous membrane through which both state and non-state actors formulate their policies and conduct their transactions. James Rosenau's attempt to interpret the emerging diversity of this shrinking yet fragmented global system by postulating the coexistence of a 'state-centric world' (constituted of 'sovereignty-bound' actors) and a 'multi-centric world' (made up of 'sovereignty-free' actors) has much to commend it. Yet, as we shall see in Chapter 9, it too underestimates the complexity of political reality and the subtle but profound ways in which sovereignty has been transformed and transferred even in the so-called state-centric world.

The emerging global security system connects not only different geographic regions of the world – in part through the functioning of the central strategic balance and the pendulum swing between superpower rivalry and co-operation – but also different social and economic strata within and between nations. The revival of nationalist sentiment and political independence on the part of many of the communities which formerly comprised the Union of Soviet Socialist Republics, each seeking to distance itself in varying degrees from Moscow's central authority, can at one level be interpreted as the reassertion of the principle of sovereignty. At another level, however, the same process may be said to challenge the Soviet state's own claim to sovereignty. The emerging picture is one of conflicting laws and competing jurisdictions shaped in part by the centrifugal dynamic arising from economic and bureaucratic paralysis on the one hand and the increasing penetration of a market mediated international division of labour on the other.

The complex web of transnational production and finance is a keystone of the global military order, offering crucial analytical insights into the dynamics of military budgets, the pattern of arms transfers, the nature of regional conflicts, and the function of great power military intervention. To put it differently, the security decisions of states are not necessarily the key independent variables of the geopolitical equation. More often than not they are the byproduct of an intricate network of subnational, supranational and transnational interests in which the primary considerations are as much economic as strategic. Issues of peace and war also contain important cultural and ideological influences and transactions, but these are just as likely to weaken as they are to reinforce the sovereignty principle. Appeals to nationalism may give the impression of a distinctive sovereign will at work, but the conditions in which such appeals are made and the consequences to which they give rise suggest instead decentred, pluralistic decision-making processes. Within them we observe competing tendencies towards centralization and decentralization, both of which qualify in different ways and at different times the principle of sovereignty, and create a multi-dimensional political space which territorial sovereignty cannot fully occupy, much less displace or illuminate.

NOTES

1. For a lucid exposition of the external meaning of sovereignty and its application to the contemporary world, see Geoffrey L. Godwin, 'The Erosion of External Sovereignty?', in James Barber and Michael Smith (eds), *The Nature of Foreign Policy: A Reader*, Edinburgh: Holmes McDougall in association with the Open University Press, 1974, pp. 45–57.
2. The state-centric analysis of the security dilemma, which dominates the international relations literature, tends to depict the relationship between rival states as a zero-sum game. See, for example, Thomas Schelling, *Arms and Influence*, New Haven, Conn.: Yale University Press, 1966; Robert Jervis, 'Co-operation under the Security Dilemma', *World Politics*, **30**, (2), January 1978, 167–214.
3. J.P. Nettl, 'The State as a Conceptual Variable', *World Politics*, **20**, 1968, 564.
4. For an analysis of the connection between the state's economic and war-making functions, see Charles Tilly, 'Reflections on the History of European State-Building', in Charles Tilly (ed.), *The Formation of National States in Western Europe*, Princeton, NJ: Princeton University Press, 1975, pp. 42, 54, 73–4; C.F. Doran, 'War and Power Dynamics: Economic Underpinnings', *International Studies Quarterly*, **27**, 1983, 419–44; George Modelski, 'The Long Cycle of Global Politics and the Nation-State', *Comparative Studies in Society and History*, **20**, April; K.A. Rasler and W.R. Thompson, 'Global Wars, Public Debts, and the Long Cycle', *World Politics*, **35**, 1983, 489–516; Immanuel Wallerstein, *The Politics of the World Economy*, Cambridge: Cambridge University Press, 1984, ch. 4.
5. Raymond Aron argues that much of modern warfare is integrally connected with the principle of legitimacy, and therefore by implication with its corollary, the principle of sovereignty. See his *Peace and War: A Theory of International Relations*, trans. R. Howard and A. Baker Fox, Garden City, NY: Doubleday, 1966, p. 156.
6. E.H. Carr, *The Twenty Years' Crisis 1919–1939: An Introduction to the Study of International Relations*, London: Macmillan, 1962, p. 228.
7. T.S. Marty, *Frontiers: A Changing Concept*, New Delhi: Palit & Palit, 1978, p. 50.
8. Friedrich Kratochwil, 'Of Systems, Boundaries and Territoriality; An Inquiry into the Formation of the State System', *World Politics*, **39**, October 1986, 35.
9. Ibid., p. 36.
10. Ibid, p. 38.
11. See J. Camilleri, 'The Cold War', in Max Teichmann (ed.), *Powers and Policies Alignments and Realignments in the Indo-Pacific Region*, Melbourne: Cassell Australia, 1970, pp. 16–24.
12. Kratochwil, 'Of Systems, Boundaries and Territoriality', p. 43.
13. See Paul Keal, *Unspoken Rules and Superpower Dominance*, London: Macmillan, 1984.
14. Bruce Russett and Harvey Starr, *World Politics: The Menu for Choice*, New York: W.H. Freeman, 1989, p. 522.
15. See, for example, Charles Pentland, 'Functionalism and Theories of International Political Integration', in A.R.J. Groom and Paul Taylor (eds), *Theory and Practice in International Relations: Functionalism*, New York: Crane, Russak, 1975; Ernst Haas, *Beyond the Nation-State*, Stanford: Stanford University Press, 1964; David Mitrany, *A Working Peace System*, Chicago: Quadrangle Books, 1966.
16. The following list is but a small sample of the many studies that seek to grapple with the transnationalization of international relations: W.F. Hanreider, 'International Organisations and International Systems', *Journal of Conflict Resolution*, **10**, September 1966, 297–313; Robert O. Keohane and Joseph S. Nye, Jr *Transnational Relations and World Politics*, Cambridge, Mass.: Harvard University Press, 1972; Oran R. Young, 'The Actors in World Politics', in James N. Rosenau, Vincent Davis and Maurice A. East (eds), *The Analysis of International Politics*, New York: Free Press, 1972; Richard W. Mansbach, Yale H. Ferguson and Donald E. Lampert, *The Web of World Politics: Non State Actors in the Global System*, Englewood Cliffs, NJ: Prentice-Hall, 1976.
17. Shirley Williams, 'Sovereignty and Accountability in the European Community', *The Political Quarterly*, **61**, (3), July–September 1990, 299.

18. See John Pinder, 'European Community and Nation-State: A Case for a Neo-Federalism?', *International Affairs*, **62**, (1), 1985–6, 41–54.

19 See William Wallace, 'What Price Independence? Sovereignty and Interdependence in British Politics', *International Affairs*, **62**, (3), 1985–6, 367–87.

20. Perhaps the standard text in this genre is Robert 0. Keohane and Joseph S. Nye, *Power and Interdependence: World Politics in Transition*, Boston: Little Brown, 1977; see also James N. Rosenau, *The Study of Global Interdependence*, London: Frances Pinter, 1980, especially chs 1, 3–4.

21. Lincoln P. Bloomfield, 'Coping with Conflict in the Late Twentieth Century', *International Journal*, **44**, (4), Autumn 1989, 777.

22. For a useful analysis of the interaction between the dynamics of social change in a Third World context and superpower rivalry, see George Modelski, 'The International Relations of Internal War', in James N. Rosenau (ed.), *International Aspects of Civil Strife*, Princeton, NJ: Princeton University Press, 1964; also Richard Little, *Intervention: External Involvement in Civil Wars*, Totowa, NJ: Rowman & Littlefield, 1975.

23. For a comprehensive outline of the principles of non-alignment, see A.W. Singham and Shirley Hune, *Non-Alignment in an Age of Alignments*, London: Zed, 1986; also Peter Willetts, *The Non-Aligned Movement*, London: Frances Pinter, 1978; K.K. Das Gupta, 'The Non-Aligned Movement and the New International Economic Order: Some Conceptual Issues', *The Non-Aligned World*, **2**, (2), April–June 1984, 273–84; M.S. Rajan, 'Non-Alignment: The Dichotomy between Theory and Practice in Europe', *India Quarterly*, **36**, January–March 1980, 43–63.

24. For a more detailed examination of these trends see J.A. Camilleri, *Civilization in Crisis*, especially chs 2 and 9; Seyon Brown, *New Forces, Old Forces and the Future of World Politics*, Glenview, Ill.: Scott, Foresman/Little, Brown, 1988, especially chs 9, 13, 14.

25. Stephen D. Krasner, 'Sovereignty: An Institutional Perspective', *Comparative Political Studies*, **21**, (1), April 1988, 89.

26. Richard Haass, 'The Primacy of the State ... or Revising the Revisionists', *Daedalus*, **108**, (4), Fall 1979, 126.

27 Ibid., p. 127.

28. James N. Rosenau, 'Patterned Chaos in Global Life, Structure and Process in the Two Worlds of World Politics', *International Political Science Review*, **9**, (4), October, p. 341.

29. For a comprehensive list see Bloomfield, 'Coping with Conflict', pp. 778–80,788–90.

30. John H. Herz, *International Politics in the Atomic Age*, New York: Columbia University Press, 1959, p. 169.

31. The multi-dimensional impact of the new technology helps to explain Herz's rethinking on the subject. See John Herz, *The Nation-State and the Crisis in World Politics*, New York: David McKay, 1976.

32. See George M. Thomson, *The Twelve Days: July 24 to August 4. 1914*, New York: G.P. Putnam's Sons, 1964; Jerome D. Frank, *Sanity and Survival: Psychological Aspects of War and Peace*, New York: Vintage Books, 1967, pp. 178–82; Ole R. Holsti and Robert C. North, 'The History of Human Conflict', in Elton B. McNeil (ed.), *The Nature of Human Conflict*, Englewood Cliffs, NJ: Prentice-Hall, 1965.

33. See Russett and Starr, *World Politics*, pp. 377–81; K.S. Holsti, *International Politics: A Framework for Analysis*, Englewood Cliffs, NJ: Prentice-Hall, 1972, pp. 317–25; Ole R. Hosti, *Crisis, Escalation, War*, Montreal and London: McGill-Queen's University Press, 1972.

34. For a penetrating exposition of this argument see Michael Howard, 'War and the Nation-State', *Daedalus*, **108**, (4), Fall 1979, 101–10.

35. Trevor Taylor, 'Defence Industries in International Relations', *Review of International Studies*, **16**, (1), January 1990, 70.

36. For an early but limited attempt to grapple with the notion see Mary Kaldor and Absjørn Eide, *The World Military Order: The Impact of Military Technology on the Third World*, New York: Praeger, 1979. A more recent but largely impressionist account is offered by Giri Deshingkar, 'Arms, Technology, Violence and the Global Military Order', in Raimo Väyrynen (ed.), *The Quest for Peace: Transcending Collective Vio-*

lence and War among Societies, Cultures and States, London: Sage, 1987, pp. 260–74; see also Albert Bergesen, 'Cycles of War in the Reproduction of the World Economy', in Paul M. Johnson and William R. Thompson (eds), *Rhythms in Politics and Economics*, New York: Praeger, 1985.

37. See Richard Falk, 'The State System and Contemporary Social Movements', in Saul H. Mendlovitz and R.B.J Walker (eds), *Towards a Just World Peace*, London: Butterworths, 1987, pp. 17–48; Nigel Young, 'The Peace Movement, Peace Research, Peace Education and Peace Building', *Bulletin of Peace Proposals*, **18**, (3), 1987, 331–49.

38. Nettl, 'The State as a Conceptual Variable', p. 575.

39. J.A. Camilleri, 'Towards an Understanding of the International System', in Teichmann, *Powers and Policies*, p. 17.

40. Fred Halliday, *The Making of the Second Cold War*, London: Verso, 1983, p. 42.

41. Ibid., pp. 42–5.

42. For a description of the structure and decision-making processes of the two alliances, see Richard W. Mansbach, Yale H. Ferguson, Donald E. Lampert, *The Web of World Politics: Non State Actors in the Global System*, Englewood Cliffs, NJ: Prentice-Hall, 1976, pp. 213–26; also Andrzej Korbonski, 'The Warsaw Pact', *International Conciliation*, **63**, May 1969, 5–73; Arnold Wolfers (ed.), *Alliance Policy in the Cold War*, Baltimore: Johns Hopkins Press, 1959; Kazimierz Grybowski, *The Socialist Commonwealth of Nations*, New Haven, Conn.: Yale University Press, 1964.

43. Mary Kaldor, *The Baroque Arsenal*, London: Abacus, 1983, p. 98.

44. This is very much the conclusion reached by Francis A. Beer in *Integration and Disintegration in NATO: Processes of Alliance Cohesion and Prospects for Atlantic Community*, Columbus: Ohio State University Press, 1969.

45. Ibid., p. 3.

46. Wallace, 'What Price Independence?', p. 370.

47. See John Kenneth Galbraith, *The New Industrial State*, Harmondsworth, Middlesex: Penguin, 1969, pp. 323–38; also G. Prins (ed.), *Defended to Death*, Harmondsworth, Middlesex: Penguin, 1983, pp. 133–68.

48. See Jane M.D. Sharp, 'NATO's Security Dilemma', *Bulletin of the Atomic Scientists*, **43**, (2), March 1987, 42–4.

49. Volker R. Hberger and Michael Zürn, *Towards Regulated Anarchy in East–West Relationship – Causes and Consequences of East–West Régimes*, Tübingen: Arbeitspapiere zur internationalen Politik und Friedensforschung, No. 11, 1989, pp. 1–2.

50. For a very helpful discussion of *détente* in the Nixon period see Stanley Hoffman, 'Détente', in Joseph S. Nye (ed.), *The Making of America's Soviet Policy*, New Haven, Conn.: Yale University Press, 1984, pp. 231–63.

51. See Bloomfield, 'Coping with Conflict', pp. 783–6, 791–4.

52. Howard M. Katchen, 'Interdependence, Convergence and the Economic Bases of Détente,' *Jerusalem Journal of International Relations*, **4**, (4), 1980, 14.

53. For a helpful exposition of the scope and limitations of East–West interdependence as it had progressed in the 1960s and early 1970s, see Franklyn D. Holzman and Robert Legvold, 'The Economics and Politics of East–West Relations', *International Organization*, Winter 1975, 274–320.

54. See, for example, Z.K. Brzezinski and S. Huntington, *Political Power: U.S.A./U.S.S.R.*, New York: Viking Press, 1965, pp. 419–38.

55. See Jan Tinbergen, *International Economic Integration*, Amsterdam: Elsevier, 1965.

56. See Starky B. Sloane, 'NATO's Future in a New Europe, An American Perspective', *International Affairs*, **63**, (3), 1990, 498.

57. Pierre Hassner, 'Europe beyond Partition and Unity', *International Affairs*, **63**, (3), 1990, 467.

58. Ian Clark, *The Hierarchy of States: Reform and Resistance in the International Order*, Cambridge: Cambridge University Press, 1989, p. 212.

7. Ecological Crisis

It is helpful here to remind ourselves that the idea of sovereignty which we have identified in this book suggests a particular view not only of the social but also of the physical world. The sovereign domain is a physical area. The sovereign state (whether ruling by itself or on behalf of the community) exercises its supreme authority not only over the people who comprise the national community but also over the course of events (both social and physical) within its domain.

For this to be so, the sovereign domain, and all that belongs to it, must be clearly demarcated from all other domains. There must not only be a clearly demarcated national territory, but also a clearly distinguished national society, economy and ecology. Further, if the state is truly sovereign, its supreme authority cannot be limited in time. It must extend backwards and forwards, having already given shape to the domain's history and now promising to shape its future.

Taken together these propositions have far-reaching implications for the theory of sovereignty. Ultimately a world partitioned into sovereign domains is a world of domains with static, uncontestable physical boundaries. Within these the state must have absolute authority, not only now but indefinitely into the future. It follows that if the world is entirely composed of sovereign states, then the boundaries of each domain are not only fixed and immutable in space, they are also fixed and immutable in time. Sovereignty is not just a theory about the past and present, but a never-ending prescription for an eternal future.

As we have already noted, the above is not a description of the actual state of affairs in nation-states. Rather it is a theoretical construct. This theory is, however, frequently invoked in the interests of describing, explaining and justifying a wide range of important policies and actions. Here the legitimacy of this sovereignty discourse derives from the extent to which the theory appears to explain reality. As the ability of the theory of sovereignty to explain the world weakens, the legitimacy of the discourse is consequently eroded. Nowhere is this clearer than in the growing gulf between the description of reality implied in the discourse of sovereignty and our emerging understanding of the ecological dynamics of the biosphere (in which we all live).

One profound deficiency in the sovereignty discourse is the suggestion that the sovereign power can exercise supreme authority over its domain. In medieval Europe, when God was considered the supreme law-giver, this was perhaps less problematic. But the modern state supposedly derives its authority from and governs on behalf of the people whose power is (comparatively) puny. The divine architect may have been presumed to be omnipotent and therefore unhindered in fashioning the universe. But people live in the universe, restricted by the natural constraints that exist between all the physical and biological processes and human activity, which together constitute the biosphere. As ecological problems impinge with increasing sharpness on our consciousness, individuals, communities and states are confronted with challenges, concepts and perspectives which are at odds with the simplified image of the world upon which the theory of sovereignty was itself originally constructed.

THE EMERGENCE OF THE ECOLOGICAL CHALLENGE

The concept of sovereignty is coming under challenge from another more 'ecological' view of the world. On the one hand we have a conception of a world divided into separate, independent communities, delineated clearly in time and space, governed by their own sovereign authority and system of law. On the other hand is a conception of a physical, ecological and social totality, a single community of humans and other species, ultimately governed equally by natural law. We have already discussed how the former – the image of a world of sovereign states – has emerged historically over some four centuries. At the same time, though perhaps less obviously, the picture of an ecologically bound world has developed through a long and parallel history.

Rich concepts of natural constraint can often be found in Christian as well as pre-Christian cultures. For example, Christian doctrine in the twelfth and thirteenth centuries held that the universe was ruled by God's principles, which in turn were reflections of divine purpose.[1] God's desire and plan were considered to be perfect and therefore unchallengeable. By contrast, humans and their values were seen as imperfect. Physical theories could be deduced from this understanding, with the natural world moving and developing in ways which attempted to overcome imperfection. For example, stones when lifted and dropped would seek to return to their natural resting place upon the ground, which was the place reserved for them in the supreme design. There developed a clear distinction between the perfection of the 'natural' design of God and the imperfection of the 'artificial' designs of human beings. Fittingly, nature, as an expression of the divine will, was also understood as presenting instructions and hidden meanings for humanity, to be read along with the Bible as a text which could reveal God's purposes. In this, humans were in subtle ways bound not only physically but even ethically by the natural order.

Christianity has been a complex doctrine subjected to and embodying diverse interpretations. Not surprisingly there has been and continues to be a debate about precisely what role Christian thought has at various times attributed or should attribute to humans in relation to the natural world. As David Pepper points out,[2] at least two contradictory elements can be discerned – one in which humanity has been seen as part of nature, and another in which humanity has assumed the role of steward over nature. In this latter view, humans may play a dominant role transforming the natural world. This interpretation, which also has deep roots, has become more prominent as the instrumental ideologies of science, progress and economic development have become more dominant. As Charles Glacken puts it:

> In the period roughly from the end of the fifteenth century until the end of the seventeenth century one sees ideas of man as controller of nature beginning to crystallise, along more modern lines... a unique formulation of Western thought, marking itself off from the other great traditions, such as the Indian and Chinese... in the twentieth century Western man has attained a breathtaking anthropocentrism, based on his power over nature, unmatched by anything in the past.[3]

Despite frequent suggestions to the contrary, 'environmentalism' too, at least expressed in terms of concern about the impact of human development on the integrity of the physical world, is not just a product of the last few decades. As Richard Grove demonstrates,[4] its roots in the West go back at least to the middle of the sixteenth century, deepening and broadening along with the unfolding of the anthropocentric view of humanity, the Renaissance, colonization, industrialization and the coherence and expansion of the capitalist market.

In Christian and Jewish culture the idea of conservation reaches back to the biblical story of the primal unsullied natural garden of Eden. During the period of European expansion at the time of the Renaissance this image was sought in the 'untouched' world which the process of exploration and colonization was beginning to penetrate. From the fifteenth century, tropical islands with their rich botanical diversity became symbols of the lost paradise. Later India, Africa and the Americas gained something of the same symbolic quality, with their inhabitants stereotyped as the 'noble savage', untouched by 'civilization'.

The process of discovery and colonization goes hand in hand with an emergent understanding that the earth's resources are not unlimited and that deliberate policies of conservation may be needed. This consciousness began to take root in the middle of the seventeenth century in the context of the commercial expansion of the Dutch and English East India Companies. The discovery of new and peculiar species of flora on St Helena and Mauritius underlined the dangers of the extinction of species in the face of human intervention. By the late eighteenth century this consciousness had given rise to full-scale experimentation, with Mauritius providing a site for systematic trials of forest conservation, pollution control and fisheries protection.

Already, in France, Germany and Britain, there was an emerging aware-ness not only of the possible danger of extinction of species, but also of soil erosion and the climatic consequences of deforestation (in particular loss of rainfall and 'desiccation' of land). The contrast between the destructive practices of colonial administrations and those of the indigenous cultures which had often maintained the land in at least quasi-stability for hundreds or thousands of years, helped develop and focus this awareness into a sharper concern. The growing influence of scientists, including botanists, in plan-ning and policy helped galvanize concern into action. Some of the first large-scale attempts at re-afforestation, as in India, with pressure from the indigenous aristocracy, were made at the end of the eighteenth century.

Concern was also rising over the global impact of industrialization. As early as 1827 the physicist-mathematician Jean Baptiste Fourier warned that human activity since the industrial revolution could seriously interfere with the earth's climate.[5] In 1858 J. Spotswood Wilson presented a paper to the British Association for the Advancement of Science on 'The General and Gradual Desiccation of the Earth and Atmosphere'. He warned that the changing ratio of carbonic acid and oxygen in the atmosphere was gradually producing a state of the earth 'in which it will be impossible for man to continue as an inhabitant'.[6] In 1896, in a landmark article ('On the Influence of Carbonic Acid in the Air upon the Temperature of the Ground') the Swedish chemist Savante Arrhenius laid the theoretical foundations for the quantitative analysis of the possibility that the release of industrial gases (and in particular carbon dioxide) could cause global warming with poten-tially significant impact on global climate. Remarkably consistent with the calculations of almost a century later, he predicted that if carbon dioxide levels in the earth's atmosphere were to double, the average surface tem-perature could increase by 4 to 6 degrees centigrade.[7]

By the 1860s, anxiety about the changes to climate and the extinction of species that could accompany Western industrialization had reached a new level of intensity, at least amongst several leading scientists. But the transla-tion of this consciousness into practical action had to be mediated by the state. It was not that the state was unreceptive to such arguments. However, from the beginning one thing was clear. As Grove remarks:

If there is one single historical lesson to be drawn from the early history of conservation under the East India Company and the ancien régime of Mauritius, it is that states can be persuaded to act to prevent environmental degradation only when their economic interests are shown to be directly threatened.[8]

During the first half of the nineteenth century many of the colonial states were particularly receptive to the frequently radical agendas of the scientific lobby on environmental issues. Operating, as it often did, with unusually centralized and far-reaching powers, the colonial state became a forum for debate about environmental controls, a development that might not have otherwise occurred. The long-term security of the state, which negative ecological effects, such as famine, threatened to undermine, often counted for more than private interests bent upon reaping maximum benefit from the land, irrespective of environmental cost.

The state's growing interest in environmental control thus developed historically side by side with the industrial and agricultural practices which accompanied the spread and intensification of capitalism. Even at this early stage significant differences in practice had emerged between the periphery (primarily comprised of colonies) and the imperial centres. The colonies provided the social structure and resources for social and environmental experimentation. The mixture of a highly centralized, technocratic decision-making structure and the availability of what was then regarded as 'virgin' land provided the opportunity and incentive for the colonial state to experiment with new forms of environmental regulation aimed at maximizing the long-term usefulness and viability of the colony. Significantly, it was Australia's colonial legislatures in Tasmania and Victoria which, in the 1860s, introduced the first comprehensive laws aimed at protecting indigenous birds from extinction.[9] In addition, frontier values helped underpin a more romantic attachment to wilderness. In the United States the Sierra Club (which became the guiding force behind the establishment of Yosemite National Park) was founded in 1892.[10]

Back in the imperial centres of the expanding capitalist market there emerged a similar and growing concern about environmental problems. Here the focus of attention was less the longevity of natural resources, and more the direct impact of industrialization. In Britain at the beginning of the nineteenth century, Thomas Malthus warned that population was growing at a rate that would exceed the growth in food supply. His attention was directed particularly to the growth of the urban proletariat.

It was the devastating local effects accompanying the shift to industrial production and the resultant rapid growth of cities which became the main focus of attention in London, the pre-eminent imperial centre of industrial capitalism. Thick palls of smoke choked such cities as the use of coal spread and intensified, giving rise to disturbing levels of local air pollution. The effects of acid from coal burning were noticed as early as the end of the nineteenth century[11] but the full impact of 'acid rain' would not become evident for another fifty years.[12]

Not long after the first acidic effects of air pollution had been officially observed, Theodore Roosevelt called the first conservation conference to be held in the White House. Convened in 1908, the conference discussed proposals for preserving various aspects of the physical environment.[13] It was the precursor of numerous government resource agencies established in the United States over the next fifty years. Though these were generally dedicated to the 'wise use' of the country's minerals, public lands, water, forests, wildlife and fisheries,[14] as with the colonial administrations, the comparative wisdom of different projects was judged mostly on the basis of potential economic gain. Conservation was still a matter of the state regulating the use of its domain to obtain maximum economic benefit, with little attention paid to the long-term economic costs associated with the loss of valuable environmental resources.

Initially, as already mentioned, it was in the colonies (the periphery) that significant steps were first taken towards environmental regulation. Later the pattern was reversed, with the metropolitan states directing more attention to the regulation of their own environments, while exporting many of the more environmentally damaging activities to the less regulated periphery. What persisted was an enduring asymmetry between core and periphery, with the pattern of environmental regulation mediated not just by the pattern of physical disruption, but also by the architecture of social and political organization. For reasons peculiar to the administration of the colonies (in particular, the centralization of authority characteristic of colonial government), it was less difficult for the colonial state to formulate an early response. Conversely, in metropolitan centres, for reasons to do with the more diffuse pattern of ownership, interest articulation and power, it was more difficult for the state to act.

The history of both core and periphery is thus one of human intervention reflecting existing patterns of social organization, but leading to the increasing disruption of the physical world. Yet that world follows physical principles and reflects a natural economy which takes no account of human perspectives. So long as the physical impact of human intervention remained largely contained within national boundaries, it was possible to believe that existing social structures could be successfully adapted to meet the challenges posed by the impact of human activity on one biosphere. However, this could not continue unchallenged indefinitely. Some eighty years after the first national environmental conference had been convened in the White House, it was already becoming clear that the political organization of a world based upon sovereign states would have to undergo substantial modification in order to grapple more effectively with global problems arising from human intervention in the biosphere.

ECOLOGICAL IMPACT AND THE SOVEREIGN DOMAIN

On 26 April 1985 in the Ukraine near Kiev, the Chernobyl reactor caught fire. As the fire raged, and then smouldered, over some ten days vast quantities of radioactive gases poured into the air. The plume of radioactive gases swept across Scandinavia, then spread southwards over other parts of Europe, moving on to contaminate parts of England, and then dispersing over an even wider area causing significant increases in radiation levels as far afield as Japan.[15] A number of governments were forced to introduce emergency measures – from monitoring radiation levels to withdrawing certain foodstuffs or advising communities to change their diet. The number of deaths that will ultimately result from the accident remains the subject of scientific controversy. What became clear from the first few days was that although national governments might construct nuclear reactors and even lay down various regulations intended to make their operation safer, the actual risk they posed extended beyond the control of any single state.

Perhaps because of its dramatic quality, the burning reactor demonstrated in a period of just a few days the large discrepancy between the sovereignty model and contemporary ecological and technological reality. In the wake of the Chernobyl accident the fixed boundaries of the national domain and the supposedly supreme authority of the sovereign state were effortlessly disregarded by the drifting clouds of radioactive gas, the hard reality of fallible technology, and the natural but profoundly threatening impact of radiation on both the biosphere and individual human bodies.

The Chernobyl accident points to the striking clash of very different constructions of reality. The traditional description of a world broken into hermetically partitioned sovereign states was confronted by a biosphere emerging ever more clearly as a single integrated whole. On the one hand, the political system was obstructing a solution to the problem posed by transnational air pollution. On the other, the system was under increasing pressure to devise a solution. It was clear that any such solution would require not only recognition of the extent to which the sovereign domain was now vulnerable to external environmental pressure, but also a readiness to surrender a degree of its authority in order to regulate the possible recurrence of accidents. Viewed as an isolated incident, the Chernobyl accident need not be seen as a challenge to the concept of sovereignty; the questions posed by it could theoretically remain unanswered. But Chernobyl represented just one in a long series of similar but increasingly frequent and serious accidents.

In the wake of the Chernobyl fire the International Atomic Energy Agency convened international conferences which drafted two new conventions setting out procedures for handling the effects of future nuclear accidents – a Convention on Early Notification, and a Convention on Assistance in the Event of a Nuclear Accident. Some sixty countries signed the two conventions, although two years after the accident only ten countries had yet ratified the first convention, with a mere six being prepared to commit themselves legally to providing the assistance required by the second convention.[16] The transfer of authority to an international regulatory regime was under way but proceeding slowly in the face of powerful vested interests and institutional inertia.

The Chernobyl accident graphically illustrates how the physical environment is now integrated with human technology on a scale which is truly global. Other examples, including the breaching of the ozone layer, the threat of the 'nuclear winter' and the danger of global warming due to the emission of greenhouse gases into the atmosphere, have given added weight to this perspective. More and more the world appears as a single technical and physical system in which technological developments in one place may produce effects virtually anywhere in the world. Rapid changes in transport and communication are making the earth appear smaller, compressing the distances that separate communities and regions. More generally the earth seems to be shrinking in relation to the escalating impact of the constantly growing processes of global industrialization. As these expand to a scale and power comparable to processes in the biosphere, they become a new part of that system, transforming its dynamics along an uncertain, but not necessarily benign, trajectory.

An environmental problem, of course, does not need to be global in extent to challenge supposedly sovereign boundaries. In Europe the burning sulphur-rich coal in one country may spread acid rain far beyond that country's boundaries. More generally, a high level of industrial pollution is borne by air and water across the continent unfettered by supposedly sovereign boundaries. As a result, different states struggle to regulate environmental problems over whose generation they have at best partial and often little or no control,[17] which explains their increasing efforts to find collaborative means to solve the common problems.

The attempts to find ways of coping with trans-boundary environmental problems in Europe must be understood within the context of the advancing process of European integration. With a significant number of advanced industrial economies tightly locked together on a single continent, national borders and independent planning and administrative institutions represent a framework which is proving progressively less and less able to fulfil their collective desire for economic development. The recognition that economic flows do not correspond with the theory and practice of sovereignty has led to slow but steady progress towards regional economic organization which removes the impediments to economic flows arising from national sovereignty. Although the first steps to overcome the constraints imposed were taken in the economic arena these have in turn helped to establish mechanisms capable of meeting other common problems. It is not surprising, then, that the attempt to deal with trans-boundary environmental problems should have led to a further elaboration of this regional political framework, opening up new areas of supranational regulation. In 1972 the EEC set up a Community environment policy. Over the next 17 years it issued over 100 directives and regulations in the area of environmental protection.

The point here is not that the trend towards supranational regulation is consummated or completely successful. Indeed, despite efforts so far undertaken and the willingness of member nations to cede key powers to the regional organization, even the problem of acid rain remains largely unresolved.[18] The point is that the very attempt to meet such problems has steadily forced the various states of the European Community, despite rhetoric to the contrary, in the direction of constructing monitoring and regional planning mechanisms which are ultimately neither predicated on nor explained by the theory of sovereignty.

THE ECOLOGICAL IMPACT OF SOVEREIGNTY

Enough has been said to suggest that the growing attention to ecological problems is beginning to pose a serious problem for the theory of sovereignty. First, the principle of sovereignty is an impediment to action designed to ameliorate critical ecological dilemmas. Secondly, it is itself a major contributing cause of the environmental problems which confront humanity. We now examine in a little more detail the nature of these two features of sovereignty.

We begin by returning again to one of the central features of sovereignty – its reliance on the use of armed force. As we have already remarked, the monopoly exercised by the nation-state over the legitimate use of force is itself eroding. Yet access to military power remains one of the central characteristics distinguishing the state from the welter of other organizations which now occupy the national and international arena. The state's use and threat of armed force continues, as we have seen, to play a key role in the sovereignty discourse, justifying the continued importance of the state in the exercise of military power in defence of the national interest and the sovereign domain. However, the claim that the state's military power is required in the interests of long-term security is now coming into conflict with the interaction of the use of military power and the properties of the biological and physical world.

The 1990 crisis in the Persian Gulf again provides a useful example. From one vantage point the whole sequence of events following Iraq's invasion of Kuwait (including the assembling of the US-led fleet of warships in the Persian Gulf, the economic sanctions imposed by the United Nations Security Council, and the subsequent war) could be interpreted as a firm endorsement of the enduring value of the theory and practice of sovereignty. But from an ecological perspective the kind of war that ensued, ostensibly in support of the principle of sovereignty, also brought to light serious difficulties inherent in the principle. In part these derived from the sheer destructive capability of the military arsenals which had massed together in readiness for combat. These included vast quantities of conventional explosives, chemical weapons and nuclear weapons. For its part Iraq made it clear that it reserved the right to use its considerable stockpile of devastatingly effective chemical weapons should the stand-off move to a shooting match. In response, the Chairman of the Senate Armed Services Committee of the US Congress, Senator Sam Nunn, made it equally clear that the United States reserved the right to use battlefield nuclear weapons as both a moral and practical option.[19] In the event the most indiscriminate weapons of mass destruction were not utilized. Nevertheless, the enormous oil slick and the deliberate ignition of oil wells that resulted from the war created a serious threat to the climate, marine ecology and water resources shared by many countries in the region.

Since the most powerful weapons of mass destruction have yet to be used, the above only suggests the direction in which war may be leading us. Nuclear war, for example, could cause far bigger volumes of smoke than the oil wells ignited in Kuwait, perhaps sufficient to generate a 'nuclear winter', which could persist in many parts of the world, perhaps for several years.[20] More generally, as the technology of war attains higher levels of destructiveness, it is not just states that become vulnerable, but the biosystem itself. The use of weapons is facilitated by the discourse of sovereignty, which constructs a world conceptually partitioned into a set of discrete and to some extent threatening and threatened communities, and by the accompanying celebration of 'states' which derive much of their authority not only from their control of military power but their readiness to use it. But as the consciousness of ecological vulnerability sharpens, the claim that the sovereignty of nations can be protected by the use of advanced weapons systems may well be undermined by the devastating impact of their use.

THE INSTRUMENTAL CHARACTER OF THE STATE

The use of military technology is only one way in which the theory of sovereignty, corresponding state action and the biosphere come into conflict. Perhaps more instructive is the strongly instrumental, even technocratic, emphasis which lies at the root of state planning and action.

In most contemporary societies the sovereign state derives much of its legitimacy in the exercise of supreme authority from its claim to justice and truth. In this we can see the legacy of an earlier period. As the canons of the councils of Toledo put it: 'The two principal royal virtues are justice and truth, (science of the reason).'[21] The claim to justice often still relies on the continued application of quite traditional processes of judicial judgement and law. In practice it is supported by a modern and increasingly sophisticated structure of experts, technological departments and elaborate scientific theories and processes. The legitimacy of the modern industrial state is now deeply dependent on its claim to expertise in economic policy, environmental control, infrastructure planning and administration. Much of the 'official discourse' of the state[22] is expressed in terms of management based on the application of technical criteria, with the organs of the state heavily dependent on either their own technical experts or hired technical consultants.

The state's assertion of the right to exercise supreme authority over the national domain derives, in no small measure, from two subsidiary claims. First, as we have already noted, it claims to represent the national interest because of a special relationship to the people (perhaps mediated through the electoral process). Secondly, it claims to represent the national interest through its access to instrumental rationality. Of all institutions, the state claims to have the best technical capabilities for assessing, enunciating and satisfying the nation's material and psychological needs. This latter claim to instrumental legitimacy is frequently matched by a pronounced tendency on the part of the state to solve problems through technical means rather than by attempting to reshape the cultural values and social, political or economic relations which may lie at the heart of those problems.

By any account, technological thinking and intervention have produced extraordinary successes. But these derive from a single-minded approach to the complex system of the biosphere, whereby much of that complexity is overlooked, leaving only that which can be readily understood and modelled.[23] This mind-set has produced extremely effective ways of transforming our immediate environment in ways which are both useful and predictable.

Yet at the same time this reductionist approach obscures from view many of the interactions which, over the longer term, have kept the entire system stable and permitted humanity's collective survival. By organizing human physical intervention as if these interactions were not important, and by

moulding the immediate physical environment to suit more narrowly conceived specifications, the tendency has been systematically to ignore the
way this weakens the fabric of stabilizing interactions. The destruction of
the ozone layer, the stripping of forests, the elimination of species, the
pollution of oceans and the threat of nuclear winter and global warming all
testify to the critical long-term ecological implications of this reductionist
instrumental approach.

Consider the problem of atmospheric pollution. Here at least some states
have been open to the idea of implementing technological solutions. Some,
for example, have begun to plan for changes in the technology of electricity
production, in part by building natural gas or nuclear power stations in place
of coal-powered stations (thereby reducing the emissions of carbon, nitrogen
and sulphur oxides). Yet states have generally proved far more reluctant to
enter into the co-operative social arrangements needed to tackle the more
fundamental problem of changing the nature, organization and values of
society in order, for example, to reduce the energy consumption which
requires the pollutants to be produced in the first place.

To put it more succinctly, the state is not only a major consumer but also
a producer of technological thinking in contemporary society. Underlying
the environmental problems which now confront humanity are the same
reductionist technological approaches to the world that we have identified as
currently underpinning the legitimacy and operation of the state. More generally, the theory of sovereignty, in which the privileged instrumental role of
the state is constructed, is itself a highly reductionist perspective, dividing
the world into compartments in a way which ignores what are now widely
understood to be vital biophysical interactions. As ecological problems pro-
liferate, and as the corresponding attention to environmental problems
sharpens, the mutually supportive relationship between the state's instrumental role and its claim to exercise sovereign power is more likely to
emerge as part of the problem than as part of the solution.

THE CONSTRUCTION OF TIME IN THE SOVEREIGN DOMAIN

Given the contemporary emphasis on the utilitarian role of the state and its
relation to the global market it is not surprising that modern states generally
have a predisposition to look favourably upon 'development' and unfavour-
ably upon anything that may be depicted as either 'standing still' or worse,
going 'backwards'. The vision of linear progress towards a high-technology
future is deeply embedded in the discourse of the modern state. The claim is
frequently made that maintaining an adequate rate of progress is necessary

for maintaining national sovereignty. Other visions are portrayed as Luddite or impractical. Alternative technological and social options are thereby pushed to the margin: the privileged course is one in which maximum change is compressed into as short a time scale as seems socially and technologically feasible.

As a consequence we may say that the theory of sovereignty is both supported by and reinforces not only a particular image of how social, biological and physical space is organized, but also a particular image of time. The concept of sovereignty conjures up a domain whose boundaries are fixed for all time. The paradox is that whilst the domain remains fixed in space, what happens within that domain is described by a dynamically evolving, modernist history. Within its sovereign domain the state presides over the process of constant demolition and reconstruction necessary to keep the nation competitive within the global system. The claim of the state to be able to facilitate this process, is, as noted in Chapter 5, critically important to the maintenance of the state's legitimacy.

So the state simultaneously supports and is constrained by a highly modernist concept of the future. Yet the rapid and accelerating rate of change that characterizes it is incompatible with the measured pace and sensitivity which is ecologically required to absorb not only the known impact of change on the physical environment, but also the unknown impact of change on the complex and only partially understood interactions that allow the biosphere to remain stable. By presiding over rapid change the state inadvertently risks rupturing the net of physical interactions and homeostatic feedback loops which have regulated the biosphere over millennia. The net effect is to intrude new uncertainties into the future behaviour of the biosphere, rendering the future both less predictable and more hazardous.

This side-effect of modernism – the creation of uncertainty in the future as a cost of simplifying and ordering the physical environment in the present – is well illustrated by the possible changes in the planet's future climate resulting from increasing levels of carbon dioxide in the atmosphere. It is not that these are well understood or open to confident prediction. Indeed, the biosphere is so complex that we are unable to forecast with any confidence just what will happen when we abruptly interfere with its normal state. There is little comfort to be derived from this, since the consequences could be anything from trivial to catastrophic.[24]

The developing uncertainty about the ecological future which is accompanying modernity has two intertwined implications. On the one hand, the uncertainty that has been created may well cause civil society to concede increased authority to the state as it looks to it for leadership in a period of crisis. This may suit the short-term interests of the state, increasing its ability to perform some of its functions within the 'sovereign' domain. But, as we have noted more than once, strength should not be confused with sovereignty. In the long run, the granting of greater powers to the state may even help erode the legitimacy of the sovereignty discourse, since it is highly probable that the state will be seen to lack not only the will but in a more general sense the ability to ameliorate the structure and pace of global development which lies at the root of the ecological crisis.

Democratic processes, which often support the legitimacy of the state, also contribute an additional element of fragmentation given the compressed time scale within which the state operates. These processes cut the state's attention span into short planning periods in line with the electoral time-table. Tied to industry by the need to adjust to the continuously changing vicissitudes of a global market and to a public opinion, which is itself modulated by the operation of media networks feeding the national community tiny, transient news grabs, the time scale of state planning shortens and fragments in parallel with the compression of the time scale of economic development.

This compressed planning horizon meshes with an equally compressed attention span created by the dynamics of the market. The valuation of the cost to future generations (who by the nature of things cannot bid in today's markets) arising from the exploitation of the environment does not normally appear in corporate calculations. The practice of devaluing the worth of natural assets by the interest rate, if their exploitation is delayed, adds further to the systematic shortening of the planning horizon.[25] Lester Thurow found that at one of America's largest corporations the average time horizon for planning was 2.8 years.[26] The short time scales of corporations, which ascribe far higher value to profits now than to future profits or losses, combine with the electoral time scales of political parties and governments to produce a process of development which is insufficiently sensitive to long-term ecological damage.

For the state, this presents a dilemma. In the short term the close planning horizon of any single government is likely to distract it from initiating those difficult changes which will produce little result by the next election, but may be essential for the amelioration of long-term environmental degradation. Yet in the long run each successive government faces a deepening contradiction between the instrumental objectives that legitimize it and the long-term net effect of neglecting the fundamental causes of the deteriorating condition of the biosphere. As this contradiction sharpens, the instrumental legitimacy of the state itself and as a result its claim to exercise, by right, supreme authority are likely to be progressively undermined.

THE PARTITIONING OF ENVIRONMENTAL ACTS

None of the above should be taken to mean that in relation to ecological problems the sovereignty discourse is by now a dead letter. The discourse is in a state of tension and transition. On the one hand, states often project themselves as sovereign and attempt to act as if they are. On the other, the image of sovereignty is undermined because those actions are not infrequently compromised or shaped by environmental, economic and social factors inconsistent with the principle of sovereignty. The tension here is between a sovereignty discourse undermined by ecological and other problems, and the residual power of the discourse to constrain actions which appear to be inconsistent with the claim to sovereignty but are increasingly considered necessary to resolve those problems. This tension is very evident in relation to the way in which the sovereignty discourse creates not only a spatial arrangement of political power, but also a corresponding partitioning of the biosphere. Although ecological problems challenge it, this conceptual partitioning of the biosphere continues to contribute to ecological deterioration. This occurs in at least four important ways:

1. *The theory and practice of sovereignty geographically insulates the state from the global effects of its actions.* Decisions which contribute to global environmental deterioration, made within its domain, can be defended as legitimate sovereign choices. As a result the state may damage the environment in ways that extend well beyond its own domain, justifying this by the belief that it is acting within its sovereign jurisdiction. The US–Canadian relationship provides an instructive example. It has been evident for some time that as much as 50 per cent of sulphur-dioxide-based acid precipitating in Eastern Canada originates in the United States. Under existing international law a customary obligation exists on parties contributing to trans-boundary air pollution to take steps to reduce its effects on all other parties. However, despite much negotiation, as of 1986 no measures had been taken by the United States specifically aimed at reducing the trans-boundary impact of US emissions on Canada.[27]

A critical factor is that each state reserves the right to make its 'sovereign' judgment on a number of complex questions (e.g. Where do the emissions come from? How much effect do they have? What would be the virtue of different control measures? Do the results of particular measures justify the costs? Is more time needed for research before concrete steps are taken?) Often parties sharing a resource (for example a fish stock) cannot even agree upon its size.[28] Whether in relation to prevention or compensation, this same demand for sovereign interpretation of what are often scientifically controversial issues leaves enormous latitude for significant, if not indefinite, prevarication.[29] For example, citing 'uncertainty about the effects of global warming and the economic impact of programs to reduce carbon emissions', the government of the United States, supported by other major contributors to greenhouse emissions, has consistently acted to block the setting of firm targets for carbon dioxide emission reductions, despite the fact that 18 European countries have independently agreed to freeze emissions of greenhouse gases.[30]

2.   *A polluter, if prevented from releasing pollution in one country may do so in another where the legislation is less strict.* This tactic is often based on the premiss that it is the sovereign right of that country to make whatever decisions it wishes. For example, it is common practice for transnational chemical corporations to establish the most polluting stages of their production in Third World countries which have much looser environmental control standards.[31]

3.   *The theory of sovereignty masks key economic and political relations which contribute to environmental degradation.* The theory of sovereignty suggests that states are independent sovereign subjects which interact in some sense on a basis of equality. This principle diverts attention from exogenous economic and political forces which often act quite unequally on states, severely limiting the range of feasible options. Relations of economic and structural dependence between nations, and the role of the market and market institutions in conditioning decisions in all countries, tend to be marginalized by the very appeal to sovereignty. By way of example, the 'decision' to accept a toxic waste dump or allow dangerous agricultural chemicals to be used in a Third World country tends to be portrayed as the rightful (if 'irresponsible') decision of its government, rather than the result of a dependent relationship for which those who benefit from that relationship are at least as, if not more, responsible.

4.   *The theory of sovereignty also masks the extent to which it is not only necessary but possible to develop new processes and structures to meet environmental challenges, as well as the extent to which such measures have in fact already been instituted.* Consider the complex relationship between France, the Netherlands and Germany. The latter two countries are adversely affected by the dumping of salt (sodium chloride) into the Rhine which has risen from 40kg/stere in 1885 up to peak values of 835 kg/stere in 1977. About one-third of this comes from potassium mines in Alsace. Accordingly France has agreed to install a system designed to reduce the discharge of salt. However 64 per cent of the cost is to be provided by the Netherlands (34 per cent) and Germany (30 per cent), although France is the principal contributor of the pollution.

It is often claimed that this sequence of events illustrates the displacement of the so-called 'polluter pays' principle by the so-called 'victim-pays' principle.[32] That is, the victim pays part or all of the costs incurred in cleaning up the pollution caused by another state. From the perspective of the theory of sovereignty it could be argued that this apparently unjust solution to the problem of trans-border pollution demonstrates the failure of the international system to provide adequate restitution to the victim. But from another perspective, it is remarkable that any solution at all has been negotiated. After all, France has, according to the principle of sovereignty, complete internal autonomy to take whatever action it wishes in relation to the Rhine as it flows within its sovereign domain.

Increasingly, the realities of integration between the countries of Europe at both the economic and environmental levels makes this an unlikely outcome. The agreement negotiated through the International Commission for the Protection of the Rhine against Pollution, a transnational regulatory structure created in 1963, displays the weaknesses of this transitional organization, whose decisions are made by consensus. Yet it also demonstrates the direction in which environmental pressure is pushing social organization. As Kiss observes, 'legal developments concerning the protection of the Rhine against pollution show that nothing can be done in this field at the national level. Pollution control in Europe requires international cooperation... . Although international cooperation exists for the Rhine, further progress is not only necessary but inevitable.'[33] In the long run the problem posed by pollution of the Rhine demonstrates the need to take the process of European integration further forward into the area of environmental regulation. It is a process for which the theory of sovereignty offers an explanatory model of diminishing utility. In addition, to the extent that the sovereignty discourse continues to enjoy enduring legitimacy it represents a significant if weakening obstruction to the political intervention which is needed. Finally, it demonstrates an increasing tension not merely between the theory of sovereignty and alternative perspectives, but between actual political formations, some of which draw their political strength and fashion their objectives from within the sovereign domain, and others whose structure, power base, aims and strategies are both reinforced by the growing concern over ecological problems, and incompatible with the obstructions created by existing national boundaries and the broader discourse of sovereignty.

STATE PROJECTS AND THE ENVIRONMENT

As the above suggests, the division of the world's social organization into notionally sovereign domains has easily identifiable ecological implications. One which may be less evident, however, is the relationship between the state and the scale of the technological developments it tends to undertake. The instrumental role allocated to the state combines with the fixed nature of its territorial domain to suggest a particular scale of technology which the state most naturally seeks to develop and manage. This has particular implications for both the biosphere and the sovereignty discourse itself. It is clear that the state is most likely to intervene in large-scale technological projects which are in some sense national in scale and can be justified as being in 'the national interest'. Multinational projects are usually left to transnational corporations or less frequently to multinational agencies, whilst small local projects are frequently left to private enterprise. Examples of the national projects often developed through the state include the construction of the national system of roads, ports and airports, major parts of the national public transport system, the development of the national communication network, and the planning and management of energy production. But it is precisely because the projects are of this scale (i.e. large and visible to many people, yet physically based within the national domain) that their environmental impact is clearly identifiable. Further, since they are projects of the state the institutions of individuals responsible for them are easily identified and the projects may readily become the focus of escalating environmental controversy.

By way of case study, it is useful to consider the nuclear industry, for here many of the processes we have examined come together. Nuclear power is pre-eminently a project executed by the national state. Born out of the nuclear weapons projects in Britain, France and the United States, nuclear power reactors were developed by the state. In most countries elements of the technology were then progressively transferred to private companies. However, in all instances, the state remains to this day directly involved in crucial aspects of the nuclear fuel cycle, and in most countries still plays the predominant role. In four of the six countries where commercial nuclear reactors are manufactured (Canada, Sweden, Britain, and France), the companies are owned either partly or wholly by the state.[34] Other areas of the fuel cycle, such as enrichment, waste reprocessing and high-level waste management, are almost invariably under government control.[35]

Not only has the metropolitan state been heavily involved in the inception, development and commercialization of nuclear power, it has also played a key role in providing the preconditions for the successful development of nuclear power. Vast amounts of research and development have been carried out and transferred to the industry free of charge, the commercial parts of the cycle have been heavily subsidized, the regulatory infrastructure has usually been provided gratis and, perhaps most importantly, the state has provided ideological support, assuming responsibility for achieving public acceptance of the nuclear project.[36]

Nuclear power development has often been justified as a central pillar in maintaining and consolidating sovereign nationhood. Especially after the steep rises in oil prices precipitated by OPEC decisions in 1972–3, different arms of the state apparatus stressed that economic growth was crucial to national sovereignty and energy independence essential for assured economic growth. Such independence could best be achieved by harnessing the most advanced energy technology. State agencies were also often instrumental in hiding from public view the magnitude of environmental threats and other hazards posed by the operation of the technology.

The history of nuclear power development, however, points less to the ways in which nuclear power has consolidated the claim to sovereign state power, than to the ways in which it has been eroded:

- The state may appear to be exercising considerable subjective autonomy when it weighs up the energy options. However, its apparent freedom in determining that there is a 'need' for nuclear power is often an illusion. First, the state usually relies on expert advice. Not infrequently, the available expert advice is conditioned by a modernist 'engineering ideology' in which 'advanced' technology is particularly valued. (In Third World countries this ideology is often imported through the overseas training of its advisers, this being reinforced after the establishment of an indigenous atomic energy authority which then lobbies enthusiastically for the expansion of nuclear power.) Secondly, states which have embarked on a nuclear programme have often been the subject of strong pressure from nuclear vendor companies, often accompanied by diplomatic pressure from their home governments.

- The decision to develop a nuclear power industry has quite often also reflected a high level of economic dependence. It has been a common strategy for the nuclear vendors to work with national banks (e.g. the US ExIm bank) to provide low-interest loans to purchasing countries on condition that the loan be used to buy nuclear reactors. This may entail a tacit subsidy of the nuclear power industry within the vendor country.[37] For the potential purchaser, often very short of capital funds, the resulting pressure to purchase nuclear reactors rather than seek other ways of handling energy problems may prove virtually irresistible.

- Once the decision to acquire foreign technology has been made, the purchasing country becomes highly dependent on external sources for fuel, maintenance, replacement parts and operating expertise. The initial purchase of a nuclear reactor may therefore be compared to a drug addict's first 'hit', establishing a habit which requires continual maintenance from the dealer.

In short, nuclear power, frequently justified in terms of its positive impact on national sovereignty, may in practice be little more than a symptom of the increasing erosion of state autonomy. This interpretation is underscored when we recall that from its very beginning the nuclear industry has carried with it a range of potent side-effects which are beyond the power of any individual government to control.[38] The most obvious is the risk of the proliferation of nuclear weapons which inevitably accompanies the spread and intensification of commercial nuclear activity.[39] A world of nations bristling with nuclear weapons, many in conflict with each other, is a dangerously unstable world – a powder keg which may be ignited at any moment by any one of a number of military flashpoints. It is precisely because of widespread international anxiety about this eventuality, not least among governments, that a number of steps have been taken towards international regulation. One result has been the adoption of the Nuclear Non-Proliferation Treaty (NPT), and the creation of the International Atomic Energy Agency (IAEA) and a corresponding regime of bilateral and multilateral treaties and agreements dealing with nuclear safeguards.

It is important to note that states have made important concessions to the need for inspection of nuclear facilities by an international regulatory body. Significantly, the international nuclear regime has been reinforced by the major nuclear armed powers, which have used their not inconsiderable economic and political muscle to establish a framework whereby nuclear technology is made available to other countries only on condition that they submit to international regulation and inspection.

It is of course true that the nuclear non-proliferation regime displays many of the characteristics of the system of sovereign states with which we are by now familiar. So as an answer to the problem of international proliferation it has many continuing inadequacies. States retain a wide range of options to limit or delay inspection of their facilities. In addition, continuing claims that NPT signatories may be developing a nuclear weapons capability (e.g. Iraq,[40] Pakistan[41]) suggest that the regime presents at best limited protection against nuclear proliferation. Its vulnerability has been highlighted in recent years by authoritative reports that India[42] and Israel[43] have developed nuclear weapons capabilities including fusion weapons, that Algeria is being assisted by China to develop nuclear weapons,[44] that Brazil and Argentina have moved some distance towards nuclear weapons development,[45] and that South Africa has acquired or is on the verge of acquiring a nuclear weapon capability.[46]

Nevertheless, inadequate as the NPT and the associated regulatory regime may be, its operation involves a considerable – part 'voluntary' and part 'involuntary' – surrender of what were once considered significant sovereign rights. As the tension between the desire to control the spread of nuclear weapons and the inadequacies of the existing regime increases, international practice in this area is likely to continue to deviate from the principle of sovereignty. It is now widely understood that nuclear proliferation is a global problem whose solution depends on internationally supported and administered processes of inspection, judicial review and international enforcement. The future development of these processes can only further undermine the legitimacy and usefulness of the theory of sovereignty.

As a case study of the relationship between the state, contemporary technological development and the theory and practice of sovereignty, nuclear power suggests one other important conclusion. Whilst the instrumental role of the state gives the concept of sovereignty much of its contemporary relevance, this relevance is itself undermined by two factors. First the state's technological intervention materially contributes to humanity's environmental predicament. Secondly, the theory and practice of sovereignty are at odds with the institutional conditions that are presumably needed to deal with that predicament. As this contradiction deepens, an oppositional response emerges, giving rise to new principles of legitimation and new forms of political organization.

From the mid-1970s to the mid-1980s opposition to nuclear power mobilized citizens drawn from a wide range of occupations and social strata and spread across much of the Western world, and as time went on in many parts of the Third World, and what was once the Soviet bloc. We have explored the history and political significance of the rise of the international movement against nuclear power much more comprehensively elsewhere.[47] Here it is important to stress the fact that the movement was indeed international not only in scale but in the way it conceived of its objectives, and worked to achieve them. The internationalism of the anti-nuclear movement was supported by formal and informal networks of scientists, engineers, trade unionists, religious groups and many others, which spanned both countries and continents. Perhaps for the first time, an environmental problem, clearly associated with an industry global in scale and organization, had given rise to a citizen opposition which also perceived itself as a global movement. The resistance to the nuclear project grew and spread to influence national policy and even the economic viability of nuclear power in a range of countries. Partly as a result of political contestation the fortunes of the nuclear industry plummeted, with projections for Western world nuclear reactor capacity for the year 2000 falling by a factor of almost ten over the decade 1974–85. For the first but certainly not the last time the ecological crisis had become a sharp focus of international consciousness and a potent vehicle for international organization.

We shall investigate the implications of the growth of the anti-nuclear movement in more detail in the next chapter, where we deal with the more general development of the 'new social movements'. Here it is sufficient to note that national boundaries were often transcended in the organization of both the industry and the movement which opposed it. National states lost control of events as citizens, often acting in concert across state boundaries, confronted the plans of industry and governments alike. Increasingly citizens saw themselves as battling not for national but international objectives in a global arena in which their state was only one protagonist among many. In short, the internationalization of the conflict – in terms of the structure of the nuclear industry, the scale of the threat, and the normative thrust of the anti-nuclear movement – was at considerable variance with the principles of sovereignty.

ECOLOGY AND THE CHALLENGE TO SOVEREIGNTY DISCOURSE

The tension between sovereignty and ecology has both a theoretical and practical dimension. The theory of a world partitioned into territorial domains under the superintendence of national states has enjoyed considerable currency over the last century, but is increasingly confronted by another equally long-standing perspective of a living planet as an integrated whole. The 'sovereign domain' is confronted by the 'biosphere', the stability of 'the nation' by the stability of 'nature', the national economy by the natural economy, and the 'world of states' by the 'global community'.

These latter concepts are not new. What is new is the increasing prominence given to them, not merely as Utopian ideals but as necessary terms in explaining problems and proposing and negotiating solutions. In the arena of human interaction, ways of thinking and speaking which we have labelled the 'discourse of sovereignty' are increasingly juxtaposed with other perspectives which we might label the 'discourse of globalism'. None of this is to say that the discourse of sovereignty has completely lost its power. But its legitimacy as a fabric of explanation is being steadily undermined as other concepts and related practices penetrate and erode that fabric. As this occurs it becomes steadily clearer that the 'sovereign state' as an institution is not adequately equipped to embody ecological principles. Its approach to the ecological dilemma is confounded by its institutional interests, instrumental role and domain of authority, which are at odds with the ecological principles and global ethos required for planetary management.

Whilst these deficiencies may first be identified with particular states, it is the system of sovereign states as a whole that is emerging as poorly equipped to meet the challenge posed by mounting ecological disruption. Paradoxically, the more advanced efforts by states to achieve some form of effective response to environmental problems help render the theoretical inadequacies of the system more visible to the naked eye. For example the OECD has developed principles for resolving trans-border pollution problems. But these are usually thwarted in practice by its inability to impose the sanctions which would be necessary to achieve significant restriction of polluting emissions. The OECD's principle of 'polluter pays', though attractive in theory, is seldom effectively applied in practice,[48] and proposals for an international pollution tax to redress the failure of the economic system to attach any cost to the pollution of common public resources (e.g. the atmosphere or oceans) may remain little more than an idea unless some international taxation authority is established, which, as Sterner reminds us, would transcend current concepts of national sovereignty.[49] Similarly, proposals to institute the sale of international pollution permits,[50] apart from running the risk of legalizing the prevalent practice of industrial countries dumping their toxic wastes in the Third World,[51] begs the question of whether states will agree to them, who is to set the permissible pollution limits, and who is to monitor and enforce them.[52]

More generally the power of a system of sovereign states to act and to conceive of actions is constrained by the increasingly powerful and pervasive dynamics of the international market. We have already discussed how the increasing transparency of international borders to financial flows, the drive for deregulation of trade, the reduction of controls over national ownership and control, the development of international communication technologies, and the increasing strength of transnational financial and commercial organizations erode the will as much as the power of the state to make sovereign decisions. This limitation is particularly evident in circumstances where the state not only confronts ecological disorders that extend beyond its domain, but is compelled to navigate powerful economic forces over which it has little or no control.

The growth of international debt provides an especially striking illustration of this latter point. Consider Brazil, where the destruction and burning of large sections of the Amazonian rainforest is proceeding at an alarming pace. Almost half of the world's rainforest has already been felled or burned, endangering or eliminating countless species and annually releasing some 6 billion tonnes of carbon dioxide into the atmosphere. Deforestation in Brazil alone, which is proceeding at the rate of one hectare every two seconds, accounts for an estimated 20 per cent of all carbon released from deforestation globally. But Brazil labours under a massive foreign debt (US $115 billion at the beginning of 1987) and a large fraction of the population is in a state 'ranging from misery to extreme poverty'. Starvation is endemic amongst the 34 million people living in the north-east of Brazil, which includes the Amazonian rainforest. At the same time the Brazilian government is under enormous international pressure to service its debt. The only way for it to do this is to increase exports and reduce public spending. This result is achieved in part by forcing peasants off their traditional land to make it available for cash crops, and by extending agricultural and industrial activity into the rainforest. Whatever the rhetoric of sovereignty, the range of practical options available to any Brazilian government committed to servicing the country's debt is limited, to say the least. It is difficult to see how, within the existing framework of economic and political constraints, the protection of the Amazonian rainforest would be able to assume a high priority.[53]

Striking though Third World examples may be, the relevance of the issues we are considering is not confined to them. It also applies, sometimes in more subtle ways, to most if not all industrialized countries. For example, the pressure for free trade which was exerted throughout much of the industrialized world in the 1980s has had a series of implications not only for sovereignty but for environmental degradation. One of the stated objectives of the negotiations over the General Agreement on Tariffs and Trade in 1990 was 'the fullest liberalisation of trade in natural resource based products', including the reduction and ultimate elimination of export and import controls.[54] As Steven Shrybman points out, the experience under the Canada–US Free Trade Agreement (FTA) provides a useful indication of the implications of this liberalization. By proscribing government regulation of energy trade between the two countries, the FTA ensures that Canadian resources are fully exploited to meet US needs at the lowest practicable cost. The result is to restrict the Canadian government's ability to regulate the rate of use of its energy resources, to reduce the pressure on the United States to decrease the high levels of waste from non-renewable energy resources, to undermine measures designed to advance the development and use of renewable and energy conservation technologies, and therefore to increase greenhouse gas emissions into the atmosphere. From a global perspective, the net effect of these measures is to reduce the pressure to conserve in the rich industrialized nations, which with 20 per cent of the world's population consume some 80 per cent of its natural resources.[55]

Similarly, the GATT negotiation process has made much of 'harmonization'. Here countries which set environmental standards above some fixed maximum would be deemed to be engaging in restrictive trade practices. As a result the ability of local or even national communities and governments to place an upward pressure on environmental standards by enacting stricter codes would be considerably reduced. For example, in late 1990 some observers were expressing concern that an early casualty of the GATT negotiations would be the Delaney clause in US food safety laws that prohibits the addition of carcinogenic chemicals to foods.[56]

Whether Third, Second or First World, the situation of states as competitors in an increasingly integrated world market profoundly confines environmental decision-making to an ever narrower range of options. Individual governments are reluctant to regulate companies if these are likely to lose national competitiveness or move their operations abroad. As the level of dependence on other nations for imports grows, so does the pressure on national governments to avoid decisions that would significantly decrease national exports. As a consequence, the range of effective options for dealing with a degraded environment, which is itself closely connected to the pattern of trade and production, is severely circumscribed.

We may summarize the argument in this chapter as follows. It is not entirely coincidental that the evolution of the theory and discourse of sovereignty should have paralleled the evolution of ecological awareness. As we have shown, there are many interactions between the two. A world comprised of sovereign states suggests a particular organization of politics and treatment of nature. And whilst the official rationale for that organization may be couched in terms of human needs, a sharp tension is developing between this method of addressing human needs and the understanding of the needs and organization of the biosphere.

It has taken 200 hundred years for environmental problems, and public consciousness of them, to begin to emerge as significant factors in global politics. At each stage of this development the possibility of effective action to head off the emerging predicament has been both shaped and restrained by political and economic conditions.

We have argued that the system of sovereign states was inadequately prepared to deal with these emerging environmental problems. Indeed it played a central role in facilitating their emergence. Sovereignty, the nation-state and the use of military force developed together in a destructive ecological spiral. First, several closely related aspects of the theory and practice of sovereignty – the instrumental character of the state, the co-option of space and time, the partitioning of environmental acts, the masking of key economic externalities, the structuring of communities as competitors and the role of state-inspired projects (such as nuclear power) – contributed to the dynamic of environmental degradation. Secondly, the dominance of the sovereignty discourse diverted attention from the many developments which undermined its rationale yet indicated possible ways in which the spiral of destruction might be stemmed and possibly reversed. Finally, the sovereignty discourse diverted attention not only from the possibility and necessity for political solutions which cut across national boundaries, but also from the limited capacity of the nation-state to formulate let alone implement effective responses.

Continued lip service to the sovereignty principle has served to obscure how distant the sovereign state is from the embodiment of ecological principles. But the reverse is also true. The emergence of an increasingly urgent environmental agenda in the closing years of the twentieth century demonstrates ever more starkly the incongruity between the physical properties of the biosphere and the image of a world partitioned hermetically, and immutably, into fixed domains of sovereign authority. The slow but steady growth of international regulation represents a hesitant but unavoidable recognition of this incongruity. The trend towards greater international institutionalization may not offer a fully acceptable or effective response to that incongruity, but it provides a clear indication that with the declining explanatory value of the theory of sovereignty and the increasing limitation on its practical expression the institutional status quo will increasingly be the subject of intense contestation, opening the way for new forms of intellectual inquiry and political action.

NOTES

1. David Pepper, *The Roots of Modern Environmentalism*, London: Croom Helm, 1984.
2. Ibid., p. 82.
3. C. Glacken, *Traces on the Rhodian Shore*, Berkeley: University of California Press, 1967, p. 494.
4. See Richard Grove, 'The Origins of Environmentalism', *Nature*, **345**, 3 May 1990, 11–13.
5. Cited in V. Ramanathan, 'The Greenhouse Theory of Climate Change: a Test by an Inadvertent Global Experiment', *Science*, **240**, 15 April 1988, p. 299.
6. J.S. Wilson, 'The General and Gradual Desiccation of the Earth and Atmosphere', Report of Proceedings, *British Association for the Advancement of Science*, 1858, pp. 155–6, cited in Grove, 'Origins of Environmentalism', p. 14.
7. Savante Arrhenius, 'On the Influence of Carbonic Acid in the Air upon the Temperature of the Ground', *Philosophical Magazine*, **41**, 1896, p. 266, table VII..
8. Grove, 'Origins of Environmentalism', p. 13.
9. Ibid., p. 14.
10. Pepper, *Roots of Modern Environmentalism*, p. 82.
11. Fred Pearce, 'Acid Rain', *New Scientist*, **116**, (1585), 5 November 1987, 1.
12. Walt Patterson, 'Nuclear Watchdog Finds its Role', *New Scientist*, 23 April 1987, 50–2.
13. Richard Frye, 'Climatic Change and Fisheries Management', *Natural Resources Journal*, **23**, (1), January 1983, 82.
14. Richard Kerr, 'Linking Earth, Ocean, and Air at the AGU', *Science*, **239**, 15 January 1988, 260.
15. Jane Simmonds, 'Europe Calculates the Health Risk', *New Scientist*, 23 April 1987, 40–3.
16. Patterson, 'Nuclear Watchdog', pp. 50–2.
17. A. Springer, *The International Law of Pollution: Protecting the Global Environment in a World of Sovereign States*, Westport, Conn.: Quorum, 1983.
18. C. Davis, 'International Affairs and the Environment', *Studia Diplomatica*, **40**, (1), 1987, 99–107; F. Pearce, 'Whatever Happened to Acid Rain?', *New Scientist*, 15 September 1990, p. 41.
19. Brian Boswell, 'Battle Plan for Limited War', *The Weekend Australian*, 11–12 August 1990, 13.
20. P.J. Crutzen and J.W. Birks, 'The Atmosphere after a Nuclear War: Twilight at Noon', *Ambio*, **11**, pp. 115–25.

21. Quoted by François Guizot, 'The History of Civilisation' quoted in L.L. Blake, *Sovereignty: Power beyond Politics*, London: Shepheard Walwyn, 1988, p. 117.

22. F. Burton and P. Carlen, *Official Discourse: On Discourse Analysis, Government Publications, Ideology and the State*, London: Routledge & Kegan Paul, 1979.

23. This argument is developed further in J. Falk and A. Brownlow, *The Greenhouse Challenge: What is to be done?*, Melbourne: Penguin, 1989, ch. 4.

24. Ibid.

25. The role of Hotelling's law and other similar considerations is discussed ibid., pp. 164–71.

26. L. Thurow, 'Revitalising American Industry: Managing in a Competitive World Economy', *California Management Review*, **XXVII**, 1984, pp. 9–41.

27. Gunther Handl, 'National Uses of Transboundary Air Resources: The International Entitlement Issue Reconsidered', *Natural Resources Journal*, **26**, Summer 1986, 443.

28. Per Magnus Wijkman, 'Managing the Global Commons', *International Organization*, **36**, (3), Summer 1982, 516–18.

29. See, for example, David Swinbanks, 'More Research Needed', *Nature*, **343**, 22 February 1990, 684; 'US, Europe at Odds on Global Warming', *Sydney Morning Herald*, 19 April 1990, 10.

30. See, for example, G. Christopher Anderson, 'Diplomatic Squalls Spoil US Climate Conference', *Nature*, **344**, 26 April 1990, 799; 'U.S. Blocks Global Pact on Greenhouse Effect', *San Francisco Chronicle*, 6 November 1990, A17; Deborah MacKenzie, 'US and Europe Could Fall Out Over Climate Change', *New Scientist*, 1 September 1990, 5.

31. Thomas Sterner, 'An International Tax on Pollution and Natural Resource Depletion', *Energy Policy*, April 1990, 300.

32. Handl, 'National Uses of Transboundary Air Resources', p. 452.

33. Alexandre Kiss, 'The Protection of the Rhine against Pollution', *Natural Resources Journal*, **25**, July 1985, p. 637.

34. See Jim Falk, *Global Fission The Battle over Nuclear Power*, Melbourne: Oxford University Press, 1982, table 3, p. 115.

35. Ibid., p. 115, table 3.

36. Ibid., pp. 74–85 and references contained therein.

37. Congressional Budget Office, *The Export Import Bank: Implications for the Federal Budget and Credit Market*, Staff Working Paper, 27 October 1976, p. 17; G.C. Duffy and G. Adams, *Power Politics: The Nuclear Industry and Nuclear Exports*, New York: Council on Economic Priorities, 1978, p. 57.

38. See, for example, Walt Patterson, *Nuclear Power* (2nd edn), Harmondsworth, Middlesex: Penguin, 1983.

39. See for example, Jim Falk, *Taking Australia off the Map: Facing the Threat of Nuclear War*, Melbourne: Penguin, 1983, pp. 177–213; Leonard Spector, *Going Nuclear: the Spread of Nuclear Weapons 1986–1987*, Cambridge, Mass.: Ballinger, 1987.

40. "When will Iraq be a Nuclear Power?", *Santa Cruz Sentinel*, 23 November 1990, A-11; *Programme for Promoting Nuclear Non-Proliferation Newsbrief*, **10**, Summer 1990, 7 and references contained therein.

41. Jonathon Power, 'Price of Pakistan's Nuclear Bomb', San Francisco Chronicle, 24 October 1990 (Z-3), 5; *Programme for Promoting*, p. 8 and references contained therein.

42. David Ottoway, 'Hydrogen Bomb Being Developed warns CIA Head', *Sydney Morning Herald*, 20 May 1989, 23.

43. John Simpson and Darryl Howlett, *The Need for a Strong Nuclear Non-Proliferation Treaty: Issues at the Fourth NPT Review Conference*, Centre for International Policy Studies, University of Southampton, Occasional Paper 8, July 1990, 14 and references contained therein.

44. 'China May Be Helping Algeria Get N-Weapons', *Sydney Morning Herald*, 13 April 1991, 17.

45. John R. Redick, *Argentina and Brazil: An Evolving Nuclear Relationship*, Centre for International Policy Studies, University of Southampton, Occasional Paper 7, July 1990, and references contained therein.

46. Leonard S. Spector, *Going Nuclear: The Spread of Nuclear Weapons 1986–87*, Cambridge, Mass.: Ballinger, 1987, p. 292.
47. See Falk, *Global Fission*; and Joseph A. Camilleri, *The State and Nuclear Power: Conflict and Control in the Western World*, Seattle: University of Washington Press, 1984, pp. 75–106, 286–93.
48. OECD, The Application of Economic Instruments for Environmental Protection, Paris: OECD, 1989.
49. Thomas Sterner, 'An International Tax on Pollution and Natural Resource Depletion', *Energy Policy*, April 1990, 302.
50. See, for example, Fred Pearce, 'Bids for the Greenhouse Auction', *New Scientist*, 4 August 1990, 47–8.
51. See, for example, Deborah MacKenzie and James Mpinga, 'Africa Wages War on Dumpers of Poisonous Waste', *New Scientist*, 23 June 1988, 30–1; Blaine Harden, 'Hostages Taken in War against Waste Dumpers', *Sydney Morning Herald*, 18 July 1988.
52. See, for example, Thomas J. Goreau, 'Balancing Atmospheric Carbon Dioxide', *Ambio*, **19**, (5), August 1990, 235 and references contained therein.
53. See Falk and Brownlow, *The Greenhouse Challenge*, pp. 179–80 and references contained therein.
54. Quoted in Deborah MacKenzie, 'Cheaper Alternatives for CFCs', *New Scientist*, 30 June 1990, p. 20.
55. Steven Shrybman, 'The Environmental Costs of Free Trade', *Multinational Monitor*, March 1990, 20.
56. 'Trading Away Rights', (editorial), *Multinational Monitor*, 6 May 1990, 6.

8.   The New Social Movements

The politics of protest is an elusive and poorly defined area of study, sitting uncomfortably between revolutionary models of structural change and pluralist/functionalist conceptions of pressure group politics. Neither of these two theoretical perspectives adequately characterizes or explains what is now a global phenomenon. Although much of the existing literature concentrates on the nature and significance of protest in advanced industrial liberal democracies, there clearly exist, despite differences in institutional setting, economic development or mode of operation, considerable linkages and similarities with oppositional politics in the Third World and what once constituted the socialist bloc.

As we shall see, protest, particularly in the context of late capitalism, is a multifaceted reality that involves a multiplicity of actors, issues and programmes. In addition to the traditional category of class pitting labour against capital recent protest movements – or to use the now widely accepted designation 'social movements' – have focused on such other categories as ethnicity, ecology, gender and personal liberation, all of which bear some relationship to but cannot fully be subsumed under or conflated with the classical Marxist dialectic.

Until recently most theoretical and empirical studies of protest have tended to highlight its deviant, aberrant or ephemeral qualities, reflecting in part the relative success of the state in using the array of rewards and punishments at its disposal to co-opt, marginalize or coerce countervailing movements. However, with the passage of time the cumulative pressures exerted by these movements have significantly impinged on the legitimacy and efficacy of state action, thereby compelling a theoretical reassessment of their origin and their relationship to state and society. Placed in a wider historical and international setting, they offer important insights into the dynamics of contemporary social conflict and reinforce the need for a reinterpretation of the concept and practice of sovereignty.

SOVEREIGNTY AND INSTITUTIONAL POLITICS

Before analysing the more salient features of the politics of protest, particularly as they relate to our understanding of sovereignty, it may be useful to begin with a characterization of the modern state, briefly restating but also elaborating parts of the argument developed in earlier chapters. Such a point of departure will help us to describe and explain the latent tensions between state and society, of which social movements are the manifest expression and which they are in the process of redefining and reshaping.

Sharply demarcated territorial boundaries have been a distinguishing feature of the system of sovereign states. The importance of boundaries derives from the need to establish with relative precision the domain within which supreme or 'sovereign' authority may be exercised. Without such agreed demarcation sovereigns are likely to be in conflict about their respective jurisdictions over given territories and populations. Alternatively, perhaps simultaneously, the prolonged absence of agreement may seriously undermine the principle of sovereignty simply by demonstrating that the uncontested exercise of sovereignty is not a *sine qua non* of effective or at least stable political organization. In this sense, it may be argued that the ideological and practical requirements of sovereignty are such that they severely restrict in space and time the domain of political action. For the territorial and historical boundaries of the state (the latter understood as the confined time-frame of the nation's history) effectively limit the scope and flexibility of institutional politics.

It is partly in order to overcome these limitations inherent in the concept that the sovereign state has felt it necessary to intervene in various areas of social and economic life, thereby assuming greater control over the space within which it exercises 'sovereign' jurisdiction. In the process, the advanced industrial state has developed an elaborate technocratic apparatus which combines military, economic, political and cultural sources of power and influences almost every aspect of social behaviour. The integrative impact of the state, most strikingly reflected in the development of a national, uniform, compulsory, public, mass educational system, has been aptly described by A.D. Smith as 'a high degree of cultural homogenisation, territorial crystallisation and social penetration'.[1] Underpinning the state's control of political space is its privileged access to information, its ability to maintain by electronic means a vast data base governing every facet of social life. This leverage is compounded by the growth of powerful bureaucratic machines and the increasing centralization of industrial and financial systems, all of which systematically erode the space for local or regional autonomy.

Nowhere is the interventionism of the state more apparent than in the economy, which is not to say that the trend is uniform across time and space.

Institutional arrangements which appear successful (functional) in conditions of rapid economic expansion may prove unsuccessful (dysfunctional) in times of severe and prolonged recession. Yet, despite considerable variations from period to period, and country to country, the growth in state intervention is a secular trend which reflects the increased social division of labour and the increased technical and administrative integration of the productive process characteristic of advanced industrialization. Though each phase of capitalist accumulation has had its own distinctive institutional features, the state has at all times been primarily responsible for overseeing the social arrangements or, as Fred Block puts it, 'the social structures of accumulation'.[2]

In the aftermath of the Second World War – a period of considerable liberalization in international trade and capital flows – the state assumed primary responsibility for overall economic management with the adoption of Keynesian principles of macroeconomic policy and the creation of the welfare state. Apart from the development of elaborate taxation and social security systems which could substantially influence levels of consumption, a comprehensive regulatory framework was established to achieve health, educational, urban planning and other social objectives. Governments were increasingly committed to providing a wide range of collectively produced social services (e.g. health, education, housing, social work) designed to achieve the reproduction of labour power but also the legitimacy of the state. As Ian Gough has argued, a variety of state initiatives were gradually supplanting the role of family and kinship structures in transferring part of the social product from the direct producers to non-working individuals.[3] As a consequence, the public sector grew significantly in most Western countries as a proportion both of Gross National Product and of the workforce.

A large and sophisticated literature has since emerged attempting to characterize the role of the capitalist state *vis-à-vis* the private sector, but to delve closely into this question would take us far beyond the concerns of this chapter. Suffice it to say that the actions of the state, while they often privilege certain powerful private interests, cannot be interpreted as directly representing those interests or even the dominant class as a whole. Nor can the state be understood simply as performing a reconciling or mediating function between the competing interests that make up the dominant class. It may be more accurate to say that the actions of the state are consistent with the rationality of the capitalist economy, that is, with the logic of the market which, as we have already seen, has over time assumed an increasingly global dimension.

In accordance with this same rationality, powerful pressures may on occasions emerge, as has happened in response to 'stagflation' in the 1970s, for a smaller public sector, resulting in recent attempts to stabilize or reduce public spending and privatize a number of public services and enterprises. Such a market-driven strategy may also aim for lower labour costs, which may in turn require higher levels of unemployment. The strategy, however, is not without political risk and is not guaranteed of success. The state may therefore be tempted to explore alternative or additional avenues, and in particular a number of 'social contract' arrangements. The essence of this option is the creation of a political structure which integrates government, trade unions and business organizations in national economic planning and incomes policy programmes.[4] The purpose of such a partnership is to negotiate on a tripartite basis the level of both the private wage and the 'social wage', thereby minimizing the likelihood of destabilizing conflicts over social and economic policy.

An important function of the modern 'social contract' may be to secure at least the tacit agreement of organized labour for the restructuring of industry, thereby hopefully laying the foundation for increased investment and the renewal of capital accumulation and economic growth. Placed in this context, social contract policies, which promise to curtail the erosion of the welfare state, may be considered as the sweetener in the otherwise bitter pill of industrial modernization, which may entail both job retrenchment and reduced real wages. No doubt the particular outcomes of such negotiated solutions will vary from country to country depending on local economic conditions, the traditions of the state, and the relation of forces between labour and capital.

The simple but inescapable conclusion to emerge is that state intervention, despite changing fashions in political ideology and practice, continues to play a pivotal role in the rationalization of production and the readjustment of the social and political structures of the world economy.

Because of the social and economic functions it performs, the national state has paradoxically been an integral part of the internationalization of trade, production, credit and information. Although territorially bound, the *sovereign* state has been transformed into a vehicle for the complex movement of money, technology, ideas and people. The result is the transnationalization of the marketplace with national economies increasingly vulnerable to external pressures. The ensuing interpenetration of national markets – a trend which has been steadily gathering momentum over more than a century – has reinforced the dominance of the market over the political process and contributed to a corresponding decline of the public sphere. At the simplest level it could be said that the progressive intrusion of the market-place into the decision-making arena has seen virtually every activity assigned a cash value. As a consequence the body of symbols, language and conventions necessary to sustain the public sphere has steadily been eroded.

In the name of consumer sovereignty, competitive individualism and the invisible hand, market principles have infiltrated the political process and achieved an ideological ascendancy over the institutions of the state. The function of citizen has largely been reduced to that of consumer, the only qualification being that policies, political campaigns and elections have themselves become objects of consumption. By turning citizenship into consumerhood, the market-place has tended to turn social problems, frustrations and grievances into 'individual afflictions with no relation to the broader social structure'.[5] Legitimacy has become associated with the satisfaction of 'privatized needs', be they expressed in terms of power, success, status, wealth or leisure. As a consequence the *public* understanding and experience of citizenship has contracted and the body politic has been deprived of the space within which it can effectively exercise sovereignty. Increasingly *state sovereignty* is identified with the authority of centralized institutions and divorced from the democratic or normative quality with which advocates of *popular sovereignty* have sought to endow the concept.

The widening gap between state sovereignty and popular sovereignty reflects the state's growing separation from civil society and ultimately threatens its own legitimacy. To pre-empt this dangerous eventuality and counteract any tendency towards division or disaffection the state may appeal to primordial ties, whether based on race, religion or nationality. For societies where the inroads of modernity coexist with still powerful attachments to tradition (particularly but not exclusively in Third World societies), the appeal to religious sentiment may be a potent instrument for reasserting the state's legitimacy (e.g. Khomeini's Iran). Generally, however, for the modern national state, the appeal to nationalism is likely to prove the more promising strategy, for it accords with the state's secular tradition which demotes the political role of religion and confines religious belief and practice to the private sphere. Instead, the state strives to establish and cement a unifying political culture, that is a value consensus based on an official interpretation of the community's past history and future destiny. A.D. Smith offers the following incisive description of the strategy: 'the state must promulgate a bureaucratic nationalism, along with a single, standardised set of values taught in a single, standardised set of public educational institutions'.[6] But it is not, as Smith suggests, simply a case of the state demonstrating to the outside world that its external policies reflect the 'will of a united nation'.

Bureaucratic nationalism serves as much a domestic as an international function. It is this latter consideration, perhaps above all others, which lies behind the 'ideology of official nationalism' and in particular the claim that the cultural and geographic boundaries of state and nation are perfectly matched, 'that the rulers of the state and nation must be the same, that state elites are interchangeable with national ones, that state and national institutions are identical and that the context of the state's culture is the same as that of the nation'.[7] Promoting cultural and ideological integration is a means of strengthening the state's unity and the legitimacy of existing institutions, all of which does not mean that the state is oblivious to external pressures, or that internal homogenization does not also serve the state's interests in its competitive relations with other states.

The ideology of 'bureaucratic nationalism' has enjoyed considerable currency, especially in times of war and crisis when the identification of external threats has been used to great effect to uphold the traditions of the state and reinforce the emotional commitment to its territorial integrity. But success is neither total nor permanent. State nationalism, despite the vast institutional and technological resources at its disposal, has often failed to subdue or neutralize the powerful myths or symbols of ethnic identity. Indeed, the supposed congruence of state and ethnic community turns out to be more the exception than the rule. Many states represent an amalgam of several nations (e.g. Belgium, Canada, the Soviet Union, Nigeria, India) and many nations are divided among the jurisdictions of several states (e.g. Kurds, Serbs, Macedonians). This distinction is a source of rising tension both within and between states.

Ironically, the very attempt of the state to bring ethnic minorities into the mainstream of economic and political life may provoke a bitter and sustained reaction. State intervention may in some instances be interpreted as well meaning but misguided, in others as an unacceptable and dangerous intrusion, in others still as a form of cultural genocide. By streamlining the educational system and encouraging the mass exodus from the countryside to the cities, the state may, albeit unwittingly, help to create the material conditions for the rise of a militant educated intelligentsia amongst ethnic minorities. This new professional class may come to see its career prospects as best served by rejection of the state's official history and civic culture, the revival of ethnic history and identity, and the assertion of political autonomy. This is presumably part of the dynamic which is currently activating the demand for ethnic separatism and independence in the Soviet Union. Attempts by the multinational state to co-opt or cajole its minorities may give it breathing space but are unlikely to provide a lasting solution.

The increasing incidence of ethnic dissent is but one manifestation, though one with far-reaching implications, of the widening gap between state and civil society. The state may be omnipresent, its tentacles may reach into every nook and cranny of social life, yet its structures, processes and policies may be far removed from the citizen's sense of identity, history and solidarity. A deep divide may separate the public and private spheres. The institutional and technical resources of the state may indeed be used for psychological or physical repression. Even in Western parliamentary democracies, the bureaucratic apparatus of government and political parties is likely, under the homogenizing influence of electoral politics and the market-place,[8] to dilute or suppress cultural and ideological diversity. The net effect must be to insulate legislative programmes and parliamentary debates from the reality of everyday life. The growing evidence of electoral abstention, the sudden shifts in voting behaviour, and mounting public cynicism towards political parties, leaders and messages point to the widespread perception of bureaucracies as one-way communication systems, engendering cultural uncertainty and political detachment.

The separation of state and society leads, then, to an essential schism within the individual between the public and the private self. The decline of meaningful political discourse, hence of the public sphere, may prompt the individual to retreat to a private world in search of meaning and reward.[9] Individual autonomy is thereby reduced to 'possessive individualism', which measures satisfaction in terms of the consumption of goods and services.[10] The autonomy of this private sphere is respected as long as it does not threaten the smooth functioning of the dominant institutions. Applying this analysis specifically to private religious belief, Luckmann reaches a conclusion that goes well beyond the confines of religion: 'By bestowing a sacred quality upon the increasing subjectivity of human existence it [autonomy] supports not only the secularization but also what we called the dehumanization of the social structure'.[11] In so far as individual autonomy is confined to self-realization in the private sphere, the state achieves much greater autonomy for its dominant institutions, thereby minimizing the threat to its legitimacy that may come with higher levels of public participation and critical scrutiny of its actions.

Such a strategy on the part of the state is not entirely devoid of risk. It is more likely to prove a double-edged sword. For, as we have already intimated, the growing distance between the public and private spheres has itself a corrosive effect. Beyond a certain threshold the subjective experience of tension may acquire a collective manifestation. Not surprisingly, the image of late capitalist society as a closed society entirely dominated by systems of manipulation and control, which Marcuse and others have articulated,[12] does not entirely accord with the available evidence. Retreat into a privatized world of self-gratification is one but by no means the only possible response. The politics of protest indicates the feasibility, perhaps probability, of a second option which, as it turns out, is mobilizing the energies of a large and growing cross-section of contemporary society. This second option, even more than the first, calls into question not merely the legitimacy but the sovereignty of the state. It is to this phenomenon that we shall now turn our attention. The new social movements are significant in this connection not necessarily because they are agents of revolutionary change, but because they represent a uniquely placed window on to a rapidly unfolding social and political reality.

CHARACTERIZATION OF NEW SOCIAL MOVEMENTS

While we have chosen to make the 'new social movements' that have sur-
faced over the last three decades, particularly in the West, the focus of our
analysis, we recognize that these movements have a much longer history and
that many of them have assumed considerable importance in the political life
of the Third World as well as of Eastern Europe and the Soviet Union. As
Claus Offe has observed, the various labels used in the literature to describe
this phenomenon – 'alternative movements', 'new protest movements', 'new
politics', 'new populism', 'neo-romanticism', 'anti-politics', 'disorderly
politics' or 'counter-institutions' – emphasize the element of rupture and
discontinuity with existing politics. Several other labels used more recently
(e.g. 'critical movements', 'anti-systemic movements')[13] tend to convey the
same idea. Offe goes on to suggest that the practice of the new social
movements implies a rejection of existing legal or institutional arrangements, in particular the dualistic conception of the private and public spheres
implicit in liberal democratic theory and the practice of the welfare state.[14]
Though he limits his analysis to the Western experience, there is no reason
to think that the same conceptual categories are not also relevant to other
societies, given the increasing integration of the world economy and the
political and cultural hegemony exercised by advanced capitalist states within
the world system.

The reader may well ask which particular movements we have in mind.
An initial list might include: the ecological, anti-nuclear, peace, feminist,
human rights, gay liberation, human potential/self-awareness, communalist
movements. However, we should also include the range of movements
struggling for local, regional, linguistic, cultural or religious autonomy,
including a number of indigenous movements, for example in the United
States, Canada, Australia and New Zealand, that have continued to resist the
intrusion of the white colonial state. To this list should be added movements
striving for urban renewal, alternative forms of economic organization, and
racial justice. In a specifically Third World context, reference must be made
to movements, both rural and urban, committed to land reform, co-operative
production and distribution, and liberation from various forms of foreign
domination. Finally, mention must be made of the many groups and communities concerned with youth, education, the workplace, rights of minorities
(e.g. elderly, disabled, ethnic groups), North–South relations, and animal
rights.

This multiplicity of movements represents an extraordinarily diverse range
of values, actors, issues and conflicts. Some movements are local, others
regional, some national, others international. Some have coalesced around
highly specific struggles (e.g. prison reform), while others embrace a wide

spectrum of social, political and economic concerns (e.g. the anti-apartheid movement). Some represent the interests of a specific social group (e.g. homosexuals) or of a geographically distinct community (e.g. New Zealand Maoris), whereas others have a presence and an agenda which spans the globe (e.g. Amnesty International). Clearly, any serious analysis must allow for the specificity of each group and each movement. Yet specificity does not negate interconnection.

In one sense there is little in common between ethnic minorities, the women's movement and urban protest. On the other hand, while careful of the dangers of overgeneralization, we may ascribe to these seemingly disparate entities and phenomena a certain commonality of experience. As Alain Touraine suggests, all dominated groups, whether indigenous communities, ethnic minorities, school students or hospital inmates, are defined by 'the exclusion, labelling, stigmatisation'[15] they suffer as victims. What makes these actors politically significant is that they are able to translate their alienation and exclusion into concrete social action. They are social movements by virtue of their ability to engender and organize social conflict.

Useful though this characterization may be, it clearly does not go far enough. Focusing for the moment our attention on the industrialised West, it emerges that social conflict generated by the new social movements deals less with labour or economic problems as traditionally understood than with cultural or ethical problems because, as Touraine puts it, 'the domination which is challenged controls not only the "means of production" but the production of symbolic goods, that is, of information and images of culture itself'.[16] Habermas too sees the main preoccupation of the social movements as the 'erosion of the life-world'. Social conflict, he tells us, arises primarily in areas of 'cultural' rather than 'material' reproduction and is manifested in 'sub-institutional, extra-parliamentary forms of protest'.[17]

For the new social movements, the critical question is not how to distribute the benefits of economic growth, but rather 'how to defend or reinstate endangered lifestyles, or how to put reformed life-styles into practice. In short, the new conflicts are not sparked by *problems of distribution*, but concern the *grammar* of forms of life.'[18] The distinction between the cultural and material spheres opens up a particularly fruitful line of inquiry, yet it must not be overstated since issues of distributive justice remain central to conflict between capital and labour in both core and peripheral states. It is not that the older dimension of conflict has ceased to be relevant but rather that a new dimension has been added to it, which in a sense transforms it, makes for new actors, new patterns of interaction and above all new forms of political life.

Strictly speaking, quite a few of the new social movements are not 'new'. As Fuentes and Gunder Frank rightly observe, 'peasant, localist/community, ethnic/nationalist, religious and even feminist/women's movements have existed for centuries and even millennia in many parts of the world'.[19] They have been traditional agents of social resistance and transformation. Moreover, the working-class/trade union movement is very much a product of the industrial revolution, and still a potent factor in regions that have recently experienced or are still on the verge of industrialization. The *newness* of the new social movements lies rather in their rejection of what Offe has described as the 'comprehensive growth–security alliance' constructed in the aftermath of the Second World War. Here a brief reference to Offe's analysis may be useful.

The alliance rested principally on the liberal-democratic welfare state consensus which in the West went virtually unchallenged for more than two decades. It assumed that family, work, leisure and the consumption-centred patterns of life would absorb the energies and aspirations of most people while participation in and conflict over public policy would be of marginal significance in the lives of most citizens. The primary objective of the economy, state and society, and of the accord between capital and organized labour, was to increase production, and with it productivity-increasing innovation. However, the growth objective was closely connected to security, which included three elements: social security (understood as adequate income and living standards for the society as a whole); military security (understood as defence against aggression and in particular expansionist communism); and political security (understood as the prevention of deviant individual or collective behaviour likely to threaten the viability of the family or the larger legal, economic and political institutions which underpinned this quasi-constitutional accord).[20]

The social movements that arose in the West as a reaction to the growth–security alliance of the 1950s and 1960s tended to highlight several key values: quality of life, individual self-realization, human rights, participation, peace and conservation. These were, after all, the values most directly threatened by the alliance. They pointed to the unacknowledged costs of economic growth and Cold War security. One of the main factors cementing an otherwise heterogeneous cluster of social movements was precisely their antipathy to growth, since they had all in different ways and to varying degrees experienced its adverse impact on everyday life. Illuminating though this analysis may be, it is unnecessarily restrictive, for the contemporary critique of the productive machine did not rest solely on the perceived destruction of health, environment and social relationships.

Even at the material level, the benefits of growth were not equally distributed. The industrial system produced a number of victims who, because of class, race, gender, age or ethnic background, were deprived of the purchasing power needed to avail themselves of the pleasures of consumption. In this sense, the various movements of resistance to emerge in many parts of the Third World, not least in the post-independence period, may also be interpreted as a reaction to the growth–security alliance, since these peripheral societies were themselves its primary victims. This may also help to explain, at least in part, why the new social movements in the affluent West and the liberation and anti-imperialist movements in the underdeveloped world were linked, despite marked cultural and economic differences, by a remarkable level of ideological and organizational solidarity.

Sensitivity to the destructive consequences of the economic and administrative complex of advanced capitalism had, however, another important characteristic. Though different in many respects, the social and political conditions fostered by bureaucratic socialism tended to provoke similar responses. What distinguished the new social movements was their understanding and mobilization of social power. They favoured flexible, adaptive, non-authoritarian and autonomous forms of organization in contrast to the structures and processes of state power. Their repudiation of institutional politics thus defines their *modus operandi* and at the same time offers them a new source of power. While heirs to the formal egalitarian principles of socialism and the universalist democratic principles of liberalism, 'they struggle in the name of autonomy, plurality and difference'.[21]

Their struggles, as we shall see, symbolize a new relationship between economy, state and society, and a new synthesis of the public and private spheres. One of their main achievements is their ability to create new political space, within which it is possible to develop new identities and articulate new demands, and where the sharp dividing line between the public and the private has largely lost its meaning. The notion that the personal is political, though most often associated with the women's movement, has achieved wide currency through a great many of the social movements. It implies a redefinition of social power which, in its confrontation with the state, necessarily also involves the reshaping of political power.

In contrast to conventional forms of political organization, the practice of the new movements is for the most part 'highly informal, ad hoc, discontinuous, context-sensitive and egalitarian', relying primarily on 'participants, campaigns, spokespeople, networks, voluntary helpers, and donations'.[22] The organizational ethos, which is generally co-operative, non-bureaucratic, non-hierarchical and participatory, has several practical ramifications, including 'a shared, often circulating leadership ... a critical stance toward professionalism ... a recognition that small may not necessarily be beautiful, but is the place to begin and the unit to build upon ... a recognition that the group is key – de-isolation is critical'.[23] This description of movement politics is no doubt an idealized version of reality. Yet, in so far as these movements establish new communities and identities, articulate new norms, rituals and language, invest existing norms with renewed vitality and urgency, and legitimize new forms of political behaviour,[24] it is reasonable to conclude that their praxis constitutes a clear break from institutional politics. Their space of action is 'a space of *non-institutional politics*' which is neither *private* (understood as 'being of no legitimate concern to others') nor public (understood as 'the legitimate object of official political institutions and actors').[25]

What, then, constitutes the political domain of the new social movements? If political parties, bureaucratic and other state institutions are ineffectual, intrusive or generally at odds with normative ends, where can these movements find a congenial space of action? These collective actors, it should be stressed, operate in, and receive their impetus from, a larger whole, namely civil society. It is civil society, not the state or the economy, which offers the new movements their preferred political terrain, 'in which the creation of norms, identities and social relations of domination and resistance are located'.[26] Unlike the state, civil society is not territorially bound. It is a field of action whose boundaries can shift to suit the requirements of new issues and changing circumstances.

To the extent that the 'life-world' provides the new social movements with their normative and political compass, it follows that their reinterpretation of civil society must be free from the constraints imposed by the state. Placed in this context, the preoccupation with the body, health, sexual identity, neighbourhood, natural environment, and even human survival represents a sharp break with the sovereignty of the state, or, to put it differently, with the conception of the state as a boundary-maintaining system. The centrality of the body for many social movements (e.g. women's, youth, homosexual, human potential, and other counter-cultural movements) is particularly significant in this respect. First, it enables the individual, freed from the integrative or manipulative tendencies of the state apparatus, to experience the body as a basic dimension of social existence. Contrary to the demands of the state and the economy, which see the body as 'a resource for use in the production of merchandise and in social reproduction', the body, understood as the place for play and eros, that is as the focus of desire, becomes also the focus of resistance.[27]

Concern with the physical and the immediate has no doubt a spatial quality about it, but here space bears a direct sensual, aesthetic or even spiritual relationship to the subject. It is mobile, flexible, personal and yet social space. It does not have the fixed boundaries, bureaucratic ethos or official status associated with the sovereign state. Here we are reminded of the postmodern condition (described in Chapter 3) and the tendency to challenge existing boundaries, deconstruct accepted categories and reinterpret official histories. These qualities are reflected in the experience of neighbourhood, but also taken a step further. Civil society is constructed or reconstructed when people in a given locality are able, through a process of mutual help, to penetrate each other's space, pursue common tasks, acquire skills, rediscover a sense of community. Neighbourhood associations, base communities and other rural or urban grassroots organizations give expression to the local dimension of civil society. As members of these communities discover the external causes of their problems, as they become exposed to new messages and images, there may emerge a consciousness of the interconnection of issues, and coalitions may form at the regional or national level.

The political domain of the new social movements is not exclusively local. The interests they have to defend often require them to act in political arenas where the technological, economic or military contest is international in scope or consequence. Yet these movements are unlikely to engage in struggle on the conventional terrain of the market-place or the battlefield. Their practice cuts across national boundaries and their messages appeal to an international audience, for their relationship to civil society is not defined by the boundaries of the sovereign state or by the actions officially sanctioned by it. In this sense, the relationship of the social movements to civil society is mediated by conflicts whose domain is fluid and responsive to a complex and rapidly changing agenda.

FUNCTIONS OF NEW SOCIAL MOVEMENTS

Enough will have been said to indicate that the new social movements cannot be adequately described, much less interpreted, within the categories of conventional sociological analysis. The case for conceptual reinterpretation has been most forcefully and incisively put by French sociologist, Alain Touraine.[28] He takes issue with the functionalist approach which purports to explain the behaviour of social movements in terms of function or dysfunction *vis-à-vis* the social system's internal processes of differentiation, integration and pattern-maintenance. According to several exponents of the functionalist school, the individual's participation in non-institutional collective behaviour stems from the experience of discontent, frustration or aggression, which itself derives from breakdown in the organs of social control or the failure of normative integration.[29] In sharp contrast to the breakdown model of collective behaviour, Touraine represents social movements as culturally oriented actors involved in structural conflict, whose goals and strategies have a social coherence and rationality of their own. In so far as new social movements have functions, these cannot be understood within the logic of the existing institutional order, since their overriding function is precisely to challenge that logic and transform the social relations which it mirrors and reinforces.

Touraine also questions the utility of resource mobilization theory, which analyses social movements in terms of strategic options and the resources they can mobilize in support of such options.[30] Such an approach may tell us something about the way social movements act and the impact of their actions,[31] but little about the meaning of these actions.

In Charles Tilly's version of modernization theory, we are offered a more sophisticated version of the link between collective action and structural change in modern everyday life. The demographic shift from the countryside to the city, the reshaping of urban life, the development of large institutions (including mass media and mass electoral politics) are viewed as factors contributing to the growth of formally organized associations and the politics of large-scale mobilization.[32] Interesting though this analysis may be, not least because of its historical perspective, it too suffers like much resource mobilization theory from an excessive focus on strategic or organizational rationality. More importantly, it precludes serious investigation of the normative status of the new social movements, or of their ideology or self-understanding as collective actors.[33]

What makes the new social movements a valuable object of sociological and political investigation is their attempt 'to socially construct new identities, to create democratic spaces for autonomous social action, and to reinterpret norms and reshape institutions'.[34] These functions are particularly relevant to our study of sovereignty because they shed new light on the nature of the modern state and its relationship to civil society. They place in context the concepts, allegiances and institutions which are central to that context. To put it differently, the new social movements, diverse though they are, may be understood primarily as a response to the cultural, technological and institutional manifestations of modernity, that is to the functioning of modern political economies and the technological apparatus, both military and civilian, which now dominates the political landscape. That response is all the more significant given that the underlying experience of deprivation and alienation is not peculiar to the membership of the new movements but is, in fact, shared by a much wider constituency which is only marginally or occasionally involved in movement politics.

Though the response to modernity, implicit in the praxis of the new social movements, takes different forms in different cultural and geopolitical environments, it would be true to say that the reaction against economic inequality does not provide its overriding impulse, at least in the industrialized world. Economic exploitation remains a potent factor, most obviously in the Third and Fourth Worlds, yet even here economic struggles are not characterized by the class specificity we associate with working-class consciousness in late nineteenth- and early twentieth-century Europe.

The experience of contemporary socioeconomic movements reflects, as in the case of other social movements, alienation from existing systems of production and profound antagonism towards notions of economic development which entail the destruction of cultures, traditions and communities, not to speak of the natural environment.[35] Many of these movements are groping for new forms of economic organization which effectively dethrone instrumental rationality and integrate the satisfaction of material needs into a larger and holistic conception of human development. As a generalization it could be said that what distinguishes the new social movements is their preoccupation with three interrelated aspects of modernity: the *experience of uprootedness*, the *societal production of technological risk*, and *institutional failure*.

The vast economic and cultural dislocations arising from the process of modernization have given rise to a powerful quest for the rediscovery of historical and cultural identities. The 'uprootedness' associated with the loss of jobs, obsolescence of skills, plant closures, mass migrations within and between countries, educational curricula unrelated to local needs, and accelerating speed of travel and information, to name but a few examples, confronts the human psyche with an environment that is unfamiliar, remote, impersonal, and therefore threatening. As Habermas puts it, the abstractions that modernity imposes on the life-world 'supersede the sensually focussed, spatial, social and temporal boundaries of complexity'.[36] The ensuing search for rootedness manifests itself in numerous and widely disparate ways (e.g. the rise of ethnic identification, the revival of religious sentiment, the growing neighbourhood movement and the return to nature as an important strand in ecological consciousness).

The connecting thread in each case is the search for identity and community – an attitude shared by a good many conservative and neo-conservative movements which are also preoccupied with the 'distancing from rooted, communal ties'. However, from the conservative viewpoint, community, rather than providing the basis for the democratic reconstitution of civil society, becomes an escape from the real world. In many instances it is little more than an attempt to recover remnants of tradition and identity from a distant part by accepting established authority while disturbing as little as possible the logic of the market-place. There is a clear dividing line between the new social movements and neo-conservative politics, not least in their ideological preferences, yet there are also connections since both are symptoms of the same social reality.

As already indicated, identification with a pre-modern ethnicity is now a widespread and increasingly potent political phenomenon. Ethnic communities enshrine a sense of togetherness (and separateness), of history (and destiny) based on shared memories and the emotive symbolism of dress, language, art, architecture, religion, custom and law.[37] These dimensions of social existence help the group and its members to position themselves in the world, both culturally and geographically. They serve as instruments of legitimation, and provide a basis for political mobilization. Although ethnic affiliation is invariably related to territory, there is, often as a result of periodic migrations, no clearly demarcated homeland. This is not to say that the system of ethnic loyalties does not often acquire considerable institutional expression or political influence, but, unlike the nationalism of the sovereign state, it is not necessarily tied to fixed boundaries. The cultural and moral soil which nurtures ethnic solidarity endows it with a spatial flexibility from which the nation-state is precluded by virtue of the legal requirements of sovereignty.

The search for identity characteristic of the women's movement has vastly different historical and sociological origins. Yet, for all these differences, the feminist struggle for autonomy and equality has also had to reconsider the myth structures of modern civilization. The critique of patriarchy, precisely because it encompasses diverse forms of exploitation, calls into question the foundations of both social and political authority. In this the demands of feminism go well beyond the goals of equal access to educational and career opportunities, equality in the workplace, or more equitable sharing between sexes of childrearing responsibilities and domestic labour generally. The feminist call for autonomy and dignity in the economic and social arenas may therefore be interpreted as an attempt to redefine the nature of work and the function of 'home'. It challenges the atomization and isolation which pervades contemporary urban life, and seeks to establish new forms of community capable of overcoming the repression and violence that arise from the sexual and economic division of labour, for which the state acts as an enforcing and legitimizing agency.[38]

From gender let us turn to the unlikely category of religion. The reader may well ask: how can religious faith, with its mythical-supernatural worldview, ritual symbolism and pre-modern conceptual and moral framework, enhance the search for identity and community? The question is particularly intriguing given the widely shared view that traditional religion is in steady decline and its social relevance severely eroded as a consequence of the twin processes of modernization and secularization.[39] There is a sense in which religious institutions have been transformed into 'marketing agencies' each desperately trying to retain its share of the market, with all that this implies for the commodification of religious beliefs and practices. Yet it is also true that religious faith, which is currently enjoying a striking revival, represents a complex and diversified response to the experience of uprootedness.

As José Casanova argues, many of the new religious movements share with the counter-culture of the 1960s 'the rejection of the capitalist world, the critique of the establishment and its logic of bureaucratic domination, instrumental rationalisation, one-dimensionality and commodification as well as the critique of bourgeois ideologies of possessive individualism, utilitarianism, careerism and the repressive work ethic'.[40] While not engaged in radical politics, many of these movements, by opting for various forms of Eastern spirituality, tend to cultivate 'pantheistic conceptions that emphasize(d) the experience of mystical illumination and the search for unity with nature and the universe in the attempt to overcome all subject-object dualisms'.[41] They express a yearning for community and security, although the authoritarian tendencies inherent in several of the Eastern sects that have recently flourished in the West make it unlikely that this version of inner-worldly mysticism will give rise to a renewed sense of human solidarity or public responsibility. Much the same conclusion applies, though for different reasons, to the bewildering array of human potential groups (e.g. Gestalt, awareness training, transactional analysis, transcendental meditation, primal therapy) which have entered the market-place offering techniques for meaningful experience and personal fulfilment.

The religious fundamentalism that has swept protestant America or Khomeini's Iran, though operating in vastly different environments and giving rise to sharply contrasting forms of political organization, represents another illuminating, though dangerous reaction to modernity. Yet this is not all there is to the revival of religious sentiment. An interesting development in this regard is the renewal of the established churches and the resulting impetus for social reform, 'including Christian-Marxist dialogue, civil rights activism, anti-war efforts, experiments in Liturgy, and re-evaluations of traditional political and moral postures'.[42] This trend must not be overstated, for it involves at best a minority movement in most mainstream churches, although it is a movement that has been particularly influential in certain pockets of Catholicism. The *aggiornamento* launched by the Second Vatican Council, while it reflects the institution's readiness to come to terms with modernity, does not regard the autonomy of the secular sphere as absolute. The conservative implications of the Catholic worldview may not have been eliminated, but 'the principle of communal ethical life' has been reasserted,[43] and with it the possibility of questioning the legitimacy of secular power and authority.

Planted in the fertile soil of Latin America, where socioeconomic oppression is rife, this principle has blossomed into a fully-fledged movement that encompasses intellectuals and peasants, base communities, as well as bishops, priests and nuns. While its impact and organizational form tend to vary from one society to another, the 'liberation theology' movement has spread to other parts of the Third World, is beginning to exert a degree of influence in the First World, and is in the process of moving well beyond the boundaries of Catholicism. The relationship of religion to modernity remains complex, ambiguous and problematic. That the sacred, the mysterious and the mystical continue to exert a powerful hold over the public imagination is clear enough. But there is reason to think that a significant element in the contemporary appeal of religion is its ability to function as 'a global myth capable of providing a foundation for the construction of an identity', enabling it to assume 'the cultural form of resistance to the instrumental rationality of the apparatus of domination'.[44] Religious or spiritual sensitivity is giving renewed impetus to the recovery of personal identity and collective solidarity.

To complete this all too brief and selective survey of the search for roots and identity, it may be useful to refer to the urban movements and communities that are confronted with 'the segregated space of ethnic fragmentation, cultural strangeness, and economic over-exploitation'.[45] Precisely because they have emerged in the wake of the modern city, these movements encapsulate in their objectives and campaigns the concerns of a great many other social movements. They crystallize the need for cultural identity, which means the 'maintenance or creation of autonomous local cultures' and in particular 'the defence of communication between people, autonomously deferred social meaning, and face to face interaction'.[46]

Despite regional and national variations, these movements cut across traditional class divisions. They are concerned not merely with the productive process but with the more inclusive sphere of consumption, communication and power. Whether it be base communities in Brazil or urban protests in Japan, the aims are essentially the same: local autonomy, decentralization and citizen participation; and the overriding project of creating self-governing communities rather than cities acting on behalf of a centralized state which is itself an instrument in a process of abstract and global integration.

So the three related themes of autonomy, identity and community are central to the praxis of the new social movements. Paradoxically, these are the very themes which underlie the state's own claim to legitimacy. The gap between promise and performance lies, in fact, at the heart of the state's crisis of legitimacy. It is this crisis which the new social movements seek to expose and exploit.

There is another dimension which, though closely connected, is nevertheless distinct. This is modern technology and the ensuing risks to life, health, security and identity that have become an integral part of advanced industrial society. Quite apart from the technologies that have a high potential for catastrophic accidents (e.g. nuclear power, nuclear weapons, genetic engineering), many others (e.g. motor cars, power lines, plastics), by virtue of the materials they require, the wastes they generate, or the hidden interactions they provoke, pose risks which may be not only global (without geographic limitation) but universal (threatening all forms of life) and possibly irreversible (threatening future generations).[47] Many of the new social movements, including anti-nuclear campaigns, urban protests against hazardous chemical industries, peace groups opposed to the development and proliferation of weapons of mass destruction, and the environmental movement generally, represent a response to the 'societal production of technological risk'.

The movements' agenda involves not only pressuring governments and other state agencies to adopt additional safeguards but gaining access to the decision-making process. The aim is to politicize technological change, to subject the choice of technical options to probing public scrutiny. The overriding impulse is not ideological opposition to technical innovation. Resistance, it is true, may be motivated by the perceived threat to jobs, status or established skills, as numerous examples of industrial conflict clearly indicate, but more often than not the motivation has to do more with the perception of risk to local communities, and its likely national and international ramifications.

The new social movements call into question the adequacy of existing technical and institutional arrangements, that is the capacity of the state to control the effects of certain technologies. Here the state has to grapple with a debilitating contradiction. It can refuse to improve or expand the complex network of safety regulations and risk being subjected to charges of incompetence or abdication of responsibility. Alternatively, it can use its authority to introduce a more comprehensive system of controls, in which case it makes itself liable to accusations of bureaucratic disregard for private initiative and civil rights, which in turn threatens to undermine the social consensus and, should the regulatory regime be draconian enough, even the process of capital accumulation. To the extent that the state itself contributes directly to the generation of technological risk, its regulatory role is doubly undermined.

The erosion of public confidence in the efficacy and impartiality of the regulatory process is graphically illustrated in the controversy that continues to dominate nuclear policy in several industrialized countries. Yet the debate about regulation reflects the much deeper conflict about the ethics of risk-taking. This unresolved conflict, itself closely related to the crisis of legitimacy, has been characterized in the following terms:

> What number of cancers and diseases, for example, ought society to trade for the economic and technological advantages promised by nuclear energy? What degree of political and economic centralisation should it tolerate in the interests of preserving current patterns of energy consumption? How in other words, could society formulate an appropriate risk-benefit analysis, and on the basis of what moral principles?[48]

In responding to this ethical dilemma the tendency of the state has been to reassert the primacy of technical expertise.

By reducing questions of human health, industrial safety or environmental protection to a series of complex technical arguments, the agencies of the state seek to blunt the sharpness of normative criticism, to exclude the performance of administrative functions from public purview, and carefully to circumscribe the level of public participation in decision-making. By contrast, one of the main functions of the anti-nuclear movement has been to develop counter-expertise and disseminate alternative scientific opinion. Even more important has been its ability to raise disturbing ethical questions about established policy and compel the state to do battle on unconventional normative terrain – a process the latter finds both risky and uncomfortable.

The intrusion of ethical considerations into the discourse of bureaucratic and technical rationality has also played a key role in the wider environmental agenda. Beyond the specific questions of wilderness and outdoor recreation, air and water pollution, land conservation and protection of forests, ecologists have raised more fundamental questions about the long-term implications of human intervention in the natural order, the appropriateness of lifestyles and the nature of work. Though far from ideologically monolithic, the environmental movement has tended to advocate a notion of sustainable development which rests on much greater levels of economic and political decentralization, a more labour-intensive mode of production, greater local and regional self-reliance, and more democratic forms of decision-making.[49]

While the new social movements have given priority to the social, cultural and ecological ramifications of modernity, their attention has also focused on the failure of dominant institutions to evaluate and internalize these ramifications. The experience of these movements, indeed their very rationale, points to 'the structural incapacity of existing economic and political institutions to perceive and to deal effectively with the global threats, risks, and deprivations they cause'.[50] In contrast to the state, with its emphasis on economic growth and technical rationality, the new social movements have developed a conception of social reality which allows for a wider understanding of deprivation and greater sensitivity to the possibility of technological and political malfunction. To use Offe's phrase, one of the main functions of the 'new politics' is the diagnosis it offers of 'blocked institutional learning capacities'.

It is not that the social movements are giving expression to an altogether different or postmodern set of values. Many of the moral principles and demands they articulate (e.g. dignity and autonomy of the individual, equality, participation, ecological balance, peace, diversity and tolerance) are clearly derived from the modern political philosophies of the last two or three centuries, not to speak of much older ethical and religious traditions.

Their innovation lies in their radical reinterpretation of these values and in the profound contradictions they expose between those values and institutionalized rules and processes.

The normative critique of mainstream institutions, notably the state, stresses in particular their repressive character. The authoritarian state, particularly in the Third World, has given rise to a wide-ranging human rights movement which operates both nationally and internationally. Repression in the periphery (e.g. Latin America) is increasingly shown to be closely connected to economic and military conditions from which metropolitan centres of power derive considerable advantage and to which they positively contribute. Even in liberal democracies, where the state is a less blatant instrument of corruption and coercion, the parliamentary process is perceived as merely disguising the assertion of bureaucratic authority. Though its ways are more subtle and the use of force less conspicuous, the state apparatus is experienced as 'a systematic structure of exclusion'.[51] The new movements generally, irrespective of their geographic location or particular focus, help to highlight the state's abuse of authority and the illegitimate closing of political and social space. They are often engaged in defensive actions aimed at recovering space lost, while at the same time trying to create new spaces, new openings for the expression of democratic values.[52]

It is not surprising, then, that the response of the new social movements to the state should be at best ambivalent and at worst hostile. On the one hand, there is a readiness to use the state's institutions where these can help to widen the available political space. Environmental organizations, for example, have expended considerable energy in securing legislative and administrative changes for the preservation of species, protection of forests and more effective pollution controls. Women's groups have fought strenuously to gain institutional acceptance of the principle of equal pay for equal work, and to have legislation introduced banning various forms of sexual discrimination. Social justice and welfare organizations are strongly pressing for a more equitable taxation system while fiercely resisting attempts to reduce the level of collective consumption. For these purposes, the new social movements are prepared to use the opportunities offered by institutional politics, including participation in public or parliamentary inquiries, actions in the courts,[53] lobbying of legislatures and political parties, pressure on government bureaucracies, especially at the local level,[54] mobilization of public opinion, and advocacy of and involvement in citizen-initiated referenda. Much could be said about the applicability of these various strategies to particular circumstances. Suffice it to say that success on any of these fronts is not assured, is unlikely to be more than partial and will seldom prove permanent.[55]

It is partly because of their limited success in using the avenues of institutional politics that the new social movements have been attracted by the prospect of electoral intervention. This strategy assumed increasing importance from the early 1970s, particularly for anti-nuclear and ecological campaigns in Europe and elsewhere. Here too, however, there are clear limitations. Quite apart from financial constraints and restricted access to the media, the electoral system may severely disadvantage small or emerging political groupings. Yet even limited electoral success may, because of the implications for co-option, generate sharp internal divisions.[56] This has been very much the experience of the German Greens who, despite their anti-statist rhetoric and practice, have found that electoral politics can become an all-consuming and sharply divisive political option.[57]

Conscious of these dangers, the new social movements have been intent on maintaining their separateness from the state, intervening in the institutional arena yet remaining at arm's length from it. For similar reasons the German Greens have sought to portray themselves as the 'anti-party party', or to put it differently, as the political arm of the new social movements. While contesting elections and deriving the benefits that come from electoral success, they have been at pains to present an alternative, if not fully elaborated, vision of plebiscitary and grassroots democracy.[58] Whatever one makes of the public declarations of the Greens and of their electoral activities, the practice of the new social movements is less open to ambiguity. While accepting that state institutions can be 'the site of democratic renewal', they are reluctant to treat them as the only or primary domain of political action. Unlike the main progressive movements of the nineteenth and early twentieth centuries, they do not see organized action as aimed at controlling or seizing state power.[59] Their overriding objective is not the capture of the state but the reconstitution of civil society.

The new social movements share with the neo-conservative movement the view that political regulation and the proliferation of bureaucratic agencies cannot in themselves resolve the underlying contradictions of advanced industrial societies. However, unlike the neo-conservative project which sees the solution in the primacy of the private sphere (e.g. private property, market, family, individualistic work ethic), the new social movements are striving for the remaking of civil society 'through practices that belong to an intermediate sphere between "private" pursuits and concerns, on the one side, and institutional state-sanctioned modes of politics on the other'.[60] They offer a notion of liberation, which, because it implies the dismantling of the power and authority of the state, bears resemblance to the Marxist 'withering away of the state'. In their case however the notion is not proposed as a hypothetical conceptualization of future society but a requirement of current practice. This is precisely the function of citizen action, hence the emphasis on mass protests, co-operative enterprises, people's inquiries and tribunals, civil disobedience and other symbolic actions of resistance, all of which are aimed at the delegitimation of state-centred authority. It is this quality, perhaps more than any other, which points to the anti-systemic tendencies of this social phenomenon.[61]

In movement politics power itself is redefined. It is no longer identified with domination or force as a condition of social order. As with kinship relations in primitive societies, power is rendered diffuse, 'defined more by the ability to do than by the possibility of forbidding, a community power viable as long as it is not monopolised by one group or institution'.[62] The mode of political action favoured by the social movements closely resembles the conception of power which Michel Foucault has clearly articulated. Instead of the traditional notion of state-centred power, of which 'sovereignty' is the logical expression (that is power located at the centre of the state, 'centred on the sole functioning of the law and on the sole functioning of prohibition'[63]), Foucault postulates the dispersal of power within the social order, in other words a plurality of powers woven into the whole fabric of society.

The experience of the new social movements, though still very much in its embryonic stage, may be considered a relatively accurate barometer of a widespread cultural crisis (the intellectual and practical ramifications of which are discussed more fully in Chapter 3) that threatens the foundations of the existing political order.[64] It represents a multifaceted response to a complex set of malfunctions or contradictions, yet the search for a new order and new forms of balance cannot but accentuate, at least for the time being, the level of systemic tension and conflict. The new social movements, then, arise from and simultaneously contribute to several trends which are antithetical to established structural forms in general and to state sovereignty in particular. They express the tensions of a political order where the accepted categories of power, authority and identity are in a state of painful transition.

REINTERPRETING TIME AND SPACE

So far we have developed the thesis that the new social movements pose a significant challenge to the political economy of modernity, of which the sovereign state is an integral part. A key aspect of that challenge relates to the way time is understood, to the role the passage of time plays in the establishment and consolidation of the political and economic order. It is not simply that the new social movements are new, but that they *move* within a time-frame radically different from that which underpins the modern system of states.

As we have stressed, the new social movements are responding to the vast social and economic transformation ushered in by modernity but are themselves part of a rapidly unfolding historical project. Moreover, they are the inheritors of earlier movements of social change, notably liberalism, socialism and nationalism. The relationship between these two sets of movements is an ambiguous one, marked as it is by both change and continuity.

By liberalism we understand that body of theory and practice which is primarily concerned with the freedom of the individual and the need for democratic processes and institutions that can protect and nurture that freedom.[65] However, another dimension of liberal doctrine is the emphasis on the free market, which in practice tends to privilege the wealthy and makes the accumulation of wealth an acceptable, even commendable, aim of private life. In the twentieth century, and especially since the Second World War, the liberal welfare state has become identified with representative democracy based on party competition and collective bargaining pursued by large, powerful and highly institutionalized interest organizations.

Socialism on the other hand, which makes equality and social justice the centrepiece of its ideology, has given rise to a number of widely diverging political projects.[66] Where it has been equated with the nationalization of the means of production, socialism has entailed a programme of structural change, at times requiring the overt use of force, with the party enjoying a virtual monopoly of power and the state acting as the primary agent of change. Trade unions have normally become an integral part of the state apparatus. Where social democracy is the preferred option, the emphasis is placed on success within a competitive parliamentary system and the establishment of the welfare state as the engine of social progress. Here the social democratic party, which initially saw itself as the political arm of the working class, generally strives for a close, often formal relationship with the trade union movement. In time, one of the key functions of social democracy would be to integrate organized labour with the apparatus of the state.

As for nationalism, we have already described the phenomenon and its underlying principles at some length. The nationalist movements that emerged first in Europe and subsequently in the colonized world represented an attempt, often grounded in different historical circumstances, to mobilize the energies of communities (i.e. nations) on the basis of shared identity and a common history. This cultural unity was seen as constituting the moral soil in which would be built a political edifice (i.e. the sovereign state) capable of preserving national independence and establishing the conditions for industrialization and material progress.

So in some ways the new social movements have adopted a good many of the values propounded by these earlier movements – most obviously the values of liberty and equality, of individual and collective rights, of identity and self-determination. Yet the new movements were also a radical departure from the statism implicit in the practice (if not the doctrine) of those older movements. Whether inspired by the idea of liberal democracy, class consciousness or national solidarity, all political actors, including trade un-ions, political parties and nationalist movements (even those most ardently professing an internationalist creed) in the end chose to pursue their objectives by identifying the state as the primary instrument of power and repository of authority.[67] Not only the workers' movement but the anti-colonial and anti-imperialist movements almost everywhere sought to overcome exploitation by placing their destiny in the hands of political parties whose strategy revolved around seizure or control of state power.[68] Yet that strategy seldom fulfilled the revolutionary objective,[69] usually for one of two reasons: either the state turned out to be incapable of achieving the desired goal – sover-eignty proved to be a mirage; or else the power of the state was soon turned against the very movements which had theoretically 'captured' the state.

The rejection by the new social movements of the statist approach to social transformation is closely related to their understanding of history, to what they perceive to be the role of the state – more specifically the modern Western state – in imposing its history on the *domestic* communities that comprise the core of its 'sovereign' jurisdiction (i.e. nation-building) and on *foreign* societies and civilizations (i.e. conquest). It is this dual process of internal and external colonization which characterizes the history of the sovereign state. The development of state nationalism normally requires the homogenization of different cultures located within the state's boundaries or at least the dominance of one culture over others. Expressed differently, the primacy of national history depends on stifling the histories of minorities and marginal communities. Similarly, the ascendancy of the colonial state rested in no small measure on the imposition of its own history on the colonized society. Such notions as 'manifest destiny', 'civilizing mission', 'modernization' and the 'march of progress' provided the ideological justifi-cation not only for Western military and economic expansion but also the legitimation for obscuring, debasing and rewriting the histories of colonized cultures and civilizations.

Underlying the history of the expanding, conquering, 'sovereign' state is the notion of continuity yet 'progress' across time, of history unfolding as 'the consolidation of cohesive territorial states out of the dispersed dynastic fragments' of former empires, as the ordering of time and space, as mastery of people and nature.[70] As the main carrier of the ideology of modernity and the key institution for the creation of national markets (and in due course a global market), the system of sovereign states was predicated on the erection of boundaries not only between geographical territories but between seg-ments of time. In addition to fostering a pervasive disjunction between the traditional and the modern, the sovereign state sought to control the flow of time by measuring, standardizing and segmenting it, by distinguishing private and public time, work time and leisure time. The application of the market principle to the workplace made possible the buying and selling of labour time, that is the commodification of time. The state provided the legal infrastructure within which the commercialization of time could flourish.

Just as significantly, the state used 'time' to bolster its own power through the conscription of armies, that is by imposing universal obligations on an entire section of the population (i.e. the young) and requiring them to place their time (anywhere from six months to two years or more) at the service of the state. Here we are indebted to Charles Maier's conceptualization of the politics of time in nineteenth-century Europe, and in particular to his interpretation of time as a political instrument designed 'to adjust human life more rationally to the constraints of an absolute time and space'.[71] Despite profound ideological differences separating the liberal and the socialist state, not to speak of the totalitarian state, the function of the political apparatus in the twentieth century has been to increase mastery and control of time. With the enormous technological resources at its disposal and the accelerating velocity of commodities, money and information, the state has been able to divide and allot time, expand and contract time, to the point where time becomes 'malleable', 'plastic', where the concreteness of experience is substituted by a bewildering flow of abstractions.[72]

The new social movements, whether consciously or otherwise, are helping to redefine the conception of history and time on which the modern state has constructed the edifice of sovereignty. To begin with, their praxis implies a rebellion against the decoupling of private and public time, against the segmentation, flattening and abstraction of time. They privilege personal relationships and forms of communal life which endow the experience of time with an organic quality and allow for a more creative coalescence of past, present and future. While remaining faithful to many of the modern values that have inspired the major emancipatory doctrines and movements of the last few hundred years, they are engaged in a project of reinterpretation which parts company with the *universalist history* as well as the *particular histories* fashioned and propagated by the modern state.

The recovery of marginalized histories, freed from the suffocating and homogenizing influence of national history, becomes a powerful psychological and political lever in the hands of the weak for resistance against the administrative and coercive intrusion of the state. For Rob Walker there is a clear parallel between the contribution the reconstruction of working-class history has made to labour movement struggles and the central role that the recovery of pre-colonial history has played in the development of national independence and liberation movements. He applies the same perspective to the recovery of women's histories, which has powerfully assisted the growing consciousness of the commonality of women's experiences across time and space.[73] Much the same dynamic is evident in the attempts of indigenous peoples, urban communities and religious movements to recover and nurture their historical roots. It is not merely that such recovery of history can give rise to a renewed sense of personal identity and self-definition, but that it offers a new compass for defining one's position in the world and, to the extent that this is a widely shared experience, enhances the community's confidence in its capacity to resist the encroachment of social life by the economy and the state.

The reinterpretation of history, and more particularly the reconceptual-ization of time, implicit in the praxis of the new social movements, endows the flow of time with an immediacy it would not otherwise have. It enables the subject to develop a deeper sense of collective purpose and become a more active member of civil society. The new attitude to time, as it impinges both on history and everyday life, facilitates the emergence of new commu-nicative structures and forms of collective identity which have both defensive and offensive implications.[74] It is not merely a question of protecting tradi-tions, allegiances and lifestyles against the incursions of modernity, but of cultivating long-term horizons, of opposing practices and projects (e.g. nuclear arms race, production of greenhouse gases) which devalue the future.

One of the distinguishing characteristics of the peace, ecological, femi-nist and other movements is criticism of existing social and political struc-tures. This criticism is wedded to a forward-looking, inventive imagination which perceives the discarded potential hidden within the present and seeks to sustain a social dynamism capable of translating that potential into politi-cal actuality. All of the critical social movements are to a greater or lesser extent animated by a radical assumption about the future, which perceives and enlivens the progressive, at times tortuous, often painful unfolding of the possibilities latent in individual and collective life. In this sense, they too give simultaneous expression to a plurality of histories and a universalist history, except that in this instance the organizing principle of plurality and universality is not the sovereignty of the state but the diversity and solidarity of human community.

Space and Society

Time and space are intimately connected. Time cannot unfold unless grounded in space. The interconnections are revealing as they are unavoidable. By considering the spatial dimension of contemporary social conflict we are better placed to evaluate the historical trajectory of the new social movements and its relationship to the evolution of the sovereign state. The importance of space cannot be overstated. It is one of the fundamental material dimensions of social life. Spatial forms are produced by human action and are a reflection of the particular mode of economic and political organization.

The system of sovereign states has clearly had a far-reaching yet contradictory and elusive impact on the structuring of both physical and social space. At the simplest level, it can be said that the sovereign state represents the vertical organization of territory in that it imposes rigidly demarcated boundaries separating one sovereign jurisdiction from another. We have already discussed at some length the security implications of territorial boundaries. The modern state seeks to establish and entrench the division of territory (on a global scale) by bringing to bear on such division the combined weight of physical force, law and culture. That is one of the principal functions of the *armed, sovereign, national state*.

The legal arrangements that are an integral part of institutionalized sovereignty (e.g. constitutions, legislature, courts) provide the basis for legal and administrative control over a given territory (and population). The principle of nationality, derived from the nurturing of *national* history, symbols and rituals (e.g. the national flag, national anthem, national festivities, system of national honours, national monuments and war memorials) reinforces the national/foreigner, insider/outsider dichotomy which territorial boundaries are meant to express and concretize. The development and deployment of military force is designed to instil confidence in the (psychological no less than physical) viability of these boundaries, to deter those who would violate them, and defend them should deterrence fail. At one level, then, the function of the sovereign state is to institute a definitive, binding and permanent relationship between the citizen and a given territory. This all-encompassing but territorially specific relationship is postulated as central to the meaning of citizenship and the task of self-definition.

What we have just outlined is, of course, little more than an idealized representation of the way physical and political space are presently organized. The doctrine of sovereignty offers us only one slice of the multifaceted reality that is modernity. Manuel Castells takes us closer to the complexity of the relationship between space and society in the following statement:

> [Spatial forms] will express and perform the interests of the dominant class according to a given mode of production and to a specific mode of development. They will express and implement the power relationships of the state in a historically defined society. They will be realised and shaped by gender domination and by state-enforced family life. At the same time, spatial forms will also be marked by resistance from exploited classes, oppressed subjects, and abused women.[75]

The arrangement of physical space (in part defined by the sovereign state) provides us with only one element of the complex equation that is the structuring of political space.

Simplifying matters a little, we may say that the organization of space in the modern period, which we take to coincide with the advent of capitalism, has been governed largely by the interaction of two agencies or principles: one operating vertically (i.e. the state) and the other horizontally (i.e. the market). This interaction has produced outcomes which are not fully explicable in terms of the logic of either agency or principle. Nowhere is this more evident than in the arena of economic organization. The growth of national economies has witnessed the centralization and concentration of the productive process and with it the 'specialisation of spatial location' in the interests of growth, profit maximization and the efficiency of production and distribution. Land has itself been commodified through the real-estate market but also through a model of metropolitan development primarily designed to serve the emerging construction and transportation markets as well as lifestyles centred on individualized consumption.[76]

Urbanization is the predictable outcome of a spatial process which stresses the mobility of population, resources, capital and information. This model usually entails rapid population shifts from the country to the city, urban sprawl, dislocation of local communities and cultures, uneven regional growth, a widening gap between the need for housing and social amenities and the availability of resources, and increasing differentiation in roles, status and power between the privileged few and the mass of society. The state is both agent and victim of this process: agent in so far as the bureaucratic apparatus performs a number of indispensable legal, administrative and economic functions; victim in that its space (i.e. national territory) becomes fully integrated into a global space governed by the internationalization of trade, production and finance. Castells refers to the spatial outcome of this form of organization as a 'space of variable geometry, formed by locations hierarchically ordered in a continuously changing network of flows'.[77] In the increasingly globalized yet abstracted system of production, in which space dissolves into flows, the state can no longer exercise effective control on the flows themselves or the outcomes of their interaction.

What effectively deprives the state of its central, overriding authority (i.e. the efficacy of its theoretical sovereignty on national space), at the same time compounds the experience of uprootedness. Old communities are disrupted, sometimes destroyed, while new ones are artificially created, all as part of the continuous restructuring of economic activity. As a consequence, urban communities are increasingly removed from the decisions which guide the ceaseless, abstract flow of labour, commodities, money and messages. Decisions, even when channelled through official institutions, are subject to pressures and demands which are often amorphous, inaccessible and unaccountable. The abstraction of decision-making mirrors the abstraction of production. Alienation is both cultural and physical as communities are separated from their histories, from the fruits of their labour, and from the decisions that shape the space in which they live.

The experience of disruption and alienation evokes varied responses: total withdrawal into private spaces on the part of some; grudging adaptation to technocratic requirements on the part of others; but also various forms of rebellion designed to defend against encroachment and discover new, more congenial spaces. Such categories as gender, class, ethnicity and neighbourhood assume greater importance as a focus of organized resistance. The examples are numerous: women who come together to share their experiences and offer each other mutual support; workers who refuse to be relocated; ethnic communities that demand better services; newcomers to big cities who establish effective social networks; neighbourhoods that breathe new life into old traditions and create alternative channels of communication.

Underlying the response of critical movements to the illegitimate intrusion of state and market is the attempt to reconstruct social space in a way that cuts across artificial boundaries. Here one has in mind not only the physical boundaries between states but also the boundaries that separate the traditional and the modern, the scientific and intuitive modes of knowledge, the knower and the known, subject and object, society and nature. The emphasis is on cultivating solidarities within and between communities, on establishing a closer match between territory (land) on the one hand, and the cultural, economic and ecological dimensions of space on the other. By way of example we may cite the experience of urban movements striving for a new conception of the city as a 'network of cultural communities', in which time and space, work and travel, health and education, are structured by its residents, in which neighbourhood becomes a self-governing entity subject neither to the dictates of a centralized state nor to the vagaries of the world market.

More or less the same connections are implicit in the thinking and practice of the peace movement, where global space becomes the main field of operation. Here we find not only the rejection of weapons of mass destruction, but an alternative conception of security which draws attention to the intricate interconnection of local, national and international influences, and widens the meaning of security to include not only military threats but other pressures – some cultural, others economic or environmental – which may disturb a society's psychological or material well-being.[78] A notion of comprehensive security gives due emphasis to the requirements of self-determination and the capacity of communities to sustain their values, traditions, lifestyles and institutions. Within such a conceptual framework, defence of national territory and of boundary-maintaining systems becomes subordinate to the elimination of social conditions (in diverse spatial contexts) which are conducive to human exploitation or environmental degradation.

Critical movements question the prevailing construction of social space not only by articulating Utopian visions or alternative policy prescriptions.

The more direct challenge lies in what they claim as their immediate field of action. The most striking feature of that field is its fluidity, evident both in the range of issues addressed and the breadth of the political terrain. The organizational expression of the new movements is both varied and dynamic. At one end of the spectrum are small groups which operate only at the local level and, often, only for a limited period. At the other end are organizations which boast a large membership, operate nationally or internationally, and have a relatively long history. Yet, despite these organizational differences, there is a striking commonality: a readiness to place a given struggle, however immediate or specific, in a wider context informed by many of the connections to which we have already alluded. It is precisely this fluid interaction at the level of ideas and analysis which explains the growing tendency towards overlapping membership, networking between movements, and coalition-building across geographical and issue boundaries. Even where particular conflicts confine themselves to one issue or locality, their intellectual and intuitive appreciation of the problem as well as their formulation of the solution will almost invariably assume a multi-dimensional discourse that cuts across conventional analytical categories.

The domain of action we are describing also has geographical fluidity: even the most local struggles demonstrate a recognition of the importance of global structures and connections. Such consciousness, however, does not imply that the various movements are advocating or mobilizing for the establishment of a global authority serviced by international institutions. Rather it points to a steady increase, both within and between movements, in international exchanges of experiences and information, regional co-ordination of events and activities, and the development of common or complementary strategies. These international networks stand in stark contrast to the strongly centralized and hierarchical forms which communist internationalism assumed in the early part of the twentieth century. Perhaps because it is structurally looser and more participatory, this mode of international interaction appears to have yielded richer results. Relevant in this regard are the numerous solidarities that have developed between North and South, and the reciprocal influence they have exerted on movement thinking 'about the meaning of life and about new paths to social transformation'.[79]

Instead of fluidity Ferenc Feher and Agnes Heller use the notion of 'transfunctionality', by which they mean the ability of modern social movements to disregard established social functions as criteria of recruitment or organization. Unlike trade unions, business organizations or professional associations, the rationale of the new movements is not to serve a particular interest or set of interests shared by all their members. This characteristic leads Feher and Heller to conclude that 'the modern social movement is consequently dynamic in that it has no *predefined* space, but flows over the whole surface of society' (italics added).[80] There is, of course, a price to be paid for such freedom of action. These collective actors do not have the relative organizational stability of conventional interest groups, because their membership is liable to greater and more sudden fluctuations. On the other hand, their greater flexibility enables them to engage the state in unconventional terrain, move quickly across the local, regional and national levels of the state apparatus, and, through a succession of forays and retreats, discover the points at which it is most vulnerable. The significance of the new social movements lies in their attempt to reconstitute civil society, partly by creating a new domain of political action but also, and perhaps more importantly, by challenging the restrictive ways in which dominant institutions, including the sovereign state, have sought to define both physical and social space.

IMPLICATIONS FOR SOVEREIGNTY

In this chapter our primary concern has been to identify the rationale, functions and mode of action characteristic of the new social movements, because they represent a set of assumptions about the nature of the political process which differ markedly from those associated with the principle of state sovereignty. Our central thesis is that the theory and therefore, to some extent, the practice of sovereignty are premised on a fundamental yet largely unresolved dualism. Part of that dualism relates to the institutional expression of the internal/external, insider/outsider dichotomy which is, indeed, one of the main functions of state boundaries.

In a system of sovereign states everyone is both a national (in one's own state) and a foreigner (in all other states). This dualism does not impinge merely on relations between states; it permeates every facet of social life within the state. By its very nature state sovereignty imposes a far-reaching division between the public and private spheres. This artificial division creates a split in the experience of everyday life by erecting a barrier between the state and the market, the citizen and the consumer, and public and private property. The state is portrayed as the repository of absolute authority, and politics as that activity which revolves around the institutions that make up or are sanctioned by the state. The public sphere is thereby equated with the centralization and bureaucratization of authority and sharply demarcated from the private sphere, which is closely connected to the atomization of civil society. In the process, state sovereignty is, except in the most formal sense, stripped of any notion of popular or democratic sovereignty.

In their intuitive and cognitive understanding of the world, no less than in their practice, the new movements reject the separation of the public and private spheres, which derives not so much from the principle of sovereignty as from the larger architecture of modernity, of which sovereignty is an integral part. Underlying the praxis of these new collective actors is the attempt to shape a new synthesis between the public and the private. Women's movements, for example, connect the personal experience of gender inequality, whether at home or at work, with the power relations that run deep through existing social, economic and political structures. The ecological movement connects the way people live, what they consume and how they travel with the prevailing systems of energy production and distribution. The anti-nuclear movements connect the widespread public uncertainty and anxiety about the future with the secretiveness of the state and the production and unequal distribution of technological risk. The peace and disarmament movements connect the deeply ingrained images of extinction, notably among the young, with the strategic discourse, weapons systems and military budgets of the world's major defence establishments. Through their vision, campaigns and organizational forms the new social movements point to a new, emerging life which, arising from the repressed fragments of the existing social order, connects personal identity and collective solidarity. In this they are contributing to the reinterpretation of the public sphere, that is to the repoliticization of civil society, in which the state is no longer sovereign.

What we have described is, of course, no more than a tendency. The critical movements are, after all, themselves both symbol and practical manifestation of society's unresolved contradictions. While their motivation may be anti-systemic, they have nevertheless to function within the 'system'. While they may reject much of the political economy of modernity, they cannot entirely escape its institutional constraints, which limit their capabilities and range of options. This explains why many of these movements often oscillate between withdrawal from the system (e.g. communitarian projects), partial accommodation with the existing mode of political bargaining (e.g. lobbying, elections), and direct confrontation with established values and authority (e.g. demonstrations and civil disobedience). More importantly, it explains why the political strategies of most movements involve a subtle mixture of withdrawal, bargaining and confrontation. Though itself weakened by tensions and cleavages, the apparatus of the modern state retains considerable resources with which to reward and to punish, and therefore to co-opt, marginalize or repress. In practice, critical movements are deeply divided by strategic, tactical and organizational differences, which in part reflect the fragmented and contradictory social space they occupy. The combined effects of these constraints limits their capacity to formulate, let alone execute, a fully coherent and comprehensive conception of the 'new politics'.

Yet, despite these intellectual and organizational limitations, the new movements point to a new interpretation of contemporary politics, around which a great many other factors are coalescing, not least the profound contradictions that underlie the whole edifice of modernity. Even when they are reactive, negative or one-dimensional, the forms of expression, organization and mobilization developed by the social movements foreshadow a new conception of politics. Their collective struggles are catalysts for the reconstruction of time as well as physical and social space.

The notion of sovereignty as absolute authority exercised by the state as the by-product of an actual or hypothetical social contract is undergoing a profound mutation. Increasingly it is being supplanted by the notion of autonomy, that is the right of individuals and collectivities to pursue their life chances without infringement by other individuals or collectivities, the state included. Contemporary social conflicts are a practical demonstration of the cultural and political potency of this idea. The redefinition of autonomy, hence of identity and community, points to a new concept of social contract, where no absolute authority is created and no rigid boundaries are erected in time or space. The multiple psychological, social and economic needs of the individual are neither defined nor satisfied by one supreme or exclusive centre of power, notably the sovereign state. Rather they are defined and satisfied by a plurality of structural forms and collective solidarities, in which none exercises sovereignty over the others. So the reconstitution of civil society involves a new set of rules which guides the interaction of these structures and collectivities. The function of the new social movements to date has been to express the need for a drastic intellectual reorientation and practical support for a new system of multiple allegiances and jurisdictions, held together not by supreme authority but by an emerging world culture and a dynamic network of communities, movements and organizations.

NOTES

1. A.D. Smith, 'Ethnie and Nation in the Modern World', *Millenium*, **14**, (2), Summer 1985, 130.
2. Fred Block, *Revising State Theory: Essays in Politics and Postindustrialism*, Philadelphia: Temple University Press, 1987, p. 177.
3. Ian Gough, *The Political Economy of the Welfare State*, London: Macmillan, 1979, p. 47.
4. See P. Schnitter, 'Still the Century of Corporatism', *Review of Politics*, **36**, January 1974; L. Panitch, 'The Development of Corporatism in Liberal Democracies', *Comparative Political Studies*, **10**, (1), April 1977.
5. Harry C. Boyte, *The Backward Revolution: Understanding the New Citizen Movement*, Philadelphia: Temple University Press, 1980, pp. 172–3.
6. Smith, 'Ethnie and Nation in the Modern World', 131.
7. Ibid., pp. 131–2.
8. See Harry C. Boyte, 'Beyond Politics as Usual', in Harry C. Boyte and Frank Riessman, *The New Populism: The Politics of Empowerment*, Philadelphia: Temple University Press, 1986, pp. 3–18.

9. The rationale and implications of privatism are discussed more fully in J.A. Camilleri, *Civilization in Crisis*, New York: Cambridge University Press, 1976, pp. 35–7.

10. See C.B. MacPherson, *The Political Theory of Possessive Individualism*, London: Oxford University Press, 1962.

11. Thomas Luckmann, 'Theories of Religion and Social Change', *The Annual Review of the Social Sciences of Religion*, **1**, 1977, 116.

12. For the best-known expositions of this analysis see Herbert Marcuse, *One Dimensional Man*, London: Routledge & Kegan Paul, 1964; also Henri Lefebvre, *Everyday Life in the Modern World*, London: A. Lane, 1971; Bruce Brown, *Marx, Freud and the Critique of Everyday Life*, New York: Monthly Review Press, 1973.

13. Claus Offe, 'New Social Movements: Challenging the Boundaries of Institutional Politics', *Social Research*, **52**, (4), Winter 1985, 826.

14. Ibid., p. 827.

15. Alain Touraine, 'An Introduction to the Study of Social Movements', *Social Research*, **52**, (4), Winter 1985, 782.

16. Ibid., p 774.

17. Jürgen Habermas, 'New Social Movements', *Telos*, **49**, Fall 1981, 33.

18. Ibid

19. M. Fuentes and A. Gunder Frank, 'Ten Theses on Social Movements', *World Development*, **17**, (2), February 1989, 180.

20. Offe, 'New Social Movements', pp. 821–5.

21. Jean L. Cohen, 'Strategy or Identity: New Theoretical Paradigms and Contemporary Social Movements', *Social Research*, **52**, (4), Winter 1985, 669.

22. Offe, 'New Social Movements', p.829.

23. Boyte and Riessman, *The New Populism*, pp. 59–60.

24. Máté Szabó, 'New Factors in the Political Socialization of Youth in Hungary: The Alternative Social Movements and Subcultures', *Praxis International*, **8**, (1), April 1988, 26–7.

25. Offe, 'New Social Movements', p. 826.

26. Cohen, 'Strategy or Identity', p. 700.

27. Alberto Melucci, 'The New Social Movements: A Theoretical Approach', *Social Science Information*, **19**, (2), 1980, 221.

28. Apart from his article in *Social Research* (1985), see Alain Touraine, *The Voice and the Eye: An Analysis of Social Movements*, Cambridge: Cambridge University Press; Alain Touraine, 'Les nouvaux conflits sociaux', *Sociologie du Travail*, **1**, 1975, 1–17.

29. Important proponents of this theoretical model include Herbert Blumer, 'Collective Behavior', in Alfred McClung Lee (ed.), *New Outline of the Principles of Sociology*, New York: Barnes & Noble, 1951; R.G. Turner and L.M. Killian, *Collective Behavior*, Englewood Cliffs, NJ: Prentice-Hall, 1957. See also W. Kornhauser, *The Politics of Mass Society*, New York: Free Press, 1959; Neil Smelser, *The Theory of Collective Behavior*, New York: Free Press, 1962.

30. For a review of resource mobilization literature, see J. Craig Jenkins, 'Resource Mobilization Theory and the Study of Social Movements', *Annual Review of Sociology*, **9**, 1983, 527–53; also Mayer N. Zald, 'Resource Mobilisation and Social Movements: A Partial Theory', *American Journal of Sociology*, **82**, May 1977. For specific application of the theory, see Steven E. Barkan, 'Strategic, Tactical and Organizational Dilemmas of the Protest Movement against Nuclear Power', *Social Problems*, **27**, (1), October 1979, 19–37; David Kowalewski and Paul Schumaker, 'Protest Outcomes in the Soviet Union', *The Sociological Quarterly*, **22**, Winter 1981, 57–68; Lewis M. Killian, 'Organization, Rationality and Spontaneity in the Civil Rights Movement', *American Sociological Review*, **49**, December 1984, 770–83.

31. Klaus Eder, 'The "New Social Movements": Moral Crusades, Political Pressure Groups or Social Movements', *Social Research*, **52**, (4), Winter 1985, 885.

32. See Charles Tilly, *From Mobilization to Revolution*, Reading, Mass.: Addison-Wesley, 1978; also Charles Tilly, Louise Tilly and Richard Tilly, *The Rebellious Century: 1830–1930*, Cambridge, Mass.: Harvard University Press, 1975.

33. Cohen, 'Strategy or Identity', p. 676.
34. Ibid., p. 69.
35. R.B.J. Walker, *One World, Many Worlds: Struggles for a Just World Peace*, Boulder, Co.:
    Lynne Rienner, 1988, pp. 65–6.
36. Habermas, 'New Social Movements', p. 36.
37. See Cynthia H. Enloe, *Ethnic Conflict and Political Development*, Boston: Little, Brown,
    1973; Arnold L. Epstein, *Ethnos and Identity*, London: Tavistock, 1978; A.D. Smith,
    The Ethnic Revival, Cambridge: Cambridge University Press, 1981.
38. Modern feminist analysis has given rise to a voluminous literature. See H. Eisenstein,
    Contemporary Feminist Thought, London: Hutchinson, 1984; J. Elshtain, *Public Man,
    Private Woman*, Oxford: Martin Robertson, 1981; J. Evans et al., *Feminism and Politi-
    cal Theory*, London: Sage, 1986; R. Hamilton, *The Liberation of Women: A Study of
    Patriarchy and Capitalism*, London: Allen & Unwin, 1978; J. Lewis (ed.), *Women's
    Rights, Women's Welfare*, London: Croom Helm, 1982.
39. See David A. Martin, *The Religious and the Secular: Studies in Secularisation*, London:
    Routledge & Kegan Paul, 1969; Bryan Wilson, *Contemporary Transformation of Reli-
    gion*, London: Oxford University Press, 1976; Peter Berger, *The Sacred Canopy*, Gar-
    den City, NY: Doubleday, 1967; Harvey Cox, *The Secular City*, Harmondsworth, Mid-
    dlesex: Penguin, 1966.
40. José Casanova, 'The Politics of the Religious Revival', *Telos*, **59**, Spring 1984, 16.
41. Ibid.
42. Robert Wuthnow, 'World Order and Religious Movements', in A. Bergesen, (ed.),
    Studies of the Modern World System, New York: Academic Press, 1980, p. 73.
43. Casanova, 'Politics of the Religious Revival', p. 25.
44. Melucci, 'New Social Movements', p. 222.
45. Manuel Castells, *The City and the Grassroots: A Cross Cultural Theory of Urban Social
    Movements*, Berkeley, Cal.: University of California Press, 1983, p. 317.
46. Ibid., p. 319.
47. Jost Halfmann, 'Risk Avoidance and Sovereignty: New Social Movements in the United
    States and West Germany', *Praxis International*, **8**, (1), April 1988, 14.
48. J.A. Camilleri, *The State and Nuclear Power: Conflict and Control in the Western
    World*, Brighton, Sussex: Wheatsheaf Books, p. 108.
49. For a conceptually more rigorous exposition of these perspectives, see Murray Bookchin,
    Post-Scarcity Anarchism, Berkeley, Cal.: Ramparts, 1971; Ivan D. Illich, *Tools for
    Conviviality*, London: Calder & Boyar, 1973; H.E. Daly (ed.), *Towards a Steady-State
    Economy*, San Francisco: W.H. Freeman, 1973; André Gorz, *Ecology and Politics*,
    London: Pluto Press, 1980.
50. Offe, 'New Social Movements', p. 847.
51. Walker, *One World, Many Worlds*, p. 16.
52. See Scott Mainwaring and Eduardo Viola, 'New Social Movements, Political Culture,
    and Democracy: Brazil and Argentina in the 1980s', *Telos*, **61**, Fall 1985, 30–32.
53. See, for example, Steven E. Barkan, 'Political Trials and Resource Molibisation: To-
    wards an Understanding of Social Movement Litigation', *Social Forces*, **58**, (3), March
    1980, 944–61.
54. For a discussion of the options open to social movements at the local government level
    see John Jensen and Kirsten Simonsen, 'The Local State, Planning and Social Move-
    ments', *Acta Sociologica*, **24**, (4), 1981, 270–91.
55. For a revealing exposition of the uneasy relationship between the environmental move-
    ment and institutional politics, see Richard P. Gale, 'The Environmental Movement and
    the Left: Antagonists or Allies', *Sociological Inquiry*, **53**, 179–99; also Richard P. Gale,
    'Social Movements and the State: The Environmental Movement, Counter-Movement
    and Government Agencies', *Sociological Perspectives*, **29**, (2), April 1986; also Hugh
    Stretton, *Capitalism, Socialism and the Environment*, Cambridge: Cambridge University
    Press, 1976.
56. Camilleri, *The State and Nuclear Power*, p. 60.
57. See Gregg O. Kvistad, 'Between State and Society: Green Political Ideology in the mid-

1980s', *West European Politics*, **10**, (2), April 1987, 222; Werner Hülsberg, *The German Greens: A Social and Political Profile*, London: Verso, 1988, pp. 140–61.

58. Kvistad, 'Between State and Society', p. 223.
59. Touraine, 'Introduction to the Study of Social Movements', p. 775.
60. Offe, 'New Social Movements', p. 821.
61. See Giovanni Arrighi, Terence K. Hopkins and Immanuel Wallerstein, 'Dilemmas of Anti-Systemic Movements', *Social Research*, **53**, (1), Spring 1986, 192–3.
62. Carla Pasquinelli, 'Power without the State', *Telos*, **68**, Summer 1986, 82.
63. See Michel Foucault, *The History of Sexuality*, New York: Pantheon, 1978, p.76; also *Discipline and Punish*, New York: Pantheon, 1977.
64. Touraine, *The Voice and the Eye*, p. 10.
65. See Lord Acton, *The History of Freedom and Other Essays*, London: Macmillan, 1907; Maurice Cranston, *Freedom: A New Analysis*, New York: Longmans, 1953; William A. Orton, *The Liberal Tradition*, New Haven, Conn.: Yale University Press, 1945; Massimo Salvadori, *Liberal Democracy*, London: Pall Mall, 1958.
66. See Harry W. Laidler, *Socialism in Thought and Action*, New York: Macmillan, 1920; G.D.H. Cole, *Socialism in Evolution*, Harmondsworth, Middlesex: Penguin, 1938; Joseph A. Schumpeter, *Capitalism, Socialism and Democracy*, New York: Harper, 1950; John Plamenatz, *Man and Society*, Vol. 2, London: Longmans, 1963; David Lane, *The Socialist Industrial State*, London: Allen & Unwin, 1976.
67. Walker, *One World, Many Worlds*, p. 59.
68. Touraine, *The Voice and the Eye*, pp. 3–4.
69. Arrighi et al., 'Dilemmas of Anti-Systemic Movements', pp. 189–90.
70. Charles S. Maier, 'The Politics of Time: Changing Paradigms of Collective Time and Private Time in the Modern Era', in Charles E. Maier, *Changing Boundaries of the Political*, Cambridge: Cambridge University Press, 1987, p. 155.
71. Ibid., p. 159.
72. Ibid., p. 165.
73. Walker, *One World, Many Worlds*, pp. 24–5.
74. Here, we are largely in agreement with Jean Cohen who takes issue with Habermas's otherwise penetrating analysis for understanding the offensive, forward-looking possibilities in contemporary forms of resistance and conflict. See Cohen, 'Strategy or Identity', pp. 710–14.
75. Castells, *The City and the Grassroots*, pp. 311–12.
76. Ibid., pp. 312–13
77. Ibid., p. 314.
78. See Johan Galtung, *There Are Alternatives: Four Roads to Peace and Security*, Nottingham: Spokesman, 1984, pp. 172–80. For specific applications of this perspective, see Mary Kaldor, 'Transforming the State: An Alternative Security Concept for Europe', *Bulletin of Peace Proposals*, **16**, (4),1985, 425–38; J.A. Camilleri, *The Australia New Zealand US Alliance: Regional Security in the Nuclear Age*, Boulder, Co.: Westview Press, 1987, pp. 199–221.
79. Scott Mainwaring and E. Viola use Brazil and Argentina as their case study to illustrate their argument ('New Social Movements', p. 35).
80. Ferenc Feher and Agnes Heller, 'From Red to Green', *Telos*, **59**, Spring 1984, 35.

9. Current Trends – Future Possibilities

In choosing sovereignty for its focus this book has sought to examine with a fresh eye one of the distinguishing themes in what has become an exceedingly influential – some would say dominant – interpretation of politics in general and world politics in particular. Like all discourses, but perhaps more than most, the sovereignty discourse constitutes a power play which obscures as much as it illuminates. It mobilizes rules, codes and procedures (but also loyalties) which privilege (and in a sense legitimize) a particular understanding of reality. Much of the conventional literature on the subject, not least in the field of international relations, treats the sovereign state as an uncontested area of modern discourse, a fact of political life, a 'sovereign presence in its own right'.[1]

This discursive practice is so deeply embedded not only in academic scholarship, but in the thinking of policy-makers, strategists, journalists and commentators, that it has come to delineate fields of study, define legitimate perspectives, and even set normative guidelines for the elaboration of concepts and theories.[2] Over time, a tight, almost unseverable link appears to have developed between the idea of sovereignty and political practice, between the notions of community within and anarchy without. The discourse on sovereignty has come to exercise a profound and pervasive influence on both knowledge and action in modern culture.

Yet the intellectual coherence and plausibility of the sovereignty principle have been in steady decline for some time. The postulated nexus between theory and practice is now decidedly tenuous. Postmodern sensibilities with their healthy suspicion of monolithic structures and grand interpretative theories reflect but also lay bare the fragmentation and discontinuity of late twentieth-century experience.

Despite the considerable ideological and institutional support it still enjoys, the paradigm, it should be said, has never been entirely free of ambiguity. It is simply that rapidly changing social and economic circumstances have made visible to the naked eye tensions and contradictions which were previously submerged. Even those long trained to see only coherence and rationality in the theory and practice of sovereignty have come to accept, however hesitantly, that the system of sovereign states cannot be equated with the totality of world politics. The question nevertheless remains: can we rely on the theoretical construct that is sovereignty to gain an insight into the nature and function of the modern state? The argument implicit in all the previous chapters is that the question cannot be adequately formulated within so limiting a framework. A more adequate analysis requires that we interpret the state in the wider context of the language, self-understanding and practice of modernity.

Sovereignty has necessarily to do with space and geopolitics, but also a great deal to do with technology, economics and culture. After all the sovereign state implies a way of partitioning the world, of allocating resources and organizing exchanges between economies, of distinguishing groups, cultures and nations. Sovereignty is no doubt central to geopolitical discourse, in war as in peacetime, establishing the 'dialectic of place attachment', whereby 'our' places and homeland are separated and differentiated from 'theirs'. But such delineation of space inevitably carries profound implications for identity, community and politics.

Geopolitical processes are not merely power plays between states, but theoretical constructs with far-reaching implications for the internal structure of states, and the relationship between state and civil society on the one hand, and between state and market on the other. The need, therefore, to problematize the sovereign state arises not just or even primarily in response to the intellectual fashion set by postmodernist thought. Rather it derives from the contingencies of contemporary political and economic life and the complex web of historical events, relationships and institutions. These cut across the inside/outside dualism of the sovereignty discourse and constitute a powerful dynamic for reinterpreting international political processes and outcomes and redefining relevant actors and agencies.

RESTATEMENT OF THE SOVEREIGNTY MODEL

Our argument leads us to conclude that a reconceptualization of sovereignty is necessary, timely and possible. Before fleshing out the implications of this conclusion, it may be helpful to restate the main elements of the sovereignty model as a way of summarizing its deficiencies, but more importantly of identifying the signposts pointing in an alternative theoretical direction.

Boundaries are central to the discourse of sovereignty. It is not merely a case of physical boundaries which separate one sovereign state from another, but of cultural boundaries which separate the 'same' from the 'other', and of conceptual boundaries which distinguish the domestic from the international, community from anarchy, and the universal from the particular. Within the boundaries imposed by the sovereign state it is possible for rights and obligations, order, freedom and other universal values to be articulated and in varying degrees given practical expression. Outside these boundaries there exists no order, no community, no framework for conducting normative discourse. All that exists is the mechanistic interaction of particular, often discordant wills, engaged in varying degrees of self-interested competition, conflict and co-operation. As Rob Walker has aptly described the dialectic, 'within states, the relation between universality and particularity may be resolvable... between states unresolvable contradiction is guaranteed'.[3]

To the international meaning of sovereignty must be added the often neglected domestic side of the equation, which, as we have seen, has far-reaching ramifications as much for *international* as for *domestic* political theory. Relevant here are the various notions of social contract which emerged in early-modern European thought in an attempt to explain the relationship between the state and civil society. The geographical or territorial extension of the state is important in that it sets the boundaries within which the contract is binding. From this actual or hypothetical social contract emerges a sovereign understood as a conscious agent located at the centre of the body politic wielding absolute power and authority. Explicitly or implicitly, the sovereign is endowed with a distinctive, identifiable will and a capacity for rational decision-making.

The enduring impact this image of the body politic has had on subsequent political thought hardly needs restating. Two influences, however, are worth noting here: one concerns the perception of space; the other the characterization of the international system. The Hobbesian view of the state, which still colours the modern understanding of sovereignty, owes a great deal to the spatial consciousness implicit in Euclidean geometry, Galilean mechanics and Newtonian physics.

The spatial qualities of the state, understood as a geometric entity with precisely demarcated boundaries, is integral to the notion of sovereignty and to international relations theory. Historical change is subordinated to the timeless abstraction that is the sovereign state. The system of sovereign states is represented as the stage from which all actors, actions and roles derive their political significance. Relations between communities are mediated by states. Sovereignty as a concept thus acquires an effective monopoly on the interpretation of international reality.

ANALYTICAL AND NORMATIVE TENSIONS

On first reading, the sovereignty paradigm appears to offer a plausible, indeed compelling, account of the modern world. Yet it does leave a great many questions unanswered. More to the point, it fails to give precise meaning and content to several central categories. Nowhere is this deficiency more apparent than in the treatment of the state itself – a deficiency to which both sociologists and political economists have recently turned their attention. Though their analysis is not yet conclusive and at times contradictory, it represents a considerable advance on the abstraction and ambiguity which surround the use of the concept in mainstream international political theory.

Sovereignty, after all, was a concept elaborated in the specific circumstances of sixteenth- and seventeenth-century Europe to explain and legitimize the rise of the centralized and absolutist state. Rapidly evolving political and economic conditions have greatly influenced the structure and function of the state, compelling us to reassess long-standing intellectual habits and assumptions.

If sovereignty is still to be regarded as an essential attribute of the modern state, the distinguishing characteristic of its *modus operandi*, then the nature of the state must be clearly and precisely formulated. Here we need to return to the discussion introduced in Chapter 2. What is it that is supposedly sovereign? What exactly is the state? Is the state at the end of the twentieth century the same political entity which emerged in sixteenth-century Europe? Is it a generic term referring to the formal institutions of government? Or does it denote the individuals and organizations canvassed by decision-making theory or foreign policy-making analysis?

Alternatively, is the true meaning of the state the more abstract 'national-territorial totality'[4] conveyed by political geography, with territory, government, population and society conflated into one entity and international relations reduced to the interaction of billiard balls? This latter definition, which most traditional theories of international relations articulate or more often assume, is obviously designed to suit the requirements of sovereignty. But such a definitional strategy runs the risk of evading or obscuring the complex and fast-changing political phenomenon it is meant to illuminate. Though still speaking of an administrative, political and military apparatus co-ordinated by a central authority, analytically more rewarding definitions of the state emphasize its relationship to the ordering and reproduction of social relations at a given historical moment. They have gained considerable currency in recent sociological studies, but have yet to leave their mark on the billiard-ball theory of international relations.

The lack of definitional clarity in the sovereignty discourse is not confined to the state. It inevitably extends to sovereignty itself. A good deal of relatively opaque abstraction surrounds the identity of the sovereign. Which contemporary institutions are the repositories of sovereign authority? In what sense and to what extent are they mechanisms of coercion and control on the one hand, or accountability and participation on the other? What, in other words, is the relationship between sovereignty and legitimacy? What does it mean today to describe sovereignty as indivisible and absolute? Is such a description premised on an exclusivist theory of political obligation? Are emerging or re-emerging religious, ideological, ethnic and other loyalties (and obligations) compatible with such a description? These largely unanswered questions reinforce the long-standing tension between *state* sovereignty and *popular* sovereignty, or more fundamentally the undefined relationship between state and civil society.

By equating the state with a notion of totality and attributing sovereignty to this catch-all abstraction, the implications of new social, economic and political arrangements are marginalized or simply ignored. The hypothetical absoluteness of sovereignty is thus preserved but only by effectively insulating it from the content, structure and history of the political process. The only category we are offered as a way of filling the ensuing conceptual void is the nation which is, however, replete with its own ambiguities and inconsistencies. The nation, understood primarily as a pre-ordained or imagined moral community, becomes little more than a synonym for civil society, and nationalism merely the cement used to fill the cracks of cultural and ideological heterogeneity and reinforce the political enclosure that is the sovereign state. Neither nation nor nationalism, divorced from concrete political practice, can bridge the gap between the state as geometric abstraction and the specific organization of civil society.

Placed in a contemporary international setting the concept of sovereignty gives rise to another series of related and equally troublesome contradictions. If all states are deemed equal by virtue of their sovereignty, how is this theoretical equality – itself the legal expression of an abstract spatial relationship – consistent with or related to the actual geopolitical inequalities associated with colonialism, domination, intervention and war? If the rationale of the sovereign state is domestic *order* in the face of actual or potential external *disorder*, how can these two conditions be reconciled? Can the internal disposition of states and societies be effectively immunized from external pressure, particularly in the age of transnational production and exchange? If state boundaries cannot effectively screen the undesired consequences of ideological and religious conflict or military and economic rivalry, then the domestic order cannot be divorced, practically let alone conceptually, from its external environment.

It is this complex and pervasive interaction of the national and international dimensions of modern social and economic life which calls into question the rigid demarcation of boundaries. If the fluctuating mix of conflict, competition and co-operation characteristic of the inter-state system is deeply influenced by the internal structure of states, and if these structures are effective channels for the projection of economic and military power across boundaries, then the questions arises: does the concept of sovereignty shed much useful light on the system of reciprocal influence? It is doubtful to say the least whether the penetration by one state into another's sovereign domain is consistent with the coherence and independence of will and action postulated by the notion of a sovereign agent.

These and related tensions evident in the discourse of sovereignty reflect more than a lack of conceptual clarity. They arise from a tendency inherent in that discourse to view the state as a frozen geopolitical entity instead of an evolving phenomenon situated in time and place. The resulting abstraction of the state obscures its role as both agent and product of a dynamic and still unfolding historical process, and its close institutional and ideological connection with the larger project of modernity and capitalist expansion. In other words, the principle of sovereignty as the defining category of international political theory, tends to overlook or understate the instrumental role of the nation-state, that is its historical function in the formation of national societies and national markets.

Here we use functionality in a strictly limited sense to denote a degree of congruence between complex processes and institutions which characterizes and helps us to interpret particular stages in the evolution of the modern period.[5] This is not to say that there are not significant historical discontinuities (reflected in the organization and conduct of the state), within as well as between stages or that relations between dominant structures and processes (e.g. between the state and the market) within a particular phase do not give rise to profound tensions and contradictions. Our argument here is simply that a historical and contextual perspective puts the theory and practice of sovereignty in a new light. It enables us to situate both the theory and practice against the background of rapid technological and economic change, and allows us to rethink the nature and function of the modern state. Most importantly, it opens up the possibility of interpreting the trajectory of the state in the second half of the twentieth century in significantly different ways from those favoured by the classical theories of sovereignty.

UNFOLDING OF HISTORICAL PROCESS

In the preceding chapters we have sought to identify some of the dimensions of historical change which bear directly on the strength and sovereignty of the state. We have not attempted a comprehensive survey. We have, for example, devoted only passing attention to the recent development of international law and its tangled web of interconnections with domestic law which now impinge on almost every major area of public policy. We have frequently referred to the steady expansion and increasingly complex fabric

of regional, supranational and international organization, but have not offered an exhaustive account of the available evidence. A more detailed
analysis of the trends implicit in the evolution of these legal and institutional
arrangements would probably confirm our conclusion about the declining
relevance and efficacy of rigidly demarcated spatial boundaries.

Instead we have chosen to highlight five discrete yet closely related phenomena that go to the heart of contemporary social and political life: the
internationalization of production, trade and finance; the homogenizing architecture of technological change; the globalization of the security dilemma; the
escalating impact of ecological change; and the rise of local and transnational
social consciousness. These interacting influences provide the context and the
impetus for the changing complexion of laws and institutions.

Though its origins lie in the Renaissance and the breakdown of the feudal
order, it is only in the twentieth century that the ideology of modernity has
achieved a universal presence. Modernity is open to varying interpretations,
but these generally include the following elements: the growth of codified
knowledge as a way of controlling the physical environment; political centralization accompanied by the expansion of highly specialized bureaucracies; continuous increases in economic production and productivity; a rapid
rate of technological change and the development of social and cultural
mechanisms designed to achieve the necessary psychological adjustment.
This ideology has come to permeate almost every national society, whose
economic and political life is as a consequence made dependent on pressures
which filter through the porous membrane of the sovereign state. Progress
centred on the unifying power of the world market has become the dominant
image of change in the capitalist world. It acts as the driving intellectual
force for the restructuring of the centrally planned economies no less than
for the modernization of the periphery. East and West, North and South,
despite economic asymmetries and ideological differences, experience the
same pull. Individual governments, irrespective of the separateness and
uniqueness conferred by state sovereignty, are homogenized by the very fact
of global technological and ideological convergence.

The growth of transnational investment, production and trade since 1945
has been accompanied by an equally spectacular expansion of international
finance. The leading American, European and Japanese banks are now integrated into the international circuit of capital. While there is considerable
ebb and flow and significant national variations in the unfolding of these
trends, integration and interpenetration have become the distinguishing features of economic organization on a global scale. The growing cross-
investment among the principal countries investing abroad and the resultant
increase in mergers and takeovers is evidence of the growing international
centralization of capital. The development of international money markets,

operating largely outside the control of state institutions, has contributed to the destruction of the Bretton Woods system created during the period of American hegemony and replaced it with an international debt economy which has hastened the integration of the newly industrializing countries and oil-exporting countries with the advanced capitalist economies. At the same time it has sharply increased the institutional constraints that sustain national and global patterns of social and economic stratification.

The political implications of the internationalization of capital are not hard to discover. There is an increasing divergence between the territorial constraints on the state and the international mobility of capital. As a consequence national governments now operate within a global environment which severely restricts their powers to gather taxes and regulate the flow of money and information, functions which are presumably central to the exercise of state sovereignty. Even more important is the emergence of an integrated world economy where a continuous process of industrial restructuring acquires a logic of its own and sets much of the agenda for national economic policy. States remain key pillars of this global edifice, but this is a far cry from the notion of a national sovereign acting as a conscious, autonomous agent or of a system of interaction explicable primarily, if not entirely, in terms of sovereign action.

Technological change is probably the most conspicuous symptom and agent of globalization. Since the Second World War, the transport and communication revolution, coupled with the computerization of knowledge, has drastically affected the productive process, enabling large enterprises to move capital and labour at relatively low cost and at vastly increased speed. The net effect has been to make 'communication universal, transport supersonic, information instantaneous and modern weaponry interplanetary'.[6] The spatial and temporal limits to human interaction have been drastically compressed, and an intricate web of interdependencies has arisen, which effectively integrates the world in a manner that has no historical precedent.

Within the emerging global architecture of power, the state has access to a vastly expanded range of coercive instruments and techniques, but access is in varying degrees also open to a large and growing number of local, international and transnational organizations. Paradoxically, technical innovations which occur within territorial boundaries, once they are fully developed, give rise to flows and movements which the state cannot effectively control but which may significantly enhance the power or freedom of action available to non-state actors. The ensuing diffusion of social control is eroding the capacity of national institutions to shape the course of events within the national domain. Similarly, the growth of communication technology has greatly increased the level of contact between societies and vastly enhanced the contribution of non-state actors to the global monitoring and dissemination of information. The state continues to play an important part in developing, organizing and integrating information linkages, but its apparent flexibility in adjusting to a rapidly changing knowledge environment cannot obscure the diminishing capacity of national boundaries to orchestrate the movement of messages and ideas.

The web of dependencies and interdependencies mediated by technological change is equally apparent in the military sphere and equally subversive of state sovereignty. National governments no longer have exclusive or even secure access to information of strategic significance. The pre-eminence of the state is also under challenge from the activity of dissident groups which have taken advantage of the relative ease with which technical know-how as well as arms and munitions can be acquired and sophisticated urban and industrial centres threatened with indiscriminate violence.

Perhaps the most important new development is the advent of weapons of mass destruction, which can travel long distances at unprecedented speeds, and inflict indiscriminate violence on civilian populations, thereby undermining conventional notions of territorial defence. States are constrained by the global threat to security and the mounting cost of advanced weapons systems, which even superpowers are finding an intolerable economic burden. Partly in order to contain these costs and to cope with the new uncertainties great and small powers alike have established integrated alliance systems and complex military production and procurement policies where the technological imperative takes precedence over traditional notions of statecraft. The state remains central to the large-scale use and threat of force since each decision requires the formal approval of one or other arm of the state. Yet increasingly the decision responds to a logic that underpins the international economic and strategic system rather than the autonomously determined values or objectives of any one of its constituent 'sovereign' units.

The economic–technological–strategic nexus we have described has now assumed added significance because of its ecological implications. At one level, it may be argued that the spatial and political forms embedded in the system of sovereign states have been conducive to the multifaceted degradation of the environment. The instrumental rationality the state brings to bear on economic policy and the competitive dynamic of the inter-state system have combined to exert increased pressure on the earth's fragile ecological systems. At another level the modern state, though directly threatening human habitability of the planet, finds itself by virtue of territorial, legal and diplomatic constraints, severely restricted in formulating, let alone implementing, an adequate response. The now commonly expressed objective of sustainable development cannot be achieved within the 'sovereign' domain of the state, for it requires ideological constituencies, policy instruments and monitoring systems which are global in scope and therefore exceed the legal and institutional competence of the state.

The sense of impending ecological crisis is symptomatic of a wider social consciousness which has emerged over the last thirty years. Evident in varying degrees in most parts of the world, it represents a response to various facets of modern life, not least the alienation produced by bureaucratic and technical rationality. The resistance implicit in the praxis of the new social movements may not yet pose a decisive threat to dominant forms of economic and political organization, but by highlighting their life-eroding consequences it is beginning to undermine their legitimacy. These movements, which we may describe as fully fledged, embryonic or latent political communities, have acquired an anti-systemic quality in that they elude traditional categories of state, nation and sovereignty. They articulate new ways of experiencing time and space; they are constructing a new sense of history and identity. For them civil society has priority over the state. The state is used instrumentally to the extent that it can further their aims. In certain circumstances, particularly in the Third World, the state may offer a useful arena for social struggle and even become a symbol of liberation. Generally, however, the conception of democratic practice favoured by critical movements, which enshrines principles of plurality, participation, inclusive membership and unfettered movement across space, stands in contradiction to the norms, rules and procedures of the sovereign state.

The contemporary historical process suggests, then, a complex interplay of material conditions and subjective perceptions, of local, national and international structures and relationships, and of systemic and anti-systemic tendencies which greatly exceed the explanatory potential of the sovereignty discourse. No doubt further refinement and elaboration of the theory will be proposed in order to accommodate a greater slice of political and economic interdependence and discount several of the less defensible claims about the nature and constitution of sovereign authority. Such attempts at conceptual flexibility may be activated by any number of motives, including intellectual habit, practical convenience or the official desire to preserve and justify the coercive and administrative apparatus of the state. Yet they are unlikely to escape for long the mounting tensions inherent in the discourse. It is the cumulative or quantitative impact of these tensions which makes it both feasible and advisable to attempt a qualitative reassessment of that discourse. This is not to imply that state-centred nationalism is rapidly declining, that the material resources available to the state will soon diminish, or indeed that new universal structures are around the corner. The low probability of revolutionary institutional change, particularly at the international level, cannot, however, be interpreted as evidence of the theoretical utility or empirical stability of sovereignty.

The state continues to perform important economic, administrative and diplomatic functions, but these must not be confused with the exercise of sovereignty. Much of contemporary social and political reality, whether reflected in the popular politics of movements and localities or economic interaction in the global domain, is not captured, much less explained, by the discourse of sovereignty. Indeed that discourse is less and less able to illuminate the functions and *modus operandi* of the state itself. The fact that some states remain relatively strong and that others may become stronger offers little support for the theory of sovereignty. State strength cannot be confused with the existence of a sovereign will. The 'strong' or 'smart' state is not necessarily able to preserve or modify its internal or external environment in line with the autonomously expressed preferences of the community it claims to represent. The contemporary world is one where community, autonomy and the division between *internal* and *external* have become sharply contested categories, where the institutional foundations of sovereignty are themselves under challenge. It may well be that the principle of sovereignty was an important, perhaps indispensable, instrument in the development of national capitalism, but that with the emergence of fully-fledged global capitalism we have entered a new historical phase which is beginning to give birth to new forms of political theory and practice.

EXTENDING OUR CONCEPTUAL HORIZONS

If the present period suggests accelerated economic and technological change and with it discontinuity of experience, search for roots, recovery of identities lost or submerged, and emergence of new consciousness, then it is reasonable to assume that established models of interpretation will be less than fully adequate. The difficulty is that continuity coexists with discontinuity, stability with crisis. Both everyday life and the political process reflect these contradictory signals, with the result that what we discern experientially and conceptually is a confused mosaic of trends and countertrends. In this transitional phase of uncertain scope and duration, it is not yet possible to specify with any confidence the contours of the new order, much less to identify a new organizing principle of political life. The best we can do is to revisit but also recast a number of theoretical insights in the hope that they will lay the foundations for more productive lines of inquiry.

World system theory in its various guises is one important element in any conceptual reconstruction of world politics. It can sharpen our analysis of the globalization of human affairs and at the same time furnish a more comprehensive and historically grounded interpretation of the state. Over the last thirty years there have been numerous contributors to systemic theory, although most of these (e.g. Kaplan, Rosecrance, Waltz) have adopted a decidedly state-centric approach. At the other end of the spectrum a few (e.g. Burton) have sought to portray the world as a system or web of transactions and communications with little or no reference to physical or political boundaries. Two more recent contributors (Rosenau and Wallerstein) deserve particular attention because they seek in different ways to depict an increasingly integrated world, yet one in which the state retains an important though not pre-eminent role. Each of these two analytical frameworks adds to our understanding of the new global order, yet neither is entirely satisfactory.

Rosenau builds his model on the eminently sensible premiss that the theoretical 'preoccupation with the locus of final authority, the existence of sovereignty, and the capacity to enforce decisions' must be abandoned in favour of a new focus on the way 'outcomes are produced and/or controlled'.[7] Yet he does not fully adhere to his own conceptual guideline. He postulates instead two systems of world politics: a highly decentralized, almost chaotic multi-centric system comprised of subnational and supranational *sovereignty-free* actors and a relatively coherent and structured state-centric world of *sovereignty-bound* actors. The problem with this conceptualization, which Rosenau was presumably trying to avoid, is the unwarranted assumption that the 'security dilemma' is the overriding concern of states in contrast to sovereign-free actors who endlessly confront an 'autonomy dilemma'. This simplistic dichotomy replicates much that is wrong with the realist state-centric model.

The state, as we have seen, is a multi-dimensional actor with administrative and economic as well as strategic functions. As Giddens clearly argues in *The Nation State and Violence*,[8] the external projection of administrative and military power is not aimed merely at the territorial integrity of the state, that is to the international conditions of its own security. It is also directed to the domestic requirements of its reproduction as an organization and to the transnational conditions necessary for the reproduction of the socioeconomic system with which it is inextricably intertwined.

The theoretical deficiencies in Rosenau's characterization of the state are paradoxically reflected in his analysis of the multi-centric world where 'implicit legitimacy and equality' are said to serve as organizing principles and the functional equivalent of sovereignty in the state-centric world. How these principles might govern relations between large transnational corporations on the one hand and ecological groups or terrorist organizations on the other is not made clear. Nor is the 'autonomy dilemma' given sufficient content to see how it would apply to the multiplicity of actors that populate the multi-centric world. Ultimately, the Rosenau model, commendable though its objective may be, seems stranded in mid-air, uncomfortably oscillating between random, incoherent diversity and the highly strained language of autonomy, equality and legitimacy reminiscent of the sovereignty discourse. What is lacking is a conceptual structure which effectively links the two systems and explains their interaction in the context of modernity and the profound social and economic transformation it implies.

It is precisely his historical perspective and keen appreciation of the structures and processes of economic internationalization which give Wallerstein's representation of the world system greater explanatory power. Within this system state power combines with efficient production for a competitive world market to produce a delicately balanced international division of labour. The ensuing pattern of global stratification, sustained by a complex web of legal, diplomatic and military relations, enables the core areas to be the principal beneficiaries of capital accumulation at the expense of the peripheral areas, which are consistently disadvantaged by the system of unequal exchange. The interaction of capitalism and the system of territorial states gives rise to a series of historical stages which plot the trajectory of the global political economy. What is attractive about Wallerstein's approach to world system theory is that it integrates three crucial interacting relationships: that between the state and the expansion of capital; that between the core–periphery division of labour and the world market; and that between states and varying configurations of power.[9]

There is nevertheless a tendency for the Wallersteinian model to explain both too little and too much. First of all, there is a sense in which the notion of a highly integrated world system overstates the equilibrium tendencies inherent in the relationship between the horizontal structure of the world market and the vertical structure of inter-state relations. The internationalization of economic activity may be greatly facilitated by the policies of the national state, but the process is seldom uniform, free of contradiction or entirely predictable. The actions of the state are not the expression of a global capitalist will. Conversely, an increasingly integrated world economy narrows the range of national policy options and may in turn diminish the efficiency, not to say legitimacy, of state intervention.

World system theory, if it is to build on the substantial foundations provided by Wallerstein and his associates, must avoid the trap of integrating all subsystemic forces and relationships into an internally coherent, harmonious, dominant world system. Moreover, the primary role ascribed to the logic of capital accumulation must be qualified to allow for the complexity, plurality, variability and open-endedness of cultural and political processes as they unfold within and between societies and civilizations. Here it is not only a case of incorporating the sociological structure of the state and the dynamic of its self-production but of going beyond the categories of state and nation to make room for the politics of localities, movements and communities whose identities, strategies, capacities and modes of interaction cut across national boundaries. There is not one but many systems, each of which interacts with the others. There is also a need to distinguish between systemic and anti-systemic norms, rules, decisional structures and modalities of action. No doubt world system theory is open to such elaboration and refinement, but the difficult task of applying the insights and heuristic tools so far devised to this wider theoretical agenda still lies ahead.

These brief observations about the value of a systemic approach brings us back to the question of boundaries. We have already indicated in several connections the need for political theory to reassess the meaning, structure and interaction of boundaries. Systemic analysis, by focusing on the varying degrees and patterns of overlap, interpenetration and reciprocal influence between systems and subsystems, lends itself particularly well to the task. Several perspectives central to our study must nevertheless be carefully integrated into any systemic framework.

The first consideration is obvious. Systems and subsystems need not be conceived exclusively in terms of territorial boundaries, or to be more precise the boundaries of states. It may well be useful to consider the relationship of individual states, clusters of states and the inter-state system as a whole to the world system. At the same time consideration must be given at the systemic and sub-systemic levels to localities, communities, movements and cultures, although their connection with physical space will differ in form, function and normative status from that which pertains to state territoriality.

Conceptual linkages between and within systems, while attentive to the relevance of physical boundaries, should not assume that all facets of civil society, all forms of community or cultural identity are contingent on the state. The representation of systemic and subsystemic relationships must not be captive to the 'politics of enclosure'. Expressed more succinctly, boundaries (hence the delineation of systems and subsystems) need not be drawn purely according to jurisdictional or even geographical criteria. A particular issue (e.g. nuclear energy), area of policy (e.g. education), or set of relationships (e.g. international finance) can each in its own way provide a useful and coherent basis of demarcation. It follows that conceptual boundaries must as closely as possible reflect the changing issues and terrain of socioeconomic organization and political conflict. They must, in other words, internalize and express the dynamics of the historical process. Theory must help us to lay bare the evolving relationship (often contradiction) between the state-centric organization of territory and the emerging patterns of cultural identification, information flows, technology transfers and movements of capital and labour.

Boundaries in any case are seldom set in concrete. They are at best theoretical tools chosen because of their descriptive or explanatory potential. A useful analytical framework must be open to the fluidity of boundaries across both time and space. It must avoid a rigid or static division between domestic and foreign policy, military and economic relations, insiders and outsiders, the public and private spheres. Only a flexible construction of systems and subsystems can be open to the decentring or fragmentation of power. It is no longer possible to identify, let alone explain, events and relationships, by concentrating simply on the policies, decisions or actions of one or more actors. It is not enough to examine how national or other actors acquire, maintain and demonstrate power. Increasingly we have to allow for more complex systems of interaction involving a variety of actors, none of whom can be regarded as pivotal to a given outcome.

The controversy that has arisen over nuclear energy policy in many parts of the industrialized world provides a good example of the polycentric nature of power and authority. It is clear that the state of the industry (e.g. the number of nuclear power plants ordered in the United States since the early 1970s) is not wholly or even primarily determined by government objectives and priorities. Numerous influences are at work, including the level of interest rates, the cost of alternative energy sources, shifts in public opinion, the regulatory environment, and the shape of the nuclear non-proliferation regime. Affecting the outcome are not only states but local communities, social movements, electricity utilities, transnational corporations, money markets and international agencies.

New concepts, then, must translate in theoretical terms the profound changes that surround both the organizational and technological basis of production and the changing cultural and political dimensions of community. We need a conceptual framework which not only identifies the processes and structures of economic internationalization but also elucidates how these processes are experienced by different national societies and different communities within each society. If international integration coincides with and fosters domestic fragmentation, our analysis of the world system must bring to light a more extensive and complicated pluralism than the one suggested by the inter-state system or even by the 'world system'. In an age of fragmenting national societies a conceptual framework is needed to explode the alleged unity and cohesion of the sovereign will, and explore the unexpected but substantial ways in which the national state may, contrary to the assumptions and predictions of conventional state-centric theory, contribute simultaneously to international integration and domestic fragmentation.

So the central issue is not the shape or size of political entities or even the demarcation of their boundaries, but the very meaning of boundaries, the very nature of the political domain. At stake is the reinterpretation of both physical and social space. The anchoring of society to a particular place and the relationship of society to other places are undergoing qualitative change. The image of a world where space is appropriated and exclusively controlled by sovereign states is a conceptual tool of doubtful utility.

A more helpful representation of the contemporary world would allow for a variety of spatial forms, not only for national space, but for local, regional and global and also functional space. National space does not preclude and may even strengthen the peasant's attachment to the village and its surroundings. Similarly, the sovereign state cannot obliterate the personal, even mystical, relationship of indigenous peoples to their land. Even within the citadel of modernity a growing number of communities are finding the claims of local space both physically more immediate and often historically and symbolically more potent than the claims of the national state. Locality is often perceived as having political primacy – precisely because its scale is more conducive to the expression of political community.

Paradoxically, there is also increasing consciousness of and even attachment to space at the other or universal end of the scale. The universalizing thrust of modernity (e.g. modern systems of communication) is compounded by the universalizing impact of the reactions it provokes (e.g. mounting concern for global ecology). But the affinity with global space, though sensitized by the material conditions of modern life, does not fully derive from them. Its source also has a normative quality, reflected in the ethos of numerous philosophical, cultural and religious traditions, all of which express in varying form a vision of humanity as a primordial moral community. This is not to negate the divisions that separate classes, states and communities, but to assert that the multiple and legitimate claims of separateness must be counterposed and reconciled with the moral claims of universality.

Our reading of the world can no longer proceed on the assumption that space is homogeneous, that it is a geometric entity to be carved up between sovereign entities. It must allow for different degrees and forms of spatiality and for complex patterns of interaction between them. While elucidating the structure of global space, as expressed through the dynamics of the world market or even of an emerging global civilization, world system theoretical models must grapple with a plurality of other spaces, each connected to the others through an increasingly complex network of flows and movements. To make the task even more demanding, the theoretical enterprise must be solidly grounded in the historical process and be sensitive to the normative impulse of the human condition. That uncertainty and confusion will surround such a theoretical enterprise for some time to come will come as no surprise to anyone.

RESHAPING THE FUTURE

But what is the purpose of theory? It must no doubt engage the intellectually curious yet do more than satisfy intellectual curiosity. Its function is to illuminate the terrain of social and political conflict, situate the clash of competing discourses, and provide a useful compass for the exploration of future options. In this book we have not sought to construct a grand alternative model of explanation. Our more modest aim has been to review and question the assumptions and conclusions of conventional political analysis. In doing this we have identified several key trends in the emerging patterns of global life. These do not allow us to predict the future but rather to see more clearly the direction in which it might or could be shaped. This is not a recipe for prediction or prescription but an invitation to an ethically sensitive evaluation of future possibilities.

The first among these trends relates to the institutional fabric of society. Here we can confidently expect increasing diversity, complexity and interaction. On the one hand, there is likely to be a proliferation of state structures not only nationally, but at the local and regional levels within the state and at the supranational and international levels between states. The inability of existing institutions to contain and mediate tensions and conflict will encourage experimentation with new institutional arrangements in unstable Third World polities but also in different parts of the industrialized world. Rationalization and expansion of local and national bureaucracies to cope with the requirements of economic restructuring will accentuate public pressure for more effective consultative mechanisms and demands by local, ethnic, religious and other communities for alternative constitutional and other decision-making arrangements.

The failure of national states to make adaptive responses to an increasingly fragile global environment will result in the further delegation of tasks and resources to international and supranational forums and agencies, which is not to say that the trend will be regular or uniform, or that it will necessarily give practical expression to the democratic impulse. This institutional outgrowth, even when directly instigated and monitored by states (i.e. governments acting in the name of states) is likely to give rise to an intricate pattern of co-operation and competition which imposes yet further constraints on the state's freedom of action. The greater the need for policy co-ordination the more difficult it will be for governments to go it alone and the greater the tendency for international institutions to place additional limitations on the practical options available to 'sovereign' states. The most probable outcome is a network of contacts, coalitions and interactions within and between national societies that escape the effective control of the central policy organs of government.

The proliferation of official institutions will not necessarily create greater opportunities for participation and accountability, unless there is a conscious effort to subject the institutional process to public scrutiny. It is not yet clear whether the new technologies for enhanced communication can be used to democratize supranational and international organizations. It remains to be seen, for example, whether the United Nations system can be radically reformed to permit much higher levels of public monitoring and control of the decision-making process. Part of the answer may lie with the new social movements and the role they play in strengthening the democratic ethos of an emerging world polity.

One thing, however, is clear: the quantitative and qualitative growth of subnational, international and transnational actors that we have outlined will of necessity entail a continuing penetration of the state's boundaries. The state may choose to respond to this potential erosion of its power base by attempting to extract additional resources from civil society (e.g. increased taxation, extension of coercive apparatus) and by proceeding with greater centralization of national institutions and decision-making processes. Yet there are clear limitations to this strategy. To begin with, the state cannot easily negate or reverse material conditions which define the emerging world system: the technological revolution in communication and transportation, the mobility of transnational capital, the global dimensions and impact of environmental damage.

The very attempt by the state to marshal its strength and defend its institutional primacy will imply a recognition that things have changed and that what was once assumed to be the preserve of the sovereign state (i.e. the national domain) is now seen as contested territory. Rising tensions between national macroeconomic policy (in industrialized states, not to speak of much weaker Third World states) and transnational corporations or international financial institutions may simply be a taste of things to come. In such contests the state may find that using the levers normally available to it (e.g. taxation, coercion) may be either irrelevant or severely limited by other considerations (e.g. the state of the economy, internal or external opposition). As Fred Block has suggested, the deepening contradictions and conflicts between state and corporate bureaucracies may produce either political paralysis or a progressive erosion of the legitimacy of dominant institutions.[10] Either way new opportunities may arise for emancipatory social and political movements.

Here, the ideological and psychological dimensions of conflict are particularly important. For sooner or later the battleground will shift as one or other of the competitors tries to maximize its position by invoking a new discourse calling into question existing loyalties and value preferences. As we indicated in the previous chapter, several of the new social movements have already embarked on this path, challenging the ethical basis of state laws, policies and procedures. This is not an altogether new phenomenon, but taken beyond a certain threshold it is likely to endanger the stability and efficacy of state authority.

The territorial state will for the foreseeable future continue to operate as an influential institution, but the presence or absence of sovereignty will be much less the defining characteristic of its structure or mode of action. What is slowly emerging is a triangular relationship between the familiar dualities of national state and world market, of state and civil society, and the less familiar (private/public) duality of market and civil society. The dialectic of these three interconnected relationships points to a new fluid pattern of fragmentation and integration which is not easily captured by or easily explicable in terms of the theory of sovereignty.

The state standing in uneasy, at times contradictory, relationship to civil society on the one hand and the world market on the other is unlikely to assert its supremacy over either. A more likely outcome is that the state will function as the principal arena of conflict, giving expression to and institutionalizing the tensions between competing values, interests and organizational principles. It will continue to provide a highly visible stage on which will be played out class and power antagonisms related to the restructuring of global economic processes and the ensuing patterns of stratification, inclusion and exclusion. In other words, the state will operate more as a vehicle of struggle than as a vehicle of sovereignty. Rather than act as a bridge between the demands of nationhood and the logic of the market through the creation of a national market – a function it performed with varying degrees of success in nineteenth-century Europe – the state will increasingly be torn between two logics. The basic contradiction will not be between national sovereignty and growing international interdependence but between two forms of interdependence: one which institutionalizes the principles of autonomy, community and identity and another which in practice negates those principles by clinging to the increasingly elusive notion of state sovereignty. One may therefore expect a deepening contradiction between emerging processes of decentralization and democratization within and between societies and the intensified centralization and bureaucratization of economic and political life.

This is not to say that the state will act as a passive or neutral agent in societal conflict. Its actions may favour systemic or anti-systemic forces, depending on the interests of those in positions of state power and the structural relationship between the state on the one hand and civil society and the international division of labour on the other. However, even when siding with particular interests and forces, the state will tend to be a vehicle for the internationalization of domestic conflict as well as the localization of international conflict. If they persist, the twin trends of globalization and its corollary, domestic fragmentation, are likely to weaken the conceptual and practical foundations of sovereignty: first, by challenging the notion that state authority is exercised exclusively or even primarily within clearly demarcated boundaries; secondly by calling into question the claim that within its territory the state's authority is unlimited and indivisible; thirdly, by suggesting a growing disjunction between state and civil society, between political authority and economic organization, and between national identification and social cohesion.

The last of these three effects may prove the most far-reaching, for it paves the way for the redefinition of civil society. Even where it has given rise to effective and cohesive nation-states, nationalism no longer seems a sufficient let alone permanent factor for social cohesion. The very centralization of the state and the integration of the national economy into the world economy are making it increasingly difficult for national society to preserve its integrity or independence. One of the dominant features of the globalization of capitalist relations is the disjuncture between the traditional and the modern, between the cultural basis of nationalism and the locus of economic decision-making. One possible consequence of such a disjuncture is a gradual transition to a new conception of civil society, a new polity cultivating a renewed sense of wholeness, with no clearly demarcated boundaries set by state territoriality or statist notions of national identity. Civil society may come to acquire a richer meaning grounded in a multiplicity of overlapping allegiances and jurisdictions where the traditional, the modern and the postmodern coexist, where local, regional and global space qualify the principle of nationality and redefine the context of community. The recovery of local and regional identities may encourage new expressions of autonomy and democratic practice and at the same time facilitate the emergence of a cosmopolitan global culture. Though its effects may be varied and not always benign, the general trend will not easily be reversed.

Central then to the reconceptualization of civil society are likely to be two at least potentially conflicting tendencies: the reassertion of cultural identity and acceptance of cultural pluralism as an organizing principle of national and international life. The search for identity and autonomy will no doubt gain in intensity but is likely to be less statist in form and inspiration than in the past, and more likely to derive from local, ethnic, religious, linguistic, social or ecological perspectives and traditions which are in some sense critical of modernity. Particularism and globalism are likely to flourish side by side in uneasy coexistence. What is less clear is whether the vastly increased mobility of messages and ideas will facilitate the cosmopolitan interaction of cultures or merely multiply the frequency and intensity of their collision.

If one accepts the view that technological and economic integration makes globalism of one kind or another an unavoidable aspect of the future, the particular form such globalism will take remains an open-ended question. Three scenarios seem plausible: globalism may be mediated primarily through economic internationalization and political fragmentation (i.e. inter-state system); or through a more localized yet mutually tolerant plurality of cultures; or again through the emergence of a distinctive world culture underpinned by a universal authority. There are powerful pressures operating in favour of each of these outcomes.

The existing world system will continue to enjoy the support of those privileged classes, strata and states which have been the principal proponents and beneficiaries of modernity. To this must be added the not insubstantial weight of institutional inertia. The option of a cosmopolitan pluralism is likely to receive considerable impetus from the perceived failure of the national state to satisfy basic needs and the praxis of the new social and political movements. The combined effect of these two factors will be to challenge the global hegemony of the West, and with it the claims of scientific objectivity and technical rationality, and in particular the sharp dualism between subject and object, knower and known, self and other, society and nature. As for the goal of a universal culture supported by international organization, it is likely to find support from social movements but also from state agencies which perceive a need for authoritative, well-resourced bureaucratic structures capable of formulating and implementing global strategies in response to the multiple crises of modern life.

It is doubtful that any of the three tendencies will achieve ascendancy in the near future. The more probable outcome is that all three will find a niche in the emerging global order. On the other hand, it is quite likely that what is now the dominant tendency, as reflected in existing institutional arrangements, will be severely weakened by various manifestations of economic crisis and environmental breakdown, and that these will considerably strengthen the revolt against Western power and with it mechanistic systems of explanation, prediction and organization. While it is unlikely that the twenty-first century will usher in a new global civilization equipped with a comprehensive system of authoritative institutions, it is entirely possible though not yet certain that we shall see a more effective dialogue of cultures and civilizations based on mutual comprehension rather than on objectification of the other. The capitalist reorganization of the world and the contradictions to which it has given rise point to the re-emergence of a cosmopolitan ethic that nurtures and draws its inspiration from a mosaic of local, regional, national, supranational and transnational spaces, loyalties and institutions. Though the state will continue to perform important administrative and other functions, the theory of sovereignty will seem strangely out of place in a world characterized by shifting allegiances, new forms of identity and overlapping tiers of jurisdiction.

NOTES

1. Richard Ashley, 'Untying the Sovereign State: A Double Reading of the Anarchy Problematique', *Millenium: Journal of International Studies*, **17**, (2), Summer, p. 231.
2. These are the very functions that Michel Foucault attributes to discursive practices in *Language, Counter-Memory, Practice*, Ithaca, NY: Cornell University Press, 1977, p. 199.
3. R.B.J. Walker, 'Sovereignty, Identity, Community: Reflections on the Horizons of Contemporary Political Practice', in R.B.J. Walker and Saul H. Mendlovitz (eds), *Contending Sovereignties: Redefining Political Community*, Boulder, Co.: Lynne Rienner, 1990, p. 175.
4. Fred Halliday, 'State and Society in International Relations: A Second Agenda', *Millenium*, **16**, (2), Summer 1987, 218.
5. By stages we refer to the various periodizations which seek to describe the evolution of modern society, and in particular the rise and development of capitalism. The emphasis here is not on the merits of any particular classification but on the need for historical perspective.
6. James N. Rosenau, 'Patterned Chaos in Global Life: Structure and Process in the Two Worlds of World Politics', *International Political Science Review*, **9**, (4), October 1988, 334.
7. Ibid., p. 346.
8. Anthony Giddens, *The Nation State and Violence: A Contemporary Critique of Historical Materialism*, Cambridge: Polity, 1985.
9. See Immanuel Wallerstein, *The Capitalist World-Economy*, Cambridge: Cambridge University Press, 1979, pp. 1–36, 152–64.
10. Fred Block, 'Beyond Relative Autonomy: State Managers as Historical Subjects', in Ralph Miliband and John Saville (eds), *The Socialist Register 1980*, London: Merlin Press, 1980, p. 240.

Select Bibliography

To assist the reader this select bibliography is divided into six sections corresponding to the main themes emerging in this study of sovereignty.

HISTORICAL AND THEORETICAL PERSPECTIVES

Acton, Lord (1920), *The History of Freedom and Other Essays*, New York: Macmillan.

Allen, J.W. (1960), *A History of Political Thought in the Sixteenth Century*, London: Methuen.

Almond, Gabriel (1989), 'The International–National Connection', *British Journal of Political Science*, **19**, (2), April.

Anderson, Benedict (1983), *Imagined Communities: Reflections on the Origin and Spread of Nationalism*, London: Verso.

Anderson, Perry (1974), *Lineages of the Absolutist State*, London: New Left Books.

Anderson, James and Stuart Hall (1986), 'Absolutism and Other Ancestors', in James Anderson (ed.), *The Rise of the Modern State*, Brighton: Wheatsheaf Books.

Aron, Raymond (1987–8), 'Postmodernism and Politics', *Social Text*, **18**, Winter.

Ashley, Richard K. (1988), 'Untying the Sovereign State: A Double Reading of the Anarchy Problematique', *Millenium: Journal of International Studies*, **17**, (2), Summer.

Attina, Fulvio (1986), 'Gerarchie Internazionale e Teoria Del Sistema Egemonico', *Politica Internazionale*, **14**, (7), July.

Austin, John (1965), *The Province of Jurisprudence Determined*, New York: Humanities Press.

Beitz, Charles B., (1979), 'Bounded Morality: Justice and the State in World Politics', *International Organization*, **33**, (3), Summer.

Benjamin, Walter (1973), *Illuminations*, London: Fontana.

Benn, S.I. and R.S. Peters (1959), *Social Principles and the Democratic State*, London: Allen & Unwin.

Berger, Peter (1967), *The Sacred Canopy*, Garden City, NY: Doubleday.

Berman, Marshall (1982), *All that is Solid Melts into Air: The Experience of Modernity*, New York: Verso.

Birch, Charles (1988), 'Eight Fallacies of the Modern World and Five Axioms for a Postmodern Worldview', *Perspectives in Biology and Medicine*, **32**, (1), Autumn.

Blumer, Herbert (1951), 'Collective Behaviour', in Alfred McClung Lee (ed.), *New Outline of the Principles of Sociology*, New York: Barnes & Noble.

Bodin, Jean (1606), *The Six Books of a Commonweale*, trans. Richard Knolles, London: Impencis G. Bishop.

Brucan, Silviu (1980), 'The State and the World System', *International Social Science Journal*, **32**, (4).

Brucan, Silviu (1982), 'The Establishment of A World Authority: Working Hypotheses', *Alternatives*, **37**, (2), Fall.

Bull, Hedley (1977), *The Anarchical Society: a Study of Order in World Politics*, London: Macmillan.

Burton, F. and P. Carlen (1979), *Official Discourse: On Discourse, Analysis, Government, Publications, Ideology and the State*, London: Routledge & Kegan Paul.

Burton, John (1972), *World Society*, Cambridge: Cambridge University Press.

Bury, J. (1960), *The Idea of Progress*, New York: Dover.

Cain, Maureen, (1983), 'Introduction: Towards an Understanding of the International State', *International Journal of the Sociology of Law*, February.

Calinescu, Matei (1987), *Five Faces of Modernity*, Durham, NC: Duke University Press.

Camilleri, J.A. (1976), *Civilization in Crisis*, New York: Cambridge University Press.

Carr, E.H. (1945), *Nationalism and After*, London: Macmillan.

Chesneaux, Jean (1987), 'Modernity: A Basic Category of Our Present Day Society', Paper presented at History of Ideas Seminar, Research School of Social Sciences, Australian National University, Canberra, April.

Claude, Inis (1962), *Power and International Relations*, New York: Random House.

Cole, G.D.H. (1938), *Socialism in Evolution*, Harmondsworth, Middlesex: Penguin.

Coplin, William D. (1965), 'International Law and Assumptions about the State System', *World Politics*, **17**, (4).

Cox, Harvey (1966), *The Secular City*, Harmondsworth, Middlesex: Penguin.

Cox, Robert W. (1981), 'Social Forces, States and World Orders: Beyond International Relations Theory', *Millenium*, **10**, (2).

Cox, Robert W. (1983), 'Gramsci, Hegemony and International Relations: an Essay in Method', *Millenium*, **12**, (2).

Cranston, Maurice (1953), *Freedom: A New Analysis*, New York: Longman.

Crough, C. (1987), 'The Nation State: the Neglected Dimension of Class', *British Journal of Industrial Relations*, **25**, (2), July.

Doyle, Phyllis (1963), *A History of Political Thought*, London: Jonathan Cape (first published 1933).

Dunne, J. (1969), *The Political Thought of John Locke*, Cambridge: Cambridge University Press.

Dyson, Kenneth (1980), *The State Tradition in Western Europe: a Study of an Idea and an Institution*, Oxford: Martin Robertson.

Eckstein, Harry (1979), 'On the "Science" of the State', *Daedalus*, **108**, (4), Fall.

Ehrenberg, Victor (1964), *The Greek State*, New York: Norton.

Ehrenreich, J. (1983), 'Socialism, Nationalism and Capitalist Development', *Review of Radical Political Economics*, **15**, (1), Spring.

Eisenstadt, S.N. (1963), *The Political Systems of Empires*, New York: Free Press.

Eisenstein, H. (1984), *Contemporary Feminist Thought*, London: Hutchinson.

Elshtain, J. (1981), *Public Man, Private Woman*, Oxford: Martin Robertson.

Evans, Judith et al. (1986), *Feminism and Political Theory*, London: Sage.

Falk, Richard A. (1975), *A Study of Future Worlds*, Amsterdam: North-Holland.

Falk, Richard A. (1980), 'The Shaping Of World Order Studies: a Response', *Review of Politics*, **42**, (1), January.

Falk, Richard A. (1986), 'Solving the Puzzles of Global Reform', *Alternatives*, **11**, (1).

Falk, Richard A. (1987), *The Promise of World Order*, Brighton, Sussex: Wheatsheaf Books.

Falk, Richard A. and Saul H. Mendlovitz (eds) (1966), *The Strategy of World Over (Vol. II: International Law)*, New York: World Law Fund.

Foucault, Michel (1977), *Language, Counter-Memory, Practice*, Ithaca, NY: Cornell University Press.

Foucault, Michel (1977), *Discipline and Punish*, New York: Pantheon Books.

Foucault, Michel (1978), *The History of Sexuality*, New York: Pantheon Books.

Frankel, Boris (1983), *Beyond the State? Dominant Theories and Socialist Strategies*, London: Macmillan.

Frankel, Boris (1987), *The Post-Industrial Utopians*, Cambridge: Basil Blackwell.

Freeman, Kathleen (1948), *Greek City-States*, London: Methuen.

Frisby, D. (1985), *Fragments of Modernity: Theories of Modernity in the Work of Simmel, Kratauer and Benjamin*, Cambridge: Polity Press, in association with Oxford: Basil Blackwell.

Galtung, Johan (1971), 'A Structural Theory of Imperialism', *Journal of Peace Research*, **8**, (2).

Gellner, Ernest (1983), *Nations and Nationalism*, Oxford: Basil Blackwell.

Giddens, A. (1985), *The Nation State and Violence: A Contemporary Critique of Historical Materialism*, Cambridge: Polity Press.

Gleik, James (1987), *Chaos: Making A New Science*, London: Cardinal.

Glover, T.R. (1944), *The Ancient World*, Harmondsworth, Middlesex: Penguin.

Goldmann, Kjell and Gunnar Sjöstedt (eds) (1979), *Power, Capabilities, Interdependence: Problems in the Study of International Influence*, Beverly Hills: Sage.

Gourevitch, Peter (1978), 'The Second Image Reversed: the International Sources of Domestic Politics', *International Organization*, **32**.

Guizot, François (1984), 'Sovereign of Right', lecture from the series 'The History of Civilizations in Europe' (translated by William Hazlitt and originally published in Bohn's Library series by George Bell and Sons), reprinted in L.L. Blake (1988), *Sovereignty: Power Beyond Politics*, London: Shepheard Walwyn.

Habermas, Jürgen (1973), 'What Does a Crisis Mean Today? Legitimization Problems in Late Capitalism', *Social Research*, **41**, (4), Winter.

Habermas, Jürgen (1985), 'Modernity: an Incomplete Project', in H. Foster (ed.), *Recodings: Art, Spectacle, Cultural Politics*, Port Townsend: Wash.: Bay Press.

Halliday, Fred (1987), 'State and Society in International Relations: a Second Agenda', *Millenium*, **16**, (2), Summer.

Harvey, D. (1984), *The Conditions of Post-Modernity: an Enquiry into the Origins of Cultural Change*, Oxford: Basil Blackwell.

Hayes, Carleton J.H. (1931), *The Historial Evolution of Modern Nationalism*, New York: Richard R. Smith.

Hegel, George W.F. (1957), *Hegel's Philosophy of Right*, trans. T.M. Knox, Oxford: Clarendon Press.

Held, David (1987), Models of Democracy, London: Polity Press.

Held, David, James Anderson, Bram Gieben, Stuart Hall, Lawrence Harris, Paul Lewis, Noel Parker and Ben Turok (eds) (1985), *States and Societies*, Oxford: Basil Blackwell.

Hinsley, F. (1966), *Sovereignty*, London: C.A. Watts.

Hintze, Otto (1975), *The Historical Essays of Otto Hintze*, New York: Oxford University Press.

Hobbes, Thomas (1968), *Leviathan*, ed. by C.B. Macpherson, Harmondsworth, Middlesex: Penguin.

Hofstede, G. (1985), 'The Interaction between National and Organizational Value Systems', *Journal Management Studies*, **22**, (4), July.

Holly, D.A., (1975), 'L'ONU, le système économique international et la politique internationale', *International Organization*, **29**, (2), Spring.

Huyssen, Andreas (1986), *After the Great Divide: Modernism, Mass Culture, Postmodernism*, Bloomington: Indiana University Press.

Illich, Ivan D. (1973), *Tools for Conviviality*, London: Calder & Boyar.

James, Alan, (1984), 'Sovereignty: Ground Rule or Gibberish?', *Review of International Studies*, **10**, (1), January.

Jameson, Frederic (1984), 'Post-Modernism, or the Cultural Logic of Late Capitalism', *New Left Review*, **146**, July–August.

Jessop, Bob (1980), 'On Recent Marxist Theories of the Law, the State, and Juridico-Political Ideology', *International Journal of the Sociology of Law*, **8**.

Jessop, Bob (1982), *The Capitalist State*, Oxford: Martin Robertson.

Jessop, Bob (1983), 'The Capitalist State and the Rule of Capital: Problems in the Analysis of Business Associations', *West European Politics*, **6**, (2), April.

Jessop, Bob (1986), 'The Nation State and Violence', *Capital and Class*, **29**, Summer.

Kahler, Miles (1987), 'The Survival of the State in European International Relations', in Charles S. Maier, (ed.), *Changing Boundaries of the Political*, Cambridge: Cambridge University Press.

Keohane, Robert O. and Joseph S. Nye (1975), *Power and Independence: World Politics in Transition*, Boston: Little Brown.

Keynes, J.M. (1933), 'National Self Sufficiency', in *Collected Works*, London: Macmillan.

Kindleberger, Charles P. (1983), 'On the Rise and Decline of Nations', *International Studies Quarterly*, **27**.

Kohn, Hans (1962), *The Age of Nationalism: the First Era of Global History*, New York: Harper & Row.

Kohn, Hans (1965), *Nationalism; its Meaning and History*, Princeton, NJ: van Nostrand.

Kornhauser, W. (1959), *The Politics of Mass Society*, New York: Free Press.

Kratochwil (1986), 'Of Systems, Boundaries, and Territoriality', *World Politics*, **39**, (1), October.

Kuhn, Thomas S. (1962), *The Structure of Scientific Revolutions*, Chicago: University of Chicago Press.

Larus, Joel (ed.) (1964), *Comparative World Politics: Readings in Western and Pre-Modern Non-Western International Relations*, Belmont, Cal.: Wadsworth.

Laski, Harold (1919), *Authority in the Modern State*, New Haven, CT.: Yale University Press.

Laski, Harold (1967), *A Grammar of Politics* (5th edn), London: Allen & Unwin.

Latouretle, Kenneth S. (1959), *The Chinese: Their History and Culture*, New York: Macmillan.

Layne, Christopher, (1980), 'The Multinational Enterprise in the International Political System: a Theoretical Consideration', *New York University Journal of International Law and Politics*, **13**, Spring.

Lefebvre, Henri (1971), *Everyday Life in the Modern World*, London: A. Lane.

Leurdjik, J.H. (1974), 'From International to Transnational Politics: a Change of Paradigm?', *International Social Science Journal*, **26**, (1).

Li, Dun J. (1965), *The Ageless Chinese: a History*, New York: Charles Scribner's Sons.

Little, R. and R.D. McKinlay, (1978), 'Linkage-Responsiveness and the Modern State: an Alternative View of Interdependence', *British Journal of International Studies*, **4**, (3), October.

Littlejohn, Gary B., Smart, J. Wakeford and N. Yuval-Davis (eds) (1978), *Power and the State*, London: Croom Helm.

Locke, John (1924), *Two Treaties of Civil Government*, Introduction by W.S. Carpenter, London: J.M. Dent.

Lyotard, Jean-François (1984), *The Postmodern Condition: a Report on Knowledge*, Minneapolis: University of Minnesota Press.

Machiavelli, Niccolò (1950), *The Prince and the Discourses*, New York: Random House.

MacPherson, C.B. (1962), *The Political Theory of Possessive Individualism*, London: Oxford University Press.

Maier, Charles S. (1987), 'The Politics of Time: Changing Paradigms of Collective Time and Private Time in the Modern Era', in *Changing Boundaries of the Political*, Cambridge: Cambridge University Press.

Maritain, Jacques (1954), *Man and the State*, ed. Richard O'Sullivan, London: Hollis & Carter.

Marx, K. and F. Engels (1950), *Selected Works*, Moscow: Progress Publishers.

Mattingly, Garrett (1955), *Renaissance Diplomacy*, London: Jonathan Cape.

Mayall, James, (1985), 'Nationalism and the International Order', *Millenium*, **14**, (2).

McHale, B. (1987), *Postmodernist Fiction*, New York: Methuen.

Mendlovitz, Saul, (1980–1), 'On the Creation of a Just World Order: an Agenda for a Program of Inquiry and Praxis', *Alternatives*, **7**, (3), Winter.

Menon, R. and J. Oneal (1986), 'Explaining Imperialism: the State of the Art as Reflected in Three Theories', *Polity*, **2**.

Michalak, Stanley J. Jnr. (1979), 'Theoretical Perspectives for Understanding International Interdependence', *World Politics*, **32**, (1), October.

Michalak, Stanley J. Jnr. (1980), 'Richard Falk's Future World: a Critique of WOMP-USA', *Review of Politics*, **42**, (1), June.

Middleton, K.W.B. (1969), 'Sovereignty in Theory and Practice', in *Defense of Sovereignty*, New York: Oxford University Press.

Miller, J.D.B. (1986), 'Sovereignty as a Source of Vitality for the State', *Review of International Studies*, **12**, (2), April.

Milliband, Ralph (1983), *Class Power and State Power*, London: Verso.

Milliband, Ralph and John Saville (eds) (1980), *Socialist Register 1980*, London: Merlin Press.

Morgenthau, Hans (1978), *Politics among Nations*, (5th edn), New York: Alfred A. Knopf.

Muller, R., (1982), 'Paradoxes of Nationalism in an Interdependent World', *Transnational Perspectives*, **7**, (1).

O'Leary, James P. (1978), 'Envisioning Interdependence: Perspectives on Future World Order', *Orbis*, **22**, (3), Fall.

Oppenheim, F. (1987), 'National Interest, Rationality and Morality', *Political Theory*, **15**, (3), August.

Orton, William A. (1945), *The Liberal Tradition*, New Haven, CT: Yale University Press.

Panitch, L. (1977), 'The Development of Corporatism in Liberal Democracies', *Comparative Political Studies*, **10**, (1), April.

Pasquinelli, Caria (1986), 'Power without the State', *Telos*, **68**, Summer.

Plamenatz, John (1965), *Man and Society*, Vol. 2, London: Longman.

Pollard, S. (1968), *The Idea of Progress*, London: C.A. Watts.

Rees, W.J. (1950), 'The Theory of Sovereignty Restated', *Mind*, **59**, (236), October.

Rejai, Mostafa and Cynthia H. Enloe (1981), 'Nation-States and State-Nations', in Michael Smith, Richard Little and Michael Shackleton (eds), *Perspectives on World Politics*, London: Croom Helm.

Renan, Ernest (1887), *Discours et Conférences*, Paris: Calman-Lévy.

Reynolds, P.A., (1979), 'Non-State Actors and International Outcomes', *British Journal of International Studies*, **5**, (2), July.

Richardson, J. (1981), 'Global Modelling in the 1980s', *Impact of Science on Society*, **31**, (4), October–December.

Rosecrance, R., A. Alexandroff, W. Koehler, J. Kroll, S. Laquer and J. Stocker (1977), 'Whither Interdependence', *International Organization*, **31**, (3), Summer.

Rosecrance, R. and Arthur Stein, (1973), 'Interdependence: Myth or Reality?', *World Politics*, **26**, (1), October.

Rosenau, James, N. (ed.) (1969), *Linkage Politics*, New York: Free Press.

Rosenau, James, N. et al. (eds) (1972), *The Analysis of International Politics*, New York: Free Press.

Rosenau, James, N. (1979), 'Muddling Meddling and Modelling: Alternative Approaches to the Study of World Politics in an Era of Rapid Change', *Millenium: Journal of International Studies*, **8**, (2), Autumn.

Rosenau, James, N. (1980), *The Study of Global Interdependence: Essays on the Transnationalization of World Affairs*, New York: Nicholls.

Rosenau, James, N. (1981), *The Study of Political Adaption*, London: Frances Pinter.

Rosenau, James, N. (1988), 'Patterned Chaos in Modern Life: Structure and Process in the Two Worlds of World Politics', *International Political Science Review*, **9**, (4), October.

Rousseau, Jean-Jacques, (1950), *The Social Contract and Discourses*, trans. G.D.H. Cole, New York: E. Dutton.

Sabine, George A. (1963), *A History of Political Theory*, (3rd edn), London: Harrop.

Sack, Robert D. (1980), *Conceptions of Space in Social Thought: A Geographic Perspective*, London: Macmillan.

Salvadori, Massimo (1958), *Liberal Democracy*, London: Pall Mall.

Schumpeter, Jospeh A. (1950), *Capitalism, Socialism and Democracy*, New York: Harper.

Schuster J. and R. Yeo (eds) (1986), *The Politics and Rhetoric of Scientific Method: Historical Studies*, Dordrecht: Reidel.

Schwarzenberger, George (1969), 'The Focus of Sovereignty', in *The Defense of Sovereignty*, ed. W.J. Stankiewicz, New York: Oxford University Press.

Seely, John Robert (1886), *Introduction to Political Science*, London: Macmillan.

Seton-Watson, Hugh (1977), *Nations and States*, London: Methuen.

Shapiro, Barry (ed.) (1990), *After the Future: Postmodern Times and Places*, New York: State University of New York Press.

Skopcol, Theda (1979), *States and Social Revolutions*, Cambridge: Cambridge University Press.

Solomon, Richard Jay (1988), 'Vanishing Intellectual Boundaries: Virtual Networking and the Loss of Sovereignty and Control', *ANNALS, American Academy of Political and Social Science*, **495**.

Spivak, Gayatri Chakravorty (1989), 'Political Commitment and the Postmodern Critic', in Aram H. Veeser (ed.), *The New Historicism*, New York: Routledge.

Strayer, R. and D.C. Munro (1959), *The Middle Ages* (4th edn), New York: Appleton-Century-Croft.

Supple, Barry (1984), 'The State and the Industrial Revolution 1700-1914', in David Held et al. (eds), *States and Societies*, Oxford: Basil Blackwell.

Targ, Harry G. (1979), 'World Order and Future Studies Reconsidered', *Alternatives*, **5**, (3), November.

Taylor, Peter J. (1986), 'An Exploration into World Systems Analysis of Political Parties', *Political Geographical Quarterly*, **5**, October.

Thompson, Kenneth W. (1981), 'Science, Morality and Transnationalism', *Interpretation*, **9**, (2–3), September.

Tilly, Charles (ed.) (1975), *The Formation of National States in Western Europe*, Princeton, NJ: Princeton University Press.

Vincent, Andrew (1987), *Theories of the State*, Oxford: Basil Blackwell.

Walker, R.B.J. (1981), 'World Politics and Western Reason: Universalism, Pluralism, Hegemony', *Alternatives*, **7**, (2), Fall.

Walker, R.B.J. (1984), 'The Territorial State and the Theme of Gulliver', *International Journal*, **39**, (3), Summer.

Walker, R.B.J. (1988), *State Sovereignty, Global Civilization and the Rearticulation of Political Space*, World Order Studies Program, Occasional Paper No. 18, Center of International Studies, Princeton University.

Walker, R.B.J. (1989), 'History and Structure in the Theory of International Studies', *Millenium*, **18**, (2), Summer.

Walker, R.B.J. and Saul H. Mendlovitz (eds) (1990), *Contending Sovereignties: Redefining Political Community*, Boulder, Col.: Lynne Rienner.

Walker, Richard L. (1953), *The Multi-State System of Ancient China*, Hamden, Conn.: Shoe String Press.

Wight, Martin (1979), *Power Politics*, Harmondsworth, Middlesex: Penguin.

Williams, Howard (1983), *Kant's Political Philosophy*, Oxford: Basil Blackwell.

Wright, Quincy (1955), *Contemporary International Law: A Balance Sheet*, Garden City, NY: Doubleday.

Yalem, Ronald J. (1978), 'Transnational Politics Versus International Politics', *Yearbook of World Affairs*, **32**.

Young, C. (1982), 'Nationalizing the Third-World State: Categorical Imperative or Mission Impossible?', *Polity*, **15**, (2).

Young, O. (1986), 'International Regimes', *World Politics*, **39**, (1), October.

Zagladin, W. and Frolon, I.T. (1982), 'Global Problems as Areas of International Co-operation', *International Social Science Journal*, **34**, (1).

ECONOMIC ORGANIZATION

Agh, Attila (1983), 'The Dual Definition of Capitalism and the Contemporary World System', *Development and Peace*, **4**, (1), Spring.

Aglietta, Michel (1978), 'Phases Of U.S. Capitalist Expansion', *New Left Review*, July–August.

Aglietta, Michel (1982), 'World Capitalism in the Eighties', *New Left Review*, **136**, December.

Amin, Samir (1974), *Accumulation on a World Scale: a Critique Of the Theory of Underdevelopment*, New York: Monthly Review Press.

Amin, Samir (1982), *The Dynamics of Global Crisis*, London: Macmillan.

Amin, Samir (1982), 'After the NIEO: the Future of International Economic Relations', *Trade and Development*, Winter.

'Anatomy of Monetary Contradictions: the World of Capital: Political Economy of the Crisis' (1981), *World Marxist Review*, **24**, July.

Andreff, Vladimir (1984), 'The International Centralisation of Capital and the Re-ordering of World Capitalism', *Capital and Class*, **22**, Spring.

Andrews, Bruce (1982), 'The Political Economy of World Capitalism: Theory and Practice', *International Organization*, **36**, (1), Winter.

Armstrong, Adrienne, (1981), 'The Political Consequences of Economic Dependence', *Journal of Conflict Resolution*, **25**, (3), September.

Aronowitz, S. (1981), 'A Metatheoretical Critique of Immanuel Wallerstein's "The Modern World System"', *Theory and Society*, **10**, (4), July.

Arrighi, Giovanni (1981), 'Multinationalization and Ungovernability of the World Economy', *Politica Internazionale*, 4–5, April–May.

Avery, William P. and David Rapkin (1982), *America in a Changing World Political Economy*, London: Longman.

Baldry, C., N. Haworth, S. Henderson and H. Ramsay (1983), 'Fighting Multinational Power: Possibilities, Limitations and Contradictions', *Capital and Class*, **20**, Summer.

Baran, Paul (1957), *The Political Economy of Growth*, New York: Monthly Review Press.

Baran, Paul (1969), *The Longer View*, New York: Monthly Review Press.

Baran, Paul and P. Sweezy (1963), *Monopoly Capital*, Harmondswoth, Middlesex: Penguin.

Barnet, Richard J. and Ronald E. Muller (1974), *Global Reach: the Power of the Multinational Corporations*, New York: Simon & Schuster.

Barone, C. (1983), 'Dependency, Marxist Theory and Salvaging the Idea of Capitalism in South Korea', *Review of Radical Political Economics*, **15**, (1), Spring.

Batra, Ravi (1986), 'The Future of International Debt?', *Review of International Affairs*, **37**, January.

Baumgartner, T. and T.R. Burns (1975), 'The Structuring of International Economic Relations', *International Studies Quarterly*, **19**, (2), June.

Bergesen Albert (ed.) (1980), *Studies of the Modern World System*, New York: Academic Press.

Bergesen Albert (1982), 'The Emerging Science of the World-System', *International Social Science Journal*, **1**.

Bergsten, Fred C. (1982), 'The U.S. and the World Economy', *Annals of the American Academy of Political and Social Science*, **460**, March.

Bergsten, Fred C. and L.B. Krause, (1975), 'World Politics and International Economics', *International Organization*, **29**, Winter.

Bernal, Richard (1982), 'Transnational Banks, the IMF and External Debt of Developing Countries', *Social and Economic Studies*, **31**, (4).

Berrios, Rubén, (1982), 'The Transideological Enterprise and the Economic East–West–South Relations', *Estudios Internacionales*, **57**, January–March.

Biersteker, Thomas J. (1980), 'The Illusion of State Power: Transnational Corporation and the Neutralization of Host-Country Legislation', *Journal of Peace Research*, **17**, (3).

Blackhurst, R. (1981), 'The Twilight of Domestic Economic Policies', *World Economy*, **4**.

Block, Fred (1986), 'Political Choice and the Multiple "Logics" of Capitalism', *Theory and Society*, **15**, (1–2).

Block, Fred (1987), *Revising State Theory: Essays in Politics and Postindustrialism*, Philadelphia: Temple University Press.

Bluestone, B. and B. Harrison (1982), *The Deindustrialisation of America?*, New York: Basic Books.

Bodenheimer, S. (1971), 'Dependency and Imperialism: the Roots of Latin American Underdevelopment', *Politics and Society*, **1**, (3), May.

Boffito, Carlo, (1979), 'The COMECON Countries and the International Economy', *Spettatore Internazionale*, **14**, (4), October–December.

Bornschier, Volker (1980), 'Multinational Corporations, Economic Policy and National Development in the World System', *International Journal of Social Science*, **1**.

Bornschier, Volker (1981), 'Dependent Industrialization in the World Economy', *Journal of Conflict Resolution*, **25**, (3), September.

Bornschier, Volker (1982), 'The .World Economy in the World-system: Structure, Dependence and Change', *International Social Science Journal*, **34**, (1).

Brada, Josef C. (1975), 'Dynamic Capitalism and the Challenge to the U.S.', *Economia Internazionale*, **28**, February–March.

Brenner, Robert (1977), 'The Origins of Capitalist Development: a Critique of neo-Smithian Marxism', *New Left Review*, **104**, July–August.

Bressand, Albert (1983), 'Mastering the World Economy', *Foreign Affairs*, **61**, (4), Spring.

Brett, E. (1983), *International Money and Capitalist Crisis*, London: Heinemann.

Brown, Andrew G. (1986), 'The Behaviour of Transnational Banks and the Debt Crisis', *Centre Transnational Corps Reporter*, Spring.

Bryant, Ralph C. (1987), *International Financial Mediation*, Washington, DC: Brookings Institution.

Brzoska, Michael (1983), 'The Military Related External Debt of Third World Countries', *Journal of Peace Research*, **20**, (3).

Calleo, David P. (1974), Business Corporations and the National State', *Social Research*, **41**, (4), Winter.

Calleo, David P. (1982), *The Imperious Economy*, Cambridge, Mass.: Harvard University Press.

Calleo, David P. (1987), *Beyond American Hegemony: the Future of the Western Alliance*, New York: Basic Books.

Cameron, Duncan (1983), 'Order and Disorder in the World Economy', *Studies in Political Economy*, Summer.

Camilleri, J.A. (1976), 'Dependence and the Politics of Disorder', *Arena*, **44–5**.

Camilleri, J.A. (1981), 'The Advanced Capitalist State and the Contemporary World Crisis', *Science and Society*, **45**, (2), Summer.

Campbell, Bruce (1985), 'Transnational Bank Lending, Debt and Balance of Payments Deficit in Third World Countries', *Canadian Journal of Development Studies*, **6**, Summer.

Caporaso, James A. (1978), 'Dependence, Dependency and Power in the Global System: a Structural and Behavioural Analysis', *International Organization*, **32**, (1), Winter.

Cardoso, Fernando Henrique (1972), 'Dependency and Development in Latin America', *New Left Review*, **74**, July–August.

Carli, Guido (1985), 'The Internationalization of Financial and Credit Systems', *Review of the Economic Conditions In Italy*, September–December.

Chase-Dunn, Christopher (1980), 'Socialist States in the Capitalist World Economy', *Social Problems*, **27**, (5), June.

Chase-Dunn, Christopher (1981), 'Interstate System and Capitalist World Economy. One Logic or Two?', *International Studies Quarterly*, **25**, (1), March.

Chase-Dunn, Christopher (1983), 'Socialist State Policy In The Capitalist World Economy', in *Sage International Yearbook of Foreign Policy Studies*, 8.

Chase-Dunn, Christopher, A. Pallas and J. Kentor (1982), 'Old and New Research Designs for Studying the World Systems', *Comparative Political Studies*, **15**, (3), October.

Chase-Dunn, Christopher and Richard Rubinson (1977), 'Toward a Structural Perspective on the World System', *Politics and Society*, **7**, (4).

Chase-Dunn, Christopher and Joan Sokolovsky (1983), 'Interstate Systems, World Empires and the Capitalist World Economy: A Response to Thompson', *International Studies Quarterly*, **27**, (3), September.

Chirot, Daniel (1980), 'The Capitalist World Economy – Review', *Social Forces*, **59**, (2), December.

Chirot, Daniel and Thomas D. Hall (1982), 'World System Theory', *Annual Review of Sociology*, **8**.

Chyba, Antonin and Linhart Karel (1977), 'New Forms of Economic Relations between Socialist and Capitalist Countries', *Czechoslovakian Economic Digest*, March.

Ciasiorowski, Mark J. (1985), 'The Structure of Third World Economic Interdependence', *International Organization*, **39**, Spring.

Clausen, A.W. (1984), 'Priority Issues for the World Economy', *International Tax and Business Lawyer*, **2**, Fall.

Cleveland, Harold Van B. and Ramachandra Bhagavatula (1981), 'The Continuing World Economic Crisis', *Foreign Affairs*, **59**, Spring.

Coakley, Jerry (1984), 'The Internationalisation of Bank Capital', *Capital and Class*, Summer.

Cohen, Benjamin J. (1977), *Organizing The World's Money: the Political Economy of International Monetary Relations*, London: Macmillan.

Corbet, Hugh (1977), 'European Integration and the Integration of the World Economy', *British Journal of International Studies*, **3**, (1), April.

(Corporate) Centre on Transnational Corporations Government Publications (1986), *Transnational Corporations in World Development: Trends and Prospects*, New York: United Nations.

Coussy, Jean (1980), 'Interpretation of Economics and Trends in Dependence Relations', *Revue Française de Science Politique*, **30**, (2) April.

Cox, Robert L. (1977), 'Labour and Hegemony', *International Organisation*, **31**, (3), Summer.

Cox, Robert W. (1979), 'Ideologies and the New International Economic Order: Reflections on Some Recent Literature', *International Organization*, **33**, (2), Spring.

Cutler K.T., J. Williams and C. Haslam Williams (1987), 'The End of Mass Production?', *Economy and Society*, **3**.

Cypher, James M. (1979), 'The Transnational Challenge to the Corporate State', *Journal of Economic Issues*, **13**, (2), June.

Dell, S. (1986), 'The History of the IMF', *World Development*, **14**, (9), September.

Diebold, William Jr. (1978), 'Adapting Economies to Structural Change: the International Aspect', *International Affairs*, (London), **54**, (4), October.

Diebold, William Jr. (1983), 'The United States in the World Economy: a Fifty Year Perspective', *Foreign Affairs*, **62**, (1), Fall.

Dolan, Michael B. and James, A. Caporaso (1978), 'The External Relations of the European Community', *Annals of the American Academy of Political and Social Science*, **440**, November.

Donges, J. (1984), 'Is European Integration Now Due to Inertia or Conviction?', *World Economy*, **7**.

dos Santos, Theotonio (1970), 'The Structure of Dependence', *American Economic Review*, **60**, May.

Dufey, Gunter (1981), 'International Capital Markets: Structure and Response in an Era of Instability', *Sloan Management Review*, **22**, Spring.

Dunning, John H. (1981), *International Production and the Multinational Enterprise*, London: Allen & Unwin.

Edwards, Chris (1985), *The Fragmented World: Competing Perspectives on Trade, Money and Crisis*, London: Methuen.

Edwards, J. and D. Romano (1983), 'Handling the Realities of Business: a Perspective of the European Societal Strategy', *Futures*, **15**, (4), August.

Ellman, Michael (1984), *Collectivisation, Convergence and Capitalism: Political Economy in a Divided World*, London: Academic Press.

Elson, D. (1982), 'The Brandt Report: A Programme for Survival', *Capital and Class*, **16**, Spring.

Evans, Peter B. (1986), 'State, Capital and the Transformation of Dependence: the Brazilian Computer Case', *World Development*, **14**, (7), July.

Evans, Peter B., D. Rueschmeyer and Theda Skocpol (1985), 'On the Road Toward a More Adequate Understanding of the State', in Peter B. Evans, David Rueschmeyer and Theda Skocpol, *Bringing the State Back In*, Cambridge: Cambridge University Press.

Evans, Trevor (1985), 'Money Makes the World Go Round', *Capital and Class*, **24**, Winter.

Feinberg, Richard E. (1985), 'LDC Debt and the Public Sector Rescue', *Challenge*, **28**, July–August.

Feldstein, Martin (1985), 'American Economic Policy and the World Economy', *Foreign Affairs*, **63**, Summer.

Frank, Andre Gunder (1969), *Latin America: Underdevelopment or Revolution* and *Capitalism and Underdevelopment in Latin America*, New York: Monthly Review Press.

Fratianni, Michele and John Pattison (1982), 'The Economics of International Organizations', *Kyklos*, **35**, (2).

Freeman, Christopher (ed.) (1981), *Long Waves in the World Economy*, London: Butterworths.

Friedman, J. (1978), 'Crisis In Theory and Transformation of the World Economy', *Review – Fernand Braudel Center for the Study of Economics, Historical Systems and Civilizations*, Autumn.

Fröbel, Folker (1982), 'The Current Development of the World Economy: Reproduction of Labour and Accumulation of Capital on a World Scale', *Review – Fernand Braudel Center for the Study of Economics, Historical Systems and Civilizations*, **5**, (4), Spring.

Fröbel, Folker, Jürgen Heinrichs, Otto Kreye and Oswaldo Sunkel (1974), 'The Internationalisation of Capital and Labour', *African Review*, **4**, (3).

Fröbel, Folker, Jürgen Heinrichs and Otto Kreye (1980), *The New International Division of Labour*, Cambridge: Cambridge University Press.

Garst, D. (1985), 'Wallerstein and his Critics', *Theory and Society*, **14**, (4), July.

George, Susan (1989), *A Fate Worse than Debt*, Harmondsworth, Middlesex: Penguin.

Gibson, Donald et al. (1980), 'Multinational Capital, Labour and the State', *Contemporary Crises*, **4**,(3), July.

Gill, Stephen (1986), 'American Hegemony: Its Limits and Prospects in the Reagan Era', *Millenium*, **15**, (3), Winter.

Gill, Stephen and David Law (1988), *The Global Political Economy: Perspectives, Problems and Policies*, Hemel Hempstead: Harvester-Wheatsheaf.

Gilpin, Robert (1973), 'Three Models of the Future', *International Organization*, **29**, (1),Winter.

Gilpin, Robert (1975), *U.S. Power and the Multinational Corporation: the Political Economy of Foreign Direct Investment*, New York: Basic Books.

Gilpin, Robert (1987), *The Political Economy of International Relations*, Princeton, NJ: Princeton University Press.

Glynn, A. (1986), 'Capital Flight and Exchange Controls', *New Left Review*, **155**, January–February.

Goodwin, Geoffrey (1977), 'The External Relations of the European Community – Shadow and Substance', *British Journal of International Studies*, **3**, (1), April.

Gordon, David M. (1988), 'The Global Economy: New Edifice or Crumbling Foundations?', *New Left Review*, **168**, March–April.

Gough, Ian (1979), *The Political Economy of the Welfare State*, London: Macmillan.

Gourevitch, Peter (1986), *Politics in Hard Times*, Ithaca, NY: Cornell University Press.

Gregory, S. (ed.) (1988), *Recent Climatic Change: a Regional Approach*, London: Belhaven.

Gutain, Manuel (1981), *Fund Conditionality*, Washington DC: IMF Pamplet Series No. 38.

Halal, W. (1984), 'Big Business vs Big Government – A New Social Contract?', *Long Range Planning*, **17**, (4), August.

Harwell, M. and A. Freeman (1988), 'The Biological Consequences of Nuclear war', *Environment*, **30**, (5).

Hawley, James P. (1979), 'The Internationalization of Capital; Banks, Eurocurrency and the Instability of the World Monetary System', *Review of Radical Political Economies*, **11**, Winter.

Hawley, James P. (1983), 'Interests, State Foreign Economic Policy and the World System: the Case of the U.S. Capital Control Programs 1961–74', *Sage International Yearbook of Foreign Policy Studies*, 8.

Hawley, James P. (1984), 'Protecting Capital from Itself: U.S. Attempts to Regulate the Eurocurrency System', *International Organization*, **38**, Winter.

Hawley, James P. and Charles Noble (1982), 'The Internationalization of Capital and the Limits of the Interventionist State: towards an Explanation of Macroeconomic Policy Failure', *Journal of Political and Military Sociology*, **10**, (1), Spring.

Heilbroner, Robert (1985), 'The State and Capitalism: how they Interact and Move Apart', *Dissent*, **32**, (4), Fall.

Helleiner, G.K. (1977), 'Transnational Enterprises and the New Political Economy of U.S. Trade Policy', *Oxford Economic Papers*, **29**, March.

Helleiner, G.K. (1982), 'The Less Developed Countries and the International Monetary System', *World Politics*, **36**, (1), October.

Hogan, W. and I. Pearce (1984), *The Incredible Eurodollar*, London: Unwin.

Hollist, W. Ladd and James N. Rosenau (eds) (1981), *World System Structure*, Beverley Hills, Cal.: Sage.

Hollist, W. Ladd and James N. Rosenau (eds) (1981), *World Systems Debates*, in special issue of *International Studies Quarterly*, **25**, March.

Holloway, Stephen K. (1983), 'Relations among Core Capitalist States: the Kautsky–Lenin Debate Reconsidered', *Canadian Journal of Political Science*, **16**, (2), June.

Hopkins, Terrence K. and I. Wallerstein (eds) (1980), *Processes of the World-System*, Beverly Hills, Cal.: Sage.

Hopkins, Terrence K. and I. Wallerstein (eds) (1982), *Immanuel World-Survey Analysis Theory and Methodology*, Vol. 1, Beverly Hills, Cal.: Sage.

Horne, J. Paul (1986), 'Structural Changes in the International Economy', *Business Economics*, **21**, January.

Hymer, Stephen H. (1979), *The Multinational Corporation: a Radical Approach*, Cambridge: Cambridge University Press.

Ikenberry, G.J. (1986), 'The State and Strategies of International Adjustment', *World Politics*, **39**, (1), October.

Itoh, M. (1983), 'The World Economic Crisis', *New Left Review*, **138**, March–April.

Jalée, Pierre (1969), *The Third World in World Economy*, New York: Monthly Review Press.

Jones, Kelvin (1984), 'Everywhere Abroad and Nowhere at Home: the Global Corporation and the International State', *International Journal of the Sociology of Law*, **12**, (1), February.

Jones, R.J. Barry (1981–2), 'International Political Economy: Problems and Issues', *Review of International Studies, Part One*, **7**, (4), October; *Part Two*, **8**, (1), January.

Junne, G. (1976), 'Multinational Banks, the State and International Integration', *German Political Studies*, **1**.

Jussawalla, M. (1983), 'International Trade and Welfare Implications of Transborder Data Flows', *Prometheus*, **1**, (1).

Jussawalla, M. (1985), 'Constraints on Economic Analysis of Transborder Data Flows', *Media, Culture and Society*, **7**, (3), July.

Kaldor, Mary (1986), 'The Global Political Economy', *Alternatives*, **11**.

Kaplan, Barbara Hockey (ed.) (1978), *Social Change in the Capitalist World Economy*, Beverley Hills, Cal.: Sage.

Karasz, Arthur (1977), 'Crisis and Reform in the World's Economy', *Review of Politics*, **39**, (2), April.

Katchen, Howard M. (1980), 'Interdependence, Convergence and the Economic Bases of Détente', *Jerusalem Journal of International Relations*, **4**, (4).

Katzenstein, P.J. (1976), 'International Relations and Domestic Structures: Foreign Economic Policies of Advanced Industrial States', *International Organization*, **30**, (1), Winter.

Kellman, M. and D. Landau (1984), 'The Nature of Japan's Comparative Advantage', *World Development*, **12**, (4), April.

Kelly, Janet (1978), 'International Capital Markets: Power and Security in the International System', *Orbis*, **21**, Winter.

Kennedy, Paul (1987), *The Rise and Fall of the Great Powers*, New York: Random House.

Keohane, Robert O. (1978), 'American Policy and the Trade Growth Struggle', *International Security*, **3**, (2), Fall.

Keohane, Robert O. (1982), 'Economic Dependence and the Self-Directed Small State', *Jerusalem Journal of International Relations*, **6**, (2).

Keohane, Robert O. (1984), *After Hegemony: Co-operation and Discord in the World Political Economy*, Princeton, NJ: Princeton University Press.

Khan, R. (1986), 'Multinational Companies and the World Economy: Economic and Technological Impact', *Impact of Science on Society*, **36**, (141).

Kimmel, M.B. (1975–6), 'The Negation of National Sovereignty: the Multinational Corporation and the World Economy', *Berkeley Journal of Sociology*, **20**.

Kimmel, M.B. (1982), 'The Modern World System, Volume 2', *Theory and Society*, **11**, (2), March.

Kindleberger, Charles P. (1973), *The World in Depression, 1929–1939*, Berkeley: University of California Press.

Kindleberger, Charles P. (1981), 'Dominance and Leadership in the International Economy', *International Studies Quarterly*, **25**, (2), June.

Kiritchenko, E. (1985), 'Certaines Particularités de la Rivalité Interimpérialiste', *La Vie Internationale*, **6**, June.

Koo, Hagen (1984), 'World System, Class and State in Third World Development', *Sociological Perspectives*, **27**, (1), January.

Korany, Bahgat (1978), 'Financial Dependence and International Behaviour', *Revue Française de Science Politique*, **28**, (6), December.

Krasner, Stephen D. (1977), 'U.S. Commercial and Monetary Policy: Unravelling the Paradox of External Strength and Internal Weakness', *International Organization*, **31**, (4), Autumn.

Krasner, Stephen D. (1978), *Defending the National Interest*, Princeton NJ: Princeton University Press.

Krasner, Stephen D. (1983), *International Regimes*, London: Cornell University Press.

Krasner, Stephen D. (1987), 'Structural Conflict: the Third World against Global Liberalism', *Journal of Politics*, **49**, (1), February.

Krause, L.B. and J.S. Nye (1975), 'Reflections on the Economics and Politics of International Economic Organizations', *International Organisation*, **29**, (1), Winter.

Krugman, Paul (1981), 'Trade, Accumulation and Uneven Development', *Journal of Development Economics*, **8**, April.

Lall, S. (1984), 'Exports of Technology by Newly-Industrialising Countries', *World Development*, **12**, (5/6), May/June.

Lane, David (1976), *The Socialist Industrial State*, London: Allen & Unwin.

Lash, S. and J. Urry (1987), *The End of Organised Capitalism*, Oxford: Basil Blackwell.

Lipietz, A. (1982), 'Towards Global Fordism?', *New Left Review*, **132**, March/April.

Lipson, Charles (1984), 'International Co-operation in Economic and Security Affairs', *World Politics*, **37**, October.

Lipson, Charles (1985), 'Bankers' Dilemmas: Private Co-operation in Rescheduling Sovereign Debts', *World Politics*, **38**, (1), October.

Lockwood, W.W. (1965), *The State and Economic Enterprise in Japan*, Princeton, NJ: Princeton University Press.

Luke, Timothy W. (1983), 'Dependent Development and the Arab OPEC States', *Journal of Politics*, **45**, (4), November.

Madeuf, Bernadette and Charles Albert Michalet (1978), 'A New Approach to International Economics', *International Social Science Journal*, **30**, (2).

Marcussen, Henrik Secher (1982), 'Changes in the International Division of Labour: Theoretical Implications', *Acta Sociologica*, **25**.

Means, G. (1988), 'Globalisation of World Markets: the CEO Response', *Washington Quarterly*, **11**, (1), Winter.

Meek, Paul (1985), 'International Financial Integration: Implications for Monetary Policy', *Federal Reserve Bank of Atlanta*, (Economic Review), **70**, December.

Menshikov, Stanislav (1986), 'Transnational Monopoly and Contemporary Capitalism', *Political Affairs*, **65**, June.

Meyer, John W. and Michael T. Hannan (eds) (1979), *National Development and the World System: Educational, Economic and Political Change 1950–1970*, Chicago: University of Chicago Press.

Minz, Beth and Michael Schwartz (1986), 'Capital Flows and the Process of Financial Hegemony', *Theory and Society*, **15**, (1–2).

Mirow, Kurt Rudolf and Harry Maurer (1982), *Webs of Power: International Cartels and the World Economy*, Boston: Houghton Mifflin.

Modelski, George (1978), 'The Long Cycle of Global Politics and the Nation-State', *Comparative Studies in Society and History*, **20**, April.

Modelski, George (ed.) (1979), *Transnational Corporations and World Order: Readings in International Political Economy*, San Francisco: W. H. Freeman.

Moffit, Michael (1984), *The World's Money: International Banking from Bretton Woods to the Brink of Insolvency*, London: Michael Joseph.

Morris, Frank E. (1986), 'The Changing World of Central Banking', *New England Economic Review*, March/April.

Morse, Edward L.(1970), 'The Tranformation of Foreign Policies: Modernisation, Interdependence and Externalisation', *World Politics*, **22**, (3), April.

Murray, Robin (1971), The Internationalisation of Capital and the Nation State', *New Left Review*, **67**, May–June.

Navarro, Vicente (1982), 'The Limits of the World Systems Theory in Defining Capitalist and Socialist Formations', *Science and Society*, **46**, (1), Spring.

Nicoll, William (1985), 'Paths to European Unity', *Journal of Common Market Studies*, **23**, (3), March.

Noble, David F. (1984), *Forces of Production*, New York: Alfred A. Knopf.

Nolan, Patrick D. (1983), 'Status in the World Economy and National Structure and Development', *International Journal of Comparative Sociology*, **24**, (1–2), January–April.

Nye, Joseph S. Jr. (1974), 'Multinational Corporations in World Politics', *Foreign Affairs*, **53**, (1), October.

Ouggard, Morten (1982–3), 'Some Remarks concerning Peripheral Capitalism and the Peripheral State', *Science and State*, **46**, (4), Winter.

Palloix, Christian (1977), 'The Self-Expansion of Capital on a World Scale', from *L'internationalisation du capital* (Paris, 1975), in *The Review of Radical Political Economics*, **9**, (2), Summer.

Perlo, Victor (1983), 'Internationalization of Economic Life', *Political Life*, **62**, September.

Petras, James F. (1976), 'State Capitalism and the Third World', *Journal of Contemporary Asia*, 4.

Petras, James F. (1981), 'Dependency and World System Theory: a Critique and New Direction', *Latin American Perspectives*, **8**, (3–4), Summer–Fall.

Petras, James F. and H. Morley Morris (1981), 'The US Imperial State', in James Petras, *Class, State and Power in the Third World: with Case Studies on Class Conflict in Latin America*, London: Zed Press.

Philip, Peter D. and Immanuel Wallerstein (1985), 'National and World Identities and the Interstate System', *Millenium*, **14**, (2), Summer.

Pinder, J. (1985), 'European Community and Nation-State: a Case for Neo-Federalism', *International Affairs*, **62**, (1), Winter.

Pool, J. and S. Stamos (1985), 'The Uneasy Calm: Third World Debt – the Case of Mexico', *Monthly Review*, **37**, (10), March.

Porter, Michael F. (1990), *The Competitive Advantage of Nations*, New York: Free Press.

Preeg, E.H. (1974), 'Economic Blocs and U.S. Foreign Policy', *International Organization*, **2**, Spring.

Pronk, Jan (1990), 'We Need a Global Mixed Economy and a Global Public Sector', *ifda dossier*, **78**, July–September.

Putnam, Robert D. and Nicholas Bayne (1987), *Hanging Together: Co-operation and Conflict in the Seven Power Summits*, London: Sage.

Radice, H. (1984), 'The National Economy: a Keynesian Myth?', *Capital and Class*, **22**, Spring.

Ray, James Lee (1983), 'The World System and the Global Political System: a Crucial Relationship?', in *Sage International Yearbook of Foreign Policy Studies*, 8.

Reese, K. (1975), 'Multinational Companies and the Nation-State', *Studia Diplomatica*, **28**, (2).

Roberts, K. (1985), 'Democracy and the Dependent State in Latin America', *Monthly Review*, **37**, (5), October.

Robertson, R. and F. Lechner (1985), 'Modernisation, Globalization and the Problem of Culture in World-Systems Theory', *Theory, Culture and Society*, **2**, (3).

Robson, Peter (1980), *The Economics of International Integration*, London: Allen & Unwin.

Roddick, J. (1984), 'Crisis, "Seignorage" and the Modern World System: Rising Third World Power or Declining US Hegemony?', *Capital and Class*, **23**, Summer.

Rostow, W.W. (1978), *The World Economy: History and Prospect*, London: Macmillan.

Ruggie, John Gerrard (1981), 'The Politics of Money', *Foreign Policy*, **43**, Summer.

Ruggie, John Gerrard (1982), 'International Regimes, Transactions and Change: Embedded Liberalism in the Postwar Economic Order', *International Organization*, **36**, (2), Spring.

Ruggie, John Gerrard (1983), 'Continuity and Transformation in the World Polity: Toward a Neo-Realist Synthesis', *World Politics*, January.

Ruggie, John Gerrard (ed.) (1983), *The Antinomies of Intedependence National Welfare and the International Division of Labour*, New York: Columbia University Press.

Russell, R.W. (1977), 'Governing the World's Money', *International Organization*, **31**, (1), Winter.

Russett, B.M. (1985), 'The Mysterious Case of Vanishing Hegemony; Or Is Mark Twain Really Dead?', *International Organization*, **39**, (2).

Rynalov, V. (1981), 'The World Capitalist Economy at the Start of the 1980s', *International Affairs*, March.

Sandler, Tom (ed.) (1980), *The Theory and Structure of International Political Economy*, Boulder: Westview Press.

Sarkar, Goutam K. (1983), *Commodities and the Third World*, Calcutta: Oxford University Press.

Sassen-Koob, Saskia (1987), 'Issues of Core and Periphery: Labour Migration and Global Restructuring', in J. Henderson and M. Castells (eds), *Global Restructuring and Territorial Development*, London: Sage.

Sassoon, Joseph (1980–1), 'Dependency and Interdependence in the International System', *Quaderni Di Sociologica*, **29**, (3).

Schmid, G. (1975–6), 'Interdependence Has Its Limits', *Foreign Policy*, **21**, Winter.

Schneider, F. and B. Grey (1985), 'Economic and Political Determinants of Foreign Direct Investment', *World Development*, **13**, (2), February.

Schnitter, P. (1974), 'Still the Century of Corporatism', *Review of Politics*, **36**, January.

Sengupta, A. (1986), 'The Functioning of the International Monetary System: a Critique of the Perspective of the Industrial Countries', *World Development*, **14**, (9), September.

Siegel, Tilla (1984), 'Politics and Economics in the Capitalist World Market: Methodological Problems of Marxist Analysis', *International Journal of Sociology*, **14**, (1).

Simai, Milhaly, (1985), 'The Role of the Socialist Countries of Eastern Europe in the World Economy', *Trade and Development*, **5**.

Sklar, H. (1980), *The Trilateral Commission and Elite Planning for World Management*, Boston: Southend Press.

Skocpol, Theda (1977), 'Wallerstein's World Capitalist System: a Theoretical and Historical Critique', *American Journal of Sociology*, **82**, (5), March.

Skocpol, Theda (1987), 'The Origins of Capitalist Development: a Critique of Neo-Smithian Marxism', *New Left Review*, **104**, July–August.

Soames, Christopher (1976), 'Europe's Wider Horizons: the External Relations of the European Community', *Round Table*, **262**, April.

Spero, Joan E. (1985), *The Politics of International Economic Relations*, London: Allen & Unwin.

Spero, Joan E. (1988–9), 'Guiding Global Finance', *Foreign Policy*, **73**, Winter.

Stewart, Francis (1985), 'The International Debt Situation and North–South Relations', *World Development*, **13**, February.

Stohl, Michael (1983), 'Imperialism and the Modern World System: the Domestic Consequences of Hegemony for Britain and U.S.', in *Sage International Yearbook of Foreign Policy Studies*, 8.

Strange, Susan (1975), 'What Is Economic Power and Who Has It?', *International Journal*, **30**, (2), Spring.

Strange, Susan (1985), 'Protectionism and World Politics', *International Organization*, **39**, (2).

Strange, Susan (1986), *Casino Capitalism*, Oxford: Basil Blackwell,

Strange, Susan (1986), 'Subnationals and the State', in John Hall (ed.), *States in History*, Oxford: Basil Blackwell.

Sylvan, David J. (1981), 'The Newest Mercantilism', *International Organization*, **35**, (2), Spring.

Teeters, Nancy (1983), 'The Role of Banks in the International Financial System', *Journal of Banking and Finance*, **7**, December.

Teune, Henry (1981), 'Human Development in a Global Political Economy', *International Studies Quarterly*, **25**, (4), December.

Thompson, H.M. (1983), 'Transnational Banking and the International Monetary Crisis', *Australian Outlook*, **37**, August.

Thompson, William R. (1983), 'The World Economy, the Long Cycle and the Question of World System Time', in *Sage International Yearbook of Foreign Policy Studies*, 8.

Thurow, Lester (1983), *Dangerous Currents: the State of Economics*, New York: Random House.

Thurow, Lester (1985), 'America, Europe and Japan: a Time to Dismantle the World Economy', *Economist*, **297**, November.

United Nations Centre on Transnational Corporations (1988), *Transnational Corporations in World Development: Trends and Prospects*, New York: United Nations.

Useem, Michael (1983), 'Business and Politics in the U.S. and U.K.: the Origins of Heightened Political Activity of Large Corporations during the 1970s and Early 1980s', *Theory and Society*, **12**, (3), May.

Van Der Pijl, Kees (1975), 'A Note on Internationalization of Capital as an Interdependent Variable in the Analysis of the International System', *Acta Politika*, **10**, (1).

Van Der Pijl, Kees (1984), *The Making of an Atlantic Ruling Class*, London: New Left Books.

Vernon, R. (1971), *Sovereignty at Bay: the Multinational Spread of US Enterprises*, New York: Basic Books.

Vernon, R. (1974), *Big Business and the State: Changing Relations in Western Europe*, Cambridge, Mass.: Harvard University Press.

Vernon, R. (1985), *Exploring the Global Economy: Emerging Issues in Trade and Investment*, Centre for International Affairs, Harvard University: Lanham University Press.

Vernon, R. and L. Wells (1986), *The Economic Environment of International Business*, Englewood Cliffs, NJ: Prentice-Hall.

Versluysen, Eugene (1981), *The Political Economy of International Finance*, New York: St Martin's Press.

Vrhunec, Marko (1983), 'The Crisis of International Economic Relations', *Review of International Affairs*, **34**, April.

Wachtel, H. (1980), 'A Decade of International Debt', *Theory and Society*, **9**, (3), May.

Wallace, W. (1986), 'What Price Independence? Sovereignty and Interdependence in British Politics', *International Affairs*, **62**, (3), Summer.

Wallerstein, Immanuel (1974), *The Modern World System*, New York: Academic Press.

Wallerstein, Immanuel (1976), 'Semi-Peripheral Countries and the Contemporary World Crisis', *Theory and Society*, **3**, (4), Winter.

Wallerstein, Immanuel (1979) *The Capitalist World Economy*, Cambridge: Cambridge University Press.

Wallerstein, Immanuel (1980), 'The States in the Institutional Vortex of the Capitalist World Economy', *International Social Science Journal*, **32**, (4).

Wallerstein, Immanuel (1980), *The Modern World System II: Mercantilism and the Consolidation of the European World Economy 1600–1750*, New York: Academic Press.

Wallerstein, Immanuel (1983), *Labor in the World Social Structure*, Beverly Hills, Cal.: Sage.

Wallerstein, Immanuel (1984), *The Politics of the World Economy: the States, the Movements and the Civilisations*, Cambridge: Cambridge University Press.

Wallerstein, Immanuel (1986), 'Braudel on Capitalism and the Market', *Monthly Review*, **137**, (9), February.

Wallerstein, Immanuel and Terence K. Hopkins (1982), *World Systems Analysis: Theory and Methodology*, Beverly Hills, Cal.: Sage.

Watz, Kenneth N. (1976), 'The Myth of Interdependence', in Charles P. Kindleberger (ed.), *The International Corporation,* Cambridge, Mass.: MIT Press.

Wheelock, J. (1986), 'Competition and Monopoly: a Contribution to Debate', *Capital and Class*, **30**, Autumn.

Whynes, David K. and Roger A. Bowles (1981), *The Economic Theory of the State*, Oxford: Martin Robertson.

Willoughby, John (1985), 'The Internationalisation of Capital and the Future of Macro-Economic Policy', *Science and Society*, **49**, (3), Fall.

Worsley, Peter (1980), 'One World or Three? A Critique of the World System Theory of Immanuel Wallerstein', in Ralph Miliand and John Saville (eds), *The Socialist Register 1980*, London: Merlin Press.

Ziebura, Gilbert (1982), 'Internationalization of Capital, International Division of Labour and the Role of the European Community', *Journal of Common Market Studies*, **21**, September–December,

TECHNOLOGICAL CHANGE

Abernathy, W., K. Clark and A. Kantrow (1983), *Industrial Renaissance: Producing a Competitive Future for America*, New York: Basic Books.

Ackerman, W. (1981), 'Cultural Values and Social Choice of Technology', *International Social Science Journal*, **33**, (3).

Ackroyd, Carol et al. (1980), *The Technology of Political Control* (2nd edn), London: Pluto Press.

Agarwal, S. (1985), 'Electronics in India: Past Strategies and Future Possibilities', *World Development*, **13**, (3), March.

Argumedo, Alcira (1981–82), 'The New World Information Order and International Power', *Journal of International Affairs*, **55**, (2), Fall–Winter.

Badham, Richard and John Mathews (1989), 'The New Production Systems Debate', *Labour and Industry*, **2**, (2), June.

Barney, G. (1980), *The Global 2000 Report to the President of the US*, London: Pergamon.

Bascur, R. (1985), 'Information in the Third World: Adjusting Technologies or Strategies?', *Media, Culture and Society*, **7**, (3), July.

Bazin, M. (1986), 'The Technological Mystique and Third World Options', *Monthly Review*, **38**, (3), July–August.

Benson, Ian and John Lloyd (1983), *New Technology and Industrial Change*, London: Kogan Page.

Berg, M. (1985), 'Government Policy and Its Impact on the Motor Industry', *Long Range Planning*, **6**, December.

Bestuzhev-Lada, I. (1987), 'High Technology and Long-term Global Problems', *Futures*, **19**, (3), June.

Bhalla, A. and A. Fluitman (1985), 'Science and Technology Indicators and Socio-economic Development', *World Development*, **13**, (3), March.

Blunden, M. (1984), 'Technology and Values: Problems and Options', *Futures*, **16**, (4), August.

Brinkman, R. (1986), 'The Genesis of a New Industrial Policy: Equity and Efficiency', *Journal of Economic Issues*, **20**, June.

Camilleri, J.A. (1984), *The State and Nuclear Power: Conflict and Control in the Western World*, Brighton, Sussex: Wheatsheaf Books.

Cavell, A. (1982), 'The Fact of Television', *Daedalus*, **III**, (4), Fall.

Caves, Richard E. and Masu Uekusu (1976), *Industrial Organisation in Japan*, Washinton: Brookings Institution.

Chombart de Lauwe, P. (1986), 'Technological Domination and Cultural Dynamism', *International Social Science Journal*, **1**.

Cohen, R. (1982), 'Science and Technology in Global Perspective', *International Social Science Journal*, **34**, (1).

Cohen, Stephen S. and John Zysman (1987), 'The Myth of a Post-Industrial Economy', *Technology Review*, **90**, (2), February–March.

Dahlnman, C. and B. Ross-Larson (1987), 'Managing Technological Development: Lessons from the Newly Industrialising Countries', *World Development*, **15**, (6), June.

Dekker, W. (1986), 'Managing a Global Electronics Company in Tomorrow's World', *Long Range Planning*, **2**, April.

Dennett, D. (1986), 'Information, Technology, and the Virtues of Ignorance', *Daedalus*, **115**, (3), Summer.

Dewar, M. (1982), *Industry Vitalization: Toward a National Industrial Strategy*, New York: Pergamon.

Dicken, P. (1986), *Global Shift: Industrial Change in a Turbulent World*, New York: Harper & Row.

Dickson, D. (1980), 'Science and Technology, North and South', *Radical Science Journal*, **10**.

Douma, S. (1984), 'Towards a New Industrial Policy', *Long Range Planning*, **17**, August.

Dyson, Kenneth and Stephen Wilks (1983), 'Conclusions' in Kenneth Dyson and Stephen Wilks (eds), *Industrial Crisis: A Comparative Study of the State and Industry*, Oxford: Martin Robertson.

Eksl, R. and G. Metayer (1986), 'Technical Modernism and Social Conservatism', *Futures*, **18**, (2), April.

Enos, J. (1986), 'Korean Industrial Policy', *Prometheus*, **4**, (2), December.

Ergas, Henry (1987), 'Does Technology Policy Matter?' in Bruce P. Guile and Harvey Brooks (eds), *Technology and Global Industry: Companies and Nation in the World Economy*, National Academy of Engineering Series on Technology and Social Priorities, Washington DC: National Academy Press.

Ernst, Dieter (1981), 'Technology Policy for Self Reliance', *International Social Science Journal*, **23**, (3).

Ernst, Dieter (1985), 'Automation and the Worldwide Restructuring of the

Electronics Industry: Strategic Implications for Developing Countries', *World Development*, **13**, (3), March.

Ernst, Dieter (1987), 'U.S.–Japanese Competition and the Worldwide Restructuring of the Electronics Industry:.a European View' in J. Henderson and M. Castells (eds), *Global Restructuring and Territorial Development*, London: Sage.

Feketekuty, G. and J. Aronson (1984), 'Meeting the Challenges of the World Information Economy', *World Economy*, **7**, (1).

Foster-Carter, A. (1985), 'Korea and Dependency Theory', *Monthly Review*, **37**, (5), October.

Frame, J. Davidson (1983), *International Business and Global Technology*, Lexington, Mass.: Lexington Books.

Fransman, M. (1986), 'International Competitiveness and the State: the Machine Tool Industry in Taiwan and Japan', *World Development*, **14**, (12), December.

Fricke, W. (1986), 'New Technologies and German Co-Determination', *Economic and Industrial Democracy*, **7**.

Gibney, F. (1982), *Miracle by Design: the Real Reasons Behind Japan's Economic Success*, New York: Basic Books.

Gough, J. (1986), 'Industrial Policy and Socialist Strategy: Restructuring and the Unity of the Working Class', *Capital and Class*, **29**, Summer.

Goulet, D. (1983), 'Science and Technology for a Global Society', *Impact of Science on Society*, **33**, (2).

Grant, P. (1983), 'Technological Sovereignty: Forgotten Factor in the High-Tech Razzamattazz', *Prometheus*, **1**, (2).

Guile, B. and H. Brooks (eds) (1988), *Technology and Global Industry*, Washington, DC: National Academy Press.

Haggard, S. (1986), 'The Newly Industrialising Countries in the International System', *World Politics*, **38**, (2), January.

Hamelink, C. (1977), *The Corporate Village:.the Role of Transnational Corporations in International Communication*, Rome: IDOC.

Hamelink, C. (1982), *Cultural Autonomy in Global Communications*, New York: Longman.

Hieronymi, O. (1987), *Technology and International Relations*, Basingstoke: Macmillan Education.

Hill, Stephen (1989), *The Tragedy of Technology: Human Liberation Versus Domination in the Late Twentieth Century*, London: Pluto Press.

Hindley, B. (1984), 'Empty Economics in the Case for Industrial Policy', *World Economy*, **7**, (3).

Hirschorn L. (1984), *Beyond Mechanisation*, Cambridge, Mass.: MIT Press.

Hoffman, K. (1985), 'Microelectronics, International Competition and

Development Strategies: the Unavoidable Issues – Editor's Introduction', *World Development*, **13**, (3), March.

Ishikawa, A. (1982), 'A Survey of Studies in the Japanese Style of Management', *Economic and Industrial Democracy*, **3**, (1).

Jacobi, O., B. Jessop, H. Kastendiek and M. Regini (eds) (1986), *Technological Change, Rationalisation and Industrial Relations*, London: Croom Helm.

Jacobsson, S. (1985), 'Technical Change and Industrial Policy: the Case of Computer Controlled Lathes in Argentina, Korea and Taiwan', *World Development*, **13**, (3), March.

Jacquemin, Alexis (1984), *European Industry: Public Policy and Corporate Strategy*, Oxford: Clarendon Press.

Johnson, C. (1982), *MITI and the Japanese Miracle, 1925–1975*, Stanford, Cal.: Stanford University Press.

Johnson, C. (ed.) (1984), *The Industrial Policy Debate*, San Francisco: Institute for Contemporary Studies.

Johnson, C. (1984), 'The Industrial Policy Debate Re-Examined', *California Management Review*, **27**, (1), Fall.

Jones, H.G. (1979), 'Government Intervention in the Economy of Sweden', in Peter Maunder (ed.), *Government Intervention in the Developed Economy*, London: Croom Helm.

Kintner, W. (1975), *Technology and International Politics*, Lexington, Mass.: Lexington Books.

Koo, Hagen (1984), 'The Political Economy of Income Distribution in South Korea: the Impact of the State's Industrialisation Policies', *World Development*, **12**, (10), October.

Kurth, James R. (1979), 'The Political Consequences of the Product Cycle: Industrial History and Political Outcomes', *International Organization*, **33**, (1), Winter.

Langdale, J. (1985), 'Electronic Funds Transfer and the Internationalisation of the Banking and Finance Industry', *Geoforum*, **16**, (1).

Lindbeck, A. (1981), 'Industrial Policy as an Issue in the Economic Environment', *World Economy*, **4**, (4).

Locksley, G. (1986), 'Information Technology and Capitalist Development', *Capital and Class*, **28**, Winter.

Lojkine, J. (1986), 'From the Industrial Revolution to the Computer Revolution: First Signs of a New Combination of Material and Human Productive Forms', *Capital and Class*, **29**, Spring.

Magaziner, I. and T. Hout (1980), *Japanese Industrial Policy*, London: Policy Studies Institute.

Mahon, R. (1987), 'From Fordism to New Technology, Labour Markets and Unions', *Economic and Industrial Democracy*, **8**, (1).

Mattelart, A., X. Delcourt and M. Mattelart (1984), *International Image Markets*, London: Comedia.

McFarlane, B. (1985), 'Industrialisation and the Changing Labour Process in SE Asia: Implications for "First World" Countries', *Economic and Industrial Democracy*, **6**.

Merrit, G. (1986), 'Multinationals: Innovators in High Technology?', *Impact of Science on Society*, **36**, (1).

Miege, B. (1987), 'The Logics at Work in the New Cultural Industries', *Media, Culture and Society*, **9**, (3), July.

Murray, F. (1987), 'Flexible Specialisation in the Third Italy', *Capital and Class*, **33**, Winter.

Nakase, T. (1981), 'Some Characteristics of Japanese-type Multinationals Today', *Capital and Class*, **13**, Spring.

Nelson, Richard R. (1984), *High-Technology Policies: A Five-Nation Comparison*, Washington: American Enterprise Institute for Public Policy Research.

Nielsen, R. (1984), 'Industrial Policy: the Case for National Strategies for World Markets', *Long Range Planning*, **17**, (5), June.

Nordenstreng, Kaarle and Herbert I. Schiller (eds) (1979), *National Sovereignty and International Communication*, Norwood, NJ: Ablex.

O'Connor, D. (1985), 'The Computer Industry in the Third World: Policy Options and Constraints', *World Development*, **13**, (3), March.

Office of Technology Assessment (1980), *The Effects of Nuclear War*, London: Croom Helm.

Parry, T. (1984), 'International Technology Transfer: Emerging Corporate Strategies', *Prometheus*, **2**, (2), December.

Pavitt, K. (1987), 'The Objectives of Technology Policy', *Science and Public Policy*, **14**, (4), August.

Pelton, J. (1983), 'The Communications Satellite: Revolutionary Change Agent?', *Columbia Journal of World Business*, **18**, (1), Spring.

Pendakur, M. (1983), 'The New International Information Order after the MacBride Commission Report: an International Powerplay between the Core and Periphery Countries', *Media, Culture and Society*, **5**, (3/4), July–October.

Piore, M. and C. Sabel (1984), *The Second Industrial Divide*, New York: Basic Books.

Ploman, E. (1979), 'Satellite Broadcasting, National Sovereignty and Free Flow of Information', in *National Sovereignty and International Communications* Norwood, NJ: Ablex.

Poirier, R. (1982), 'Literature, Technology, People', *Daedalus*, **3**, (4), Fall.

Poznanski, K. (1984), 'Technology Transfer', *World Politics*, **37**, (1), October.

Prentice, J. (1984), 'Competing with the Japanese Approach to Technology', *Long Range Planning*, **17**, (2), April.

Rehn, G. (1987), 'State, Economic Policy and Industrial Relations in the 1980s: Problems and Trends', *Economic and Industrial Democracy*, **8**, (1).

Roncaglio, R. (1985), 'Information and Transnational Culture: Directions for Policy Research', *Media, Culture and Society*, **7**, (3), July.

Ryscroft, R. and J. Szyliowicz (1980), 'The Technological Dimension of Decision Making', *World Politics*, **33**, (1), October.

Sabel, C. (1982), *Work and Politics*, Cambridge: Cambridge University Press.

Salinas, Raquel and Leena Paldán (1979), 'Culture in the Process of Dependent Development: Theoretical Perspectives', in Kaarle Nordenstrong and Herbert I. Schiller (eds), *National Sovereignty and International Communications*, Norwood, NJ: Ablex.

Salvaggio, Jerry L. (ed.) (1989), *The Information Society: Economic, Social and Structural Issues*, New Jersey: Lawrence Erlbaum.

Saxonhouse, G. (1983), 'What is All This about Industrial Targetting in Japan?', *World Economy*, **6**, (3).

Schiller, Herbert (1973), 'Madison Avenue Imperialism', *Trans-Action*, March–April.

Schiller, Herbert (1979), 'Transnational Media and National Development', *National Sovereignty and International Communications*, Norwood, NJ: Ablex.

Schiller, Herbert (1979), 'Transnational Corporation. The International Flow of Information, Challenges to National Sovereignty', *Current Research on Peace and Violence*, **2**, (1).

Schiller, Herbert (1981), *Who Knows: Information in the Age of the Fortune 500*, Norwood, NJ: Ablex.

Schiller, Herbert (1984), *Information and the Crisis Economy*, Norwood, NJ: Ablex.

Schiller, Herbert (1985), 'Privatising the Public Sector: The Information Connection', in B.D. Ruben (ed.), *Information and Behaviour*, Vol. 1, New Brunswick: Transaction.

Shaiken, H. (1984), *Work Transformed*, New York: Holt, Rinehart & Winston.

Shapley, D. (1982), 'The Media and National Security', *Daedalus*, **111**, (4), Fall.

Singh, K. and B. Gross (1981), 'McBride: the Report and Response'. *Journal of Communication*, **31**, (4), Autumn.

Smith, A. (1982), 'Information Technology and the Myth of Abundance', *Daedalus*, **111**, (4), Fall.

Smith, A. (1985), 'The Influence of Television', *Daedalus*, **114**, (4), Fall.

Smith, A. (1986), 'Technology, Identity, and the Information Machine', *Daedalus*, **115**, (3), Summer.

Smythe, Dan (1977), 'Communications: Blindspot of Western Marxism', *Canadian Journal of Political and Social Theory*, **1**, Fall.

Soete, Luc (1985), 'International Diffusion of Technology, Industrial Development and Technological Leapfrogging', *World Development*, **13**, (3), March.

Streeck, W. (1987), 'Industrial Relations and Industrial Change: the Restructuring of the World Automobile Industry in the 1970s and 1980s', *Economic and Industrial Democracy*, **8**, (4).

Sussman, G. (1984), 'Global Telecommunications and the Third World: Theoretical Considerations', *Media, Culture and Society*, **6**, (3), July.

Thurow, Lester (1984), 'Revitalizing American Industry; Managing in a Competitive World Economy', *California Management Review*, **27**, (1).

Tisdell, C. (1983), 'The International Realpolitik of Science and Technology Policy', *Prometheus*, **1**, (1), June.

Tomassini, Luciano (1980), 'Industrialization, Trade and the International Division of Labour', *Journal of International Affairs*, **34**, (1), Spring–Summer.

Tomassini, Luciano (1982), 'Interdependence and National Development', *Estudios Internacionales*, **58**, April–June.

Tracey, M. (1985), 'The Poisoned Chalice? International Television and the Idea of Dominance', *Daedalus*, **114**, (4), Fall.

Williams, K., T. Cutler, J. Williams and C. Haslam (1987), The End of Mass Production?', *Economy and Society*, **16**, (3), August.

Zegveld, W., (1987), 'Technology and Change in Industrial Societies: Implications for Public Policy', *Technovation*, **5**, (4), February.

Zysman, J. (1983), *Governments, Markets and Growth*, Ithaca, NY: Cornell University Press.

Zysman, J. and L. Tyson (1983), *American Industry in International Competition*, Ithaca, NY: Cornell University Press.

SECURITY AND THE USE OF FORCE

Albrecht, U. (1983), 'Military R&D Communities', *International Social Science Journal*, **35**, (1).

Alker, Hayward R., Jr and Thomas J. Biersteker (1884), 'The Dialectics of World Order: Notes for a Future Archaeologist of International Savoir Faire', *International Studies Quarterly*, **28**, (2), June.

Altfield, Michael F. (1984), 'Measuring Issue-Distance and Polarity in the International System: a Preliminary Comparison of an Alliance and an Action Flow Indicator', *Political Methodology*, **10**, (1).

Alting Von Gesau and A.M. Frans (1981), 'Détente and the Changed

Balance of Power in Europe', *Jerusalem Journal of International Relations*, **5**, (3).

Arkin, William A. and Richard W. Fieldhouse (1985), *Nuclear Battlefields: Global Links in the Arms Race*, Cambridge: Balinger.

Aron, Raymond (1966), *Peace and War: a Theory of International Relations*, trans. Richard Howard and Annette Baker Fox, Garden City, NY: Doubleday.

Aron, Raymond (1983), *Clausewitz, Philosopher of War*, London: Routledge & Kegan Paul.

Beer, F.A. (1969), *Integration and Disintegration in N.A.T.O.: Processes of Alliance Cohesion and Prospects for Atlantic Community*, Columbus: Ohio State University Press.

Beres, Louis René (1983), *Mimicking Sisyphus: America's Countervailing Nuclear Strategy*, Lexington, Mass.: Lexington Books.

Beres, Louis René (1984), *Reason and Realpolitik: U.S. Foreign Policy and World Order*, Lexington Mass.: Lexington Books.

Brecher, M. and J. Wilkenfeld (1982), 'Crises in World Politics', *World Politics*, **34**, (3), April.

Camilleri, J.A. (1987), *The Australia New Zealand US Alliance: Regional Security in the Nuclear Age*, Boulder, Col.: Westview Press.

Charles, D. (1987), 'NATO Looks for Arms Control Loopholes', *Bulletin of the Atomic Scientists*, **43**, (7), September.

Cooling, Benjamin Franklin (ed.) (1981), *War, Business and World Military Industrial Complexes*, New York: Kennikat Press.

Cypher, James M. (1974), 'Capitalist Planning and Military Expenditures', *Review of Radical Political Economy*, **6**, (3).

Dalby, Simon (1990), *Creating the Second Cold War: the Discourse of Politics*, London: Frances Pinter.

Deutsch, Karl W., Lewis J. Edlinger and Roy C. Macridis (1967), *France, Germany and the Western Alliance*, New York: C. Scribner's Sons.

Domke, William K., Richard C. Eichenberg and Catherine M. Kelleher (1987), 'Consensus Lost? Domestic Politics and the "Crisis" in NATO', *World Politics*, **39**, (3), April.

Galtung, Johan (1984), *There are Alternatives: Four Roads to Peace and Security*, Nottingham: Spokesman.

Hassner, P. (1974), 'How Troubled a Partnership?', *International Journal*, **29**, (2), Spring.

Holsti, D.A., P.I. Hopman, and J.D. Sullivan (1981), 'Unity and Disintegration in International Alliances: Comparative Studies', *Journal of Conflict Resolution*, **25**, (4), December.

James, B. (1985), 'Alliance: the New Strategic Focus', *Long Range Planning*, **18**, (3), June.

Jönsson, Christer (1984), *Superpowers: Comparing American and Soviet Foreign Policy*, London: Frances Pinter.

Kaldor, Mary (1983), 'Military R&D: Cause or Consequence of the Arms Race?', *International Social Science Journal*, **1**.

Kaldor, Mary (1985), 'Transforming the State: an Alternative Security Concept for Europe', *Bulletin of Peace Proposals*, **16**, (4).

Kaldor, Mary and Edie Asbjørn (eds) (1979), *The World Military Order: the Impact of Military Technology on the Third World*, New York: Praeger.

Kamo, Takehiko (1979), 'International Integration and the Dynamics of Peace: Behavioural Trends in the European Community', *British Journal of International Studies*, **5**, (2), July.

Kegley, C.W. and E.R. Wittkopf (eds) (1985), *The Nuclear Reader Strategy, Weapons, War*, New York: St Martin's Press.

Kick, Edward L. (1983), 'World System Properties and Military Intervention – Internal War Linkages', *Journal of Political and Military Sociology*, **11**, (2), Fall.

Klapp, Merrie G. (1984), 'Industrial Policy Offshore: the International Boundaries of State Enterprises', *Journal of Commonwealth and Comparative Studies*, **22**, (1), March.

Lévesque, Jacques (1982), 'The U.S.S.R. and Her Allies: Military Activity in the Third World', *International Journal*, **37**, (2), Spring.

Lockham, Robin (1977), 'Militarism: Arms and the Internationalization of Capital', *IDS Bulletin*, **8**, (3), March.

Luck, Edward C. (1977), 'The Arms Trade', *Proceedings of the Academy of Political Science*, **32**, (4).

Lumsden, Malvern (1978), 'Global Military Systems and the N.I.E.O.', *Bulletin of Peace Proposals*, **9**, (1).

Neuman, Stephanie G. (1986), 'The Arms Trade in Recent Wars: the Role of the Superpowers', *Journal of International Affairs*, **40**, (1), Summer.

Nuechterlein, Donald E. (1983), 'Convergence and Divergence in the North Atlantic Relationship', *The World Today*, **39**, (5), May.

Nuechterlein, Donald E. (1984), 'The Widening Atlantic: NATO at Another Crossroads', *The World Today*, 40, (8–9), August–September.

Nye, Joseph S. (ed.) (1984), *The Making of America's Soviet Policy*, New Haven, Conn.: Yale University Press.

Perlo, Victor (1982), 'Militarism and Inflation', *Political Affairs*, **61**, July.

Sengas, D. (1987), 'Dismantle Offense, Strengthen Defense', *Bulletin of the Atomic Scientist*, **43**, (10), December.

Sloan, Stanley R. (1980), 'Crisis In Détente – Crisis in the Atlantic Alliance?', *Europa-Archiv*, **35**, (13), July.

Sloan, Stanley R. (1984), 'European Co-operation and the Future of NATO:

in Search of a New Transatlantic Bargain', *Survival*, **26**, (6), November–December.

Smith, R.P. (1977), 'Military Expenditure and Capitalism', *Cambridge Journal of Economics*, **1**, (1), March.

Smyth, Dan (1978), 'Rivalry and Realignment in NATO', *Current Research on Peace and Violence*, **1**, (1).

Thompson, William R. (1983), 'Uneven Economic Growth, Systemic Challenges and Global Wars', *International Studies Quarterly*, **27**, (3), September.

Toumi, Helena (1981), 'Transnational Military Corporations: the Main Problems', *Current Research on Peace and Violence*, **4**, (3).

Väyrynen, Raimo (1977), 'Transnational Corporations and Arms Transfers', *Instant Research on Peace and Violence*, **7**, (3–4).

Willenbrock, F. Karl (1985), 'Technology Transfer and National Security', *IEEE Technology and Society Magazine*, September.

THE ENVIRONMENT AND ITS POLITICS

Ackerman, T. and W. Cropper (1988), 'Scaling Global Climate Projections to Local Biological Assessments', *Environment*, **30**, (5).

Anderson, Christopher G. (1990), 'UN Fragments over Treaty', *Nature*, **343**, February, 6259.

Anderson, Perry (1990), 'Diplomatic Squalls Spoil US Climate Conference', *Nature*, **344**, April, 26.

Bell, A. (1987), 'Prepare Now for Climate Change, Scientists Warn', *Ecos*, **53**, Spring.

Bell, A. (1988), 'A Legacy of Heavy Metals', *Ecos*, **55**, Autumn.

Bell, A. (1988), 'Chlorine Blamed for Growing "Ozone Hole"', *Ecos*, **56**, Winter.

Blake, D. and S. Rowland (1988), 'Continuing Worldwide Increase in Tropospheric Methane', *Science*, **239**, March.

Blechman, B. (1988), 'A Minimal Reduction of a Major Risk', *Bulletin of the Atomic Scientists*, **44**, (3), April.

Bramwell, Anna (1989), *Ecology in the 20th Century: A History*, New Haven, Conn.: Yale University Press.

Buttel, F. (1986), 'Sociology and the Environment', *International Social Science Journal*, **3**.

Council on Environmental Quality and United States Department of State (1980), *The Global 2000 Report to the President: Entering the Twenty-First Century*, 1, Washington DC: US Government Printing Office.

Crutzen, Paul and John Birks (1982), 'The Atmosphere after a Nuclear War: Twilight at Noon', *Ambio*, **11**.

Daly, H.E. (ed.) (1973), *Towards a Steady-State Economy*, San Francisco: W.H. Freeman.

Davis, C. (1987), 'International Affairs and the Environment', *Studia Diplomatica*, **40**, (1).

El-Sabh, M. and T. Murty (eds) (1986), *Natural and Man Made Hazards*, Boston: Reidel.

Falk, Jim and Andrew Brownlow (1989), *The Greenhouse Challenge: What Is To Be Done?*, Melbourne: Penguin.

Flood, M. and R. Grove-White (1976), *Nuclear Prospects*, United Kingdom: Friends of the Earth.

Flowers, Sir Brian (chairman) (1976), 'Nuclear Power and the Environment', *Royal Commission on Environmental Pollution*, 6th report, ch. VII, London: Her Majesty's Stationery Office.

Goldman, M. (1987), 'Chernobyl: a Radiobiological Perspective', *Science*, **238**, 30 October.

Goreau, Thomas J. (1990), 'Balancing Atmosphere Carbon Dioxide', *Ambio*, **19**, (5), August.

Grove, Richard (1990), 'The Origins of Environmentalism', *Nature*, **345**, (May), 6279.

Handl, Gunther (1986), 'National Uses of Transboundary Air Resources: the International Entitlement Issue Reconsidered', *Natural Resources Journal*, **26**, (3), Summer.

Handle, P. (president, National Academy of Sciences) (1975), letter to Dr F.C. Ikle, 12 August 1975, accompanying presentation of report to the Arms Control and Disarmament Agency, of US National Academy of Sciences, *Long-Term World-Wide Effects of Multiple Nuclear-Weapons Detonations*, Washington, DC: US National Academy of Sciences.

Hohenemser, C. and O. Renn (1988), 'Chernobyl's Other Legacy', *Environment*, **30**, (3).

Kerr, Richard (1988), 'Linking Earth, Ocean, and Air at the AGU', *Science*, **239**, 15 January.

Kiss, Alexandre (1985), 'The Protection of the Rhine against Pollution', *Natural Resources Journal*, **25**, (3), July.

Lindley, D. (1988), 'CFCs Cause Part of Global Ozone Decline', *Nature*, **332**, (March), 6162.

MacKenzie, Deborah (1988), 'Coming Soon: the Next Ozone Hole', *New Scientist*, **119**, (1628), September.

Maddox, J. (1988), 'Jumping the Greenhouse Gun', *Nature*, **334**, (July), 6177.

Mintzer, Irving (1987), *A Matter of Degrees: the Potential for Controlling the Greenhouse Effect*, Research Report S, Washington DC: World Resources Institute, April.

Nanda (1982), 'Global Climate Change and International Law', *Impact of Science on Society*, **32**, (3), July–September.

Nisbet, E. (1988), 'The Business of Planet Management', *Nature*, 333, (16 June), 6174.

O'Riordan, T. (1981), *Environmentalism* (2nd edn), London: Pion.

OECD (1989), *The Application of Economic Instruments for Environmental Protection*, Paris : OECD.

Onuf, N. (1983), 'Reports to the Club of Rome', *World Politics*, **36**, (1), October.

Parker Frisbie W., L. Krivo, R. Kaufman, C. Clarke and D. Myers (1984), 'A Measurement of Technological Change: an Ecological Perspective', *Social Forces*, **62**, (3).

Patterson, Walt (1983), *Nuclear Power* (2nd edn), Harmondsworth, Middlesex: Penguin.

Pearce, Fred (1990), 'Bids for the Greenhouse Auction', *New Scientist*, 4 August.

Pearce, Fred (1990), 'Whatever Happened to Acid Rain', *New Scientist*, 15 September.

Pittock, Barrie A. (1987), *Climatic Catastrophies: the International Implications of the Greenhouse Effect and Nuclear Winter*, Working Paper No. 20, Canberra, Australian National University, July.

Purnell, J. (1988), 'The Global Environment', *Environmental Science Technology*, **22**, (1), January.

Rodgers, C. (1988), 'Global Ozone Trends Reassessed', *Nature*, **332**, (17 March), 6161.

Saleti, E. and P. Vose (1984), 'Amazon Basin: a System in Equilibrium', *Science*, **225**, (July), 4658.

Shiva, V. (1987), 'Forestry Myths and the World Bank', *Ecologist*, **17**, (4–5), July–November.

Simmonds, Jane (1987), 'Europe Calculates the Health Risk', *New Scientist*, 23 April.

Simon, J. and H. Kahn (1984), *The Resourceful Earth: a Response to Global 2000*, Oxford: Basil Blackwell.

Smil, V. (1987), 'A Perspective on Global Environmental Crises', *Futures*, **19**, (3), June.

Spinrad, B. (1988), 'US Nuclear Power in the Next Twenty Years', *Science*, **239**, 12 February.

Springer, A. (1983), *The International Law of Pollution: Protecting the Global Environment in a World of Sovereign States*, Westport, Conn.: Quorum.

Stretton, Hugh (1976), *Capitalism, Socialism and the Environment*, Cambridge: Cambridge University Press.

Trainer, T. (1985), *Abandon Affluence!*, London: Zed Books.

Trainer, T. (1986), 'A Critical Examination of "The Resourceful Earth"', *Technological Forecasting and Social Change*, **30**, (1), August.

Turco, R. and G. Golitsyn (1988), 'Global Effects of Nuclear War', *Environment*, **30**, (5).

US National Academy of Sciences (1975), *Long-Term World-Wide Effects of Multiple Nuclear-Weapons Detonations*, Washington, DC: US National Academy of Sciences.

Voltz, A. and D. Kley (1988), 'Evaluation of the Montsouris Series of Ozone Measurements Made in the Nineteenth Century', *Nature*, **332**, (17 March), 6161.

Waldrop, M. (1984), 'An Inquiry into the State of the Earth', *Science*, **226**, (October), 4675.

Wijkman, Per Magnus (1982), 'Managing the Global Commons', *International Organization*, **36**, (3), Summer.

World Commission on Environment and Development (1987), *Our Common Future*, Oxford: Oxford University Press.

Worster, Donald (1985), *Nature's Economy: A History of Ecological Ideas*, Cambridge: Cambridge University Press.

NEW SOCIAL MOVEMENTS

Arrighi, Giovanni, Terence K. Hopkins and I. Wallerstein (1986), Dilemmas of Antisystemic Movements', *Social Research*, **53**, (1), Spring.

Bahro, R. (1982), *Socialism and Survival*, London: Heretic.

Bahro, R. (1984), *From Red to Green*, London: Verso.

Bahro, R. (1986), *Building the Green Movement*, Philadelphia: New Society Publishers.

Barkan, Steven E. (1979), 'Strategic Tactical and Organizational Dilemmas of the Protest Movement against Nuclear Power', *Social Problems*, **27**, (1), October.

Barkan, Steven E. (1980), 'Political Trials and Resource Mobilisation: towards an Understanding of Social Movement Litigation', *Social Forces*, **58**, (3), March.

Bookchin, Murray (1971), *Post-Scarcity Anarchism*, Berkeley Cal.: Ramparts.

Boyte, Harry C. (1980), *The Backyard Revolution: Understanding the New Citizen Movement*, Philadelphia: Temple University Press.

Boyte, Harry C. (1986), 'Beyond Politics As Usual', in Harry C. Boyte and

Frank Reissman, *The New Populism: the Politics of Empowerment*, Philadephia: Temple University Press.

Bozeman, Adda B. (1960), *Politics and Culture in International History*, Princeton, NJ: Princeton University Press.

Brown, Bruce (1975), *Marx, Freud and the Critique of Everyday Life*, New York: Monthly Review Press.

Camilleri, J.A. (1986), 'After Social Democracy', *Arena*, **77**.

Capra, F. and C. Spretnak (1984), *Green Politics*, London: Hutchinson.

Casanova, José (1984), 'The Politics of the Religious Revival', *Telos*, **59**, Spring.

Castells, Manuel (1983), *The City and the Grassroots: A Cross-Cultural Theory of Urban Social Movements*, Berkeley, Cal: University of California Press.

Cerny, Phillip G. (ed.) (1982), *Social Movements and Protest in France*, London: Frances Pinter.

Cohen, Jean L. (1985), 'Strategy or Identity: New Theoretical Paradigms and Contemporary Social Movements', *Social Research*, **52**, (4), Winter.

Eder, Klaus (1985), 'The "New Social Movements": Moral Crusades, Political Pressure Groups, or Social Movements?', *Social Research*, **52**, (4), Winter.

Enloe, Cynthia H. (1973), Ethnic Conflict and Political Development, Boston: Little, Brown.

Epstein, Arnold L. (1978), *Ethos and Identity*, London: Tavistock.

Falk, Jim (1982), *Global Fission:the Battle over Nuclear Power*, Melbourne: Oxford University Press.

Feher, Ferenc and Agnes Heller (1984), 'From Red to Green', *Telos*, **59**, Spring.

Fuentes, M. and Gunder Frank (1989), 'Ten Theses on Social Movements', *World Development*, **17**, (2), February.

Gale, Richard P. (1986), 'Social Movements and the State: the Environmental Movement, Countermovement and Government Agencies', *Sociological Perspectives*, **29**, (2), April.

Gorz, André (1980), *Ecology and Politics*, London: Pluto Press.

Habermas, Jürgen (1981), 'New Social Movements', *Telos*, **49**, Fall.

Halfmann, Jost (1988), 'Risk Avoidance and Sovereignty: New Social Movements in the United States and West Germany', *Praxis International*, **8**, (1), April.

Hall, Stuart and Martin Jacques (eds) (1989), *New Times: the Changing Face of Politics in the 1990s*, London: Lawrence & Wishart in association with *Marxism Today*.

Hamilton, R. (1978), *The Liberation of Women: a Study of Patriarchy and Capitalism*, London: Allen & Unwin.

Hülsberg, Werner (1988), *The German Greens: a Social and Political Profile*, London: Verso.

Jenkins, Craig J. (1983), 'Resource Mobilization Theory and the Study of Social Movements', *Annual Review of Sociology*, **9**.

Jensen, John and Kirsten Simonsen (1981), 'The Local State, Planning and Social Movements', *Acta Sociologica*, **24**, (4).

Killian, Lewis M. (1984), 'Organization, Rationality and Spontaneity in the Civil Rights Movement', *American Sociological Review*, **49**, December.

Kowalewski, D. and P. Schumaker, (1981), 'Protest Outcomes in the Soviet Union', *The Sociological Quarterly*, **22**, Winter.

Kvistad, Gregg O. (1987), 'Between State and Society: Green Political Ideology in the Mid-1980s', *West European Politics*, **10**, (2), April.

Lewis, J. (ed.) (1982), *Women's Rights, Women's Welfare*, London: Croom Helm.

Luckman, Thomas (1977), 'Theories of Religion and Social Change', *Annual Review of the Social Sciences of Religion*.

Mainwaring, Scott and Eduardo Viola (1984) 'New Social Movements, Political Culture and Democracy: Brazil and Argentina.in the 1980s', *Telos*, **61**, Fall.

Marcuse, Herbert (1964), *One Dimensional Man*, London: Routledge & Kegan Paul.

Martin, David A. (1969), *The Religious and the Secular: Studies in Secularisation,* London: Routledge & Kegan Paul.

Melucci, Alberto (1980), 'The New Social Movements: a Theoretical Approach', *Social Science Information*, **19**, (2)

Mendlovitz, Saul H. (ed.) (1987), *Towards a Just World Peace*, London: Butterworth.

Mosco, Vincent and Andrew Herman (1980), 'Communication, Domination and Resistance', *Media, Culture and Society*, **2**.

Offe, Klaus (1985), 'New Social Movements: Challenging the Boundaries of Institutional Politics', *Social Research*, **52**,(4), Winter.

Pankoke, Eckart (1982), 'Social Movement', *Economy and Society*, **11**, (3), August.

Pepper, David (1984), *The Roots of Modern Environmentalism*, London: Croom Helm.

Porritt J. (1984), *Seeing Green*, Oxford: Basil Blackwell.

Smelser, Neil (1962), *The Theory of Collective Behaviour*, New York: Free Press.

Smith, A.D. (1981), *The Ethnic Revival*, Cambridge: Cambridge University Press.

Smith, A.D. (1985), 'Ethnie and Nation in the Modern World', *Millenium*, **14**, (2), Summer.

Szabò, Máté (1988), 'New Factors in the Political Socialization of Youth in Hungary: the Alternative Social Movements and Subcultures', *Praxis International*, **8**,(1), April.

Szecsko, T. (1986), 'Mass Communication and the Restructuring of the Public Sphere. Some Aspects of the Development of "Information Culture" in Hungary', *Media, Culture and Society*, **8**, (2).

Tilly, Charles (1978), *From Mobilization to Revolution*, Reading, Mass.: Addison-Wesley.

Tilly, Charles, Louise Tilly and Richard Tilly (1975), *The Rebellious Century: 1830–1930*, Cambridge, Mass.: Harvard University Press.

Touraine, Alain (1974), 'Mouvements sociaux et idéologies dans les sociétés dépendantes', *Tiers Monde*, January–March.

Touraine, Alain (1975), 'Les nouveaux conflits sociaux', *Sociologie du Travail,* **17**, (1), January–March.

Touraine, Alain, (1981), *The Voice and the Eye: an Analysis of Social Movements,* Cambridge: Cambridge University Press.

Touraine, Alain (1984), 'Les Mouvements sociaux: objet particulier ou problème central de l'analyse sociologique?', *Revue Française de Sociologie*, **25**, (1), January–March.

Touraine, Alain (1985), 'An Introduction to the Study of Social Movements', Social Research, **52**, (4), Winter.

Turner R.G. and L.M. Killian (1957), *Collective Behaviour*, Englewood Cliffs, Prentice-Hall.

Vergani, Shinoda and Kesler (1987), 'The Culture of Fragments – Notes on the Question of Order in a Pluralistic World: towards a Structure of Difference', *PRECIS*, **6.**

Walker R.B.J. (1988), *One World, Many Worlds: Struggles for a Just World Peace,* Boulder, Col.: Lynne Rienner.

Wallerstein, Immanuel (1986), 'Marxisms as Utopias – Evolving Ideologies' *American Journal of Sociology*, **91**, (6).

Weston, J. (ed.) (1986), *Red and Green: the New Politics of the Environment*, London: Pluto Press.

Wilson, Brian (1976), *Contemporary Transformation of Religion*, London: Oxford University Press.

Zald, Mayer N. (1977), 'Resource Mobilisation and Social Movements: a Partial Theory', *American Journal of Sociology*, **82**, May.

Index